World Religions in Practice

Praise for *World Religions in Practice*

"In an age when religion is increasingly in the news, but often for all the wrong reasons, the need for a balanced, sympathetic, and objective educational tool has never been greater. Paul Gwynne has provided an accessible introduction to religion. His approach is refreshingly obvious: it is through the understanding of what people are doing that we discover what they are thinking."

Douglas Pratt, University of Waikato, New Zealand

"An exciting and intriguing approach, taking central categories in religion and indicating how they show up in different religions pragmatically . . . the table of contents inspired me to dive right in and read."

Dr Darren J. N. Middleton, Texas Christian University

". . . this is an impressive accomplishment that presents a moving and engaging encounter with the religious traditions of the world."

Kim Paffenroth, Iona College, USA

"A carefully crafted and comparative approach to major religions, often serving to separate human populations, as templates of how humankind in so many varied places has had such similar needs, desires and hope. Gwynne's book represents a very creative turn in this field."

Marjorie Snipes, University of West Georgia

"A very efficient, dynamic and useful tool in an approach to the five major religions of the world."

Alexandria Egler, St Francis College, USA

"A thoughtful and accessible approach to the religions from a phenomenological point of view. The book promotes the desirable end of understanding and sympathy between religious practitioners, and is an attractive choice as an introductory textbook."

George Sumner, University of Toronto

"This book treats the great traditions with a vividness and immediacy which have seldom if ever been equalled. Instead of placing the main emphasis on doctrines, beliefs and their claims to truth, Paul Gwynne selects those aspects of life where religions become practical and guides us to an appreciation of each which is aesthetically pleasing as well as providing useful information. Surely one of the best ways to come to know a faith tradition different from one's own is to live among its adherents. Reading this book is the next best thing. It should prove invaluable for educators and students as well as interested laypeople in a variety of professions."

John D'Arcy May, Irish School of Ecumenics, Trinity College Dublin

World Religions in Practice

A Comparative Introduction

Paul Gwynne

Blackwell
Publishing

© 2009 by Paul Gwynne

BLACKWELL PUBLISHING
350 Main Street, Malden, MA 02148–5020, USA
9600 Garsington Road, Oxford OX4 2DQ, UK

The right of Paul Gwynne to be identified as the author of this work has been asserted in
accordance with the UK Copyright, Designs, and Patents Act 1988.

First published 2009 by Blackwell Publishing Ltd

1   2009

Library of Congress Cataloging-in-Publication Data

Gwynne, Paul.
    World religions in practice : a comparative introduction / Paul Gwynne.
        p. cm.
    Includes bibliographical references and index.
    ISBN 978-1-4051-6702-4 (hardcover : alk. paper)—ISBN 978-1-4051-6703-1
(pbk. : alk. paper)   1. Religions.   I. Title.

    BL80.3.G89 2009
    200—dc22

                                                    2007042456

A catalogue record for this title is available from the British Library.

Set in 10.5/13pt Minion
by Graphicraft Limited, Hong Kong
Printed and bound in Singapore
by C.O.S. Printers Pte Ltd

The publisher's policy is to use permanent paper from mills that operate a sustainable forestry policy,
and which has been manufactured from pulp processed using acid-free and elementary chlorine-free
practices. Furthermore, the publisher ensures that the text paper and cover board used have met
acceptable environmental accreditation standards.

For further information on
Blackwell Publishing, visit our website at
www.blackwellpublishing.com

For Kim, Kirindy, Bonnie, and Sally

CONTENTS

BOXES AND TABLES

TABLES

FIGURES

NOTE ON SCRIPTURAL REFERENCES

The following versions of scriptural and traditional texts have been used:

Access to Insight: Readings in Theravada Buddhism, ed. John Bullitt, sutta translations by the Venerables Bhikkhu Bodhi, Acharya Buddharakkhita, Bhikkhu Khantipalo, Nanamoli Thera, Ñanavara Thera, Narada Thera, Nyanaponika Thera, Soma Thera, Thanissaro Bhikkhu (Phra Ajaan Geoff), and Sister Vajira; I. B. Horner, John D. Ireland, K. R. Norman, and F. L. Woodward. At www.accesstoinsight.org.

Babylonian Talmud, ed. Rabbi Dr Isidore Epstein. London: Jews' College. Also available at www.come-and-hear.com/talmud.

Bhagavad Gita, trans. Juan Mascaro. London: Penguin, 1962.

The Holy Bible: New Revised Standard Version with Apocrypha. New York: Oxford University Press (1991). Copyright 1989, Division of Christian Education of the National Council of the Churches of Christ in the United States of America. Used by permission. All rights reserved.

The Hadith, USC-MSA Compendium of Muslim Texts, University of Southern California, at www.usc.edu/dept/MSA/fundamentals/hadithsunnah.

The Holy Koran, trans. Mohammed H. Shakir. New York: Tahrike Tarsile Qur'an Inc., 1983. Also available at www.usc.edu/dept/MSA/fundamentals/hadithsunnah.

ACKNOWLEDGMENTS

I wish to thank the following academic colleagues for their invaluable feedback on the draft manuscript:

Professor John D'Arcy May, Irish School of Ecumenics, Trinity College, Dublin
Associate Professor Douglas Pratt, Department of Philosophy and Religious Studies, University of Waikato, New Zealand
Dr Heather Foster, School of Education, University of South Australia, Adelaide
Peta Jones Pellach, Director of Adult Education, Shalom Institute, Sydney
Amna Hansia and the staff of the Australian Islamic College, Perth
Associate Professor Constant Mews, Director of Centre for Studies in Religion and Theology, Monash University, Melbourne

I am also very grateful for the professional advice and support of the Blackwell staff and their associates, especially Rebecca Harkin, Karen Wilson, Bridget Jennings, Anna Oxbury, and Jacqueline Harvey.

Paul Gwynne
Sydney

CREDITS FOR PHOTOGRAPHS AND MAPS

1.1 Photo © istockphoto.com; 1.2 Photo © Damir Cudic / istockphoto.com; 1.3 Photo © Murat Sen / istockphoto.com; 1.4 Photo © istockphoto.com; 1.5 Photo © Henry Fu / istockphoto.com; 2.1 Photo © Teresa Hurst / istockphoto.com; 2.2 Photo © Shawn Harris / istockphoto.com; 2.3 Photo © James Rodkey / istockphoto.com; 2.4 Photo © Nancy Louie / istockphoto.com; 2.5 Photo © Wael Hamdan / istockphoto.com; Chapter 3 title, statue of Moses, photo © istockphoto.com; 4.1 Photo © Terry Healey / istockphoto.com; 4.2 Photo © Odelia Cohen / istockphoto.com; 4.3 Photo © istockphoto.com; 4.4 Photo © World Religions Photo Library / Alamy; 5.1 Photo © World Religions Photo Library by Nick Dawson; 5.2 Photo © Alan Crawford / istockphoto.com; 5.3 Photo © istockphoto.com; 5.4 Photo © Tulay Over / istockphoto.com; 5.5 Photo © istockphoto.com; 6.1 Photo © Israel images / Alamy; 6.2 Photo © Sally and Richard Greenhill / Alamy; 6.3 Photo © Russell McBride / istockphoto.com; 6.4 Photo © Anders Ryman / Alamy; 7.1 Photo © Christine Gonsalves / istockphoto.com; 7.2 Photo © Ravi Tahilramani / istockphoto.com; 7.3 Photo © istockphoto.com; 7.4 Photo © Vladimir Grishin / istockphoto.com; 7.5 Photo © Ashley Cooper / Alamy; 8.1 Photo © Alan Tobey / istockphoto.com; 8.2 Photo © istockphoto.com; 8.3 Photo © World Religions Photo Library by Louise B. Duran; 8.4 Photo © Anneclaire Le Royer / istockphoto.com; 8.5 Photo © Lorenzo Pastore / istockphoto.com; 9.1 Photo © Steven Allan / istockphoto.com; 9.2 Photo © Franky De Meyer / istockphoto.com; 9.3 Photo © Jean-Yves Benedeyt / istockphoto.com; 10.1 Photo © Pattie Calfy / istockphoto.com; 10.2 Photo © istockphoto.com; 10.3 Photo © World Religions Photo Library / Gapper; 10.4 Photo © Alison Stieglitz / istockphoto.com; 10.5 Photo © Itani / Alamy; 11.1 © Elnur Amikishiyev / istockphoto.com; 11.2 Photo © Lily Rosen-Zohar / istockphoto.com; 11.3 Photo © Yuri Hnilazub / istockphoto.com; 11.5 Photo © Jeremy Edwards / istockphoto.com; 11.6 Photo © Lorenzo Pastore / istockphoto.com; 12.1 Map by Sally Host; 12.2 Photo © Alan Tobey / istockphoto.com; 12.3 Map by Sally Host; 12.4 Photo © World Religions Photo Library / Alamy; 12.5 Map Sally Host; 12.6 Map by Sally Host; 12.7 Photo © Moti Meiri / istockphoto.com; 12.8 Photo © Mark Weiss / istockphoto.com; 12.9 Photo © World Religions Photo Library by Camerapix; 12.10 Map by Sally Host

INTRODUCTION

Few would deny that religion constitutes a vital piece of the jigsaw when it comes to fully understanding human societies and their members, both past and present. It is a key influence on a host of cultural activities around the globe, from weddings and funerals to public holidays and festivals. Religious belief is frequently a source of inspiration for works of literature, art, and architecture, and can significantly shape everyday life at the level of diet and clothing. Even in highly secularized Western society, the legacy of centuries of religious tradition has left its distinctive and enduring mark on language, symbol, and custom. Sadly, religious motives are also an ingredient in many political conflicts and even acts of terrorism that currently dominate the world stage. For better or for worse, religion is still very much a part of the human story and cannot be ignored if we hope to explain fully what makes individuals and communities think and act in the way that they do.

Moreover, the contraction of the world from an array of far-flung continents to a single global village has brought a wide spectrum of religious beliefs firmly within our horizon wherever that may be. In Western societies, mass immigration programs have meant a reversal of colonial times and the arrival of large numbers of adherents of "other faiths." The world has come to us and its religions are no longer exotic phenomena in distant lands, but the defining world views of neighbors and work colleagues. Conversely, the relative ease and affordability of travel provides an unprecedented opportunity for today's tourist to visit cultures where ceremonies, festivals, artworks, and buildings express religious ideas in both recognizable and unrecognizable ways.

In such a world, an appreciation of different religious traditions is arguably more pertinent than ever. Without diluting or compromising one's own fundamental philosophical, spiritual, or religious persuasions, an interested and respectful study of different religious systems affords an opportunity to complete the picture. The comparative study of religion provides the broader context into which more familiar faith systems can be situated and thus better understood. It can highlight the distinctive features that render each religion truly unique, while at the same time revealing fascinating areas of intersection between faiths.

This book is an attempt to explore those similarities and differences, hopefully contributing something to the quest for a deeper understanding and a more profound appreciation of the common ground between all religions. To this end, a phenomeno-logical approach has been adopted. In other words, it is not primarily concerned with the veracity or credibility of the religious claims involved. Nor is it about demonstrating that one religion is more advanced or complete than another. Although absolute objectivity is an impossible ideal in any discipline, apologetic issues are deliberately set aside in an attempt to present each religion in a respectful and accurate manner.

The major religions dealt with in this book are Hinduism, Buddhism, Judaism, Christianity, and Islam. The decision to restrict the study to these five in no way implies that the list is exhaustive. There are other religious and quasi-religious systems that could be considered global such as Taoism, Confucianism, Sikhism, Jainism, Baha'ism, and Zoroastrianism but the scope and approach of the book meant that a limit had to be imposed at some point. The five that have been chosen are frequently the subject of textbooks and courses on "world religions" and for good reason. Four of them represent the largest religious denominations according to approximate current statistics: Christianity (2.1 billion), Islam (1.2 billion), Hinduism (900 million), and Buddhism (380 million). With about 14 million adherents, Judaism admittedly involves much smaller numbers, but it is included in the main five due to its significant age, widespread influence, and fundamental links to the other two Abrahamic faiths, Christianity and Islam.

The approach taken in this book is somewhat different from that of standard works in two ways. First, most introductory works on the world's major religions adopt a serial approach whereby the author outlines the key features of each religion in turn. Thus chapters tend to be organized according to the religions themselves and the reader is escorted on a journey of discovery through various aspects of the faith system in question. The bibliography at the end of this book contains many such examples. The advantage is that a reasonably coherent overview of each religion is provided in discrete units. However, an alternative method has been used for this work. Rather than organizing religions in linear fashion and treating each one as a separate whole, a more lateral approach has been adopted whereby a range of general themes is explored across the religions. The result is a series of cross-sections that reveal how a particular theme, such as sacred writing or holy days, is expressed in each religion. Such an approach is able to generate greater levels of explicit comparison between the religions, uncovering not only the unique qualities that differentiate them, but also an assortment of interesting overlaps and connections.

Second, most books on the world's major religions tend to focus on either their historical development or their theological beliefs while (with a few exceptions) paying little or no attention to the actual living out of the faith. Several decades ago, Ninian Smart proposed that all religions contain, to a greater or lesser extent, seven fundamental dimensions: doctrinal-philosophical; experiential-emotional; mythical-narrative; ethical-legal; social-institutional; practical-ritual; and material. The themes chosen for this book belong primarily to Smart's last two categories (with one chapter devoted to the ethical dimension). Thus we will be looking mainly at how the five religions are expressed in practice. Our principal interest lies more in customs than in creeds, in external actions than in inner attitudes. Nevertheless, an examination of the ritual and material dimension of these five religions inevitably touches on Smart's other dimensions, including the doctrinal-philosophical. A study of religious practices cannot avoid consideration of the theological foundations that underpin them. The practical features of religions, such as the use of images and texts in worship, the donning of special clothing, or the design of sacred buildings, reflect deeper doctrinal positions regarding the world and our place in it. In this respect, the old Latin adage rings true: lex orandi lex credendi [the law of praying is the law of believing]. In other words, the practical is a mirror to the theoretical. Religious custom is a reflection of religious belief and vice versa.

The 12 practical themes are themselves arranged and linked under an overarching motif: the sanctification of the ordinary. As Smart rightly pointed out, religion is a complex, multi-dimensional phenomenon that has proved to be notoriously difficult to pin down. This is clear from the myriad of definitions available (for a sample see box 0.1). Some definitions stress the individual while others stress the social; some the psychological, others the cultural; some the moral, others the political. However, most definitions of religion contain the reference to a reality beyond time and space, which can be denoted in many ways: "the divine"; "the sacred"; "the supernatural"; "the spiritual"; "the Holy"; "ultimate being"; "God"; "Allah"; "Brahman"; "eternal dharma"; and so forth. Whether this reality actually exists or is merely the product of the human imagination is one of the most burning of all philosophical issues. But apart from the question of its factual or fictional status, faith in transcendent reality clearly has a profound impact on the way in which believers interpret and live out human existence. Whatever the designation, Hindus, Buddhists, Jews, Christians, and Muslims all see it as the answer to the most important questions of all: Where did we come from? Why are we here? And where are we going? Consequently, belief in transcendent reality casts a new light on all aspects of life, even the most mundane. Ordinary realities such as food and clothing, birth, marriage, and death, even time and space itself, are given a more profound, extraordinary meaning through the eyes of religious faith. Familiar objects, activities, moments, and places become part of the provision of ultimate meaning and thus take on a sacred, transcendent quality.

Box
0.1

SOME DEFINITIONS OF RELIGION

The belief in a superhuman controlling power, especially in a personal God or gods entitled to obedience and worship. (*Concise Oxford Dictionary*)

A belief system that includes the idea of the existence of an eternal principle that has created the world, that governs it, that controls its destinies or that intervenes in the natural course of its history. (*Random House Dictionary*)

Homo religiosus always believes that there is an absolute reality, the sacred, which transcends this world but manifests itself in this world, thereby sanctifying it and making it real. (Mircea Eliade)

Religion, in the largest and most basic sense of the word, is ultimate concern. It gives us the experience of the Holy, of something which is untouchable, awe-inspiring, an ultimate meaning, the source of ultimate courage. (Paul Tillich)

A system of symbols which acts to establish powerful, pervasive and long-lasting moods and motivations in men by formulating conceptions of a general order of existence and clothing these conceptions with such an aura of factuality that the moods and motivations seem uniquely realistic. (Clifford Geertz)

Religion implies that human order is projected into the totality of being. Put differently, religion is the audacious attempt to conceive of the entire universe as being humanly significant. (Peter Berger)

Religious ideas are illusions, fulfilments of the oldest, strongest and most urgent wishes of mankind. Thus the benevolent rule of a divine Providence allays our fear of the dangers of life; the establishment of a moral world-order insures the fulfillment of the demands of justice, which have so often remained unfulfilled in human civilization; and the prolongation of earthly existence in a future life provides the local and temporal framework in which these wish-fulfilments shall take place. (Sigmund Freud)

Religion is the sigh of the oppressed creature, the heart of a heartless world, just as it is the spirit of a spiritless situation. It is the opium of the people. The abolition of religion as the illusory happiness of the people is required for their real happiness. (Karl Marx)

The 12 themes are organized into three clusters which constitute the three sections of the book. Part I looks at two principal religious ways in which the reality that lies "beyond time and space" can be accessed: the visual image and the written or spoken word. The use (or non-use) of these two bridges to transcendent reality not only constitutes an important starting point for our comparison of practice but also reveals something about how each religion understands transcendent reality itself. Part II focuses on human existence "within time and space." It opens with a brief survey of moral duty in each religion and then proceeds to examine three main rites of passage (birth, death, and marriage) that are frequently marked by religious ritual. This section also takes the two most basic necessities of life (food and clothing) and examines how they are also given sacred meaning by religious faith. Part III looks at the very fabric of spatial-temporal existence, and explores how each of the five religions sanctifies time and space itself. Themes of the holy day, the annual calendar, the sacred building, and pilgrimage are examined in each religion. Of course, the choice of these 12 themes does not imply that the list is complete. There are other practical themes that could be added such as healing, initiation, and prayer. However, these 12 themes resonate effectively across the five religions, thus representing a useful sample that serves well the comparative and practical purpose of the book.

Given the limited size of such a book, there is simply not enough space to delve into the intricate details of the chosen themes. The beliefs and practices discussed here are merely the tips of many icebergs that can be adequately fathomed only in more specialized works. Moreover, the five religions themselves are far from monochrome, consisting of a spectrum of subdivisions, sects, and traditions whose beliefs and practices can vary significantly at times, especially in the case of Hinduism. Thus the danger of generalization hovers constantly over such a project, including the inherent limitations of the term "world religion" itself. Consequently, the author has endeavored to focus on broadly typical characteristics of each major religion, accompanied by the acknowledgment of variations and exceptions where relevant. Admittedly a picture painted with broad brush strokes must ignore small things, but there is some value in stepping back at times and taking a more panoramic view. In short, this book is more concerned with forests than trees, especially what the forests look like from above and where their boundaries touch.

The primary audience of the book is the tertiary or senior secondary student in religious studies courses as well as the layperson who has an interest in major religions and their interrelationship. Although the book is introductory in nature, a basic familiarity with the five religions will be advantageous since each religion is encountered thematically along with others. Accordingly, a brief vignette and timeline for each religion has been provided at the end of this Introduction. The effect of the comparative approach is akin to a thematic tour, but the road is more reminiscent of a meandering track than a straight highway. The order in which we travel through the five religions will vary from chapter to chapter, depending on where the bridges seem to occur naturally. It should be noted that the particular order in which the religions are dealt with in each chapter is not intended to imply any kind of priority or superiority, nor is it the only possible one. The tour itinerary is not binding, but hopefully it is one that will provide fresh views and interesting landscapes.

Words in bold type are included in the Glossary at the end of the book.

HINDUISM ॐ *Key facts*	
No. of adherents (approx.)	900 million
Origins	Hinduism has no historical founder but its origins are usually linked to the Aryan invasion of the Indus Valley civilization around 1500 BCE, which resulted in a socio-religious caste system and the emergence of the Vedas as primary sacred texts.
Subdivisions	Hinduism is a general term embracing a complex spectrum of religious sects. It can be subdivided according to the principal form of Brahman which is worshiped:
	• Vaishnavism (600 million): worship of Vishnu and his incarnations such as Krishna and Rama;
	• Shaivism (200 million): worship of Shiva;
	• Shaktism: worship of Shakti (Mother Goddess) and her manifestations such as Parvati, Durga, and Kali.
	There are also many recent movements such as the Arya Samaj, which was founded by Dayananda Saraswati in the late nineteenth century.
Transcendent reality	The term *Brahman* refers to the one absolute reality that embraces the entire cosmos. Brahman is beyond all finite categories but is manifest and worshiped in the form of different gods and goddesses such as Vishnu, Shiva, or the Mother Goddess. Thus Hinduism is difficult to classify and is described variously as polytheistic, pantheistic, henotheistic, or monistic.

Key facts (cont'd)

Human existence	Hindus believe in samsara (reincarnation) whereby the atman (soul) of the deceased is reborn into the world according to the law of karma. The cycle can last hundreds or thousands of lifetimes but it is hoped that all individuals will eventually be released from the cycle of rebirth and attain moksa (final liberation). For some Hindu philosophers, such as Shankara, moksa involves the dissolution of the atman back into Brahman. For others, such as Ramanuja, the liberated atman retains some degree of individual existence in perfect communion with Brahman and other beings. There are three main paths to moksa: • jnana-marga: the path of knowledge and meditation; • karma-marga: the path of moral action; • bhakti-marga: the path of devotion and worship of a particular deity.
Sacred texts	There are two main categories of Hindu sacred writings: • shruti (primary revelation): the Vedas and the Upanishads; • smriti (secondary revelation): there are many works in this category of which the most prominent are the two great epics (the Mahabharata and the Ramayana), the poetic Puranas, and legal codes such as the Laws of Manu.
Key rituals	The 16 traditional life-cycle rituals (samskaras) include many prenatal and childhood ceremonies, as well as initiation into adulthood (sacred thread), marriage, and funeral rites.

Timeline	
1500–1200 BCE	Aryans invade Indus Valley
1200–900	Earliest Vedas composed
900–600	Emergence of Brahmanical Hinduism with caste system
800–300	Upanishads composed
500–100	Ramayana and Mahabharata epics composed
150	Bhagavad Gita composed
200 BCE–200 CE	Laws of Manu composed
300–500	Many Puranas composed; Vishnu and Shiva emerge as major deities
600–900	12 alvars (Tamil saints) compose many devotional poems
810	Shankara develops the Advaita Vedanta philosophy
1000–1200	Muslim invasions of northern India
1200–1600	Spread of devotional (bhakti) movements
1498	Vasco da Gama arrives in India
1526	Mughal Empire commences
1556–1605	Akbar (third Mughal ruler) shows tolerance to Hindus
1658–1707	Aurangzeb (sixth Mughal ruler) destroys many Hindu temples
1757	Robert Clive establishes a British protectorate in Bengal
1828	Ram Mohan Roy founds the Brahmo Samaj
1829	Widow-burning (sati) banned by the British
1831–7	Thuggees suppressed by the British
1850	First English translation of the Rg Veda

Timeline (cont'd)

1875	Theosophical Society promotes Hinduism in the West; Dayananda Saraswati founds the Arya Samaj
1880	Beginning of large-scale emigration of Indian workers
1885	Foundation of the Indian National Congress Party
1897	Vivekananda establishes the Ramakrishna Mission
1913	Rabindranath Tagore wins Nobel Prize for Literature
1947	India gains independence
1948	Gandhi assassinated
1950	Constitution of the Republic of India

BUDDHISM ☸
Key facts

No. of adherents (approx.)	380 million
Origins	Siddhartha Gautama (c.560–480 BCE) was born into the royal family of the Sakya kingdom (near the current Indian/Nepal border). He married and had a son, but upon experiencing the Four Sights (old age, sickness, death, and a holy man) left his family and spent seven years as a wandering ascetic. Meditating under a tree at Bodhgaya, he grasped the Four Noble Truths and became Buddha [Enlightened One]. He delivered the First Sermon to his five companions at Sarnath and thereafter traveled around northern India, teaching and attracting followers until his death at Kusinegara.

Key facts (cont'd)

Subdivisions	• Theravada (Way of the Elders) has about 130 million followers located mainly in Sri Lanka, Burma, Thailand, Cambodia, and Laos. It is sometimes called "Hinayana" (Lesser Vehicle) by the Mahayana tradition. Theravada Buddhism stresses the importance of the monastic community and the need for self-discipline in order to attain nirvana. • Mahayana (Greater Vehicle) has approximately 200 million followers located mainly in China, Mongolia, Japan, Korea, and Vietnam. It has more readily incorporated elements from local cultures and stresses compassion, especially in the form of the bodhisattva, a holy person who postpones nirvana to assist others. • Vajrayana (Diamond Vehicle) has about 20 million adherents and is the dominant form of Buddhism in Tibet. It is characterized by mystical rituals and elements including tantras, mantras, and mandalas.
Transcendent reality	Buddha rejected the Hindu concepts of Brahman (transcendent being) and atman (soul). The main focus of his teaching is on personal liberation from craving (greed, hatred, and ignorance) which binds us to the wheel of reincarnation. Thus many argue that Buddhism should not be classified as a religion, although it has many features that are similar to other religions.

Key facts (cont'd)

Human existence	Buddhists believe in reincarnation according to the law of karma. However, the self is illusory and what is reborn each time is a reconfiguration of basic energies. Liberation from the wheel of samsara is attained by embracing the Four Noble Truths:
	1 suffering is universal; 2 the root of suffering is craving for transient things; 3 nirvana is the end of suffering and reincarnation; 4 the way to nirvana is the Noble Eightfold Path: right knowledge, right attitude, right speech, right action, right livelihood, right effort, right mindfulness, and right meditation.
	The Pancasila (Five Precepts) is the Buddhist list of fundamental ethical principles that should be followed.
Sacred texts	The Tipitaka (Three Baskets) is a threefold collection of the Buddha's sayings, the monastic rule, and a philosophical system. It is the most important text in Theravada Buddhism. Other texts are given equal or greater status in Mahayana and Vajrayana schools, such as Lotus Sutra and the Tibetan Book of the Dead.
Key rituals	Buddhism has no universal ceremonial system. Its rites of passage are profoundly influenced by local culture and custom. Monastic life involves ordination ceremonies, alms rounds, and a range of meditation practices.

Timeline	
560 BCE	Birth of Siddhartha (traditionally 620 BCE)
525	Siddhartha gains Enlightenment and becomes the Buddha
480	Death of Siddhartha (traditionally 544 BCE); First Buddhist Council at Rajagaha
360	Second Buddhist Council at Vaisali
272–231	Mauryan emperor Ashoka actively promotes Buddhism
250	Third Buddhist Council and Great Schism; Mahinda introduces Buddhism to Sri Lanka
1–100 CE	Lotus Sutra and other Mahayana texts composed
50	Tipitaka completed in Sri Lanka
50–100	Buddhism enters China
200	Nagarjuna founds the Madhyamaka (Middle Path) School in India
200–300	Buddhism expands into southeast Asia
400	Pure Land Buddhism emerges in China Sacred tooth relic of Siddhartha brought to Sri Lanka
500–600	Buddhism enters Japan and Korea
600–700	Buddhism enters Tibet
618–907	Golden age of Buddhism in China under Tang dynasty
800	Construction of Borobudur Temple (central Java)
1100–1200	Construction of temple complex at Pagan (Burma); Buddhism virtually extinct in India; Zen Buddhism appears in Japan
1150	Construction of Angkor Wat (Cambodia)
1200–1300	Shinran and Nichiren found Buddhist schools in Japan

Timeline (cont'd)

1578	Sonam Gyatso given the title "Dalai Lama"
1800–1900	Extensive Western translations of Buddhist writings
1949	Bodhgaya Temple site returned to Buddhist control
1950	World Fellowship of Buddhists founded
1959	Dalai Lama goes into exile
1965–80	Buddhist monks protest against Burmese government
1989	Dalai Lama receives Nobel Peace Prize

JUDAISM ✡
Key facts

No. of adherents (approx.)	14 million
Origins	Judaism traces its origins to the covenant between God and Abraham (c.1800 BCE) who left his homeland in Mesopotamia and settled in the land of Canaan (Israel). The covenant was passed on to his son (Isaac) and his grandson (Jacob). The most important event in Jewish history is the miraculous escape (the Exodus) of the Israelites from Egypt (c.1250 BCE) under the leadership of Moses. The Torah (Law) was subsequently revealed to Moses on Mount Sinai. After 40 years in the wilderness, the people entered the land of Canaan and established an independent kingdom with priesthood and temple.

Key facts (cont'd)

Subdivisions	• Orthodox Judaism upholds the value of tradition, stressing the ongoing importance of biblical commandments such as those pertaining to diet and the Sabbath. It is the official form of Judaism in Israel. • Reform Judaism is more liberal toward contemporary culture and thus more willing to adapt traditional teaching to new situations. For example, it allows vernacular language in worship and women's ordination. • Conservative Judaism takes a middle position between the Reform and Orthodox movements. There are also Jewish cultural streams such as Ashkenazi (from central and eastern Europe) and Sephardic (from the Iberian peninsula, northern Africa, and the Middle East).
Transcendent reality	Judaism professes faith in one, supreme, personal God who created the universe. God has revealed his will via Moses and the prophets, and has intervened at key moments in history to save his chosen people. God is infinite and utterly beyond human imagination; thus idolatry is a grave sin and a constant danger.
Human existence	Humans are created in the image of God, and their destiny is to share eternal happiness with their creator in heaven. Most Jews believe that human persons are born and die just once, after which everyone faces divine judgment although some accept a limited form of reincarnation (gilgul). Jews are required to keep the divinely revealed Law, especially the 613 explicit commandments found in the Torah.

Key facts (cont'd)

Sacred texts	The Jewish Bible, or Tanach, consists of the 5 books of the Law (Torah), the 8 books of the Prophets (Neviyim), and the 11 books of the Writings (Ketuvim). The Talmud is a detailed commentary on Tanach composed in two main forms around 500 CE.
Key rituals	The main rites of passage are circumcision, bar mitzvah, marriage, and the funeral service. The sabbath (Saturday) is set aside as a day of strict rest.

Timeline

1800 BCE	Abraham, Isaac, and Jacob (the patriarchs)
1250	The Exodus
1200–1050	Occupation of Canaan by Hebrew tribes
1050–930	United kingdom of Israel under Saul, David, and Solomon
950	Solomon constructs the First Temple
920	Kingdom divides into Israel (north) and Judah (south)
722	Assyria conquers northern kingdom; ministry of Isaiah
586	Destruction of the Temple and Exile in Babylon; ministry of Jeremiah
537	Return from Exile; ministry of Ezekiel
520–510	Construction of the Second Temple
165	Rededication of the Temple under Judas Maccabeus
63 BCE	Palestine becomes part of the Roman Empire
70 CE	Destruction of the Second Temple (Av 9)

Timeline (cont'd)

100	Canonization of Tanach
135	Bar Kokhba rebellion defeated by the Romans
200	Rabbi Judah writes the Mishnah
450	Palestinian Talmud
550	Babylonian Talmud
1204	Death of Maimonides
1290	Jews expelled from England
1492	Jews expelled from Spain
1560–70	Joseph Caro writes the Shulhan Aruch
1740	Hasidism founded
1800–1900	Orthodox, Reform, and Conservative movements
1861	Zionist movement begins
1882–1900	First Aliyah (migration to Israel)
1917	Balfour Declaration supports formation of a Jewish state
1938–45	The Holocaust
1948	State of Israel established
1950	Israeli Parliament passes the Law of Return
1967	Six Day War
1972	Ordination of the first female rabbi
1983	Reform Judaism accepts patrilineal Jewish descent

CHRISTIANITY †
Key facts

No. of adherents (approx.)	2.1 billion
Origins	Jesus of Nazareth (c.6 BCE–30 CE) is considered by Christians to be the long-awaited Jewish Messiah and also the incarnate Son of God. In a short public life that began with his baptism in the Jordan, Jesus preached the imminent coming of the kingdom of God in which sinners would find divine mercy and forgiveness. He is said to have worked many miracles in the tradition of Moses and Elijah, especially healing the sick. His message and person aroused serious opposition from the religious and political leadership and he was condemned to death by crucifixion. Christians believe that he was raised from the dead and appeared to his followers, commissioning them to continue his message and work.
Subdivisions	The main subdivisions of Christianity are a result of two historical moments: • Eastern Christianity (centered on Constantinople) and Western Christianity (centered on Rome), formally separated in the Great Schism of 1054. The Eastern churches are now known collectively as Orthodox Christianity (250 million). • The sixteenth-century Reformation led to a further division of Western Christianity into the (Roman) Catholic Church (1 billion) and many Protestant churches (850 million) such as the Lutheran, Anglican, Calvinist, and Baptist traditions.

Key facts (cont'd)

Transcendent reality	Christianity is essentially monotheistic in that it professes faith in one, supreme, personal God. However, the belief that Jesus is the human incarnation of God led to the concept of the Trinity: three divine persons, or modes of existence (Father, Son, and Holy Spirit) in the one divine essence (God).
Human existence	Human persons are born and die once, after which they face divine judgment. The virtuous enjoy heaven, which is a state of perfect, eternal bliss in communion with God and other beings. The wicked are condemned to hell, which is a state of eternal alienation from the creator. Christianity accepts the ongoing validity of the Ten Commandments as a fundamental moral guide but interprets them as imitation of Jesus who is the supreme model for human life.
Sacred texts	The Christian Bible consists of the Jewish Tanach (renamed as the Old Testament) and the 27 Christian books of the New Testament. Catholic Bibles also include a number of works found in the ancient Greek version of the Jewish Bible (the Septuagint) but not in Tanach.
Key rituals	Catholic and Orthodox churches recognize seven sacraments that are considered to have been established by Christ: baptism, confirmation, the Eucharist, holy orders, marriage, reconciliation, and anointing of the sick. Protestant churches tend to recognize only two such rituals as having an explicit basis in the New Testament: baptism and the Eucharist.

Timeline	
6 BCE	Birth of Jesus
30 CE	Death of Jesus
50–120	New Testament written
65	Death of Peter and Paul
65–312	Periodical persecutions of Christians
270	Christian monasticism begins
313	Edict of Milan legalizes Christianity
325	Council of Nicea defines Jesus as fully divine
380	Christianity becomes official religion of the Roman Empire
400	Jerome produces the Vulgate (Latin Bible)
430	Death of Augustine
451	Council of Chalcedon defines Jesus as divine and human
525	Christian calendar introduced
787	Second Council of Nicea rejects iconoclasm
1054	Great Schism between Western and Eastern Christianity
1095–1291	The Crusades
1163	Construction starts on Notre Dame Cathedral (Paris)
1274	Thomas Aquinas composes the *Summa Theologica*
1453	Ottomans conquer Constantinople
1455	First printed Bible by Gutenberg
1478	Spanish Inquisition begins
1508–12	Michelangelo paints the Sistine Chapel
1517	Martin Luther initiates the Protestant Reformation

Timeline (cont'd)

1534	Henry VIII establishes the Church of England
1545–63	Council of Trent responds to the Reformation
1609	John Smyth establishes a Baptist Church in America
1729	John and Charles Wesley begin the Methodist movement
1869–70	Vatican I defines papal primacy and infallibility
1899	Gideons International founded
1947	Dead Sea Scrolls discovered
1948	World Council of Churches formed
1962–5	Vatican II reforms the Catholic Church

ISLAM ☪
Key facts

No. of adherents (approx.)	1.2 billion
Origins	Muhammad (c.570–632 CE) was a successful merchant based in Mecca. When he was about 40 years old, he received the first of a series of divine revelations, which continued until his death. Muhammad's monotheistic message met with opposition in Mecca, and eventually his small community was forced to migrate to Medina in 622 CE (the Hijra). Muhammad proved to be a successful leader in Medina where Islam consolidated and grew. After a series of battles, Mecca surrendered in 630 CE and Muhammad transformed its central shrine, the Ka'bah, into a symbol of the new faith. He died in 632 and is buried in Medina. His companion Abu Bakr was elected as the first caliph.

Key facts (cont'd)

Subdivisions	The main subdivision in Islam is between the Sunni majority (950 million) and the Shi'ite minority (150 million). Sunnis accept the election of Abu Bakr and his three successors (Umar, Uthman, and Ali) as legitimate leaders (caliphs) of the early community. Shi'ites claim that the leadership should have passed immediately to Ali, who was Muhammad's son-in-law and cousin. Thus Ali, his wife (Fatima), his sons (Hasan and Hussain), and the line of true leaders (imams) have an important status in Shi'ite Islam.
Transcendent reality	Islam stresses the absolute oneness and transcendence of God (Allah). Thus, idolatry (shirk) is one of the gravest sins for a Muslim. God reveals his will through the prophets, of whom Muhammad is the last and greatest. God's will is encapsulated in the Qur'an.
Human existence	Islam believes that humans are born and die once. On the day of judgment at the end of the world, all will be held accountable: the just will be rewarded with the joys of Jannah (Paradise) while the wicked will be punished in Jahannam (hell).
Sacred texts	The holiest text in Islam is the Qur'an, which is a collection of the revelations received by Muhammad during his lifetime. The Qur'an is considered to be the literal word of God. Its authority is complemented, but not rivaled, by official collections of the sayings and example of the Prophet, which are known as hadith.

Key facts (cont'd)

Key rituals	Islam ritually marks key moments in life such as birth, marriage, and death. The Five Pillars of Sunni Islam are also an important aspect of practice:
	• shahadah: declaration of faith in God and his Prophet • salat: formal prayers five times per day • zakat: a percentage of income given to the poor • sawm: daylight fasting during the month of Ramadan • hajj: pilgrimage to Mecca

Timeline

570 CE	Birth of Muhammad
610	Muhammad receives first revelation
622	Hijra: Muslim community leaves Mecca for Medina; Islamic calendar begins
624	Muslims defeat Meccans in Battle of Badr
630	Mecca surrenders to Muhammad
632	Death of Muhammad; Abu Bakr chosen as first caliph
633–42	Muslim armies conquer north Africa, Syria, Palestine, and Mesopotamia
634	Umar becomes second caliph
644	Uthman becomes third caliph
650	Uthman organizes written edition of the Qur'an
656	Ali becomes fourth caliph
661	Murder of Ali and beginning of Umayyad Caliphate in Damascus

Timeline (cont'd)

680	Death of Hussain at Karbala
700	Arabic becomes official language of the Muslim Empire
732	Battle of Tours: Muslim Empire reaches its furthest western extent
754	Abbasid caliphs rule from Baghdad
750–850	Four main Sunni schools of law founded
874	Occultation of twelfth Shi'ite imam (Muhammad al-Mahdi)
1100	Al Ghazali's writings promote Sufism Islam spreads to southeast Asia via merchants and missionaries
1187	Saladin defeats Crusaders at the Battle of Hattin
1258	Mongols sack Baghdad and end the Abbasid caliphate
1299	Osman founds the Ottoman Empire
1453	Ottomans conquer Constantinople
1520–66	Reign of Suleiman the Magnificent – zenith of the Ottoman Empire
1744	Muhammad Abd al-Wahhab and Muhammad bin Saud found the kingdom of Saudi Arabia
1918	End of the Ottoman Empire
1947	Foundation of Pakistan
1948	Arab–Israeli War
1979	Iranian Revolution
1988	Ahmed Salman Rushdie writes *The Satanic Verses*
1996	Taliban regime gains power in Afghanistan
2001	September 11 attacks in the USA

Note: Many earlier dates in the above timelines are only approximate and still a matter of scholarly debate.

Part I

BEYOND TIME AND SPACE

Chapter 1

IMAGE

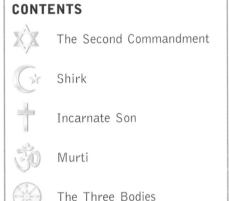

Introduction

At the heart of religion lies the belief in a transcendent reality that provides an overarching context for human life and all that it contains. Seen through religious eyes, this visible world is not the full story. There is a dimension beyond the visible that holds the key to the origin, the purpose, and the ultimate destiny of the cosmos and its inhabitants. Where religions tend to diverge is on the specific nature of this dimension. Is it personal or impersonal? Is it one or many? Is it masculine or feminine? Is it fundamentally similar to or different from us? The answers to such questions can be found by investigating one of the principal practical ways in which Hindus, Buddhists, Jews, Christians, and Muslims access the transcendent — their use or non-use of the sacred image.

The Second Commandment

At the beginning of the twentieth chapter of the book of **Exodus**,[1] the second book of the Jewish Bible, the reader suddenly encounters one of the most important and celebrated shortlists of religious-ethical principles in Judaism. The scene is an awe-inspiring theophany shrouding the desert mountain called Sinai, into which **Moses**, the leader of the recently emancipated Hebrew slaves, has been beckoned. Amid the clamorous thunderclaps and flashing lightning, the God of Israel delivers his moral blueprint for the newly liberated faith community. In rabbinic Hebrew the items of that list are called Aseret ha-Dibrot [The Ten Statements]; in English they are better known as the **Ten Commandments**.

The order in which the commandments are delivered and conventionally listed is far from random (see chapter 3 for details). Jewish tradition divides the Aseret ha-Dibrot into two halves: the first five concern the vertical relationship between humanity and God, while the remaining five concern the horizontal relationship between human persons themselves.[2] According to Judaism, the first commandment consists of the indicative statement "I am the Lord your God," which requires the response of religious faith. Belief in God is the first and foremost step. But it is the second commandment that holds the key to the Jewish understanding of the nature of the divine reality. It begins with the phrase: "You shall have no other gods before me."[3]

For many commentators, the words of the second commandment are ambiguous in that it is not clear whether the text is speaking of strict **monotheism** or **henotheism**.

Box 1.1	THE 13 PRINCIPLES OF THE JEWISH FAITH (MAIMONIDES)
	1 God exists.
	2 God is one.
	3 God is incorporeal.
	4 God is eternal.
	5 God alone should be worshiped.
	6 God has communicated through the prophets.
	7 Moses was the greatest of the prophets.
	8 The Torah is the word of God.
	9 The Torah is authentic and cannot be changed.
	10 God is aware of all of our actions.
	11 God rewards the just and punishes the wicked.
	12 The Messiah will come.
	13 The dead will be resurrected.

The former refers to belief in the existence of one God only. The latter designates worship of a single god while accepting the existence of other gods.[4] The exact nature of early Hebrew faith and the precise origins of monotheism have been a matter of scholarly debate for some time. Such historical issues aside, the traditional Jewish interpretation of the second commandment for over 2,000 years has been unequivocally monotheistic. In other words, Judaism professes exclusive belief in and worship of the one God. Conversely, one of the most serious sins in Judaism is the interposing of "other gods" before the One – idolatry.

The monotheistic bedrock of Judaism is manifest in a host of religious writings and practices, a classical example of which is the 13 Principles of the Jewish Faith (see box 1.1) enumerated by the outstanding twelfth-century philosopher Moshe ben Maimon, otherwise known as **Maimonides**. His summary of the key elements of Jewish faith was initially criticized but a poetic version known as the Yigdal hymn was eventually incorporated into the daily Jewish prayer book. Each morning in synagogues across the world, devout Jews chant:

> Exalted be the Living God and praised.
> He exists – unbounded by time in His existence.
> He is One – and there is no unity like His Oneness.
> Inscrutable and infinite is His Oneness.

Another striking statement of monotheism in the daily **liturgy** is the prayer that is considered by many to be the most important in Judaism: the **Shema** (see box 1.2). Taken from the book of **Deuteronomy**, it opens with the declaration "Shema Yisrael Adonai Eloheinu Adonai Echad" [Hear, O Israel: The LORD our God, the LORD alone].[5] The text goes on to exhort believers to love the one God with all of their being and to bring these words to mind "when you lie down and when you rise."[6] In obedience to the command, the rabbinic tradition has incorporated the Shema

---

THE SHEMA

Box 1.2

Hear, O Israel: The LORD is our God, the LORD alone. You shall love the LORD your God with all your heart, and with all your soul, and with all your might. Keep these words that I am commanding you today in your heart. Recite them to your children and talk about them when you are at home and when you are away, when you lie down and when you rise. Bind them as a sign on your hand, fix them as an emblem on your forehead, and write them on the doorposts of your house and on your gates. (Deuteronomy 6:4–9).

into official evening and morning prayers. As the sun rises and sets each day, God's oneness is proclaimed by Jews at prayer in all corners of the world.

The Shema is not only verbally expressed on a regular basis at prayer, but is also literally worn on the body and fixed to doorways as a constant reminder of the divine unity. The same Deuteronomy text exhorts the believer to bind these words "as a sign on your hand, fix them as an emblem on your forehead, and write them on the doorposts of your house and on your gates."[7] Once again, in literal obedience to the divine command, the Shema is inscribed in black ink on parchment from the skins of **kosher** animals and placed inside special containers known as the tefillin and the mezuzah. The tefillin are small black boxes that are strapped to the forehead and left arm at weekday morning prayers, while the mezuzah is fixed to the doorposts of Jewish homes at eye level as a constant reminder of the oneness of God each time the believer passes. So essential is the idea of God's unity that it is placed before the Jewish mind and heart when they are stationary in prayer or on the move with their ordinary daily routine.

Given that Judaism is committed to belief in one God, how do Jews conceive of the deity? What images come to mind? The next line of the Yigdal hymn provides the beginning of an answer: "He has no semblance of a body nor is He corporeal; nor has His holiness any comparison." Although the Jewish scriptures and the **Talmud** occasionally refer to God's hands, eyes, mouth, and other bodily parts, Jewish theology insists that such anthropomorphisms are metaphorical in nature and in no way imply that God is actually physical or bodily in some sense. Maimonides stressed the point by including the statement "God is incorporeal" among his 13 fundamental principles. The principle itself is concise, but Maimonides dedicates most of the first book in his major work, *Guide for the Perplexed*, to outlining the figurative nature of such biblical language and insisting on the absolute metaphysical difference between the creator and creation. Human minds may legitimately use familiar concepts such as bodily features to imagine the divine, but to interpret that language literally would be to fail to appreciate the otherness of God and fall into idolatry. It would be to project finite qualities onto the infinite. God is, by definition, divine not human.

The principle that it is absolutely beyond our ability to express the fullness of God in word or form stands behind the remainder of the second commandment:

> You shall not make for yourself an idol, whether in the form of anything that is in heaven above or that is on the earth beneath or that is in the water under the earth. You shall not bow down to them or worship them; for I, the Lord your God, am a jealous God.[8]

The prohibition on images is not only aimed at avoiding worship of other gods, which would naturally undermine the monotheistic principle, but is also concerned with fatally flawed attempts to depict the one true God. The ultimate mystery that shrouds the deity should never be forgotten. Among the world religions, Judaism in particular stresses the otherness and invisibility of God which is the original meaning of the term *kadosh*, usually translated as "holy" but perhaps more accurately rendered "different." The God of Judaism is truly transcendent and any attempt to depict the Holy Other is doomed to failure. It can only lead to misinterpretation and idolatry. The biblical episode that perhaps best captures the Jewish concern not to reduce God to something finite via an image or idol is when Moses destroys the golden calf that the Israelites had fashioned while he was on the heights of Sinai. The text tells us that not only does Moses melt the statue, but he also grinds it into powder and casts the remains into the waters which the apostate community must then drink.[9] The point is thrust home in graphic fashion that any form of idolatry is intolerable.

Thus, it is not surprising that one will never see statues, paintings, or similar realistic imagery in Jewish synagogues and homes. This is not to say that Judaism is devoid of an artistic tradition. However, given the suspicion toward icons, Jewish art has understandably focused on more abstract patterns and elaborate decorations. Artists poured their aesthetic energies into ceremonial objects such as candelabra, scrolls, and containers. All of these can be an aid to prayer but, when a Jew turns to worship, there

Figure 1.1
Interior of a
Jewish synagogue

is no mediating image or tangible object that represents God or connects the believer with the divine. At the far end of a synagogue, toward which the congregation faces, there is no statue or painting or altar. Instead, there is a receptacle, decorated and marked by a burning candle, inside which are kept the scrolls of the Jewish scriptures: divine words not divine images.

The synagogue itself is usually oriented toward the holy city, Jerusalem, where the **Temple** once stood. The last Temple was destroyed by the Roman armies in August 70 CE.[10] There is a legend that when the Roman general Titus entered the **Holy of Holies** – the inner sanctum into which only the high priest would go once a year on the Day of Atonement – he expected to find either immense treasure or a statue of some sort that portrayed the God of this stubborn, resistant people. Instead he found nothing: the room was empty. The God of Israel is one and transcendent, indivisible and invisible.

In fact, the Holy of Holies did once house an important object that disappeared into the mists of history long before Titus arrived on the scene. It was a long rectangular chest known as the **Ark of the Covenant**. Over it were fixed two winged seraphs facing each other from either end, creating a space known as the Seat of Mercy. According to Jewish belief, the Ark contained the very tablets that Moses received from God on Sinai with the Aseret ha-Dibrot inscribed on them: again, divine words not divine images. As for the symbolic Seat between the seraphs on which the God of Israel was "enthroned" as king – it was empty. No man-made image was ever placed there. For the Jewish faith past and present, God is indivisible and invisible. But Judaism is not the only religion in which empty space stands as the most appropriate symbol of the divine transcendence. Something very similar can be found in the town of Mecca.

Shirk

In the center of the courtyard of the great mosque of **Mecca** stands one of the most recognizable structures in the Islamic world – the **Ka'bah**. As the name vaguely suggests, it is cubic in shape, standing about 50 feet above a marble base. Constructed from gray stone, it is usually covered by the kiswa, a black cloth embellished with golden calligraphy. Islamic tradition tells us that it was built by Adam based on a celestial prototype and subsequently rebuilt by the **patriarch** Abraham and his son Ishmael after being destroyed in the waters of the Flood. The Ka'bah was already the focus of religious practice in pre-Islamic Arabia. Local tribes would make annual pilgrimages to the shrine which contained, at the time, more than 300 statuettes representing the pantheon of local gods. Some say that there was a statue and a god for every day of the year.

In the year 630, when **Muhammad** returned triumphant to his native town after nearly a decade as governor of Medina, he ordered all the statuettes to be destroyed.

But the Ka'bah was retained and transformed into the axis of a new religious world. Five times a day, every day of the year, 1 billion Muslims recite their daily prayers facing toward the Ka'bah as they fulfill one of the most fundamental requirements of their religion. It is a powerful global gesture unifying worshipers across a myriad of cultures and nations. The question is: What are they all facing? With what symbol did Muhammad replace the hundreds of pre-existing pagan statues inside the Ka'bah? The answer is illuminating – nothing. Apart from some hanging lanterns and a small table for perfumes, there is no sacred object or religious icon of any sort that attempts to portray God inside the Ka'bah.[11] Like the Holy of Holies in the ancient Jewish Temple, at the heart of Islam lies an indivisible and invisible mystery.

Muhammad's destruction of the multiplicity of statues in the Ka'bah reflects the first key theological principle concerning the nature of God in Islam. It is a principle succinctly expressed in the **shahadah** – the first of the Five Pillars of Islam (see box 1.3) and its fundamental credal statement.

> I bear witness that there is no god but God;
> I bear witness that Muhammad is His prophet.[12]

In direct and unambiguous terms, the shahadah announces Islam's unshakeable belief in the oneness and uniqueness of God – the principle known as tawhid. Alongside the Jewish faith, Islam stands as a resolute voice of unqualified monotheism, asserting that there is only one absolute and that it is by nature undifferentiated and without equal.

It is no coincidence that such a bedrock article of faith is woven inextricably into daily practice. The shahadah itself constitutes a key component of the haunting call from the tops of **mosques** that beckons Muslims to turn from their mundane activities and face Mecca in daily prayer. The same assertion of monotheism constitutes the gateway to Islam, since to utter the shahadah with clear-minded intention

THE FIVE PILLARS OF SUNNI ISLAM		BOX 1.3
shahadah	the witness of faith	
salat	the five daily prayers	
zakat	the religious tax	
sawm	the Ramadan fast	
hajj	the pilgrimage to Mecca	

before two witnesses is sufficient for one to convert to Islam. Embracing the concept of tawhid is the key to joining the Muslim religious community. Tawhid is also one of the major recurring themes in Islam's holiest book, the **Qur'an**. An oft-quoted text is the brief 112th chapter appositely entitled "Al Ikhlas" [The Unity]:

> Say: He is Allah, the One,
> Allah is He on whom all depend,
> He does not beget, nor is He begotten,
> And (there is) none like Him.[13]

The converse of tawhid is **shirk** which literally means "making a partner or an equal" and is conventionally translated into English as "idolatry." The attribution of partners or equals to Allah is to deny the principle of God's uniqueness and unity, undermining the very foundations of the religion. As such, shirk is the gravest sin in Islam.[14] In Islamic jurisprudence, it is equivalent to unbelief and Muslims who profess it are to be ousted from the community with their legal rights suspended until they renounce their erroneous beliefs or practices.

The pre-Islamic Arabic religious pantheon is a classical example of shirk against which Muhammad's monotheistic message was aimed. The smashing of the idols of the Ka'bah is symbolic of the assertion of God's utter uniqueness over any form of **polytheism**. Furthermore, theologies of God that seem to compromise the inner unity of the godhead, such as the Christian Trinity, are also rejected as shirk by the Qur'an.

> O followers of the Book! do not exceed the limits in your religion, and do not speak (lies) against Allah, but (speak) the truth; the Messiah, Isa son of Marium is only an apostle of Allah and His Word which He communicated to Marium and a spirit from Him; believe therefore in Allah and His apostles, and say not, Three. Desist, it is better for you; Allah is only one God.[15]

The dangers of idolatry lurk not only in other religious systems which speak of many gods or a plurality within the godhead. For many Muslims the sin is committed even when one approaches Allah via the intercession of another being.[16] In the strict Saudi Arabian **Wahhabi** school, shirk can occur when Muslim pilgrims display excessive devotion at the graves of saints, including Muhammad's tomb in **Medina**. Even **Mawlid an-Nabi** [Birthday of the Prophet], a festival that the outsider might expect to be one of the most celebrated in the Islamic calendar, has no special prayers or services and is even somewhat downplayed for fear of deifying Muhammad. The founder of Islam is considered to be the Seal of the Prophets and the greatest human ever to have lived, but in the end he is human not divine. There is no God but Allah, and Muhammad is his Prophet – nothing more.

The insistence on the unity of God does not imply that there is no richness in God. Islamic tradition stresses the simplicity of God but also speaks of the 99 divine "names" – a litany of qualities that traditionally begins with the two attributes that preface every chapter of the Qur'an: "In the Name of Allah, the most compassionate, the most merciful." The names are recited in private meditation by Muslims with the assistance of the tasbih with its three sections of 33 beads. As in the case of Catholic and Buddhist rosaries, the beads are turned as the believer mentally moves along the list, although the tasbih today often serves more secular purposes such as worry beads for restless hands or as a fashion accessory.

If Muhammad's destruction of the idols of the Ka'bah reflects the key Islamic principle of monotheism, his decision not to replace them with any tangible symbol or icon reflects another key principle: **aniconism**. Allah is beyond all images. The prohibition of shirk means not only that there is no equal to God but also that there can be no finite image or object that is worthy of representing the infinite One or through which the worshiper seeks a more palpable experience of the deity's presence. When Muslims enter into the sacred moment of official prayer five times a day, the only physical requirements are that they stand on clean ground and face Mecca. There is no icon or statue or altar between them and the focus of their adoration. Even if the prayers are recited inside a mosque, the only tangible object toward which the congregation faces is a decorated niche in the wall known as the **mihrab**. The mihrab is usually designed in the shape of a doorway or an arch but it does not lead to any room or inner sanctum. It is basically an architectural device indicating the **qibla** – the direction of Mecca. The minds of the worshipers who stand before the mihrab focus beyond the walls of their mosque to the distant Ka'bah which itself is devoid of any sacred symbol or object. The God of Islam lies beyond any earthly horizon, which renders our attempts to portray him futile.

As in Jewish synagogues, a visitor to a **mosque** might be struck by the notable absence of religious images, pictures, statues, and icons. The rejection of any artistic form that can lead to idolatry is manifest in the ambience of Islam's places of prayer. Instead of portraits and anthropomorphic figures, one finds instead more abstract themes such as geometric forms, floral designs, and calligraphic patterns. The latter typically draw on verses from the Qur'an and other Islamic literature, capitalizing on the graceful, flowing style of Arabic script. The aesthetic dimension is far from absent in Islamic culture, but it tends to be expressed in written rather than pictorial form.

A striking example of the Islamic duty to avoid all potential forms of shirk in its sacred buildings is the case of the Hagia Sophia (Holy Wisdom) in Istanbul, the city once known as Constantinople. Originally constructed as a Christian basilica by Justinian I in 537, its internal walls were adorned with a magnificent array of holy mosaics. When the city fell to the Ottoman Turks in 1453, the building was converted into a mosque and, because of the iconoclastic demands of the new faith, its mosaics covered in plaster. One must admire the broadmindedness of the Ottoman sultans who periodically removed the plaster in order to maintain the artwork beneath. After nearly 500 years, the secular Turkish government turned the building into a museum in 1934, and commenced the process of restoring many of the original Christian mosaics as well as retaining much of the Islamic calligraphic art.[17] The initial decision to cover the icons was not based on an inherent Islamic disdain for art or beauty as such, but rather on a deep-seated theological conviction that there can be no images in a house of prayer. With regard to the insistence on strict monotheism and the general ban of images in worship, Jews and Muslims are in fundamental agreement – God is utterly

Figure 1.2
Interior of the
Blue Mosque,
Istanbul

one and ultimately transcendent – but what is the position of the original Christian builders of the Hagia Sophia?

 ## Incarnate Son

In the year 726, the Byzantine Emperor Leo III published an edict declaring that all holy images were in direct contravention of the second commandment and, as idols, should be destroyed. Soldiers immediately began to implement his orders. Their removal of a popular image of Christ from the gate of the imperial palace in Constantinople sparked a general riot and constituted the first act in what historians call the Iconoclastic Controversy. The term *iconoclast* literally means "image-breaker," and the controversy itself refers to two distinct periods of Byzantine imperial opposition to the veneration of religious images during the eighth and ninth centuries. Coincidentally, it was the female regent who brought an end to the conflict in both periods. In 787 the Empress Irene organized a council of bishops that condemned **iconoclasm** as heresy. The decision was endorsed by the papacy and the council came to be recognized by all Christians as the seventh and last genuinely **ecumenical council** of the Church.[18] Similarly in 843 it was the Empress Theodora who restored the icons to churches, and since that date **Eastern Christianity** has commemorated the event on the First Sunday of Greater Lent which is known as "The Triumph of Orthodoxy."

Historians suggest that there were a number of reasons for Leo's initial move against religious icons: military reversals against the Muslims; an eruption of the volcanic island of Thera interpreted as divine displeasure at images; a desire to control the monasteries which were bastions of icon veneration; and the sense that images were a hindrance to the conversion of Jews and Muslims. But behind these practical issues were several key theological arguments, the primary one being that the veneration of images is in violation of the second commandment. Although it eventually dispensed with many of the ritual obligations contained in the Jewish scriptures, Christianity never abandoned the essence of the religious and moral principles given to Moses on Sinai. Thus, it was argued that the ban on making and revering images remained in force. It would seem that Christians share the same conviction as Muslims and Jews, that God is utterly transcendent and beyond any visual depiction. So how did the opponents of iconoclasm possibly counter such an argument and prevail?

The key protagonist against the ban on icons was a monk living in Muslim-controlled Syria named John of Damascus. Ironically, the fact that his place of residence was beyond the control of the Christian emperor gave John freedom to resist the imperial ban, even though his Muslim neighbors would have been in total sympathy with the iconoclasts' religious agenda. John argued that the commandment forbidding images of God had been superseded by nothing less than the Incarnation. What did John mean by that? Something about the Christian understanding of divinity itself overturns the once valid biblical conviction that God cannot be portrayed in any finite material manner. For Christians, something has actually changed in God and it is here that Christianity begins to part ways with its monotheistic cousins, Judaism and Islam.

The Christian modification of traditional Jewish monotheism was not a sudden decision or a smooth journey. It took several centuries for Christians to agree on both the concept itself and the most appropriate language to express it. One of the most widely accepted and frequently recited versions of the eventual redefinition of God is found in the words of the **Nicene Creed** (see box 1.4).[19] What strikes the reader is that apart from four short assertions at the end,[20] the entire Creed is concerned with the true identity of **Jesus** and his relationship to the one God of Israel, designated by Christians as "the Father."

For many the answer to the question of the founder's identity is summed up in his most common epithet, which now functions as a surname: **Christ**. However, far from a surname, *Christos* is a Greek term that literally means "anointed one," a direct translation of the Hebrew term *Masiah* (Messiah). "Jesus Christ" is thus properly rendered "Jesus the Christ." The phrase is actually a claim that the carpenter of Nazareth is the long-awaited **Messiah** or king of Israel. This claim in itself constitutes one of the most fundamental differences between Christianity and Judaism, but it does not quite explain why the Christian idea of divinity and the use of images in worship vary from the Jewish and the Islamic vision of one invisible God. Ultimately, the Jewish Messiah is a human figure, a descendant of **King David** who, in the last days, will restore Israel to its former glory and righteousness. But the Nicene Creed goes much further than this. It opens with an affirmation of monotheism that Jews and Muslims would have few problems accepting:

> We believe in one God,
> the Father, the Almighty,
> maker of heaven and earth,
> of all that is, seen and unseen.

However, the next statement touches on the very heart of the matter and spells out the true nature of the Christian claim about Jesus more explicitly than even the title "Christ":

> We believe in one Lord, Jesus Christ,
> the only son of God,
> eternally begotten of the Father,
> God from God, Light from Light,
> true God from true God,
> begotten, not made,
> of one being with the Father.

THE NICENE CREED

Box 1.4

We believe in one God,
the Father, the Almighty,
maker of heaven and earth,
of all that is, seen and unseen.

We believe in one Lord, Jesus Christ,
the only son of God,
eternally begotten of the Father,
God from God, Light from Light,
true God from true God,
begotten, not made,
of one being with the Father.
Through him all things were made.
For us and for our salvation
he came down from heaven:
by the power of the Holy Spirit
he became incarnate from the Virgin Mary,
and was made man.
For our sake he was crucified under Pontius Pilate;
he suffered death and was buried.
On the third day he rose again
in accordance with the Scriptures;
he ascended into heaven
and is seated at the right hand of the Father.
He will come again in glory
to judge the living and the dead,
and his kingdom will have no end.

We believe in the Holy Spirit, the Lord, the giver of life,
who proceeds from the Father [and the Son].
With the Father and the Son
he is worshipped and glorified.
He has spoken through the Prophets.
We believe in one holy catholic and apostolic Church.
We acknowledge one baptism for the forgiveness of sins.
We look for the resurrection of the dead,
and the life of the world to come. AMEN.

The Creed is essentially a response to Jesus's monumental question to his disciples "Who do you say I am?"[21] The conciliar answer is that Jesus is an incarnation of the divine Son who has existed from before creation itself ("eternally begotten of the Father") and who is as fully divine as the Father ("God from God"; "of one being with the Father"). In fact, it was not the application of the title "Christ" to Jesus that led the bishops to utter this most elevated claim. Historically, it was another title also used by his followers in the earliest years of the new religion. The seeds of the Nicene Creed were already present when the first generation of Christians began to worship Jesus as Kyrios [Lord]. This was the same term used in Greek translations of the Jewish scriptures for the Hebrew *Adonai*, a sacrosanct title reserved exclusively for the one God.

One can see the tension building as the Creed progresses. Christians believe in "one" God but are compelled to say more. The assertion of the full divinity of Jesus leads naturally to a revision of their understanding of God. There is talk of a divine Son who is distinct from the divine Father and who, unlike the Father, becomes enfleshed as a human person in time and space. Something of God remains utterly transcendent (Father) while something becomes incarnate (Son). The Creed goes on to complete the classical picture by introducing the third element (Spirit) who is described by many Christian theologians as the perfect reciprocal love between the other two divine "persons." God is one and yet God is also three: Father, Son, and Holy Spirit. This is the essence of the Christian doctrine of the **Trinity**, and it is a direct consequence of the declaration of Jesus's divine status. Christians still count themselves as monotheists alongside Jews and Muslims, but belief in a God who is simultaneously one and three makes it a modified monotheism.

Despite the esoteric nature of the doctrine of the Trinity and the struggle by generations of Christian theologians to make sense of this mystery of mysteries, it is very much woven into everyday Christian language and practice. Many churches, colleges, and other Christian institutions around the world bear the name "Trinity." Catholic and Orthodox Christians make a sign of the cross during private and public prayer by touching their forehead and each shoulder in turn[22] with accompanying words that signify the Father, Son, and Holy Spirit. Christian clergy bless their congregations with the same cruciform gesture in the name of the three divine persons. Young and old neophytes are baptized into the Christian faith with water and an ancient formula that makes specific reference to the Trinity.

However, the Trinity has never been a major theme in Christian art, and when it is the subject of a painting or icon, or more rarely a statue, problems quickly arise. The artist usually has no difficulty in portraying the Son but it is a different matter when it comes to the other two persons. The traditional use of a gray-bearded figure to represent the Father and a dove the Spirit may solve the artist's dilemma but it is poor theology. In one sense, only the Son can truly be depicted in finite worldly form since, in Christian theology, only the Son becomes part of the finite world.

It was the doctrine of the Incarnation that John of Damascus appealed to in his battle with the iconoclasts. In response to the accusation that the veneration of sacred images was a violation of the second commandment, John argued that the prohibition on holy images had been abrogated by the Incarnation itself. If the Son of God has truly taken on human nature and become a part of the created world in a real sense, then the images are legitimate. They depict not an idol but the reality of the God-man. In John's thinking, the real danger of iconoclasm was that it failed to grasp the significance of the most important event in human history. For the Christian, the invisible, transcendent God had become visible and incarnate. God now had a human face.

It was not the last time in the Christian story that iconoclasm was an issue. Sixteenth-century Protestant reformers such as **Calvin** and Zwingli expressly condemned the potential idolatry linked to the use of statues, relics, and other holy objects.[23] The climax of Reformation iconoclasm was the Beeldenstorm when, in the summer of 1556, several monasteries were attacked and statues destroyed in what is now the Netherlands and Belgium. **Protestant Christianity** is still wary, and its preference for churches without statues and icons is reminiscent of the synagogue and the mosque. On the other hand, **Orthodox** and **Catholic** Christianity embraced the eighth-century victory over iconoclasm and their churches are typically characterized by mosaics, murals, stained-glass

Figure 1.3
Christian mosaics in the Hagia Sophia, Istanbul

windows, frescoes, paintings, and statues. Many of these may depict human figures such as Mary and the saints, but the most prominent place is usually reserved for an image of Christ. It may be as an infant at his mother's breast, as dying victim on the cross, or as glorious risen Lord, but the principle is the same – the incarnate Son is the visible icon of the invisible God.

Although it is often categorized together with the other monotheistic faiths of Judaism and Islam, on closer inspection Christianity has a different hue. In the sense that it admits a plurality within the one godhead, the conceivability of divine incarnation in human form, and the widespread use of sacred images in worship, it actually resembles not so much its cousin religions of the Middle East but that ancient religious system of the Orient, beyond the Indus river.

Murti

In the ancient Hindu texts known as the Shilpa Shastras [Treatises on Art], which date from the first or second centuries BCE, one finds highly detailed instructions on how to design and make a sacred statue. Prescriptions depend upon the divine subject whose image is being created, and include meticulous guidelines with regard to posture, shape, features, hand gestures, color, symbols, and so forth. The artist is directed as to which type of wood or stone should be used, how to clean the raw material, and what rituals should be carried out during the carving and painting processes. Once complete, the image is still not ready for use in worship until a special consecration ceremony is held. Priests recite the blessing formula and purify the image with substances such as honey and butter. By touching various parts of the statue and breathing into it, the sacred minister facilitates the "installation" of divine presence in the object. The high point comes when the priest uncovers the sealed eyes, often with a special ceremonial needle. The entire ritual is appropriately named prana pratistha – the infusion of breath. From this moment, what was merely dead wood or stone becomes for the worshiper a sacred icon and a channel for divine blessings – a **murti**.

For many Hindu schools, it is almost impossible to envisage worship without the murti.[24] In most Hindu traditions, the sacred image is an integral component of ritual adoration whether in the public space of a temple or the private sphere of a home. It is the center of attention and the heart of all symbolic acts during the service. Typically a statue will be kept concealed in the inner sanctum of a temple or behind a simple curtain or cabinet door in homes. At the time of worship, a portable murti will be brought out into a special viewing room in the temple, or simply uncovered in the domestic context.

The fact that the climax of the consecration ceremony involves uncovering the eyes indicates the importance of the visual for the Hindu. Seeing is all important and the eyes of the murti are often disproportionately large or highlighted in some way. In fact, Hindus often refer to the practice of worshiping before a murti as **darshana**, which literally means "an audience." The believer comes to the deity just as a humble subject might come before the king, in the hope that they will be granted a hearing for their concerns. The royal encounter theme is also reflected in the ritual actions performed on the murti during worship. Each gesture is meant to represent the cordialities that one would normally extend to an important visitor in one's house. First, the face, arms, and feet of the statue are washed or sprinkled with water, just as a weary traveler might cleanse and refresh themselves after a tiring journey. The murti is then dressed in splendid clothing and adorned with jewelry, flowers, and perfumes. Finally a meal is prepared and placed before the special guest for their consumption. Moreover, the term *darshana* can also connote "religious vision"; it is the fervent hope of the worshiper to actually "see" the deity through the image in a powerful, mystical sense.

Given the prominent role the murti plays in Hindu worship, it is not surprising that adherents of the Semitic monotheistic religions have often branded the practice as idolatrous. However, the Hindu devotee is fully aware that the infinite cannot be captured or exhausted by a finite man-made statue. The murti itself is not the object of adoration and prayer, but functions as a tangible sign of the presence and power of transcendent reality. For the Hindu, the murti is the physical channel of divine energy, a visible point of access between heaven and earth. Although Hindus would agree with Jews and Muslims that the Absolute is beyond all worldly forms, nevertheless, along with many Christians, they also assert that it can be effectively encountered via sacred symbols and images. Hinduism, like much of Christianity, is a highly sacramental religion in which concrete signs are the conduits of divine favor and effective symbols of the divine presence.

In Hindu theology, the justification for the use of visible images to symbolize invisible divinity is based on the twin concepts of nirguna and saguna. The former refers to the utterly transcendent nature of the Absolute, which is beyond form or attribute or any quality that can be envisaged by the human mind. Nirguna is the ineffable, incomprehensible, elusive nature of the Absolute that remains forever shrouded in mystery, beyond images and imagination. However, in order for the human mind to approach and worship ultimate mystery, it is appropriate to symbolize it in concrete form – saguna. In this way what is abstract and transcendent is conceived of and worshiped in a form that is more recognizable such as the humanlike deities **Vishnu**, **Shiva**, or the **Mother Goddess**. For the various Hindu traditions that worship one of these main manifestations of the Absolute, there is both dissimilarity and similarity between transcendent reality and the empirical world. Divinity will always transcend the image depicted by the murti, but something of divinity is authentically captured in the artistic representation as well.

The difference–likeness tension is also reflected in the features of the murti itself. Sometimes the object is non-anthropomorphic such as sacred stones or the phallic **linga** of Shiva. More often the murti is anthropomorphic and each particular deity is identifiable by symbols and features specified in the Shilpa Shastras. For example, Vishnu is usually recognizable by blue skin and the four symbols he carries: a conch, a mace, a discus, and a lotus.[25] On the other hand, Shiva is usually depicted with white skin, a crescent moon in his hair, carrying a trident and a drum.[26] Yet even though the Hindu deity is generally portrayed as humanlike, there are also non-human and superhuman features such as the elephant head of the popular **Ganesha** or the many arms that hold various objects – another reminder that there is still a significant difference between the divine and the human.

Figure 1.4
Sacred image (murti) of the Hindu goddess Durga

Mention of Vishnu, Shiva, and the Mother Goddess raises another aspect of Hinduism that is often of concern to monotheistic outsiders: its apparent polytheism. In the town of Mandore, just five miles from the city of Jodhpur in Rajasthan, lie the ruins of the old capital of Marwar. Among the buildings and gardens, the visitor comes across a more recent construction housing enormous figures of many Hindu gods and local heroes. It is known as the Shrine of Three Hundred Million Gods. The number is astronomical, almost bizarre, and yet, according to tradition, that is the number of gods in Hinduism. Indeed, the visitor to any Indian temple would notice that the statues and carvings depict a bewildering array of different divine characters. Reasonably familiar names such as Shiva, Vishnu, Brahma, Ganesha, Krishna, Rama, Skanda, Lakshmi, Parvati, Durga, Kali, Varuna, Indra, Agni, and Garuda are just the tip of the iceberg. The full Hindu pantheon is truly overwhelming and at first glance the religion seems to be unmistakably polytheistic. However, things are not always as they seem, especially in the Hindu universe. In fact there are good reasons why Hinduism could just as legitimately be described as an example of monistic theism or henotheism.

In actual practice, individual Hindus tend to devote themselves to one particular divine figure or ishta devata, rather than worship the entire pantheon or turn to several of the major Hindu gods simultaneously. For example, in the **Shaivite** and **Vaishnavite** traditions of Hinduism, the figure of Shiva or Vishnu respectively is considered to be the one true divine being while other characters of the pantheon are secondary spirits, incapable of bringing definitive liberation. The principle is succinctly expressed in a verse from one of the most widely read texts in the vast library of Hindu literature, the **Bhagavad Gita** [Song of the Lord]. Lord Vishnu, incarnate in human form as **Krishna**, speaks:

> Even those who in faith worship other gods, because of their love they worship me, although not in the right way. For I accept every sacrifice, and I am their Lord supreme. But they know not my pure Being, and because of this they fall.[27]

So, although the heavens are full of various quasi-divine beings, there are traditions within Hinduism that profess an ultimate single deity who is the proper object of worship above them all.

In the other major Hindu theological tradition, the **Advaita**, each of the many gods provides an insight into the one ultimate mystery. In this school, divine figures such as Shiva, Vishnu, or the Mother Goddess[28] are like the multiple colors of a beam of light refracted through a prism. Each captures something of the richness of the one ultimate reality. Moreover, the One possesses such inexhaustible richness that 300 million light beams are needed just to begin to reflect its profundity. The term in Hinduism that best denotes the One above the gods is **Brahman**. It is the one ultimate source of all truth and goodness, one fundamental ground of all existence, the origin and end of all things. It is even beyond personification and is better understood as an impersonal Absolute rather than a personal God as in the **Semitic religions**. *Brahman* is the highest and holiest word in Hinduism. Moreover, it has been a part of Hindu theology from early days. The notion is discussed in the **Upanishads**, the earliest of which were composed prior to 500 BCE. There are even earlier hints of a fundamental **monism** lying beneath the ostensible polytheism of the **Rg Veda**, an ancient anthology of hymns to various Hindu gods:

> They call him Indra, Mitra, Varuna, Agni,
> and he is heavenly noble-winged Garutmat.
> To what is One, sages give many a title,
> they call it Agni, Yama, Matarisvan.[29]

Just as the concept of Trinity suggests that Christianity is not simply monotheistic, so too the concepts of ishta devata and Brahman suggest that the many religious traditions that are categorized under the generic title of Hinduism cannot simply be described as polytheistic. Both religions acknowledge a mix of singularity and plurality within transcendent reality. Unity and differentiation coincide within absolute being.

This is not the only interesting connection between Hinduism and Christianity with regard to practical worship and its implications for a theology of transcendent reality. The widespread use of sacred images in both faiths presumes a fundamental similarity between divinity and humanity. This similarity is expressed in concrete terms via the notion of **incarnation**. In Christianity, the incarnation of a divine person in human nature has occurred once, and only once, in all of history. It is a salvific event of unparalleled proportion that has transformed both divine and human nature forever. In Vaishnavite Hinduism, there has been a series of incarnations as part of the gracious activity of Lord Vishnu who takes on creaturely form in times of crisis in order to save the world:

> For the salvation of those who are good, for the destruction of evil in men, for the fulfilment of the kingdom of righteousness, I come to this world in the ages that pass.[30]

Hindus call these incarnations the **avatars** of Vishnu. Over 20 are mentioned in Hindu literature,[31] but tradition highlights nine major ones, with a tenth expected at the end of this age. Commentators have noted how the list seems to reflect an evolutionary progress from sea creature to terrestrial animal to human (see box 1.5). Although there are clear differences between the 10 mythological avatars of Hinduism and the claim to a single historical incarnation in Christianity, nevertheless both religions accept the notion that the metaphysical gulf between the divine and the human can be bridged by the gracious descent of the divine into our world. Just as Jewish and Islamic iconoclasm underlines the fundamental difference between the divine and the human, the Christian icon and the Hindu murti attest to a genuine similarity as well.

Box 1.5

THE 10 AVATARS OF VISHNU

1   Matsya, the fish
2   Kurma, the tortoise
3   Varaha, the boar
4   Narasimha, the man-lion
5   Vamana, the dwarf
6   Parashurama, the hero with the ax
7   Rama
8   Krishna
9   Buddha (or Balarama)
10 Kalki, the one to come

A person perusing the list of avatars for the first time might be surprised by the ninth name. In some Hindu sources it is recorded as Balarama, the brother of Krishna. However, in the more common version it is the famed Indian prince who forsook the comfort of palace life, found Enlightenment under the bodhi tree, and became founder of one of the world's great religions. For Hindus, the Buddha is one of a series of divine incarnations, but what do Buddhists believe about their founder?

 ## The Three Bodies

The first period of explicit Buddhist art commences with the reign of the Mauryan emperor **Ashoka** (c.273–232 BCE), who converted to Buddhism and promoted the new faith through extensive construction projects. What is striking in this earliest period is the absence of any human representations of the founder. Typically, the **Buddha** is represented by abstract symbols such as a wheel (symbolizing his teaching), the bodhi tree (under which he received **Enlightenment**), a lion (a popular theme under Ashoka), a lotus plant (Buddha's purity in a soiled world), a footprint (his impact on the world), or even an empty throne (his absence). Some speculate that the early avoidance of any likeness springs from the Buddha's own wish that there be no representations of his physical form after his death. The trend changes dramatically in the first century CE in northern India when anthropomorphic statues and sculptures suddenly begin to appear. To this day tens of millions of Buddha images adorn temples and homes throughout the world.

The most common posture for the Buddha image is a meditation position with legs crossed, although sometimes he is depicted reclining in death, sitting on a chair, or walking on a missionary journey. The facial expression is usually one of serenity and calm, a result of the advanced state of mind that comes from Enlightenment. At first, the sitting Buddha images may look monotonously identical, but upon closer inspection the onlooker notices that the positions of the hands vary. These are the **mudras** of a Buddha statue and, like the posture, they carry different meanings: resting in the lap (meditating); holding a bowl (seeking alms); touching the earth (resisting temptation); raised in front of the chest (teaching).

All of these are natural human features, but there is also a supernatural aspect to the Buddha statues that reflect the special status of their subject. According to tradition, a Buddha has the 32 major and 80 minor marks of a superior being. For example, one of these marks is the ushinisha – a bump on the top of the head in either the form of fire, representing spiritual energy, or the shape of stubble resulting from the cutting of his hair on the night he renounced his old life. Another example is the urna, which is a mark in the center of the forehead symbolizing the third eye of wisdom. The images of an eight-spoked wheel are also found on the soles of the feet, indicating the Noble Eightfold Path to final liberation.

Figure 1.5
Buddha statue at Kamakura, Japan

So the question arises: who is the subject depicted by these images that blend natural and supernatural qualities? The immediate answer is the sixth-century BCE figure named **Siddhartha Gautama**, at times referred to as **Sakyamuni** [Sage of the Sakya People] but better known as the Buddha. Like the term *Christ*, *Buddha* is not a surname but an epithet, in this case meaning "Enlightened One." However, in Buddhist thinking, there is more than one Buddha. The **Theravada** tradition[32] speaks of at least 28 Buddhas

Table 1.1   The Five Wisdom Buddhas of Tibetan Vajrayana Buddhism

	North	*South*	*East*	*West*	*Center*
Name	Amoghasiddhi	Ratnasambhava	Akshobhya	Amitabha	Vairocana
Color	green	yellow	blue	red	white
Element	air	earth	water	fire	ether
Hand position	protection	giving	touching earth	meditation	teaching

prior to Sakyamuni, who is the Buddha for our age. In the **Mahayana** tradition[33] there is not only a series of Buddhas throughout the great ages but also a host of celestial figures known as Buddhas and bodhisattvas, all of whom are vividly portrayed in statues and images across the Buddhist world.[34] Some of these heavenly figures resides in a "pure land" or Buddha field where believers go after death provided they have faithfully expressed their devotion during this life. The pure land is not quite final liberation, but is the penultimate stage of the spiritual journey, for there are no further impediments to complete enlightenment in such a perfect world.

Tibetan Buddhism has developed the notion of the Five Wisdom Buddhas who inhabit pure lands at the cardinal points of heaven: north, south, east, west, and center (see table 1.1). Each Buddha is recognizable by a particular color, mudra, symbol, cosmic element, vehicle, and so on. Arguably the most popular of these celestial Buddhas, not only in Tibet but throughout Asia in general, is the Buddha of the Western Pure Land – **Amitabha**.[35] The second most eminent religious figure in Tibet, the **Panchen Lama**, is considered to be his incarnation. In fact, so popular was Amitabha that historical tensions have arisen between Buddhist schools over whether Amitabha or the historical Sakyamuni is more important and thus the true center of devotional practice.[36]

Each of the Five Wisdom Buddhas is accompanied by a **bodhisattva** (wisdom being). These are beings that have gained perfection and are ready for final liberation. However, they postpone **nirvana** out of compassionate concern and linger in this world in order to assist with the liberation of others. The ideal of selfless consideration embodied in the bodhisattva reflects the notion that spiritual liberation has a communitarian dimension. It is about *us* rather than just me. Moreover, the idea that there are generous, caring beings available to help is a deeply consoling one for struggling believers. The first of the four traditional bodhisattva vows eloquently captures the idea:

> However innumerable beings are, I vow to save them;
> however inexhaustible the passions are I vow to extinguish them;
> however immeasurable the dharmas are I vow to master them;
> however incomparable the Buddha-truth is, I vow to attain it.

The most popular bodhisattva is **Avalokiteshvara**, companion to Amitabha of the Western Pure Land. Personified as the female **Kwanyin** in China and the male **Kwannon** in Japan, Avalokiteshvara is the one who looks down in compassion. In Buddhist art, he/she is usually portrayed in Hindu style, with thousands of arms, capable of reaching all in need. Indeed, the **Dalai Lama** of Tibet is believed to be an incarnation of Avalokiteshvara and the most popular Tibetan **mantra**, uttered by millions every day, is addressed to this bodhisattva: "Om Mani Padme Hum" [Hail to the Jewel in the Lotus].

So the serene Buddha figures that are found in temple and home might represent a historical human figure or a group of transhistorical heavenly beings. But are they in any way *divine* images like the Christian icon or the Hindu murti? Are the celestial Buddhas in some sense *gods* like the Hindu deities who manifest a particular aspect of infinite Brahman? Is the historical Sakyamuni some sort of divine incarnation, similar to how Hindus understand him to be the ninth avatar of Vishnu?

On one hand, the answer to such questions must be negative. Buddhism is generally considered an exceptional case among the five major world religions in that it is not clear whether Buddhists actually believe in a supreme being. In this sense Buddhism is oxymoronic – an agnostic religion – which is why some prefer to categorize it as a philosophy. According to the sources, Sakyamuni was silent on the question of the existence of God. The core of his message, summarized as the **Four Noble Truths**, provides a diagnosis of the source of human suffering as well as a lasting remedy. His primary concern is to map out a reliable path to ultimate liberation from all forms of suffering – physical, psychological, or existential. This path does not require belief in or devotion to a supreme being. Sakyamuni does not explicitly deny the existence of God but neither does he affirm it. It seems to be a far cry from Judaism and Islam. If they are religions of one God and no images, Buddhism seems to be a religion with images but no God.

On the other hand, there is a doctrine in Buddhism that not only outlines the deeper theological significance of the Buddha images but also points to a concept that is very close to divinity. It is the teaching of the Three Bodies or Trikaya. According to this concept, a Buddha has three bodies. The first is the nirmana-kaya [created body], which is physical manifestation in time and space, such as the actual body of Sakyamuni that was eventually cremated. The second body is the sambhoga-kaya [enjoyment body], that which is usually depicted in the Buddha statue. It has a combination of human and superhuman qualities that symbolize the superior nature of the enlightened ones. This is reputed to be what is seen in advanced states of meditation. The third body is the dharma-kaya [reality body], which is an abstract and absolute principle beyond any historical or transhistorical figure – the **dharma** or Buddha-truth. The Indian prince known as Sakyamuni, the many heavenly figures that await us in their pure lands, and the bodhisattvas who come to our aid and accompany us to those lands are all manifestations of one supreme dharma truth in spatio-temporal form. That ultimate transcendent reality is admittedly not the personal God of the Semitic religions, whose image is strictly prohibited in Judaism and Islam, but justified in Christianity. It is more akin to the non-personal absolute Brahman of Hinduism which stands behind the multiple forms symbolized in the Hindu murti. Similarly, the transcendent dharma truth is made accessible and conceivable to finite minds via the enjoyment bodies depicted in the Buddha statues. Buddhists do not worship the statues but, as in Hinduism and sections of Christianity, they are powerful sacramental representations of a higher principle that pervades the cosmos, providing intelligibility, meaning, and liberation.

SUMMARY

While all five religions share a fundamental belief in a transcendent dimension to reality, there are both similarities and differences concerning their understanding of its true nature and the ways in which it is appropriately envisaged and represented. This chapter has focused on the use or non-use of the sacred image as a means of investigating those similarities and differences.

One of the most striking features of the synagogue and the mosque is the obvious lack of statues, paintings, and icons depicting divinity. While artistic energy tends to be expressed via abstract symbolism and calligraphic design, Judaism and Islam are both absolutely insistent that there is no place for the sacred image in the house of worship. Such strong iconoclastic practice is grounded in the Jewish and Muslim emphasis on the invisibility and otherness of God. The taboo on images reflects their common stress on the transcendent nature of ultimate being. The creator cannot be compared to or portrayed as anything within creation. Any attempt to do so is doomed to failure, since the infinite cannot be captured by the finite. Such an object would undermine the true nature of the deity and its use would be unavoidably idolatrous. Consequently the condemnation of false images is deeply entrenched in both faiths. The rejection of idolatry constitutes the second of the Ten Commandments of Judaism, while shirk is considered to be the most serious of all sins in Islam.

Moreover, Judaism and Islam not only champion the invisibility of God but also God's indivisibility. Idolatry not only fails to appreciate the elusiveness and mystery that shrouds the divine face, but also undermines the monotheistic foundation of both religions. The second Jewish commandment implies that the God of Israel is the only true God, and Islam's first pillar is the proud declaration that there is no God but God. Both Judaism and Islam are truly described as **Abrahamic religions** in that they are both heirs to the legacy of the biblical figure who is considered by many to be the first to embrace an explicit and uncompromising faith in the oneness of God.

There is no doubt that Christianity endorses the ten Jewish commandments including the profession of one God and the rejection of idolatry. But there are interesting differences with Judaism and Islam when it comes to the use of sacred images. In the tradition of the Jewish second commandment and the Islamic rejection of shirk, Protestant Christianity is also suspicious of physical icons and tends to keep such potential idols out of its churches. In contrast, Orthodox and Catholic Christianity warmly endorse such artworks and treat the statue, the painting, and the mosaic as valid components of worship. On this point, these Christian traditions not only move away from the Jewish and Islamic practice, but also reflect a distinctive element in Christian belief that is employed as a justification for the use of the sacred image. That belief is the central Christian claim that God has become incarnate in the person of Jesus. In Christian thinking, the infinite transcendent God has assumed finite human nature forever. God now has a human face, and thus the image of the human Christ is not an idol but a window on divinity. If Jewish, Muslim, and Protestant Christian avoidance of the sacred image reflects the genuine difference between creator and creature, the Orthodox and Catholic use of the sacred image stresses a basic similarity between the divine and the human, which renders the concept of incarnation paradoxical but conceivable.

The Christian belief that Jesus is the incarnate Son of God not only constitutes a key element in the argument about the use or non-use of sacred images, but also has profound consequences for Christian monotheism. The idea that one aspect of God has taken on human nature (Son) while a second distinct aspect of God remains beyond the human (Father) leads naturally to the idea of three "persons" in one God. The Incarnation is the basis for the Christian doctrine of the Trinity. Thus, although Christianity is described as the third sibling in the Abrahamic family of monotheistic religions, the concept of a triune God means that it is a nuanced monotheism: a unity-in-plurality.

In so far as Christianity professes a mix of singularity and plurality within transcendent being, claims that divinity has assumed human form via an incarnation, and (at least in certain Christian traditions) endorses the use of sacred images, it resembles not so much its Semitic cousins as Hinduism. The sacred image or murti is an integral part of worship in many Hindu traditions. Fashioned according to ancient guidelines and consecrated via the infusion of sacred breath, the murti represents a tangible point of contact between the profane and the sacred. Reminiscent of the Christian position, the use of the murti in Hinduism is justified by the doctrine of nirguna/saguna which acknowledges that ultimate being is simultaneously dissimilar and similar to the visible world. This paradox is reflected in the combination of non-anthropomorphic and anthropomorphic features in most statues and paintings. Moreover, the similarity is further supported by the tradition of Vishnu's avatars (incarnations). Although there are 10 traditional incarnations rather than one, and some of these are animal, nevertheless Hindus share the belief with Christians that the ontological gulf between divine and human is not so unbridgeable that the divine cannot assume human form.

The multiplicity of different figures represented by murtis also reflects the vastness of the Hindu pantheon, traditionally placed at 300 million gods. Such a staggering number tends to reinforce the popular notion that Hinduism is polytheistic. However, nirguna is a reminder that the many Hindu deities are ultimately particular manifestations of ultimate being itself (Brahman). Moreover, most Hindus tend to devote themselves to one particular form (ishta devata) of Brahman such as Vishnu, Shiva, or the Mother Goddess. Again, like Christianity, Hinduism sits easily with the notion that transcendent reality involves both the one and the many.

Finally, Buddhism's agnosticism with regard to the existence of a personal God or even Brahman itself sets it apart from the other four faiths and leads many to question whether it is in fact a religion at all. Nevertheless, everyday Buddhist practices are ostensibly religious, including the widespread use of the Buddha image for meditation and supplication. In this sense Buddhism is the converse of Judaism and Islam. If the latter are religions with one God and no images, the former is a religion with images but no God. Yet even this is not the full picture since many Buddha images in Mahayana practice do not depict the historical founder but celestial beings (Pure Land Buddhas and bodhisattvas) who are committed to assisting struggling believers on earth. These transcendent beings are accessed by devotion through the tangible Buddha image with the purpose of gaining assistance on the journey to liberation. Furthermore, even the statues that depict the historical Buddha suggest that there is more here than meets the non-believing eye. Many of the superhuman features that are incorporated into the image reflect the doctrine of the Buddha's three bodies (Trikaya), implying that Sakyamuni was more than merely a wise teacher from the past and in fact represents a historical personification of an eternal, transcendent truth.

The idea of an eternal, absolute truth that pervades the universe and is made manifest in time and space touches on a second principal way in which religious believers, especially in the iconoclastic religions of Judaism and Islam, access transcendent reality – not via the visual sacred image but via the words of a holy book.

DISCUSSION TOPICS

1   What is the difference between monotheism, monism, henotheism, and polytheism?
2   Are humans made in the "image of God" or is there an unbridgeable difference between humanity and divinity?
3   Why are images banned in Judaism and Islam? Are there exceptions?
4   What are Sufism and the Kabbalah? Why are they sometimes seen as undermining Islamic and Jewish monotheism?
5   What does the traditional iconography of Vishnu, Shiva, or the Mother Goddess tell us about the Hindu understanding of divinity?

6 Compare and contrast the Christian Trinity (Father, Son, and Holy Spirit) and the Hindu "Trinity" (Brahma, Vishnu, and Shiva).

7 Compare and contrast the notion of divine incarnation in Hinduism and Christianity.

8 How have Christ and Buddha been portrayed in religious art throughout history? What does this tell us about how they are perceived in their respective religions?

9 Is it appropriate to depict divinity in feminine as well as masculine form?

10 Should Buddhism be called a religion if it does not profess faith in a supreme being?

FURTHER READING

Cohn-Sherbok, Dan (2003). *Judaism: History, Belief and Practice*. London: Routledge, pp. 343–56.

Corrigan, John, et al. (1997). *Jews, Christians, Muslims: A Comparative Introduction to Monotheistic Religions*. Upper Saddle River, NJ: Prentice Hall, pp. 75–152.

Eck, Diana (1998). *Darsan: Seeing the Image in India*. 3rd edn. New York: Columbia University Press.

Gordon, Matthew S. (2002). *Understanding Islam*. London: Duncan Baird, pp. 22–35.

Grimes, John (2004). "Darshana," in Sushil Mittal (ed.), *The Hindu World*, Abingdon: Routledge, ch. 23.

Harvey, Peter (1990). *An Introduction to Buddhism: Teaching, History and Practices*. Cambridge: Cambridge University Press, ch. 8.

Hertzberg, Arthur (ed.) (1998). *Judaism*. New York: Free Press, pp. 63–76.

Klostermaier, Klaus (1994). *A Survey of Hinduism*. 2nd edn. Albany, NY: SUNY Press, ch. 20.

Knott, Kim (2000). *Hinduism: A Very Short Introduction*. Oxford and New York: Oxford University Press, pp. 50–9.

Morgan, David (2005). *The Sacred Gaze: Religious Visual Culture in Theory and Practice*. Berkeley and Los Angeles: University of California Press.

Reynolds, Frank E., & Carbine, Jason A. (eds.) (2000). *The Life of Buddhism*. Berkeley and Los Angeles: University of California Press, ch. 2.

Swearer, Donald K. (2004). *Becoming the Buddha: The Ritual of Image Consecration in Thailand*. Princeton, NJ: Princeton University Press, chs. 1–2.

Zibawi, Mahmoud (1993). *The Icon: Its Meaning and History*. Collegeville, MN: Liturgical Press.

NOTES

1 The Ten Commandments are also found in Deuteronomy 5:6–21.

2 Jewish tradition includes the commandment to respect one's parents as part of the divine category.

3   Exodus 20:3.

4   The term *henotheism* was coined by the nineteenth-century German scholar Max Müller.

5   Initially the Shema consisted only of two verses: Deuteronomy 6:4–5 (see Talmud Sukkot 42a and Berachot 13b). However, the liturgical recitation of the Shema usually includes three other biblical passages: Deuteronomy 6:6–9; 11:13–21; and Numbers 15:37–41.

6   Deuteronomy 6:7.

7   Deuteronomy 6:8–9.

8   Exodus 20:4–5.

9   See Exodus 32:20.

10   The destruction of both the First Temple by the Babylonians (586 BCE) and the Second Temple by the Romans (70 CE) is commemorated in the Jewish calendar on **Tisha B'Av**, the ninth day of the month of Av.

11   Pilgrims in Mecca endeavor to reach out and touch the black stone (Al-hajar Al-aswad) which is set into the exterior of the Ka'bah at one corner. The object predates Islam and is considered to be a symbol of the covenant between God and Abraham.

12   Rather than designate a proper name for the deity, "Allah" is the Arabic term for "the one God" and is used by Christian and Jewish Arabs as well as Muslims. Scholars believe that it is etymologically linked to the Hebrew word "El," which appears as a divine name in the Jewish scriptures.

13   Qur'an 112:1–4.

14   Qur'an 4:48 states: "Surely Allah does not forgive that anything should be associated with Him, and forgives what is besides that to whomsoever He pleases; and whoever associates anything with Allah, he devises indeed a great sin."

15   Qur'an 4:171.

16   Qur'an 21:98.

17   A more recent and radical example of the Islamic abhorrence for idolatrous images is the destruction of the ancient Buddha statues of Bamyan, Afghanistan in May 2001 by the extremist Taliban regime.

18   It is known as the Second Council of Nicea. The Catholic Church counts another 14 subsequent councils as "ecumenical" (representative of the entire Church) but these are not recognized as such by Orthodox and Protestant Christians.

19   The formal statement of Christian faith issued by the First Council of Nicea (325) and revised at the following Council of Constantinople (381). The majority of Christian churches today are in fundamental agreement on its content. The creed is recited during Sunday services in many churches including the Catholic, Orthodox, and Anglican traditions.

20   The creed ends with very succinct statements concerning the Church, baptism, resurrection, and the world to come.

21   Mark 8:29.

22   Orthodox Christians touch their right then left shoulder, while Catholics begin with the left shoulder.

23   For example, see Calvin's *Institutes of the Christian Religion*, book 1, ch. 12.

24   There are exceptions such as the **Arya Samaj** movement which banned the use of the sacred image in favor of the ancient Vedic fire ritual.

25 Traditionally the conch represents creativity, the mace existence, the discus mind, and the lotus liberation.

26 The moon symbolizes the ephemeral nature of reality, the trident the three fundamental forces of nature (creation, preservation, and destruction), and the drum the rhythm of Shiva's eternal dance which sustains the universe in existence.

27 Bhagavad Gita 9:23.

28 A fourth major tradition in Hinduism worships the One in the form of the Mother Goddess. Even in the Vaishnavite and Shaivite traditions, the feminine aspect of divinity is explicitly acknowledged via **Lakshmi** and **Parvati**, the female consorts of Vishnu and Shiva respectively. In Hindu spirituality, the active female principle complements the passive male principle.

29 Rg Veda 1.164.46.

30 Bhagavad Gita 4:8.

31 For example, see Bhagavata Purana, canto 1, ch. 3.

32 The Theravada, or Southern, school of Buddhism is predominant in countries such as Sri Lanka, Burma, Thailand, and Cambodia. It is also known as the Hinayana (Lesser Vehicle) tradition but the term is generally avoided due to its pejorative connotation.

33 The Mahayana, or Northern, school of Buddhism is prevalent in China, Japan, Korea, and Vietnam. The Tantric or Vajrayana (Diamond Vehicle) school of Tibet is sometimes identified as a third major division, although doctrinally it can be considered an extension of the Mahayana School.

34 Although the concept of bodhisattva is primarily a feature of Mahayana Buddhism, the Theravada tradition admits one such being, **Maitreya**, who will become the Buddha at the end of our present age. Sakyamuni is considered to have been a bodhisattva in his previous lives which are narrated in the **Jataka Tales**.

35 Amitabha is known as Amida in Japan and O-Mi-To-Fu in China.

36 For example, the medieval Japanese schools founded by Shinran and Nichiren stressed devotion to Amitabha and Sakyamuni respectively.

Chapter 2

BOOK

CONTENTS

Introduction

Whether a religion supports or condemns the use of sacred images, each of the five major religions possesses a set of written texts that are considered to be uniquely holy and authoritative. If not all faiths accept the validity of visual access to the transcendent via a painting or an icon, there is a greater willingness to accept the legitimacy of verbal access. Religions may disagree as to whether the divine face can be depicted, but there is a broad consensus that the divine voice can be heard and the divine word captured in human language. In this chapter we shall explore the sacred books of each religion. What are their form and contents? What is the basis of their authority? Who were the human authors involved? Who may read the texts and how are they used in ritual and daily practice?

ॐ Shruti and Smriti

In common English parlance a pundit is an expert in a particular field of knowledge, whose opinion is therefore regarded as highly informed and authoritative. The word is derived from the Hindu term *pandit* – someone who chants hallowed texts from memory at official religious sacrifices. For the Hindu, the gesture of offering food and drink to the gods must be accompanied by the sound of the sacred words if the ceremony is to be efficacious. Sign is accompanied by word; the visual is complemented by the verbal. Naturally, the art of memorizing the words and singing them to designated melodies and rhythms is both demanding and highly respected. In one sense, the pandit truly is an expert in holy writ.

The special texts that are memorized and chanted by the pandit are many and varied, but for many Hindu sects the holiest and most authoritative books are a set of writings known as the **Vedas**. The Sanskrit term *Veda* literally means knowledge and may be etymologically linked to the Latin word for "vision." The Vedas are generally considered to be the earliest and most esteemed part of the vast library of Hindu religious writings. Scholars estimate that they may have been composed anywhere between 1500 and 500 BCE, a period often referred to as the Vedic Age of Hinduism.

The Vedas comprise four works written in ancient Sanskrit:

Rg Veda (The Veda of Verses)
Sama Veda (The Veda of Chants)
Yajur Veda (The Veda of Sacrificial Prayers)
Atharva Veda (The Veda of the Fire Priests)

The oldest and most important is the **Rg Veda**, which is a collection of over 1,000 hymns to early Hindu deities such as Indra (god of war), Varuna (god of law), and Agni (god of fire). Later classical gods such as **Shiva** and **Vishnu** appear only briefly and as minor characters at this stage of development.[1] The Yajur Veda gathers together formulas used at sacrifices while the Sama Veda is an anthology of mantras drawn from the Rg Veda and rearranged for musical recital at formal ceremonies. Finally, the Atharva Veda is somewhat different from the other three in that it contains magic spells and incantations that have little to do with the sacrificial system and are more typical of popular folk religion.

Each Veda contains not only a core collection of hymns (samhita) but also attachments known as brahmanas. These are essentially rubrics and instructions that insure the ritual is carried out in the proper manner. Thus the first two layers of the Vedic texts form an extensive hymnbook and manual for Hindu ritual. However, the brahmanas are not the only texts attached to the hymnodies. Each Veda also has appendixes known as Aranyakas (forest treatises) and **Upanishads** [Sitting at the Feet]. As the terms imply, these are works that were composed not in connection with official village ceremonies, but rather in the quiet refuge of the forest where the student sat at the feet of a spiritual master and learnt wisdom beyond mere ritual orthodoxy (see box 2.1).

Box 2.1	THE PRINCIPAL UPANISHADS (AND CORRESPONDING VEDAS)	
	1 Aitareya	Rg
	2 Kausitaki	Rg
	3 Chandogya	Sama
	4 Kena	Sama
	5 Maitrayani	Sama
	6 Brhadaranyaka	Yajur
	7 Isa	Yajur
	8 Katha	Yajur
	9 Shvetashvatara	Yajur
	10 Taittiriya	Yajur
	11 Mandukya	Atharva
	12 Mundhaka	Atharva
	13 Prashna	Atharva

The Aranyakas and the Upanishads contain philosophical musings set in dialogue form that explore classical themes such as the meaning of human existence, the identity of the self, and its relation to the absolute. In fact, it is in the Upanishads that we find, for the first time, serious speculation about post-death existence and the emerging notion of **reincarnation**. For some, these writings correspond to the advanced stages of an ideal Hindu existence, where the believer is expected to relinquish family ties and retire to the forest in order to devote himself to meditation and spiritual inquiry. The Hindu theological tradition that draws inspiration from the Upanishads is known as **Vedanta**: the *end* of the Vedas in the sense of fulfillment rather than mere termination. In this tradition, the Upanishads are understood as the completion of the Vedas, bringing them to their ultimate purpose.

This fascinating combination of devotional hymns, **liturgical** guidelines, and existential musings has enjoyed a traditional pre-eminence in Hindu religious literature. Consequently the contents of these texts are described as **shruti**. The term literally means "that which is heard," implying that the ultimate source of the ideas encapsulated in these books lies beyond the human. "That which is heard" is from above, from the heavens: these are divine, not human words. According to Hindu tradition, the Vedas were revealed to sages in an ancient era, a distant mythical past. These privileged ones, known as **rishis**, received the divine knowledge while in an advanced state of meditation, the product of years of dedication and study. The Rg Veda implies that this state of mind exists on another plane of mental awareness, in the world of the gods: "the rishis abide in the immutable supreme ether where are seated all the gods."[2] This inspired knowledge was translated into **Sanskrit**, considered to be the most perfect of human languages, and handed on for the benefit of posterity.

In contemporary Hindu sects that acknowledge the Vedas as revealed truth, these hymns are often read through the lens of the Upanishads and subsequent theological development. Rather than being interpreted literally as songs addressed to personified natural forces and processes, they are seen as metaphors of the soul's quest for ultimate union with **Brahman**. It is often pointed out that the authors of the Upanishads are themselves also anonymous, with the implication that their content is also independent of the human writer. Like the Vedas they possess a knowledge that transcends the original historical context and is relevant to all generations. The true author is beyond the human instrument and the message is an unchanging truth that must be handed on from generation to generation.

What is striking about the Vedic tradition within Hinduism is that this revealed knowledge is not for everyone's eyes or ears. Shruti literature is restricted to a specific audience. According to the ancient legal code of Hinduism, the **Laws of Manu**, only adult males from the upper three classes are considered worthy to read this most sublime genre of sacred writing.[3] Those who belong to this privileged social group are known as the **twice-born**, since they participate in an initiation ceremony at the end of childhood that is analogical to a second, spiritual birth. The Vedas become their second mother, metaphorically. The underlying presumption is that only the twice-born possess the spiritual maturity necessary to appreciate and appropriate the wisdom found in the shruti writings.

Thus it is considered inappropriate for women and children, as well as male members of the lower classes, to access these works. This means that the majority of believers do not have direct access to the holiest set of religious writings. How does Hinduism justify such disenfranchisement from the very source of wisdom needed for ultimate liberation? The traditional response is that, in the Hindu world view, the twice-born are considered to be at a more advanced stage on the spiritual journey and are thus more capable of appreciating the profundity of the shruti writings. Moreover, this advancement is the result of the build-up of good **karma** over many previous lives. That they are male members of the upper classes at this point in their journey is a consequence of the law of karma which states that the extent to which a person fulfills the duties of this particular life determines the form in which they will be reincarnated in the next. The shruti texts are for those who are nearing the end of that epic journey.[4]

However, the ban does not imply that those who are not twice-born have no spiritual resources whatsoever to draw on. As mentioned earlier, the size and extent of the full corpus of Hindu religious writings is quite staggering. The shruti texts themselves constitute many bound volumes, but there are hundreds of other writings that are worthy of study and are also used in private and public worship. This is the vast category of **smriti** writings, a term that means "remembered." In contrast to shruti literature, which is divine wisdom "heard" by the sages during deep meditation and subsequently handed on, smriti literature is a mix of both divine inspiration and human composition. Thus smriti is considered to be less authoritative than shruti. Nevertheless, because smriti is not restricted to the twice-born, it is actually more familiar to the average Hindu. Some of the most important smriti texts include poetic tales of the classical gods Shiva and Vishnu, known as the **Puranas** and the two great epics, the **Ramayana** and the **Mahabharata**.

Deep in the heart of the Mahabharata[5] lies arguably the most popular and influential religious text in India today – the **Bhagavad Gita** [Song of the Lord]. The Gita is a 700-verse poem that depicts a conversation between **Arjuna**, one of the heroes of the Mahabharata, and **Krishna**, an avatar of Vishnu, who is disguised as his charioteer. The scene takes place on the eve of a great battle during which Krishna advises Arjuna on the importance of both duty and devotion, subsequently revealing himself in his divine glory. Although it is technically part of the smriti literature, the Gita has acquired the status of shruti in most Hindu sects. Indeed its dialogue style and its profound musings on the meaning of life are reminiscent of the Upanishads. For many, its contents are an abiding synthesis of the various theological traditions within Hinduism, especially its teaching of the four ways to liberation: meditation (raja yoga), selfless action (karma yoga), wisdom (jnana yoga), and loving devotion (**bhakti** yoga).

It should also be noted that not all Hindu sects consider the Vedas to be the most important repository of divine truth. For example, Hindu **tantric** sects, whether dedicated to Vishnu, Shiva, or the Mother Goddess, recognize their own sets of writings

Figure 2.1
Rama and Hanuman in Ramayana battle scene

as superior to the Vedas, testifying to the amazing degree of variation within Hinduism itself. Nor is this a recent trend. As long ago as 500 BCE, an Indian spiritual master repudiated the canonical authority and restricted status of the Vedas, declaring that he had found the eternal truth of the universe after an intense night of meditation. The Enlightenment that he gained under a bodhi tree would be eventually be expressed in human language, gathered into "three baskets," and made available to anyone who genuinely sought it, irrespective of age, gender, or class.

The Three Baskets

Soon after the death of Buddha **Sakyamuni** around 480 BCE, about 500 of his disciples gathered at the Saptaparni caves near Rajagaha in northern India. The assembly was presided over by Mahakasyapa, one of Sakyamuni's most revered followers. One of the principal aims of this First Buddhist Council was to identify and accurately record the master's teachings for posterity. According to tradition, the Council turned to two monks renowned for their amazing powers of memory. **Ananda**, the Buddha's cousin and personal assistant, had traveled extensively with the founder and witnessed many

Figure 2.2
Buddha preaching to the first five disciples at Sarnath

of the sermons and discourses to various audiences over the years. It is said that Ananda recited the entirety of the Buddha's teachings for the Council, prefacing each sermon with the declaration: "Thus have I heard on one occasion." A second monk named Upali, who was famous for his diligent commitment to the way of the Buddha, summarized the rules of monastic life.

Although the historical Buddha had passed from this world and was no longer physically present to his community, his doctrinal vision and his practical guidelines for living had been captured and recorded for generations to follow. Monks would memorize the words and teach them diligently to their novices, establishing an unbroken chain of oral transmission. About 100 years later, historians note that a third collection of teachings appeared in which the Buddha's ideas were more logically analyzed and fashioned into a philosophical system. Thus a threefold form of the Buddha's teachings emerged: a collection of Sakyamuni's sayings; an extensive list of his prescriptions for community life; and a systematic analysis of reality as seen through Buddhist eyes. The oral tradition was eventually committed to writing in Sri Lanka around the year 30 CE under the command of King Vattagamani, and so appears the first official written anthology of Buddhist religious texts – a Buddhist canon.

The dominant school of Buddhism in Sri Lanka at the time was the **Theravada** and its scribes used **Pali**, a language that probably originated in western India. Pali was more of a literary language than one used for common speech. In fact, the word *pali* means a line or verse from an authoritative work, indicating that the name may have been derived at a later time when it had already come to designate the sacred text. The canon was also translated in other schools using other languages including Sanskrit, but, because the Theravada school alone survived the demise of Buddhism in India and is now the predominant form of the religion in south and southeast Asia, its canon has acquired widespread acceptance among all Buddhists. Understandably, it is referred to as the "Pali Canon" but because of its tripartite form it is also commonly called **Tipitaka**, or the "**Three Baskets**"[6] (see box 2.2).

The imagery of baskets has several theoretical explanations. Some scholars focus on the ancient method of storage, arguing that the scriptures were originally written on long narrow palm leaves, stitched together at the edges and literally kept in three separate baskets, one for each part of the total collection. Others point to the metaphor of construction workers passing baskets along lines at building sites, thus stressing how the tradition is handed on from generation to generation. Whatever the origin of the analogy, the threefold arrangement is the most salient feature. So what exactly is in each of the baskets?

In the traditional ordering, the first basket is called the **Vinaya Pitaka**, or the Basket of Discipline. It is the smallest of the three and, as its title implies, it consists essentially of lists of disciplinary rules for monastic life. This is the collection that can be traced back to Upali's recitation at the First Council. In total there are 227 regulations

---

THE THREE BASKETS OF BUDDHISM (TIPITAKA) **Box 2.2**

Vinaya Pitaka: The Basket of Discipline
 Suttavibhanga (basic rules)
 Khandhaka (rules and sayings)
 Parivara (summaries)

Sutta Pitaka: The Basket of Threads
 Digha Nikaya [Long Discourses]
 Majjhima Nikaya [Medium Discourses]
 Samyutta Nikaya [Grouped Discourses]
 Anguttara Nikaya [Enumerated Discourses]
 Khuddaka Nikaya [Minor Discourses]

Abhidhamma Pitaka: The Basket of Higher Teaching
 Dhammasangani (phenomena)
 Vibhanga (treatises)
 Dhatukatha (elements)
 Puggalapannatti (individuals)
 Kathavatthu (points of controversy)
 Yamaka (pairs)
 Patthana (relations)

---

for monks (**bhikkhus**) and 311 for nuns (**bhikkhunis**). The rules are designed to insure that monks and nuns live according to the ideals of material simplicity, celibacy, and inoffensiveness. Punishments vary from immediate expulsion for serious offenses to simple acts of penance and confession for relatively minor transgressions. The greater number of rules for females might today be considered as evidence of inherent patriarchy but these were essentially aimed at insuring the well-being and protection of the nuns in times when women were considered to be more vulnerable. In fact, the acceptance of women into monastic life was a revolutionary decision in a Hindu world. Buddhist nuns date back to the very earliest period when the Buddha himself, at Ananda's insistence, agreed to allow his own stepmother to take the habit. The inclusion of women and lower-caste men in the monastic community from the beginning was an important declaration that spiritual advancement is independent of gender and **caste**.

The second basket is the Sutta Pitaka, or the Basket of Threads. The Pali term sutta (or **sutra** in Sanskrit) means a thread, and in both Hinduism and Buddhism it refers to authoritative teachings that were literally sewn together in written collections. Such teachings "sew" together the apparently disparate and disconnected aspects of human existence, investing life with purpose and meaning. In the Pali Canon, this second basket is the largest of the three, containing over 10,000 sayings attributed to the historical Buddha and memorized by Ananda. The Sutta Pitaka is usually divided into five sections or nikaya: (1) long (digha) discourses; (2) medium length (majjhima) discourses; (3) grouped (samyutta) discourses; (4) enumerated (anguttara) discourses, which are arranged according to themes or topics; and (5) minor (khuddaka) discourses.

In one sense, the Sutta Pitaka constitutes the heart of the Pali Canon. Its sayings are considered by Theravada Buddhists to be Buddhavacana, the actual words of Sakyamuni. Typically each teaching is prefaced by Ananda's phrase "Thus have I heard," and the place and occasion of the discourse is provided. As each sermon concludes, the text tells us that the listeners were overjoyed at the wisdom that had been imparted to them. Two of the most beloved and widely read sections of the Sutta Pitaka are the **Dhammapada** and the **Jataka Tales**. The Dhammapada [Verses on the Truth] is an anthology of over 400 short ethical maxims ascribed to the historical Buddha. It plays an important role in the religious life of religious and lay Buddhists and has enjoyed extensive popularity in the West, not unlike the Bhagavad Gita. Its key themes are characteristic of the Buddhist world view such as the quest for inner peace, tolerance toward others, and firm advocacy of non-violence. The Jataka Tales are stories concerning the Buddha's former lives. Although only the oldest poetic sections are considered canonical, the later prose additions recount the gradual spiritual development of the person who was destined to be eventually reincarnated as the Enlightened One for our epoch. The themes of the Jataka Tales are graphically depicted in the bas-reliefs of Buddhist shrines such as Borobudur in Java and Bharhut and Sanchi in central India.

The third basket is the Abhidhamma Pitaka, or Basket of Higher Teaching. Scholars generally agree that this is a later addition to the original two collections that emerged from the First Council. Its contents represent subsequent reflection on, and a more philosophical elaboration of, earlier doctrine. The familiar world of humans, animals, plants, and matter is redefined in terms of fleeting abstract phenomena. Its esoteric themes and its dense, demanding style mean that the Abhidhamma is not widely read except in monasteries and by those who wish to probe Buddhism in a more scholarly fashion. Even Buddhist myth acknowledges that these are not words that were spoken by Sakyamuni during his earthly life. The Abhidhamma is considered to be a pure and highly advanced form of the Buddha's teaching that was revealed from the heavenly realms only after his death.

The idea that there are revealed truths that may not actually have been uttered by Sakyamuni during his lifetime is a key aspect in the other major school of Buddhism: the **Mahayana**. If the Theravada school looks to the Three Baskets for its most authoritative texts based on the presumption that these are the words of Sakyamuni, then the Mahayana school looks to other writings as well but with the same justification for their authority – somehow these works also contain the teaching of the Buddha.

While recognizing the authenticity and authority of the Three Baskets, Mahayana Buddhism adds a series of other writings that express typical Mahayana concepts such as the figure of the **bodhisattva** and liberation via the devotional path. One of the most prominent examples is the Lotus Sutra (Saddharmapundarika Sutra) which probably dates from the first century CE and is widely used throughout east Asia. In fact, most of the additional writings are also described as sutras – threads of truth as in the case of the Sutta Pitaka.[7] These are works that were composed much later in the story of Buddhism, as it was gradually exported to new cultural contexts such as China, Japan, and Tibet. However, the general belief is that they contain sermons that the Buddha Sakyamuni preached to assemblies of bodhisattvas and other celestial figures in a transhistorical plane of reality. Eventually, these truths have been revealed to us in time and space either by Sakyamuni himself or by celestial Buddhas and other beings. Sometimes Ananda's phrase "Thus have I heard" is affixed to the texts to indicate a connection with the Buddha, thus underpinning their canonical authority. There are also Buddhist traditions that bypass the written texts altogether, such as the **Zen** school which professes an oral transmission of sublime truths from generation to generation outside of the scriptures.

The doctrine of the Three Bodies (discussed in chapter 1) expresses the idea that the historical Sakyamuni is ultimately a particular manifestation in time and space of an eternal principle of truth – the **dharma**. This absolute cosmic principle has been expressed in human language via the words of Sakyamuni, memorized by Ananda and Upali, and recorded in the Three Baskets. Even the later texts of the Mahayana schools are seen as authoritative articulations of that same eternal dharma, which has been revealed to the wise by the Buddhas and bodhisattvas of their visions. The belief that a timeless truth has become incarnate in a historical founder, and that the official record of that person's words and deeds carries enormous importance for the believing community, is applicable not only to the followers of the Enlightened One but also to the followers of the Anointed One.

 New Testament

In the year 367 CE Athanasius, bishop of Alexandria, wrote an Easter letter to his congregation nominating 27 literary works as inspired by God and thus authoritative for Christians. This was the list of what was to become the Christian section of the canon. It may seem surprising that it took three centuries for the Church to sort out precisely which books were worthy of inclusion in its Bible, but the process involved more than just the official endorsement of ecclesiastical leaders. Prior to this, the books had to be composed in the first place, as well as widely used and accepted at the grass roots among Christian communities. Even in Athanasius's day there were still concerns in some parts of the Church regarding one or two of the books,[8] but eventually the list was accepted as definitive by mainstream Christianity and came to be known as the **New Testament** (see box 2.3).

Box 2.3	THE BOOKS OF THE NEW TESTAMENT
	Matthew
	Mark
	Luke
	John
	Acts of the Apostles
	Romans
	1 Corinthians
	2 Corinthians
	Galatians
	Ephesians
	Philippians
	Colossians
	1 Thessalonians
	2 Thessalonians
	1 Timothy
	2 Timothy
	Titus
	Philemon
	Hebrews
	James
	1 Peter
	2 Peter
	1 John
	2 John
	3 John
	Jude
	Revelation

Although there are 27 books in the New Testament, it is not an enormous work, constituting a rather slim publication on a bookshelf. Moreover, none of the books were actually written by the founder himself, **Jesus** of Nazareth. In fact, the New Testament is a modest-sized anthology of writings composed by a generation of Christian authors during the mid to late first century and early second century CE. Upon opening a copy, the reader will immediately notice that the two main literary forms are "gospel" and "letter": four gospels and 21 letters, to be precise.[9]

Traditionally the order of contents begins with the gospels. Assigning them pride of place is no coincidence, for these four works immediately take the reader to the very heart of the Christian religion. A **gospel** is essentially a short biography of the founder, a life of Jesus seen through the eyes of Christian faith; and, for the Christian, it is a life of enormous significance. The English term "gospel" is derived from the old English word *godspell*, itself a translation of the original Greek *evangelion* which means "good news." Christians see these four books as a way of encountering the message and the deeds of someone who is the epitome of good news for humankind.

The question arises as to why there are four versions of that one crucial life. Several attempts were made to harmonize the four into one single synthesis, the most notable being the Diatessaron of Tatian.[10] However, the Church favored the retention of the four distinct accounts as the will of God. Bishop-theologian Irenaeus of Lyons was one of the first to insist on the validity of a fourfold gospel, arguing that it made logical sense given that there are four corners of the earth and four winds.[11] Quaint analogies aside, there seems to have been a general wisdom that each gospel contributes something unique and valuable to the overall portrait of Jesus, complementing the others and completing the picture. But it was not only a question of whether there should be one gospel or four. The burning issue was also whether there should be more than four, given that dozens of other gospels had been produced in the early centuries of the Christian era, all purporting to be an accurate record and interpretation of the life of Jesus. Many bear an apostolic title that is meant to imply an eyewitness authority: the gospel of Thomas, the gospel of Philip, the gospel of Peter, and so on. In the end, the four traditional gospels alone prevailed, their canonicity being based on claims of more orthodox teaching, more reliable apostolic authorship, and more widespread use by major Christian communities. The rejected versions became known as **apocryphal** gospels, a term that originally meant hidden and esoteric, but finally came to mean spurious and misleading. These were versions that did not make the grade although scholars today point out that they contain a treasure trove of information about Christianity in its infancy.

The authors of the four canonical gospels are named by tradition as Matthew, Mark, Luke, and John,[12] although none of the gospels themselves explicitly identifies its author. The only exception is probably the "beloved disciple" of Jesus who claims to be the key witness to the events recounted in the fourth gospel, but his identification as the apostle John is not explicit.[13] Despite the ambiguity surrounding the precise identity of the four evangelists, scholars tend to agree that the gospels are the final written product of a decades-long process of oral transmission, traceable back to the original eyewitnesses and ultimately to Jesus himself. Each of the final editors – Matthew, Mark, Luke, and John – has selected, arranged, and molded the material to generate their own distinctive portrait of the founder tailored for their particular audience. It is the same Jesus, but seen through different eyes and presented to a different readership.

Although it is usually listed second in the order, scholars tend to agree that **Mark**, the shortest gospel, is also the earliest, probably being finalized before the fall of Jerusalem in 70 CE. Mark's gospel is replete with stories about Jesus's miraculous healings but there is not a great deal of his teachings. Mark's original version is a non-stop narrative from Jesus's baptism in the river Jordan to his eventual arrest and execution in Jerusalem, with only minimal reference to the most significant claim of all: Jesus's resurrection from the dead.

The gospels of **Luke** and **Matthew**, which were written a decade or two later, reproduce Mark's stories in basically the same order but with two interesting additions. First, in contrast to Mark, both gospel writers include blocks of Jesus's teachings that are essentially the same. This curious fact (i.e., material common to Matthew and Luke but not found in Mark) led experts to posit the existence of a written collection of Jesus's sayings that was employed by both Matthew and Luke independently. The hypothetical work was called "Q" by nineteenth-century scholars after the German word *quelle* meaning "source." Moreover, because the first three gospels are so closely related in terms of general layout and borrowed contents, they are referred to as the **synoptic gospels**.

Second, again in contrast to Mark, both Matthew and Luke commence their gospel with the conception and birth of Jesus. The well-known Christmas motifs find their origin in the infancy stories at the beginning of these two gospels. There is a common kernel that includes Jesus's miraculous conception without a human father, the names of his parents, his birth in Bethlehem, and his home in Nazareth. But there are also differences. Only Matthew mentions the three **magi**, the star, and the escape of the family to Egypt. On the other hand, only Luke refers to the shepherds in the fields, the appearance of the angel to **Mary**, and the circumcision and naming ceremony in the Temple eight days after the birth. The subtle differences continue throughout the two gospels and suggest that each has been composed for very different groups of early Christians. Constant references to the Jewish scriptures, a genealogy of Jesus that starts with **Abraham**, and the famous **Sermon on the Mount**, which portrays Jesus as a new Moses on a new **Sinai** dispensing a new Law, all suggest that Matthew's audience were Jewish converts. In contrast, Luke's references to pagans who are attracted to Jesus's message, a genealogy of Jesus that extends back to Adam, the first human being, and an opening sentence revealing that the gospel is written for "your excellency Theophilus" all suggest a non-Jewish audience. Matthew and Luke remind us that the early Church was a mixture of Jew and **gentile**, and that the Christian "good news" was intended not only for the people of Israel but for the entire human family. The canon confirms that Christianity's universal missionary vocation was in existence from the very earliest stage.

The fourth gospel stands on its own as very different from the first three. For example, in contrast to the dozens of miracles recorded in the synoptic gospels, **John** mentions just seven signs – a number that signifies perfection in the Jewish tradition. Moreover, after each miracle Jesus delivers an extensive discourse that develops a theological theme. It is clear that the fourth gospel is a result of a much longer process of reflection about the person and significance of Jesus. Consequently it is often dated to the end of the first century CE. Most significantly, it does not begin at the Jordan with an adult Jesus as in Mark, nor at the conception and birth of Jesus as in Matthew and Luke. The opening phrase of John's gospel takes the reader back to a moment before the creation of the universe itself, echoing the book of Genesis:

> In the beginning was the Word, and the Word was with God, and the Word was God.[14]

What is implicit in the synoptic gospels becomes resoundingly explicit in the fourth gospel. The subject of this biography is not merely a Jewish **prophet**, or a royal child miraculously conceived, or an amazing miracle worker, but the eternal and divine

Word who pre-exists time itself. "Word" here is a translation of the original Greek *Logos* from which is derived the common English suffix of academic disciplines such as geo*logy*, bio*logy* and psycho*logy*. In Greek philosophy, Logos is the all-pervading intelligibility of the universe, which makes it possible for the inquiring human mind to investigate and make sense of the world around us. Logos is what renders the world a rational place. It is the difference between cosmos and chaos, and thus is the basis of all scientific inquiry. A few verses later, the fourth gospel goes on to state the most profound of Christian beliefs: "And the Word became flesh and lived among us."[15] Here is a highly developed answer to the question that all gospels are written to answer: who is Jesus of Nazareth?

It is not really surprising that the four gospels have primacy of place in the Christian canon. The four biographies are the official record of the teachings, the actions, indeed the life of the one whom Christians regard as none other than the human incarnation of transcendent truth and intelligibility. As such, the gospels are words that capture the memory of the Word and that must be proclaimed to all as good news. Here we are not that far from the concept of dharma truth personified in the historical person of Sakyamuni and the gathering of that truth into three "baskets" for the benefit of posterity. The status of the gospels is borne out by liturgical practice. In official acts of worship for many mainstream Christian churches, the gospel is traditionally the last in any series of biblical readings; the congregation is often invited to stand as the Book of Gospels is carried aloft to the pulpit; and only certain persons ordained for the purpose (deacons) may proclaim a gospel.

The second main literary type is epistle, or letter. There are 21 epistles in the New Testament, each a piece of correspondence that provides a window into the beliefs and practices of the early Christians. Like the gospels, the epistles bear apostolic names that are meant to establish a link to Jesus himself via those who were closest to him during his life: Peter, James, John, Jude. It is difficult to say whether the Aramaic-speaking apostles actually wrote these Greek epistles which deal with a range of issues and circumstances in the earliest communities. It is possible that the original apostle's authority stands behind the actual epistle writer in some sense. What is striking is that the majority of the epistles do not bear the name of the one of the 12 disciples of Jesus. Rather their author is a convert from Judaism who probably never met Jesus during his life but turned out to be one of the most indefatigable missionaries ever – **Saint Paul**. The titles of many of the Pauline letters reflect the extent of his journeys aimed at establishing nascent Christian communities in towns and regions across the Roman Empire: Corinth, Thessalonica, Philippi, Galatia, Ephesus, Colossus, and

Figure 2.3
Statue of Saint Paul carrying the double-edged sword of God's word at the Basilica San Paolo, Rome

Rome. Moreover, with 13 letters in the official canon, Paul's theological influence on Christianity is as undeniable as it is enormous. The letters of Paul and the other New Testament authors may be one degree removed from the figure of Jesus but they are still considered inspired writings that channel divinely sanctioned ideas and commands to the Christian believer.

The New Testament constitutes only about a quarter of the Christian Bible. The other three-quarters are equally considered to be divinely inspired. In the second century a Christian named Marcion enthusiastically proposed that, although Christianity had begun as a movement within Judaism, the Father of Jesus Christ was not the same as the God of Israel. Christianity had to sever ties with its mother religion in every respect. For Marcion this also meant expunging from the emerging Christian canon anything that looked remotely Jewish including the gospel of Matthew and, of course, rejecting the validity of all existing Jewish scriptures. Had Marcion prevailed, the Christian Bible would have been much slimmer: essentially the gospel of Luke and Paul's letters. However, orthodox Christianity decided against his insistence on the radical novelty of the new Israel (the Church) and the obsolescence of the old Israel. Instead it acknowledged Christianity's Jewish heritage and accepted the authenticity of the Jewish holy books as God's preparation for the coming of his **Messiah**. As a result, Christian Bibles contain not only the 27 Christian writings known collectively as the New Testament but also a slightly rearranged version of the great religious corpus of Judaism, known to Christians as the **Old Testamen**t but referred to by Jews in its original format as Tanach.

Tanach

In mid to late October each year, at the end of the week-long feast of **Sukkoth**, Jews celebrate what is known as **Simhat Torah** [Rejoicing with the Law].[16] On this day, the solemn mood of a **synagogue** service is transformed. Instead of removing only the scrolls to be used for the public reading, all scrolls are removed, accompanied by vigorous dancing and singing that sometimes even flows out into the streets. As the buoyant procession moves about the synagogue, participants jump up and down shouting "Moshe emet u'Torato emet!" [Moses is true and his Torah is true!]. Children join in, often carrying flags that symbolize the 12 tribes of Israel, while chocolates and sweets are handed out much to their delight. The festive atmosphere and high-spirited behavior mark the day on which the annual cycle of scriptural readings comes to an end. During the morning service, the last chapters of the book of **Deuteronomy** are proclaimed and are followed immediately by the first chapters of the book of **Genesis**, and thus the cycle begins anew. The festival reveals the depth of emotion and respect with which Jews regard the most sacred part of their scriptures – the **Torah**.

The Hebrew word *Torah* can be translated in various ways including "teaching," "instruction," and most commonly "law." Although the term can mean the entire contents of Jewish law, more specifically it refers to the first five books of the Jewish Bible. In Hebrew the names of the books are taken from the first words in each: Bereishit, Shemot, Vayikra, Bamidbar, and Devarim. In English they are usually referred to as Genesis, **Exodus**, **Leviticus**, **Numbers**, and Deuteronomy.

These five writings constitute the oldest and most sacred stratum of the Jewish scriptures, and their contents are an interesting mix of narrative and commandment – lore and law. The books of Genesis, Exodus, and Numbers contain the classical biblical stories of the creation of the world, Adam and Eve, Noah and the Flood, Abraham and his family, the escape from Egypt under Moses, the 40 years of wandering in the desert and the eventual arrival at the borders of the promised land. In contrast, the books of Leviticus and Deuteronomy (which is Greek for "second law") are essentially a collection of divine laws that are binding on Israel. These are the rules and regulations that constitute the holy covenant between God and his people.

The narrative books themselves are not without prescriptions and proscriptions either, including the famous **Ten Commandments** which are listed in Exodus as well as Deuteronomy. Torah is thus an apposite title given the pervasive presence of legal injunctions throughout. So great was the concern to know precisely what the creator required that the rabbinic tradition undertook the task of identifying and enumerating each specific divine command in the Torah. The result is the traditional list of 613 **mitzvot** [commandments] that are considered to have been given to **Moses** either in one extraordinary moment on Mount Sinai or over a series of encounters in the Tent of Meeting.[17] Some rabbis sought a symbolic meaning in the number, for example Rabbi Simlai who taught that the 365 negative commandments correspond to the number of days in the year, and the 248 positive commandments to the number of bones and joints in the human body.[18]

The Torah is also known as the Five Books of Moses, which hints at the traditional belief that Moses himself was its author, or to be more specific, that God revealed these words to the people through Moses. Modern biblical scholarship argues that the Torah actually consists of four distinct literary strata reflecting the hand of different editorial schools over time: the Yahwist and Elohist editors dating back to about 1000 BCE and differentiated by the name for God preferred by each (YHWH or Elohim); the Deuteronomic editor in the sixth century BCE; and finally the Priestly editor from the period after the return from Babylonian captivity (post-537 BCE). However, most Orthodox Jews do not accept such theories and still insist on the Mosaic source of the total contents of all five books. Behind Moses stands the supreme authority of God. Thus the Torah is not a man-made literary construct, but divine thought expressed in human language. It may have been revealed in time and space but it had always existed in the mind of the creator from before creation itself. It is truly *Torah min ha-shamayim*, the Torah from heaven.

The annual cycle of Torah readings that begins and ends on Simhat Torah is part of the regular synagogue service on **sabbath** (Saturday) morning, when participants are invited to read a section of the day's text for the congregation. The act of "going up" to read the Torah is called an **aliyah**, a biblical term that refers to a pilgrim making the journey up to Jerusalem for a festival, or the return of the **Babylonian exiles** to the promised land.[19] It now signifies the migration of Jews to reside in modern Israel. In other words, the honor of stepping up to read from Judaism's most revered text is likened to an exile's long-awaited return to his or her homeland, or the pilgrim's joyous and relieved arrival at the gates of the holy city after an arduous journey. In one sense, the reader is on holy ground when standing before the word of God and uttering the sacred sounds for their fellow worshipers. Traditionally the reader whispers the text while an expert cantor chants the same verses to a traditional melody. The number of aliyot varies according to the week day, but there are usually seven readers on a sabbath, the first of whom is a **cohen**[20] and the second a **levite**.[21]

The significance of the Torah is further highlighted by other practices and customs that surround it. For the synagogue readings, a Torah scroll, or Sefer Torah, is used

rather than a bound book. Over 300,000 characters are meticulously copied with a quill and ink by an expert scribe (sofer) onto a scroll of special parchment called gevil, according to very strict standards. A single error can render the scroll unworthy of use in official ritual. As a result, the entire process can take more than a year and be extremely costly. The gevil parchment consists of animal hide treated with salt, flour, and special resin.[22] The scroll is usually adorned with beautiful fabric and ornamental silver breastplates, and reserved in an ornate container at the end of the synagogue called the **aron ha kodesh**, or holy ark. The **Pentateuch**, an alternative term for Torah often used in biblical scholarship, means "the five containers" and refers to the traditional manner of keeping Torah scrolls in special cases. During the reading, a small wooden or metal pointer called a yad is used not only to protect the parchment from contact with the skin but also to symbolize the respectful distance that should be kept in the presence of God's holy word.

Fundamental and authoritative as they are, the five books of the Torah are not the only literature that constitutes the Jewish canon of scriptures. The Hebrew Bible actually consists of 24 books grouped into three sections (see box 2.4):

Figure 2.4 A Jewish boy reads from a Torah scroll using a yad

the 5 books of the Law (Torah), the 8 books of the Prophets (Neviyim), and the 11 books of the Writings (Ketuvim). Although these latter books do not carry the same authority as the Torah, they are nevertheless considered to be divinely inspired and thus have their proper place in synagogue worship, devotional piety, and theological study.[23] The formal word for the entire collection of 24 canonical books is Mikra [Readings], but the more common term is an acronym formed from the first syllables of the Hebrew names of the three sections: **Tanach**.

When was the Jewish canon fixed? The scholarly consensus is that the books of the Torah were considered to be divinely inspired from the earliest times and that the prophetic books achieved canonical status soon after their composition, the latest of which probably dates to the period after the Babylonian Exile (586–537 BCE). The book of Sirach, which dates from about 180 BCE, includes a list of the names of great men from Israel's history in the same order as these figures are found in the Torah and the Neviyim. However there is less clarity about precisely when the third section of Tanach, the Ketuvim, was admitted to the canon. For many Jews, Tanach was closed soon after the construction of the Second **Temple** in the late sixth century BCE. For others, including many Christian scholars, the process took a few more centuries. For example, Heinrich Graetz advanced the hypothesis in the late nineteenth century that a council of rabbis had met in Jamnia around the year 90 CE and officially recognized Ketuvim as canonical. Indeed the late first century was a time of consolidation for the Jewish faith after the destruction of the Second Temple by the Romans in 70 CE. However, many argue today that there is insufficient evidence to sustain Graetz's theory.[24] The Talmud itself suggests that it was **Rabbi Akiva** (second century CE) who had the final say. The threefold division of Tanach is not explicitly mentioned in works such as the Septuagint (a first-century BCE Greek translation of the Jewish scriptures), the **Dead Sea Scrolls**, or the writings of Philo of Alexandria. The first-century CE historian **Josephus** speaks of a threefold division, although he only mentions 22 books. The first reference to a 24-book canon is found in 2 Esdras, a

---

THE 24 BOOKS OF THE JEWISH SCRIPTURES (TANACH)   **Box 2.4**

The Law (Torah)
  Genesis
  Exodus
  Leviticus
  Numbers
  Deuteronomy

The Prophets (Neviyim)
  Joshua
  Judges
  Samuel
  Kings
  Isaiah
  Jeremiah
  Ezekiel
  The 12 minor prophets

The Writings (Ketuvim)
  Psalms
  Proverbs
  Job
  Song of Songs
  Ruth
  Lamentations
  Qoheleth
  Esther
  Daniel
  Ezra–Nehemiah
  Chronicles

Jewish-Christian apocryphal work from the early second century CE, and even this claim is debatable.[25]

Regardless of the historical quest for exact dates, at some stage between the construction of the Second Temple and the first century CE, the full collection of 24 Jewish writings was recognized as divinely authored and thus demanding the highest level of reverence and obedience. God had spoken his irrevocable word through the prophets, the greatest of whom was Moses. As the age of the prophets passed, so the inspired books ceased to be written and the canon was closed. From then on it was a matter of sifting through the pages of Tanach in order to quarry its immense riches and spell out in more and more precise ways what the 613 mitzvot required. That enormous challenge was taken up by the rabbis and, in time, led to the composition of Judaism's classical and complex application of biblical commandments to everyday life, the **Talmud**. Meanwhile the inspired, revelatory nature of Tanach was recognized not only by Christianity, which renamed it the Old Testament, but also by a new religion whose founder saw himself as the final prophet in that same long line.

Qur'an

One night during the month of Ramadan in the year 610 CE, a middle-aged Arabian merchant was meditating in a cave on Mount Hira, just outside the town of Mecca. According to tradition, he was suddenly overwhelmed by the presence of another being whose voice commanded him:

> Read in the name of your Lord Who created.
> He created man from a clot.
> Read and your Lord is Most Honorable,
> Who taught (to write) with the pen
> Taught man what he knew not.[26]

The events of that evening would prove to be a turning point not only for **Muhammad** but for religious history. The encounter was to be the first in a series of such experiences that would last until his death 22 years later. Muhammad's initial reaction was fear and confusion. However, the sympathetic support of his wife **Khadijah** and other close associates, as well as the continuing nature of the auditions,[27] would eventually convince him that he was being called to be a prophet. The contents of those auditions would eventually be collected into a single volume, constituting the holiest text in Islam – the **Qur'an**.

The term *Qur'an*[28] refers to the collection of recitations that came about as a result of iq'ra, which literally means to read or to recite – the very command that Muhammad received in his first revelatory experience. As with any prophet, Muhammad's role was to recite a divine message in human language for his hearers. Given that the auditions were experienced from time to time over a long period, the fragmentary nature of the Qur'an is not surprising. Far from a systematic treatise of Islamic belief, it consists of poetic utterances of varying length whose meaning may or may not be immediately apparent to the reader. The Qur'an is traditionally divided into 114 **surahs** (or chapters) that are more or less organized in descending order according to their size, other than the first which is a short surah in the form of an introductory prayer. It is not clear why such an arrangement was originally chosen but it has persisted. Paradoxically, the effect is that the chronological order of chapters is often reversed, since the shorter chapters, which are more likely to be located later in the Qur'an, are considered by many scholars to be the earlier utterances of Muhammad. In most printed versions, each surah is prefaced by a phrase indicating whether it stems from the period during which Muhammad lived in Mecca (610–22) or the period during which he resided in Medina (622–32), although dating individual surahs and verses is a particularly challenging task.

Each surah opens with the phrase "Bismillah ir-Rahman ir-Rahim"[29] [In the name of **Allah**, the Beneficent, the Merciful], reminding the reader that the sacred words they are about to encounter are a result of divine favor. Moreover, each surah also carries a traditional name that is derived from a striking word or particular incident described in the chapter itself and is a popular means of referencing. Some examples are Surah 1 which is appropriately called "The Opening," Surah 4 ("Women"), and Surah 96 ("The Clot").

The Qur'an is about the same size as the Christian New Testament and contains over 6,000 verses or ayats – a term that literally means a divine sign or miracle. It is a significant word since there is no developed tradition of miracle-working for Muhammad, as for Sakyamuni and Jesus. When challenged to explain this apparent lack of evidence for Muhammad's divine calling, Muslims tend to point to the one miracle that authenticates their founder. For them, the Qur'an itself is the undeniable proof since it would have been impossible for an illiterate Muhammad to have produced such an exquisite and profound literary masterpiece without divine involvement.[30] In fact the Qur'an was one of the first written works in Arabic and, like Luther's German translation of the Christian Bible, had a considerable impact on the language itself. The Qur'an is neither prose nor poem but something in between – a style of Arabic known as saj, which uses rhyme but no regular meter. Scholars also notice a shift from a succinct, vivid style in the earlier passages to a more prosaic, doctrinal style in the later.

As with Sakyamuni and Jesus, Muhammad was not the actual writer of the holy book that bears the founder's stamp. Muhammad "recited" the divine words that came to him in his revelatory experiences, while his followers memorized them and eventually noted them down on materials such as parchment, stone, palm leaves, and papyrus.

There is some debate as to the precise historical process that led to a written Qur'an, but scholarly opinion tends to agree that an official version was commissioned around the year 650 during the reign of **Uthman**, the third **caliph**. Uthman appointed a committee headed by Zaid ibn Thabit, a close associate of the Prophet, to reconcile the different versions of the Qur'an that were in circulation at the time. The final product was then distributed widely throughout the caliphate, and orders given for the destruction of all other copies. The Qur'an today is essentially Uthman's edition in terms of content and layout, its eventual reception possibly being facilitated by the fact that it was linked to Medina, the town in which the prophet spent the last 10 years of his life and in which he is buried.[31]

Unlike Sakyamuni and Jesus, Muhammad is not considered by Islamic faith to be the original author of the words. Muslims often stress that Muhammad is merely the conduit through which God transmitted a divine message. The tradition is that Muhammad entered a trance-like state, during which he would often fall to the ground, sweat profusely, and become oblivious to his surroundings. When he regained normal consciousness, he would speak the words that he had heard in this altered state to those present. The Qur'an itself describes the actual revelatory experience as occurring "by suggestion, or from behind a veil, or by sending a messenger to suggest what he pleases."[32] The implication is that Muhammad did not see God or even hear God's voice. God remains transcendent even as he communicates with humanity in the process of revelation. The Prophet was given insight into the divine mind only indirectly ("behind a veil"), or via the mediation of a "messenger" or angel.[33] In Islam, the voice that Muhammad actually heard was that of the angel Gabriel (Jibreel).[34] In Jewish tradition, Gabriel is the archangel who appeared to the prophet Daniel and explained the hidden meaning of his mysterious visions.[35] In Christianity, it is Gabriel who figures in the Annunciation, informing Mary that she is pregnant with the Christ-child.[36] In the **Semitic religions**, Gabriel and his fellow angelic beings bridge the gap between the infinite God and finite humans, assisting in the process of divine communication.

Gabriel is not the only Jewish or Christian figure that appears in the pages of the Qur'an. Prominent persons who are explicitly mentioned include Noah, Abraham, Moses, David, and Jesus.[37] Although the Islamic creed, the **shahadah**, succinctly declares that Muhammad is *the* Prophet of God, this is always understood to mean the final prophet in a long series. The message of the prophets of Israel, especially their insistence on themes such as monotheism and social justice, is acknowledged by Islam to be divinely inspired. Jews and Christians are described as **People of the Book** – the book being that same history of divine revelation that comes to a close with the Seal of the Prophets and finds its ultimate expression in the words of the Qur'an.

In the end, Gabriel and Muhammad are but intermediaries. The true author of the Qur'an is God himself and the fundamental belief in its divine origin underpins the Islamic attitude toward this holiest of books. One Islamic tradition speaks of the **Night of Power**, when the entire Qur'an was "sent down" by God during the month of Ramadan.

Another tradition holds that the Qur'an was gradually revealed to Muhammad and the first community over more than two decades. Moreover, some later revelations seem to qualify or even replace earlier ones that led to the theological notion of "abrogating" and "abrogated" verses.[38] In other words, like a good teacher, God only slowly unveils the fullness of his revelation to Muhammad and his young community of faith, taking into account their need for time to digest its complexities and demands. This approach retains the idea of a Night of Power on which the Qur'an was sent down but only to the lowest heaven whence Gabriel revealed it in stages to the Prophet.

The descent of the Qur'an on the Night of Power is also linked to the belief that the Arabic Qur'an that was dictated to Muhammad by Gabriel is an earthly copy of a heavenly original. This is very close to the Jewish idea of a pre-existing Torah that was always with God, even before creation itself. Several Qur'anic verses support the notion of an uncreated Qur'an:

> I swear by the Book that makes things clear: Surely we have made it an Arabic Qur'an that you may understand. And surely it is in the original of the Book with Us, truly elevated, full of wisdom.[39]

The idea has its opponents within Islam who fear that an uncreated Qur'an, somehow distinct from God himself, too closely resembles the Christian idea of a pre-existing Word distinct from the Father, and thus verges on idolatrous **polytheism** (**shirk**). Others justify the idea by insisting that the eternal book is God's speech, a quality of the one God, similar to his willing and knowing.

Because of the belief in its divine authorship, Muslims are generally reluctant to promote translations of the Qur'an. The old adage "Every translation limps" is particularly pertinent when dealing with the word of God. Published translations often have the Arabic and the vernacular juxtaposed. Arabic is always used in official worship and public ceremonies even though the majority of Muslims are not arabophone. The believers may not speak Arabic, but they are familiar with the Qur'anic text in its original form. There are also millions of believers around the world who have memorized all 80,000 words of the Qur'an and as a result are highly respected members of their local faith community. Such a person is called a hafiz which, appropriately, means a "guardian."

The Qur'an is intricately woven into Islamic life and practice. In place of sacred images, verses from the Qur'an adorn mosques and public buildings with full calligraphic flourish. Thousands of pages of Qur'anic commentaries sit on the shelves of Islamic libraries and colleges. The book itself is treated with the utmost respect and **ablutions** have to be performed before handling it if one is not in a state of religious purity. Desecrating or insulting the word of God in human language is considered a serious form of blasphemy. There are even appropriate and inappropriate methods for disposing of old texts.

BOX 2.5 ## AL-FATIHA: THE OPENING CHAPTER OF THE QUR'AN

In the name of Allah, the Beneficent, the Merciful.
All praise is due to Allah, the Lord of the Worlds.
The Beneficent, the Merciful.
Master of the Day of Judgment.
Thee do we serve and Thee do we beseech for help.
Keep us on the right path.
The path of those upon whom Thou hast bestowed favors. Not (the path) of those
    upon whom Thy wrath is brought down, nor of those who go astray.

Figure 2.5
Qur'an with
prayer beads

As noted above, the word *Qur'an* itself is derived from the verb "to recite," and today
the Qur'an is recited on a daily basis by millions of believers around the globe. The
recitations are usually informal but there are also seven official types of Qur'anic chant.
Apart from the traditional 114 surahs, the text is also divided into equal sections for
regular daily recitation during the month of Ramadan. Moreover, its opening surah,
Al-Fatiha (see box 2.5), and other select Qur'anic passages are an integral part of official
daily prayers and rites of passage.

SUMMARY

The existence of a sacred, authoritative collection of writings that definitively shapes belief and practice is a common feature in all five religions. Such texts are held in the highest esteem by believers, who see them as priceless repositories of eternal truth and wisdom: divine thought captured in human language for posterity. Consequently these texts play a vital role in religious study, meditation, and ritual. They are diligently perused by those who seek a higher form of knowledge, and reverently recited in formal public worship and private prayer. Although some of these religions reject the use of the holy image as tantamount to idolatry, all accept the notion that ultimate being can be effectively accessed through the words of the holy book – a verbal gateway to the transcendent. But apart from this basic level of intersection, what similarities and differences exist between the religions in terms of the form, content, and use of the sacred text?

Hinduism is characterized by the vast number of holy books and its peculiar lack of a universally accepted canon – a testimony to the utter diversity within Hinduism. However, many Hindu traditions recognize the unique religious status of an ancient stratum of writings categorized as shruti. The term is often translated as "heard," suggesting that these works are the product of a direct process of illumination experienced by seers in profound states of meditation long ago. At the core of the shruti literature are the four Vedas, anthologies of hymns and ritual instructions that have been used throughout the centuries for ceremony and worship. Attached to these ritual-centered documents are the Upanishads, with their contrasting emphasis on philosophical speculation and the individual's quest for truth concerning the self and the world. Shruti is a fascinating mixture of texts that pertain to public ritual and private spirituality. Moreover, Hinduism is also unique among the religions in that access to its most sacred writings is dependent on age, class, and gender. Traditionally only the twice-born males of the upper three classes were deemed worthy of reading the Vedas. The holiest of texts were meant only for the eyes of the advanced on the journey to final liberation. This limitation of access has led to widespread use of the other category of Hindu writings known as smriti which includes such diverse forms of writing as the law code of Manu, the poetic Puranas, and the two great epics known as the Ramayana and the Mahabharata. In particular, a work set deep within the Mahabharata is arguably the most beloved and influential text among the general Hindu populace today – the Bhagavad Gita.

Many sects within Hinduism did not accept the classical Vedic tradition and thus developed their own specific texts for study, meditation, and ceremony. One such sect eventually blossomed into a major world religion. Although it retained many Hindu concepts drawn from the Upanishads, Buddhism rejected the Vedas and the practice of restricted access, replacing them with its own collection of authoritative texts known as the Three Baskets, which are available to all who seek enlightenment. What is different here is not just the relaxation of access to the holiest writings but that the authority of these writings is grounded not in mystical knowledge revealed to sages in a distant past but in the credible eyewitness accounts of the teachings and actions of the historical **Buddha** as provided by his closest companions. The justification for the elevation of these writings to canonical status lies in their connection to the founder himself who is regarded as the supreme channel of transcendent truth for our epoch. Even in Mahayana schools of Buddhism, where later texts were subsequently added to or even surpassed the importance of the Three Baskets, the tendency is to understand these writings as further elaborations presented by the Buddha from a transcendent sphere of reality.

This emphasis on the teaching and example of the founder as the source of the holy book's authority is also characteristic of Christianity which regards Jesus as the incarnation of eternal truth, the "Word made Flesh." Thus the record of his words, deeds, and entire life is of supreme importance to Christians. Like the historical Buddha, Jesus did not actually write a book but his sayings and actions were eventually recorded by those who claimed access to eyewitness accounts from within the circle of the first disciples. From the dozens of biographies that emerged over the subsequent decades of the early Church, four were chosen as official and placed at the head of the Christian canon. Not only do the works of Matthew, Mark, Luke, and John enjoy primacy in the order of the New Testament books, but they are also typically given pride of place in Christian ritual and worship. Like the Three Baskets in Buddhism, so too the Four Gospels in Christianity provide access to the founder through whom transcendent truth and meaning are revealed to humankind. The remainder of the New Testament is primarily a collection of epistles whose inclusion in the canon was based not only on the orthodoxy of their content but also on their purported apostolic authorship, or at least their link to an apostle who is supposed to have enjoyed a personal knowledge of the founder.

What is unique about the Christian Bible is that it not only contains the 27 Christian writings collectively known as the New Testament but also a much longer section that acts as a preamble and is thus entitled the "Old" Testament. This preamble is in fact the entire canon of the Jewish faith, known in that tradition as Tanach – surely one of the most significant intersections between any of the five religions. Its inclusion in the Christian Bible reflects the self-understanding of Christianity as the new Israel, bringing to completion, but not totally abrogating, all that went before in the religious experience of the ancient people of God.

The acronym "Tanach" refers to the threefold subdivision of the Jewish Bible into the Law, the Prophets, and the Writings. Unlike Christianity and Buddhism, the Jewish canon is not primarily centered on the life of a founder who is seen as an incarnation of divine truth. The Jewish scriptures were gradually revealed over 1,000 years of history and were definitively closed at about the same time as the Christians finalized their Bible. The first and most fundamental section of the Jewish canon is the Law (Torah) which is traditionally understood to have been revealed in the theophanies associated with the desert mountain Sinai. The divine words that have been captured in the ancient Hebrew of the sacred page are deemed to have always existed in the mind of God from before creation itself. In one sense the Torah is eternal, but it has come down to earth via the mediation of the greatest of all prophets, Moses. While the figure of Moses towers above all other spokespersons for God in the Jewish tradition and stands as the key human authority behind the Torah, nevertheless he is not considered the founder of Judaism or the personification of transcendent truth, as with Sakyamuni or Jesus. Thus the emphasis in Judaism is not so much on Moses, but on the divine words that were dictated to him on the holy mountain and subsequently recorded on the page of the holy book. It is the Torah itself rather than Moses that represents the most sublime yet tangible locus where such truth is directly encountered. Jewish practice reflects the highest honor and respect for such holy texts in its insistence on impeccably transcribed Torah scrolls which are stored in the most sacred place in the synagogue, carried in solemn procession during worship, and buried with dignity when damaged.

On the one hand, Islam is unique among the religions in that its canon consists of only one book associated with just one prophet. On the other, it is similar to Christianity in that it sees itself as the true fulfillment of the Jewish prophetic line. Although Islam does not include Tanach in its canon, the Qur'an frequently refers back to significant religious figures of Israel and indeed to Jesus himself. Moreover, there are strong resonances with the Jewish understanding of sacred scripture. The rejection of visual images of God is a feature of both Judaism and Islam, and it is not surprising to find the same strong emphasis placed on the holy book by Muslims as well as by Jews. In one sense, the lack of the visual is compensated by the highlighting of the verbal. Thus, like the Torah, the Qur'an is also considered to be a pre-existing reality in the mind of God that became incarnate in time and space via the mediation of the last of the prophets, Muhammad. As in Judaism, the Prophet is not an incarnation of divine truth but a mouthpiece through which the thoughts of God are revealed in human language. Thus it is in the sacred book itself, containing the very words of God, where the Muslim can most closely approach the divine on earth. Consequently, the Qur'an is regarded with extreme reverence by Muslims, many of whom memorize its entire contents in the hope of appropriating its essence.

The sacred writings of each religion provide an important verbal access to the transcendent. Although there are important differences in the extent, content, and significance of the holy books in each religion, these texts constitute a point of contact with ultimate being. But the sacred texts also constitute an enduring litmus test for orthodox belief and a guide for practice. The sacred writings of each faith shape not only the creeds but also the moral life itself as well as customs that mark key moments such as birth, death, and marriage or daily habits such as food and clothing. The holy book, which reveals so much about that which lies beyond time and space, also significantly determines how human beings are to live their religious lives within time and space. It is to such themes that we turn in the next section.

DISCUSSION TOPICS

1 Discuss the relative importance of written scriptures in each major religion.
2 Should religious scriptures always be interpreted literally? How else can they be interpreted?
3 Why are the Vedas and Upanishads not accepted by all Hindu traditions? Explore alternative holy writings in various Hindu schools and sects.
4 Identify the main scriptures of the Mahayana and Tibetan Buddhist traditions. What is the status of the Tipitaka in these traditions?
5 Compare the central message of the Bhagavad Gita and the gospel of John.
6 Identify the main apocryphal gospels and discuss why they were omitted from the Christian canon.
7 How and why do Catholic and Protestant Bibles differ?
8 How do Jews and Christians differ in the way they interpret Tanach or the Old Testament?
9 Compare the visionary experience and missionary role of Muhammad with Jewish prophets such as Moses, Isaiah, Jeremiah, or Ezekiel.
10 What are the Satanic Verses? What do they tell us about how the Qur'an was revealed?
11 What are the Talmud and the Hadith? How do they complement Tanach and the Qur'an respectively?

FURTHER READING

Bhaskarananda, Swami (2002). *The Essentials of Hinduism.* 2nd edn. Seattle: Viveka, pp. 11–21.
Brown, Daniel James (2003). *A New Introduction to Islam.* Oxford: Blackwell, ch. 5.
Brown, Raymond (1997). *An Introduction to the New Testament.* New York: Doubleday, part 1.
Cook, Michael (2000). *The Koran: A Very Short Introduction.* Oxford: Oxford University Press.
Corrigan, John, et al. (1997). *Jews, Christians, Muslims: A Comparative Introduction to Monotheistic Religions.* Upper Saddle River, NJ: Prentice Hall, pp. 3–73.
De Lange, Nicholas (2000). *Introduction to Judaism.* Cambridge: Cambridge University Press, pp. 45–65.
Gordon, Matthew S. (2002). *Understanding Islam.* London: Duncan Baird, pp. 36–45.
Hauer, Christian E., & Young, William A. (2000). *An Introduction to the Bible: A Journey into Three Worlds.* 5th edn. Upper Saddle River, NJ: Prentice Hall.

Kramer, Kenneth (1986). *World Scriptures: An Introduction to Comparative Religions.* Mahwah, NJ: Paulist Press.

McGrath, Alister E. (1997). *An Introduction to Christianity.* Oxford: Blackwell, pp. 36–100.

Michaels, Axel (2003). *Hinduism: Past and Present.* Princeton, NJ: Princeton University Press, pp. 47–66.

Mittal, Sushil (ed.) (2004). *The Hindu World.* Abingdon: Routledge, chs. 2–5.

Powell, Barbara (1996). *Windows into the Infinite: A Guide to the Hindu Scriptures.* Fremont, CA: Asian Humanities Press.

Pratt, Douglas (2005). *The Challenge of Islam: Encounters in Interfaith Dialogue.* Aldershot: Ashgate, ch. 3.

Renard, John (1996). *Seven Doors to Islam: Spirituality and the Religious Life of Muslims.* Berkeley and Los Angeles: University of California Press, pp. 1–34.

Sandmel, Samuel (1978). *The Hebrew Scriptures: An Introduction to their Literature and Religious Ideas.* New York: Oxford University Press.

Sangharakshita (1985). *The Eternal Legacy: An Introduction to the Canonical Literature of Buddhism.* Birmingham: Windhorse.

NOTES

1 For example, certain traits of Shiva are recognizable in the earlier Vedic deity Rudra.
2 Rg Veda 1.164.39.
3 See the Laws of Manu IV.99: "He (the twice born) must never read (the vedas) in the presence of the shudras (servant class)."
4 It should be noted that in contemporary India the absolute ban on women and lower-class Hindus reading or studying the Vedas is increasingly being relaxed or even ignored.
5 Mahabharata, Bhishma Parva, chs. 23–40.
6 The Sanskrit form is "Tripitaka."
7 A huge number of Mahayana and tantric writings enjoy canonical status, including the Perfection of Wisdom, Saddharma-Pundarika, and Pure Land Sutras, to name but a few.
8 For example, the Eastern Church was reluctant to canonize the Apocalypse of John (otherwise known as the book of Revelation) due to its enigmatic language and style, while the Western Church admitted the Letter of James only belatedly because of doubts about the authenticity of its apostolic authorship. The canonical status of the latter was again called into question by Luther during the sixteenth-century Reformation, on the basis of its claim that faith cannot save without accompanying works.
9 The remaining two works are the Acts of the Apostles (an account of the early Church by Luke) and the book of Revelation (an apocalyptic work that portrays the final cosmic battle between good and evil in heavily symbolic language).
10 Tatian's Diatessaron was composed around 175 CE in Syria.
11 Irenaeus, *Adversus Haereses*, 1.11.8.
12 The four gospel writers are often symbolized in Christian art by the four animals mentioned in the book of Revelation: a man, a lion, a bull, and an eagle (Revelation 4:6–7).
13 See John 13:23–5; 21:20–5.

14 John 1:1.

15 John 1:14.

16 For Orthodox Jews living in Israel and for most Reform Jews, Simchat Torah is marked on the eighth day of Sukkoth, otherwise known as Shemini Atzeret. For Orthodox Jews living outside of Israel, it is celebrated on the day following Shemini Atzeret.

17 See Talmud Yoma 80a.

18 See Talmud Makkoth 23b–24a.

19 See also Genesis 50:14; Numbers 32:11; Ezra 2:1.

20 A member of the priestly line, descended from Aaron, the high priest, at the time of the Exodus.

21 A member of the biblical tribe of Levi, one of the 12 tribes of ancient Israel.

22 Maimonides, *Hilkoth Tefillin*, 1:8, 14.

23 The Five Scrolls (Hamesh Megillot) from the Ketuvim are feature readings at important Jewish festivals throughout the year: Song of Songs at Passover; Ruth at Shavuot; Lamentations at Ninth of Av; Qoheleth at Sukkoth; and Esther at Purim.

24 See Jack Lewis, "Council of Jamnia," in *The Anchor Bible Dictionary* (New York: Anchor Bible, 1992), vol. III, pp. 634–7.

25 In some versions of 2 Esdras 14:45, Ezra the scribe works with five assistants for 40 days and nights and produces 94 books. God commands him to make the first 24 public and to reserve the remaining 70 for the wise. However, in other versions the total number of books produced is 204.

26 Qur'an 96:1–5.

27 The term "audition" is preferred to "vision" as a description of Muhammad's ecstatic experiences since the emphasis is on hearing rather than seeing.

28 Also written in English as *Koran*.

29 The one exception is Surah 9 which scholars think may originally have belonged to Surah 8.

30 The verse from Surah 96 that refers to "teaching man the use of the pen" is often quoted in this context. See also Qur'an 10:38 which challenges the skeptic to find a comparable work: "Let them come then with a surah like it."

31 Some oft-mentioned versions of the Qur'an at the time were those of Ibn Mas'ud in Kufa, Ubayy ibn Ka'b in Syria, and Abu Musa in Basra.

32 Qur'an 42:50–2.

33 The Hebrew term is *malach* which literally means a messenger, as does the Greek *angelos*.

34 Qur'an 2:97.

35 Daniel 8:15–17; 9:20–4.

36 Luke 1:19.

37 See Qur'an 6:83–90.

38 One example of the principle of "abrogating and abrogated verses" is the issue of alcohol which is initially acknowledged as a gift from God (16:67), then presented as a danger to the spiritual life (2:219), and finally condemned as the work of **Satan** (5:90).

39 Qur'an 43:3. See also Qur'an 85:21–2 which speaks of a well-preserved or guarded "tablet."

Part II

WITHIN TIME AND SPACE

Chapter 3

ETHICS

CONTENTS

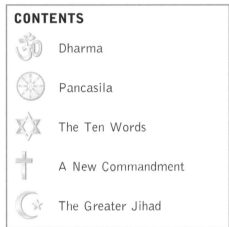

Introduction

Religion not only concerns the nature of transcendent reality and its connection with our world, but also constitutes a comprehensive socio-cultural framework that provides members with ultimate meaning and purpose. In this respect, religion makes sense of human existence within time and space, casting a transcendent hue on the most ordinary aspects of life such as food and clothing, birth and death. In the following chapters we shall explore such themes, commencing here with the sense of ethical duty found in all cultures. How is the human experience of the "moral ought" expressed in the five religions? How does each religion understand the basic nature and purpose of moral life? How does morality relate to transcendent reality? What are the main sources of moral teaching? Do the religions share any fundamental moral principles?

ॐ Dharma

The **Bhagavad Gita** is indisputably one of the most popular and influential texts in Hinduism. Set on the eve of a great battle between good and evil, its 18 chapters relate the conversation between the hero-prince **Arjuna** and his charioteer, who is revealed as none other than Lord **Krishna** himself. Arjuna is troubled by the prospect of fighting his own cousins on the field of Kurukshetra but Krishna advises him to ignore such fears for several reasons. For one thing, the body may be destroyed but the **atman** (spiritual essence) survives. Moreover, he will be considered a coward if he does not fight. But the most telling argument advanced by the divine counselor is that Arjuna is bound as a warrior to fight, even if the enemy is kin.[1] Put simply, he must do his duty. The need to fulfill one's obligations is a constantly recurring theme in the Bhagavad Gita, reflecting the importance of duty for Hindus in general. Like Arjuna, every Hindu experiences an all-embracing sense of religious, moral, and social duty that is best encapsulated in the term **dharma**.

Dharma is a rich and complex term that can be translated into English in a variety of ways: duty, obligation, law, virtue, and ethic. In fact, the term is broader than these, for it touches on not only the rules and regulations that pertain to human society but also the very fabric of the material world itself. The origins of dharma lie in the ancient Vedic idea of r'ta, which refers to the harmony, regularity, and order of the physical universe. The early Hindu deity Varuna was its caretaker, insuring that the planets kept to their proper paths and the seasons progressed on time.[2] It is the cosmic principle that holds all things together and enables them to run their course. Contemporary science knows it as "the laws of nature" such as the fundamental forces of gravity, electromagnetism, and nuclear attraction. In Hindu thinking, the dharma of the sun is to rise in the east; the dharma of water is to flow downstream; and the dharma of a flower is to blossom in spring.

Apart from the regular processes of nature, dharma also refers to the laws that govern human activity. Hinduism sees a vital connection between the two, for the failure of humans to live by their dharma can have a deleterious effect on the physical world itself. When people ignore their duties, the cosmic order is threatened and the universe slides toward chaos and disintegration. In Hindu thinking, proper behavior literally keeps the world from falling apart. But what sort of behavior does human dharma involve? Traditional Hindu thought differentiates between two main types of dharma: vishesha dharma, which pertains to one's particular situation in life; and sadharana dharma, which consists of universal moral norms.

Vishesha dharma concerns the socio-religious obligations that are primarily determined by factors such as one's gender, class, and age. Such obligations differ for men and women, upper class and lower class, young and old. The classical Brahmanic formulation of such duties is summed up in the term *varna ashrama dharma*, where **varna** stands for the four traditional social classes and **ashrama** the four traditional life stages (see box 3.1). It is varna dharma that Krishna refers to in the Bhagavad Gita when he urges Arjuna to do his duty as a member of the warrior class. Vishesha dharma underpins a world view in which each member of society contributes something valuable to the whole. Thus it is the dharma of the priest to teach, of the warrior to defend, of the merchant to generate commerce, and of the servant to serve. Ideally it is the dharma of an upper-class boy to study, of a young man to marry and beget children, and of an aging person to retire to the forest as a celibate mystic. Desiring the station of another is a serious threat to the social harmony generated in such a system, and not surprisingly Krishna insists several times in the Gita:

> And do thy duty, even if it be humble, rather than another's, even if it be great. To die in one's duty is life; to live in another's is death.[3]

At this level, dharma is relative to the particular situation of the individual concerned and thus it is difficult to speak in terms of absolutes. The taking of life is permissible, even obligatory for the **kshatria** in certain circumstances, while the duty of the ascetic is non-violent resistance and even martyrdom. However, there is another form of dharma, beyond the contingencies of gender, class, and age. Apart from vishesha dharma, Hindu thought also acknowledges the existence of general moral norms that are considered applicable to all human beings irrespective of religious affiliation or historical-cultural conditioning. The sadharana dharma is literally "universal" in its relevance as a guide for human behavior. This type of dharma is the ethical bedrock of Hinduism, which finds resonance in many other great religious traditions. But what precisely does the sadharana dharma prescribe?

For many, the most fundamental principle on which a superstructure of more explicit moral rules can be erected is the Golden Rule: treat others as you would have them treat you. The idea is not absent from Hinduism and can be found in a number of places in the Hindu holy writings, for example in the Mahabharata: "One should not behave toward others in a way which is disagreeable to oneself. This is the essence of morality. All other activities are due to selfish desire."[4] But

---

TRADITIONAL HINDU CLASSES (VARNA) AND LIFE STAGES (ASHRAMA)   Box 3.1

Varna

brahmin	the priestly class
kshatria	the warrior class
vaishya	the merchant class
shudra	the servant class
(dalit	the untouchable class)

Ashrama

brahmacarin	the student
grihasthin	the householder
vanaprasthin	the forest-dweller
sannyasin	the ascetic

how is that essential notion spelled out in more detail? There are many lists of moral prescriptions and proscriptions throughout the extensive volumes of Hindu sacred literature. One of the most oft-quoted comes from the Taittiriya Upanishad. Framed as the final discourse from a guru to his pupil, it recommends truthfulness, righteousness, learning, alms-giving, hospitality, respect for parents and teachers. Similarly the sixteenth chapter of the Bhagavad Gita enunciates the qualities of the virtuous person such as charity, self-control, non-violence, truthfulness, and many others.[5] But one of the most convenient catalogues of the key ethical principles of Hinduism appears among the eight "limbs" of classical yoga in Patanjali's Yoga Sutra. Before the practitioner commences with the well-known bodily positions and breathing techniques associated with yoga, the first two "limbs" consist of the five yamas [restraints] and the five niyamas [relaxations]. As the term implies, the yamas restrain or control immoral behavior by identifying activities that should be avoided. According to Patanjali, these are:

1 *ahimsa*: the avoidance of violent thought and action;
2 *satya*: the avoidance of dishonesty and betrayal;
3 *asteya*: the avoidance of theft and covetousness;
4 *brahmacariya*: the avoidance of lust, drunkenness, and bad company;
5 *aparigraha*: the avoidance of greed and desire.[6]

Whereas the negatively phrased yamas represent vices to be rejected, the positively phrased niyamas represent virtues to be cultivated or values to be unleashed. According to Patanjali, the five niyamas are:

1 *saucha*: purity in body, mind, and speech;
2 *santosha*: contentment with one's possessions;
3 *tapaha*: endurance and perseverance;
4 *svadhyaya*: scriptural study and the quest for wisdom;
5 *ishvarapranidhana*: devotion, worship, and meditation.[7]

Together, the yamas and the niyamas form two sides of the moral coin. One set proscribes while the other prescribes; one set reins in destructive activity while the other releases goodness.

As with all forms of dharma, these ethical principles are not decreed by an external creator god who imposes them as moral laws and judges according to the degree to which they have been obeyed. Although it is a type of "law," dharma is a natural law that is intrinsic to the universe. Even the Hindu gods are subject to dharma rather than being its source or author. Similarly, humans do not create the rules of moral and socio-religious life. The dharma is discovered rather than invented, discerned rather than devised. So important is this all-pervasive, multilayered reality that Hindus prefer to call their religion sanatana dharma (the eternal and universal law). Moreover, living according to the dharma is listed as the first of the Five Constant Duties (Panca Nitya Karmas) that define Hindu religious life: dharma (virtuous living); upasana (daily worship); utsava (festivals); tirthayatrai (pilgrimage); and **samskaras** (life-cycle rituals). The rich and varied ways in which Hindus practice their religion includes a fundamental commitment to the moral life. Religious practice is hollow without an ethical dimension, while the ethical dimension is taken up and given new meaning by religious faith.

Given the immense diversity within the Hindu world, it is especially difficult to speak of "the Hindu position" in contemporary ethical debates concerning abortion, birth control, euthanasia, sexuality, and so on. Different Hindu schools and sects often disagree on practical matters even though they are all grounded in a common belief in the sanatana dharma. There are a number of sources to which the Hindu believer will turn for moral guidance. The sacred teachings of the **shruti** and **smriti** literature are fundamental, especially the classical law codes or **dharmashastras**, the best-known of which are the **Laws of Manu**. Hindus also look to outstanding persons of virtue who have left an example to be emulated, as well as the sagacious advice of spiritual counselors and gurus.

The need to know and live out the dharma is important not simply because it constitutes a vital aspect of moral, social, and religious life. The extent to which such obligations are fulfilled has significant long-term consequences, beyond death itself. In the reincarnational world view of Hindu faith, the form in which a deceased person is reborn into this world is directly affected by the extent to which he or she conformed to the dharma during their lifetime. This causal link between actions and their effects is known as **karma**. Those who heed Krishna's advice to Arjuna and complete their dharmic duties build up good karma and are thus likely to be reborn into more auspicious circumstances on earth or at a higher level in the cosmic hierarchy. Those who fail to do so generate bad karma and may find themselves reborn into a lower social class or even a lower form of life. Hindus may not live in fear of divine judgment at the end of their days, but the element of accountability is very real. The moral imperative may not be driven by apprehension about meeting one's maker, but concerns for a better rebirth and ultimately liberation from the wheel of reincarnation itself are powerful incentives for Hindus to take their dharmic responsibilities seriously.

Of course, the conviction that moral duty plays an important part in religious life and carries transcendent significance in the process is not limited to Hinduism. The belief that fulfilling one's ethical and religious duties greatly determines one's progress on the wheel of reincarnation is also a salient feature of its daughter religion. Moreover, the same recognition of the fundamental value of life, property, honest communication, sexual propriety, and control of desire can be found in Buddhism's famous list of five basic moral principles.

Pancasila

Seven weeks after Prince **Siddhartha Gautama** achieved complete **Enlightenment** and became the Buddha for our epoch, he met up with his five former ascetical companions at a deer park at **Sarnath**. There, he delivered his First Sermon, sharing the profound wisdom he had received under the tree at **Bodhgaya**. The contents of that initial discourse are known as the **Four Noble Truths**, which represent the very essence of Buddhist belief (see box 3.2).

Briefly, the First Noble Truth notes that human existence is full of suffering (dukha) at every level of our being: physical pain and debilitation; emotional troubles and anxieties; and a chronic existential unease resulting from the apparently pointless cycle of birth, death, and rebirth. The Second Noble Truth identifies the cause of all suffering as the misplaced desire for transient realities that can never fully satisfy the human mind or heart. It is this that binds us to the wheel of **reincarnation**. The Third Noble Truth holds up the hope of ultimate liberation (**nirvana**) from the apparently endless cycle and the cessation of all pathological cravings that shackle us to it. The Fourth Noble Truth outlines eight strategies that should be undertaken to make progress toward nirvana:

> Now this, monks, is the noble truth of the way leading to the cessation of suffering: It is this Noble Eightfold Path: that is, right view, right intention, right speech, right action, right livelihood, right effort, right mindfulness, and right concentration.[8]

The Buddhist understanding of existence is very similar to that of Hinduism which also sees the ultimate goal of the human person as liberation from the wheel of reincarnation. For the Hindu the key to making progress toward final liberation is adherence to the dharma as both universal moral norms and particular obligations linked to **caste**, gender, and age. It is at this point that Buddhism differs from its parent religion in its rejection of the relevance of the varna ashrama dharma. For Buddhists, dharma is not about adherence to caste laws and life-cycle rituals. Rather, dharma refers to the sublime truth that was rediscovered by Prince Siddhartha on the night of his Enlightenment and imparted to the earliest followers in the First Sermon. The essence of the dharma is the Four Noble Truths – the key that unlocks the dilemma of human existence and leads to ultimate liberation. Thus, the dharma (the teaching) combined with the Buddha (the teacher) and the Sangha (the community that is taught) make up the **Three Jewels** of Buddhism.

Commentators often divide the eight aspects of the last Noble Truth into three subcategories. The first two "paths" – right view and right intention – are categorized under wisdom (panna) since these involve intellectual acceptance of the Buddha's teaching and volitional commitment to his way. The last three – right effort, right

> ## THE FOUR NOBLE TRUTHS
>
> **Box 3.2**
>
> 1 Suffering: Now this, monks, is the noble truth of suffering: Birth is suffering, ageing is suffering, sickness is suffering, death is suffering; union with what is displeasing is suffering; separation from what is pleasing is suffering; not to get what one wants is suffering; in brief, the five aggregates subject to clinging are suffering.
> 2 The Source of Suffering: Now this, monks, is the noble truth of the origin of suffering: It is this craving which leads to renewed existence, accompanied by delight and lust, seeking delight here and there; that is, craving for sensual pleasures, craving for existence, craving for extermination.
> 3 The Cessation of Suffering: Now this, monks, is the noble truth of the cessation of suffering: It is the remainder-less fading away and cessation of that same craving, the giving up and relinquishing of it, freedom from it, and non-reliance on it.
> 4 The Way to the Cessation of Suffering: Now this, monks, is the noble truth of the way leading to the cessation of suffering: It is this Noble Eightfold Path: that is, right view, right intention, right speech, right action, right livelihood, right effort, right mindfulness, and right concentration.

mindfulness, and right concentration – are usually regarded as key elements of the art of meditation (**samadhi**) which is a necessary means to liberation. The remaining three paths – right speech, right action, and right livelihood – are classified under the heading of virtue (sila) since all three involve moral choices pertaining to relationships with others. Right speech demands that one's words are not deceitful, abusive, or divisive. Right action is a general call to live with uprightness in all aspects of morality. Right livelihood acknowledges that certain occupations may be morally unacceptable and should thus be avoided.[9] In other words, three of the eight fundamental ways that the Buddha presents as being crucial to attaining final liberation touch on the ethical dimension of life.

Like Hinduism, the Buddhist understanding of morality is not based on command-ments issued by a transcendent God and that are to be observed by human subjects. In such a system, God defines what is good and evil, and it is the moral duty of the believer humbly to obey the unquestionable divine law. Without clear belief in a personal supreme being, Buddhism grounds morality in the degree to which thoughts and actions either advance or impede progress toward final liberation. For this reason, Buddhists prefer to speak of actions as "skillful" (kausalya) or "unskillful" (akausalya) rather than as right or wrong. It is not a question of whether or not a certain act is in accordance with the will of a divine being. It is more a question of whether a certain act will contribute to eventual emancipation from the enslaving wheel of reincarnation. An action is also skillful if it is carried out with a pure intention and brings about positive effects such as happiness and harmony.

There is no shortage of material in Buddhist literature when it comes to specific moral principles that provide practical guidance for people in their everyday lives. The life of Sakyamuni himself is presented as a model that Buddhists should emulate on their journey toward nirvana. Most Buddhist schools uphold the belief that Sakyamuni, like all Buddhas throughout the ages, was devoid of any moral fault and thus constitutes a paragon of goodness and virtue. This is certainly true of his final reincarnation, but his earlier lives, narrated in the **Jataka Tales**, are also considered to be invaluable sources of moral inspiration and direction. In terms of teachings, the Golden Rule of ethics can also be found in the pages of Buddhist holy writings: "Comparing oneself to others in such terms as 'Just as I am so are they, just as they are so am I,' he should neither kill nor cause others to kill."[10] But beyond that one general principle, the Buddhist heritage also contains a number of useful lists that sum up the main aspects of sila. The most prominent is known simply as "the five precepts" or **Pancasila** (see box 3.3).

Box 3.3	**THE BUDDHIST PANCASILA**
	I refrain from destroying living creatures
	I refrain from taking that which is not given
	I refrain from sexual misconduct
	I refrain from false speech
	I refrain from intoxicants which lead to carelessness.

The Pancasila is considered to be the basic moral code for all believers, not just monks, and it plays a prominent role in Buddhist practice. Lay persons often explicitly recommit themselves to the five fundamental principles on the Buddhist monthly holy day known as **uposatha** (see chapter 9). The Pancasila is an important part of the chanted recitations by monks at crucial moments such as birth, marriage, and death, and is frequently the topic of sermons to visitors at monasteries. The laity themselves often recite the Pancasila on a daily basis as a constant reminder of their moral obligations.

There are various ways in which the Pancasila can be understood. The term itself reflects the idea that these are five "virtues" or qualities that characterize the spiritually advanced person. When a person embraces Buddha truth and begins to assimilate its insights into his or her life, it becomes less and less possible for that person to contravene any of the five precepts. The wise and virtuous believer "naturally" lives out the five rules since they are the fruits of inner peace and harmony. In this sense the Pancasila provides a basic definition of goodness or skillfulness in terms of the Buddhist faith. Another way of understanding the Pancasila is reflected in the fact that the Buddha sometimes referred to the list as the "five training rules" (pancasikkha). Rather than perceiving them as commandments imposed from on high, the Pancasila provides practical guidelines by which the believer is able to mold attitudes, actions, and ultimately moral character itself toward a more integrated and liberated state of being.

The five precepts are phrased in negative terms: "I refrain from" a certain action. Like the Hindu yamas, the Pancasila identifies actions that are to be avoided because they impede progress toward nirvana. These ideas represent a minimum threshold beneath which one should not venture. But Buddhists often point out that each precept also contains a positive value that complements the negative language and urges the believer to strive for a higher ideal. It is not just a matter of conforming to the precepts. It is about using them as a springboard in order to reach greater ethical heights. Thus the first precept requires the Buddhist to refrain from harming living beings, which is understood to include not only human but also animal and even plant life. This makes sense in the Hindu–Buddhist world where individuals may be reincarnated as other life forms, thus blurring the sharper boundaries that normally apply in Western thinking. On the positive side, one finds values such as lovingkindness, compassion, and generosity. For example, a popular form of spiritual exercise in Buddhism is the metta meditation where the practitioner cultivates thoughts of lovingkindness (metta) toward other beings, commencing with the self, and then moving out in ever widening concentric circles to embrace friends, acquaintances, enemies, and finally the entire cosmos. The same ideal of lovingkindness for all beings is manifest in the Mahayana concept of the **bodhisattva** who defers nirvana and remains present in this world in order to save all beings. The first precept also lies behind the widespread Buddhist practice of vegetarianism, as well as playing a key role in Buddhist ethical debates concerning more controversial issues such as abortion, euthanasia, and capital punishment.

The second precept concerns theft in its many forms, including obsession with material goods which can lead to stealing. The positive virtue implied here is generosity, not only in terms of money but also in terms of time and talent. Alms-giving is an important aspect of Buddhist life, especially material support of the monastic community by the laity. Similarly, the monks' renunciation of physical possessions and comforts is a radical expression of detachment from what are seen as false treasures. The third precept recognizes that sexual desire is one of the most powerful, and thus potentially one of the most dangerous drives in the human person. Buddhism acknowledges the existence of a sexual ethic involving both actions and thoughts, and built on integrity, fidelity, and concern for the other. Although sexual activity is not considered unskillful or immoral per se, it is generally assumed that final progress toward nirvana eventually requires the adoption of the celibate way of life. The fourth precept specifies that lying and deceit are unacceptable and that all communication should be not only honest, but also sensitive and constructive. Truth is an indispensable element on the path to ultimate liberation. Finally, the fifth precept focuses on the need for mental clarity which is a critical part of the Buddhist quest for wisdom via study and meditation. Consequently, all forms of alcohol, drugs, and other intoxicating substances, which have the potential to cloud the mind and undermine responsibility, are considered unskillful. This can also include shallow and addictive forms of entertainment.

The fifth precept is somewhat unusual and distinctive to Buddhism in that the concern for the deleterious effects of alcohol and drugs is not explicitly articulated in the Hindu yamas. But the first four precepts certainly are: violence, dishonesty, theft, greed, and lust in their manifold forms are identified in Hinduism and Buddhism as morally unacceptable. Respect for life, property, truthfulness, and sexual propriety are recognized in both traditions as the very heart of ethical behavior. But this intersection between religions is not confined to these two great Oriental traditions. The same shared fundamental moral principles from the Hindu–Buddhist tradition are also found in the ethical heritage of the **Semitic religions** although the origin, context, and motivation may differ.

The Ten Words

The Jewish biblical book named after the eighth-century BCE prophet Amos contains a startling passage:

> I hate, I despise your festivals, and I take no delight in your solemn assemblies. Even though you offer me your burnt-offerings and grain-offerings, I will not accept them; and the offerings of well-being of your fatted animals I will not look upon. Take away from me the noise of your songs; I will not listen to the melody of your harps. But let justice roll down like waters, and righteousness like an ever-flowing stream.[11]

It is an impassioned outburst from the God of Israel via his human mouthpiece, vehemently condemning any form of pious ritualism devoid of moral righteousness. While the sacrificial cult was considered a central part of official worship and a key expression of religious faith, what God ultimately wants is, according to Amos, not external religious formalities but ethical integrity in both thought and action. There is no point worshiping in the **Temple** while exploitation, oppression, and perversion of justice prevail outside. It is an instructive passage because it is not unique to Amos. The strident call to justice and ethical behavior is a common theme in the message of most of Israel's **prophets**.[12] No wonder these inspired spokespersons have often been labeled the conscience of Israel since "learn to do good" is their constant refrain.[13] While the prophetic books emphasize the importance of the social dimension, individual morality is stressed in other biblical books such as Proverbs and **Psalms**. The person who is truly pleasing to God is not only "wise" (hakham) but also "righteous" (tzaddik) and "upright" (yashar). The rabbinic tradition of Judaism also upheld the importance of ethical thought, and the **Talmud** is replete with legal and non-legal discussion of moral issues. An entire tractate, Pirkei Avoth (Ethics of the Fathers) is dedicated to such themes, declaring at one point: "The world stands on three things: Torah, divine service and acts of loving kindness."[14] As with Hinduism and Buddhism, the obligation to live a moral life is an indispensable part of Jewish religious practice.

The moral principles of the biblical prophets and the post-biblical rabbis are grounded in the first five books of the Jewish scriptures known collectively as the **Torah**. Its dramatic stories of the creation, the **patriarchs**, and the escape from Egypt are filled with disturbing cases of disobedience, murder, treachery, deceit, and corruption, as well as edifying examples of trust, courage, generosity, hospitality, and forgiveness. But it is in the Torah's extensive legal codes that the foundation of Jewish moral teaching is to be found. As with most religions, the duty to be ethical in one's thoughts and actions is an integral part of Jewish religious life and its moral principles are ultimately derived from the 613 **commandments** that were distilled from the Torah by the rabbinic tradition. This means that moral duty for a Jew is different from a purely secular system based on human freedom, the voice of conscience, or a set of philosophically derived values. While these aspects of moral life are generally accepted by Jewish thinking as valid, belief in a supreme creator God adds a completely new dimension. Right and wrong, goodness and evil, are defined not only in terms of human relationships but also in terms of the will of the creator who designed the world in the first place. Jewish morality is ultimately about faithful obedience to that divine will. Moreover, the final fate of every individual is determined by the divine judge who holds each individual morally accountable for their actions during life.

On this point, Judaism admits the existence of general moral norms available to all human beings outside the Jewish tradition. According to the Talmud, God gave seven fundamental laws to Noah prior to the Flood that were to be the moral basis for future humanity. Thus, long before the Torah was revealed to Moses, the Noahide Laws were already available to all persons of goodwill. The seven laws are prohibitions against false gods, murder, theft, sexual immorality, blasphemy, cruelty to animals, and corruption of the justice system.[15]

On one hand, Judaism is different from Hinduism and Buddhism, neither of which finds the ultimate source of morality in an external God who seeks obedience from his subjects. On the other hand, the divine will in Judaism is not some extraneous law imposed unjustly upon humankind. On the contrary, Judaism sees the divine commandments as reliable guideposts on the way to humankind's true destiny of eternal communion with God beyond death. Thus Judaism agrees with the Hindu–Buddhist conviction that leading a moral life is a sure path to definitive fulfillment. The commandments of the Lord may seem restrictive and limiting at first but, like the dharma, they are in the best interests of the human subject in the end. It is as if the external moral law, which comes as a divine edict, finds an echo in the inner nature of the human person who has been designed for communion with his or her maker.

There is a further dimension to the Jewish understanding of morality. The moral life is not only about obeying divine laws designed for the benefit of the human person in the first place. It is also about emulating the law-giver and creator-designer. Jewish faith holds that, although infinite and utterly beyond our imagination, nevertheless God is a personal being with traits similar to those found in humans, only perfect.[16] Thus the rabbinic tradition sees morality as an imitation of God, in whose image we are created.[17] The idea of imitating God's goodness is also reflected in the rabbinic idea that the most powerful incentive to upright conduct is the sanctification of the divine name (kiddush ha-Shem). Traditionally this was done in three ways: prayer, martyrdom, and good conduct. Thus, a Jew should be willing not only to surrender his or her life as a witness to the faith but also to so behave from day to day that God's name is honored by non-believers. In this way, Israel fulfills her vocation to be a "light to the nations."[18]

So what does God demand in terms of moral behavior? Is it possible to summarize the biblical commandments in terms of a few basic principles or norms? The rabbis often searched for a kelal or summary statement of the entire Torah. In a well-known Talmudic passage,[19] Rabbi Simlai notes that the 613 commandments given to Moses are reduced to 11 in Psalm 15. These are further abbreviated to six principles by Isaiah; three by Micah ("Act justly, love mercy and walk humbly with God"), two again by **Isaiah** ("Keep justice and do righteousness"), and finally one by Habakkuk ("The just man lives by his faithfulness").[20] Jewish tradition also contains the Golden Rule, classically expressed by the first-century BCE teacher Hillel as follows:

> A certain heathen came before Shammai and said to him, "Make me a proselyte, on condition that you teach me the whole Torah while I stand on one foot." Thereupon he repulsed him with the builder's cubit which was in his hand. When he went before Hillel, he said to him, "What is hateful to you, do not to your neighbour: that is the whole Torah, while the rest is the commentary thereof; go and learn it."[21]

Hillel's teaching draws on **Leviticus** 19:18 which succinctly declares: "Love your neighbor as yourself." But the classical summary of the Jewish moral law is the list said to have been engraved by God himself on two stone tablets and given to Moses on the holy mountain Sinai for all posterity. Although popularly known as the **Ten Commandments**, the biblical term *Aseret ha-D'vareem* is better translated as "Ten Words," hence the commonly used Greek term *Decalogue*.[22]

Considered by many to be the quintessence of the Torah, the **Decalogue** can be described as a list of broad obligations into which all of the other commandments can be conveniently placed. Consequently the number 10 has come to symbolize completeness and totality in the Jewish tradition. There was a time when the Ten Words were recited as part of official daily prayers, although the rabbis discontinued the practice out of a concern that believers would mistakenly think that there were only ten commandments and thus neglect the other 603.[23] Nevertheless, the Ten Words still play a vital part in Jewish moral education and their revelation is the major theme of the festival of **Shavuot** (Pentecost). In the synagogue the congregation traditionally stands when the biblical passages containing the Ten Words are read, and the image of the two stone tablets is a popular theme in synagogue art.

The Ten Words are listed in two places in the Hebrew scriptures: once in Exodus and a slightly longer version in **Deuteronomy**.[24] In abbreviated form, the traditional Jewish order is:

1   I am the Lord your God who brought you out of the land of slavery.
2   You shall have no other gods before me.
3   You shall not misuse the name of the Lord your God.
4   Remember the Sabbath day and keep it holy.
5   Honor your father and mother.
6   You shall not murder.
7   You shall not commit adultery.
8   You shall not steal.
9   You shall not bear false witness against your neighbor.
10   You shall not covet.

Such an arrangement allows for a neat division into two groups of five commandments, reflecting the use of two tablets in the biblical story. The first tablet concerns the vertical relationship with God. Thus the first commandment, which is in indicative rather than imperative form, is interpreted as requiring belief in the existence of God. The second emphasizes the unity of God and the dangers of any form of idolatry; the third reflects the Jewish concern for the divine name; and the fourth sets aside one holy day of rest each week. The fifth commandment, which concerns respect for parents, may seem more appropriately listed on the second tablet, but Jewish tradition sees the parent–child relationship as a mirror of the relationship between God and humankind.

The second tablet lists the basic moral norms that underpin most human cultures and societies. As with almost all of the Ten Words, the last five are phrased as negative imperatives identifying certain activities as inherently immoral: murder, adultery, theft, lying, covetousness. The list is strikingly reminiscent of the same fundamental ethical principles concerning relations between humans outlined in the Hindu yamas and the Buddhist Pancasila. Like the yamas and the Pancasila, the Ten Words are only general moral norms, from which more specific positions on a range of ethical issues are derived, such as abortion, euthanasia, genetic engineering, war, contraception, and sexual activity. These positions and teachings can vary significantly within Judaism, depending on the particular tradition such as **Reform**, **Conservative**, or **Orthodox**. Yet, despite diverse positions in particular cases, all agree that the broad principles enunciated in the Ten Words are a key part of the moral argument and cannot be overlooked.

The complementary relationship between the vertical and the horizontal axes, symbolized by the two tablets, is a vital aspect of Jewish moral understanding. In fact, traditional teaching suggests that if there is a conflict between duty toward God and duty toward neighbor, it is the latter that should take precedence. The point is well made in a story from the book of **Genesis** where Abraham interrupts his prayer to offer hospitality to three strangers.[25] Paradoxically, the strangers turn out to be God in disguise. This is precisely Amos's concern (quoted at the start of the chapter): worship of God in heaven is futile if not accompanied by justice and peace on earth. The same concern to marry the two tablets was a key motif in the life of another Jewish prophet who is portrayed by his followers as the new Moses who taught a new law for a new Israel.

A New Commandment

> One of the scribes came near and heard them disputing with one another, and seeing that he answered them well, he asked him, "Which commandment is the first of all?" Jesus answered, "The first is, 'Hear, O Israel: the Lord our God, the Lord is one; you shall love the Lord your God with all your heart, and with all your soul, and with all your mind, and with all your strength.' The second is this, 'You shall love your neighbor as yourself.' There is no other commandment greater than these."[26]

The above incident from the gospel of Mark tells of the occasion when Jesus was invited, like many rabbis, to present his kelal or summary statement of the Torah. In response, he quotes two of the 613 commandments, treating them as if they were one commandment, but the greatest of them all. The obligation for all Jews to love God first and foremost with all of their being is found in Deuteronomy[27] while the imperative to love one's neighbor as oneself is taken directly from Leviticus.[28] There is nothing new or unique in either of the individual commandments cited or even the combination. Jesus is basically reiterating the fundamental link between the vertical and horizontal axes of religious life symbolized by the two tablets of the Decalogue. What it does reinforce is the fact that Christian moral teaching is utterly grounded in the Jewish tradition, although the daughter religion sees itself somehow moving beyond what it calls the "Old Testament."

Christian thinking agrees with the Jewish idea that the world is the work of a benevolent and wise God who has created humans with a specific destiny in mind: namely, eternal communion with God. An essential aspect of the path to that destiny is moral behavior, since it is one of the main criteria against which each individual will be held accountable by the divine judge on the last day. As in other religions, Christianity admits that fundamental moral norms are potentially available to all human beings, irrespective of whether they have religious faith or not. Saint Paul refers to this innate sense of morality in his letter to the Romans:

> When Gentiles, who do not possess the law, do instinctively what the law requires, these, though not having the law, are a law to themselves. They show that what the law requires is written on their hearts, to which their own conscience also bears witness.[29]

Christian churches disagree over the extent to which this natural sense of right and wrong is distorted by human sinfulness thus rendering it unreliable. **Protestant** and **Orthodox** Christians tend to treat non-religious sources of ethics with a certain suspicion, while the **Catholic** tradition in general has been more accepting of the validity of secular moral reasoning and traditionally included "natural law" in its treatises on moral theology. Yet all Christians agree that the revealed word of God, recorded in the pages of the scriptures, provides a clearer guide to moral life. The Jewish scriptures, referred to as the **Old Testament** by Christians, is an essential first step. Although many ancient Jewish customs and practices, such as circumcision, **kosher**, and **sabbath** laws, were eventually abandoned by the early Church, the moral core of the biblical tradition was retained. When asked what is needed to achieve eternal life, Jesus simply refers to the Decalogue,[30] which has subsequently become the most widely used framework for Christian moral teaching throughout the ages.

This represents an extremely important point of intersection between the Jewish and Christian traditions. Closer inspection reveals that the Christian listing of the Ten Commandments varies slightly from the Jewish tradition (see table 3.1). Moreover, the version used by the Orthodox churches and most Protestant groups is different again from the Catholic and **Lutheran** version. The first difference is that the indicative statement, which functions as the first commandment in the Jewish version, is considered a preamble in both Christian versions. Thus the first Christian commandment concerns the oneness of God and the ban on any forms of idolatry. The second variation is that the Orthodox and Protestant version separates out the ban on graven images as a commandment distinct from the general prohibition against other gods. Highlighting the dangers of images in this way makes sense given the general Protestant aversion to statues and icons, although it is unusual for the Orthodox Church which has championed the use of the sacred image for most of its history. The effect of these two subtle differences early in the list is that the traditional numbering of the following commandments are the same for Jews, Orthodox Christians, and Protestant Christians but slightly different for Catholics and Lutherans. The latter make up the

Table 3.1   The Ten Commandments in its different forms

	Jewish	Catholic and Lutheran	Orthodox and Protestant
1	*I am the Lord your God who brought you out of the house of slavery.*	I am the Lord your God and you shall have no other gods before me.	I am the Lord your God and you shall have no other gods before me.
2	You shall have no other gods besides me.	You shall not misuse the name of the Lord your God.	*You shall not make for yourself any graven image.*
3	You shall not misuse the name of the Lord your God.	Remember to keep holy the Lord's Day.	You shall not misuse the name of the Lord your God.
4	Remember the Sabbath day and keep it holy.	Honor your father and mother.	Remember to keep holy the Lord's Day.
5	Honor your father and mother.	You shall not kill.	Honor your father and mother.
6	You shall not murder.	You shall not commit adultery.	You shall not kill.
7	You shall not commit adultery.	You shall not steal.	You shall not commit adultery.
8	You shall not steal.	You shall not bear false witness against your neighbor.	You shall not steal.
9	You shall not bear false witness against your neighbor.	*You shall not covet your neighbor's wife.*	You shall not bear false witness against your neighbor.
10	You shall not covet anything that belongs to your neighbor.	You shall not covet your neighbor's goods.	You shall not covet anything that belongs to your neighbor.

Note: Italic denotes variation in the list.

number 10 by dividing the ban on covetousness into separate commandments concerning the neighbor's wife and his goods. For many the Catholic–Lutheran version, which can be traced back to Saint Augustine, has the advantage of acknowledging the wife as a human person, clearly distinct from the neighbor's material possessions.[31] At the same time, the effect is to place greater emphasis on sexual transgressions since two commandments now touch on this aspect of morality: the sixth understood as covering sexual acts and the ninth covering sexual thoughts. The other noteworthy difference between the Jewish and Christian versions of the Decalogue is the commandment concerning the taking of life. In the original Hebrew, what is prohibited is murder but the Christian tradition has translated the verb as "kill," which is a broader category and not quite the same thing.

Important as the Ten Commandments are as a practical list of moral norms, there is a strong element in Christian thinking that these guidelines are insufficient in themselves. Stemming from the writings of Saint Paul, the law of Moses, which is summarized in the Decalogue, is seen as good and holy but somehow imperfect. It supplies the essential information necessary for the moral life but lacks the motivating force needed to carry it out. In Paul's thinking, what is needed is a "new law" which not only provides the content but also the psychological drive to be virtuous. That drive can come only through faith in **Jesus** as the incarnate Son of God and Savior of humankind. Thus Christian morality is essentially christocentric, but what does this mean?

The central role of Jesus in Christian morality parallels the importance of Sakyamuni in Buddhism. His example provides an invaluable guidepost and a powerful source of inspiration for the faithful. Like the Buddha, the Christ is considered to be sinless and thus the perfect model for all to emulate. Furthermore, the gospels are full of Jesus's teachings on a range of issues including morality. The classical collection of such teachings is the **Sermon on the Mount**, constituting chapters 5 to 7 of the gospel of Matthew. Standing on a Galilean hill surrounded by attentive crowds, Jesus is portrayed by the first evangelist as a new Moses proclaiming a new Decalogue for a new Israel. The "sermon" opens with a list of blessings known as the Beatitudes in which Jesus praises those who are pure, meek, merciful, peaceful, and willing to suffer for justice. What follows is Jesus's own critique of the Decalogue itself which opens with a confirmation of its perennial validity: "Do not think that I have come to abolish the law and the prophets; I have come not to abolish but to fulfill."[32] But he then proceeds to push its application well beyond the letter of the law:

> You have heard that it was said to those of ancient times, "You shall not murder"; and "whoever murders shall be liable to judgment." But I say to you that if you are angry with a brother or sister, you will be liable to judgment; and if you insult a brother or sister, you will be liable to the council; and if you say, "You fool," you will be liable to the hell of fire . . .
>
> You have heard that it was said, "You shall not commit adultery." But I say to you that everyone who looks at a woman with lust has already committed adultery with her in his heart . . .
>
> You have heard that it was said, "An eye for an eye and a tooth for a tooth." But I say to you, do not resist an evildoer. But if anyone strikes you on the right cheek, turn the other also . . .

> You have heard that it was said, "You shall love your neighbor and hate your enemy."
> But I say to you, Love your enemies and pray for those who persecute you.[33]

For many, the language of some verses seems too quixotic to be a workable basis for day-to-day ethics in the real world. Yet it basically corresponds to the call for moral excellence found in most religious traditions. Just as Hindus, Buddhists, and Jews are encouraged to transcend the minimum standards of the yamas, the Pancasila, and the Decalogue, so too Christians are invited to embrace virtue enthusiastically rather than to avoid vice perfunctorily. In Christian thinking the key motivation for such supererogation is "love." Of course, "love" can have many levels of meaning including romance, family relationships, and friendship. But the New Testament uses the unusual Greek term *agape* to refer to a higher love than any of these.[34] Agape is God's love for humankind, made manifest in the life of his incarnate Son. This divine love constitutes the heart of an eleventh commandment which Jesus bequeaths his followers: "I give you a new commandment, that you love one another. Just as I have loved you, you also should love one another."[35] The Jewish idea that morality is an imitation of the transcendent God of love and mercy evolves into the Christian idea of imitating that same God in human form. According to Paul, the discovery of that infinite love is the power and inspiration needed to awaken the human heart to love God and neighbor in return. Even the Golden Rule, explicitly endorsed by Jesus ("In everything do to others as you would have them do to you; for this is the law and the prophets"[36]), is given a new interpretation. Now acts of kindness to others are also seen as acts toward the God-man himself: "Truly I tell you, just as you did it to one of the least of these who are members of my family, you did it to me."[37]

These are the general principles on which most forms of Christian moral teaching are based. Their application in specific ethical issues can vary considerably from church to church and within churches. For example, official Catholic morality is extensively shaped by the tradition of papal teaching, while Orthodox churches place great emphasis on Church Fathers,[38] and Protestant communities stress a close reading of the biblical text. However for most branches of Christianity the moral life is grounded in the divinely revealed commandments of the Old Testament, viewed in a new perspective in the context of the life and teaching of Jesus. A similar process can also be observed in Islam where the legacy of the Decalogue is absorbed and reinterpreted through the prism of the Qur'anic text and the example of the Prophet.

The Greater Jihad

There is a much quoted tradition in Islam that relates how **Muhammad**, upon returning from a battle, declared: "We now go from the lesser jihad to the greater jihad."

The term **jihad**, commonly understood as "holy war," has become one of the most recognizable and notorious religious words today. Indeed in the mainstream **hadith** tradition, jihad usually means a military encounter fought on behalf of the faith. However, the Arabic word literally means "struggle" and, although the authenticity of the above saying is questionable, many Muslims, especially **Sufis** and **Shi'ites**, acknowledge its basic point: that apart from the possibility of a justified armed struggle on behalf of Islam (the al-jihad al-asghar, or "lesser jihad") there is a more important form of "struggle" that takes place within the soul of every individual (the al-jihad al-akbar, or "greater jihad"). Whereas the former is external, physical, and occasional, the latter is internal, spiritual, and constant. Some commentators further differentiate its various forms. The jihad of the soul refers to the fight against evil in the mind; the jihad of the tongue is waged by the spoken word, such as preaching; the jihad of the pen is the struggle to gain greater knowledge of Islam through study; and the jihad of the hand is carried out via ethical behavior. Whatever the differentiations, the idea is clear: the greater jihad is the everyday moral struggle against temptation that is an essential part of being a Muslim. As with other religions, Islam acknowledges the importance of the moral life and considers it inseparable from the life of faith. A Muslim's whole existence is permeated by ethical demands. But what are the guidelines for the Muslim who aspires to seek good and to avoid evil?

As with other major religions, Islam is aware of the Golden Rule. According to the hadith: "None of you truly believes until he loves for his brother what he loves for himself."[39] Moreover, like the Hindu dharma, the Jewish Noahide Laws, and the Christian natural law, Islam admits that a universal knowledge of the moral law is discernible by natural intelligence and forms a basis for the final judgment. One Qur'anic text hints at this innate sense of right and wrong:

> I swear by the Sun and its brilliance . . .
> And the soul and Him who made it perfect,
> Then He inspired it to understand what is right and wrong for it;
> He will indeed be successful who purifies it,
> And he will indeed fail who corrupts it.[40]

However, Muslims share the conviction with other religions that natural knowledge of good and evil is unreliable and that only by special enlightenment or revelation can the human mind clearly and fully obtain truth including moral truth. Like its Jewish and Christian cousins, Islam holds that God has revealed his eternal will via a special line of prophets, thus rendering the content of the moral law more detailed and reliable. Moral duty is not just about establishing a society of justice and peace on earth. It is also about fulfilling the divine plan that destines humans for eternal communion with God. The word "Islam" itself literally means "submission," not in the sense of capitulation to an oppressive force but in the sense of trusting obedience to the creator who knows what is best for us.

Given that morality stems from the overarching divine plan for the world and its human inhabitants, the primary source of moral teaching for Muslims is the sacred book in which that divine plan for subsequent generations is stored. The **Qur'an** is the definitive measure of good and evil as stated in the opening of its twenty-fifth chapter, aptly named "Al-Furqan" [The Criterion]: "Blessed is He, Who sent down the Furqan (criterion) upon His servant that he may be a warner to the nations."[41] As in Christianity, the Qur'an builds on truths already revealed through Muhammad's predecessors, the prophets of Israel. Thus Islam approves of the moral teachings of the Jewish scriptures, including the Decalogue, although Muslims believe that the original texts have been corrupted over time. Consequently, the Decalogue does not appear as such in the Qur'an although one can find Qur'anic verses that support the main ideas of the Ten Words: the ban on idolatry (47:19) and swearing (2:224); the need to keep the holy day (62:9); respect for parents (17:23); and the prohibition of murder (5:32), adultery (17:32), theft (5:38–9), deceit (2:283), and covetousness (20:131).

One particular passage from the seventeenth chapter ("The Children of Israel") is frequently described as the Islamic equivalent of the Decalogue. As with the Jewish text, the list of moral precepts can be divided in different ways. One possible combination is the following list of 10 basic principles:

1   Do not worship another god but God.
2   Be kind to your parents, and care for them.
3   Give to your relatives what is their due.
4   Do not be miserly or extravagant with your possessions.
5   Do not abandon your children out of fear of poverty.
6   Do not fornicate.
7   Do not kill anyone whom God has forbidden except for a just cause.
8   Do not steal from orphans but deal with others honestly and justly.
9   Do not follow what you do not know.
10 Do not act with arrogance.[42]

Although the precepts do not coincide exactly with the Decalogue, there is considerable overlap, including the emphasis on monotheism, respect for parents and family, as well as the forbidding of unjustified killing, sexual impropriety, theft, injustice, and an unhealthy preoccupation with material possessions.

The second main source of Islamic moral teaching is the Prophet himself. While the contents of the Qur'an are understood to be the literal words of God, Muhammad's own sayings and the example of his life complement the revealed truths found in the sacred text itself. It is as if Muhammad were a living commentary on the Qur'an, applying its ideals to his own words and deeds. As with Sakyamuni and Jesus, Muhammad is held up as a model to be followed: "Certainly you have in the Apostle of Allah an excellent exemplar for him who hopes in Allah and the latter day and remembers Allah much."[43] Moreover, like Sakyamuni and Jesus, there is a tradition within Islam that considers Muhammad to be morally impeccable and thus the most perfect of models. While all Muslims profess that Muhammad was without fault in the reception and transmission of the words of the Qur'an,[44] the Shi'ite tradition in particular holds that Muhammad, his daughter **Fatima**, and the twelve imams in his bloodline were recipients of God's ismah, or protection from moral fault. Hence, a profound knowledge and appreciation of the founder provides incalculable moral guidance and motivation to millions of Muslims today. Moreover, in contrast to Jesus, there is a considerable volume of biographical information about Muhammad, at least from the last two decades of his life, which has been passed down to posterity. This information, known as the hadith, contains the words and deeds of the Prophet that have been validated by reliable witnesses and organized into official collections. The six classical **Sunni** hadith collections are:

Sahih Bukhari
Sahih Muslim
Sunan Abu Dawud
Sunan al-Tirmidhi
Sunan al-Sughra
Sunan Ibn Majah

Not only do believers have the wisdom and insight of Muhammad's teachings, but also the practical example of his actions.

Despite many relevant references in the Qur'an and the hadith, Islamic moral teaching is most explicitly enunciated in **shari'a** – the Islamic law. Shari'a lies at the very heart of Islamic practice including moral behavior. For the Muslim, everyday ethical behavior is an integral part of one's religious life that is defined and shaped by the religious law. The eternal law of God is rendered accessible through the shari'a which encompasses the social and the individual, the civil and the criminal, the ritual and the ethical. Morality and legality coincide, and what is right and wrong is defined for the Muslim by the divine law. As the term *shari'a* suggests, this is the truest "path" to humanity's eternal destiny.

In a manner reminiscent of the twofold division of the Jewish Decalogue, shari'a is traditionally divided into two main sections: al-ibadat (our relationship with God), which deals with religious practices such as daily prayer, the sacred tax, fasting, and pilgrimage; and al-mu'amalat (our relationships with others), which includes marriage and inheritance, business, crime and punishment, and so forth. Both the vertical and horizontal axes of existence are an equally vital part of lived religious praxis. Within this twofold structure, all actions are placed into one of five fundamental categories. The first category (fard) pertains to all acts that are considered compulsory, such as the five daily prayers, the fast of **Ramadan**, and payment of the sacred tax. The second category (mandub or mustabah) contains actions that are recommended but not obligatory, such as personal prayer and other forms of devotion. It is also the category into which Islam places virtues such as voluntary alms-giving to the poor, acts of courage, or gestures of unsolicited kindness. The third category (mubah) denotes acts that are morally neutral, including one's preference in terms of food, leisure activities, or choice of dress provided these are within general moral parameters. The fourth category (makruh) comprises actions that are disapproved but permissible, such as divorce. The final category (**haram**) refers to acts that are forbidden. Many of these are equally condemned in other religious traditions, such as murder, adultery, theft, blasphemy, and deceit, but some are peculiar to Islam, such as the consumption of pork or alcohol and breaking the Ramadan fast.

The development of shari'a since the time of Muhammad is as complex a subject as Christian canon law or Jewish Talmudic history and well beyond the scope of this work. However, it should be noted that while most Muslims are in broad agreement on matters of religious practice and morals, Shi'ite and Sunni Muslims have their own legal systems. Even within the Sunni world, there are at least four classical

---

Box 3.4

THE FOUR MAIN SUNNI SCHOOLS OF LAW

- The **Hanafi** school is the oldest, largest, and most liberal school, granting more importance to human reason than the other schools. It is predominant in Turkey, Syria, Egypt, Iraq, as well as central and south Asia.
- The **Shafi'i** school emphasizes the strict application of principles and tends to avoid speculation. It is predominant in east Africa and southeast Asia.
- The **Maliki** school considers the practice of the early Medina community as an important source of law, sometimes taking precedence over the hadith. It is predominant in north and west Africa.
- The **Hanbali** school is the most conservative, stressing the primacy of the Qur'an and using analogy only with great caution. It is predominant in the Arabian peninsula.

All four schools recognize the Qur'an as the primary source of law, followed by the collected sayings and example of the Prophet (hadith), the consensus of the elders (ijma), and analogical reasoning (qiyas).

schools of jurisprudence (madhabs) named after prominent scholars who lived and wrote during the eighth and ninth centuries CE: the Hanafi, Shafi'i, Maliki, and Hanbali schools (see box 3.4). Despite the plurality of schools, Sunnis accept all four as legitimate and often point out that the variations between them are usually minor. What the evolution of the four schools does indicate is that, while the Qur'an and the hadith represent fixed sources that do not change with time, Islamic legal reasoning also admits factors that allow for a degree of ongoing interpretation and application. One such factor, generally accepted by Sunni scholars at least, is analogical reasoning (qiyas) which applies the timeless principles of the past to new situations that are not explicitly dealt with by the tradition. The plurality of legal schools also reflects the fact that Islam, like other major religions, has no single central authority that speaks for all Muslims on matters of ethics, which thus makes it misleading to speak of "the Islamic position" on a particular issue. Nevertheless, the Qur'an, the hadith, and the shari'a constitute a solid threefold foundation on which Islamic moral teaching is based. The revealed word of God, the shining example of the Prophet, and the detailed applications of the law provide the guidance and the orientation necessary for fulfilling one's moral duty.

SUMMARY

The sense of moral duty, which is such a fundamental aspect of being human, constitutes an important practical dimension of all five major religions. Each in its own way incorporates the "ought" of conscience into the broader framework of a religious world view and thus adds a special layer of significance to the basic duty of doing good and avoiding evil. Although not all decisions and actions are moral, those that are have their place firmly within the world of belief. Seen through the eyes of faith, the moral life is an integral part of religious life and moral obligations are often interwoven with other forms of religious obligation. For example, in Hinduism, the varna ashrama dharma embraces a complex range of social, cultural, and ritual rules that vary according to personal circumstances. Yet, along with the more general sadharana dharma, these are still part of the all-encompassing cosmic law that must be fulfilled. Similarly, the 613 commandments of the Jewish Torah are a mixture of moral and ritual-cultic prescriptions, all of which are considered sacred and all of which must be obeyed with diligence and commitment.

Once moral duty is placed within a religious context and given a religious interpretation, certain implications arise. The most obvious is the connection between moral behavior in this life and one's ultimate fate beyond death. This link and the powerful motivation it generates are features of all five religions. Doing the right thing now has serious consequences in the long term. Thus in Hinduism, following the dharma and storing up good karma by way of ethical actions is one of the three traditional ways of obtaining ultimate liberation from the cycle of reincarnation. Similarly, three of the eight elements of the Buddha's Noble Eightfold Path that leads to nirvana highlight the need for ethical behavior. Virtue, as well as wisdom and meditation, is the key to final release. Although the Semitic religions in general do not embrace the Hindu–Buddhist notion of reincarnational existence, nevertheless moral actions in this present life have **eschatological** repercussions. Jews, Christians, and Muslims all believe that individuals will be held accountable for their actions before the judgment seat of the creator and that moral character will be one of the most important criteria.

The connection between moral behavior and one's final destiny highlights an important difference between Hinduism–Buddhism and the Semitic religions. In the latter, the ultimate source of moral right and wrong is the transcendent, personal creator God. Thus moral duty takes the form of compliance with an eternal divine law that defines good and evil. Although there are other reasons for acting morally, not the least of which is respect for other beings, the **Abrahamic religions** profess that morality is also about trusting obedience. These religions claim that the divine law in question is not some oppressive, alien system of constraint imposed unfairly upon humankind. Rather, it is a guide offered by the one who designed humans with a particular end in mind: namely, eternal communion with God. In contrast, the Hindu–Buddhist world view sees moral duty arising out of the cosmic order. The dharma is an eternal law but not the decree of a creator God. Rather, it is an intrinsic part of the universe itself that needs to be understood and followed for one's own benefit. Even the many gods of the Hindu pantheon are subject to the dharma, although there are moments in the Bhagavad Gita when Krishna is presented as the loving source of the dharma in a similar way as God is the loving source of the moral law in the Semitic faiths.

Despite such differences, there is a considerable degree of agreement when it comes to the fundamental moral norms that underpin social and individual life. Each religion has its own list of core principles, whose content are remarkably similar in essence. Admittedly there are differences of emphasis, such as the Buddhist concern to protect all forms of life (not just human) in contrast to the Jewish and Islamic understanding that not every form of "killing" is necessarily immoral. But the Hindu yamas, the Buddhist Pancasila, the Jewish and Christian versions of the Decalogue, and the seventeenth chapter of the Qur'an all identify murder, theft, sexual impropriety, dishonesty, and greed as the most serious categories of immoral thought and action. Even the Golden Rule – treat others as you would have them treat you – can be identified within all five traditions (see box 3.5). Of course, these are broad principles, and differences arise very quickly when one moves into more detailed ethical issues, not only between religions but also between the various subdivisions within them.

Finally all traditions agree that such lists are only an indication of a minimum threshold of appropriate behavior. Ideally, the believer should seek to cultivate the positive values that constitute the reverse of the moral coin for each prohibition. One should

---

THE GOLDEN RULE OF ETHICS IN EACH RELIGION

Box 3.5

One should not behave towards others in a way which is disagreeable to oneself. This is the essence of morality. All other activities are due to selfish desire. (Mahabharata)

Comparing oneself to others in such terms as "Just as I am so are they, just as they are so am I," he should neither kill nor cause others to kill. (Sutta Pitaka)

What is hateful to you, do not to your neighbor: that is the whole Torah, while the rest is the commentary thereof; go and learn it. (Talmud)

In everything, do to others as you would have them do to you; for this is the law and the prophets. (Gospel of Matthew)

None of you truly believes until he loves for his brother what he loves for himself. (Hadith)

---

maximize virtue rather than merely avoid vice. An important part of that quest is the example of religious figures from the past, especially the founder. In this respect, Sakyamuni, Jesus, and Muhammad all play a very important role in the moral life of Buddhists, Christians, and Muslims. In each case, the founder is considered a sinless paragon of virtue to be emulated. Not only their teaching but the practical example of their lives provides inspiration and motivation for believers in the struggle to be good. But the practice of religion is not only a question of moral uprightness. Beyond ethical duty there lies a fascinating array of symbolic actions, customs, times, and places that help to define religious identity, express religious faith, and give transcendent meaning to the human journey from birth to death. It is to such themes that we turn in the following chapters.

DISCUSSION TOPICS

1   Do all religions agree on the fundamental moral norms for humanity?
2   How does each religion explain the origin of evil in the world?
3   Can there be a system of ethics that is not based on religious faith?
4   Do human persons have real freedom of choice or are we ultimately victims of fate? What do the world religions teach on this issue?
5   How does each religion explain why innocent persons suffer?
6   What is the position of each religion on contemporary moral "life" issues such as abortion, euthanasia, capital punishment, and warfare?

7   Compare the Hindu–Buddhist belief in karma with the Jewish, Christian, and Islamic belief in divine judgment.

8   What are the arguments for and against belief in reincarnation?

FURTHER READING

Bhaskarananda, Swami (2002). *The Essentials of Hinduism*. 2nd edn. Seattle: Viveka, pp. 97–105.

Burke, T. Patrick (2004). *The Major Religions: An Introduction with Texts*. 2nd edn. Oxford: Blackwell (see relevant sections on "ethics").

Cohn-Sherbok, Dan (2003). *Judaism: History, Belief and Practice*. London: Routledge, pp. 564–71.

Corrigan, John, et al. (1997). *Jews, Christians, Muslims: A Comparative Introduction to Monotheistic Religions*. Upper Saddle River, NJ: Prentice Hall, pp. 277–339.

Crook, Roger (2006). *Introduction to Christian Ethics*. 5th edn. Upper Saddle River, NJ: Prentice Hall, part 2.

Gordon, Matthew S. (2002). *Understanding Islam*. London: Duncan Baird, pp. 60–71.

Harvey, Peter (1990). *An Introduction to Buddhism: Teaching, History and Practices*. Cambridge: Cambridge University Press, ch. 9.

Keown, Damien (2000). *Buddhism: A Very Short Introduction*. Oxford and New York: Oxford University Press, ch. 8.

Keown, Damien (2001). *The Nature of Buddhist Ethics*. Basingstoke: Palgrave Macmillan, chs. 1–2.

Newman, Louis E. (2004). *An Introduction to Jewish Ethics*. Upper Saddle River, NJ: Prentice Hall, chs. 2–4.

Renard, John (1996). *Seven Doors to Islam: Spirituality and the Religious Life of Muslims*. Berkeley and Los Angeles: University of California Press, pp. 75–106.

Sangharakshita (1985). *The Eternal Legacy: An Introduction to the Canonical Literature of Buddhism*. Birmingham: Windhorse, pp. 127–44.

Singer, Peter (ed.) (1993). *A Companion to Ethics*. Oxford: Blackwell, chs. 4–9.

NOTES

1   Bhagavad Gita 2:30–3.
2   Rg Veda 1.15.1–21; 2.28.1–11.
3   Bhagavad Gita 3:35; see also 18:47.
4   Mahabharata, Anusasana Parva XIII.113.8.
5   Bhagavad Gita 16:1–3.
6   Yoga Sutra, Sadhana Pada 2.35–9.
7   Yoga Sutra, Sadhana Pada 2.40–5.
8   Samyutta Nikaya 56.11.
9   Samyutta Nikaya 45.8.

10 Khuddaka Nikaya, Sutta Nipata 705; Samyutta Nikaya 5.353.

11 Amos 5:21–4.

12 See Hosea 2:13; Isaiah 1:11; Micah 6:6–8; Jeremiah 6:20.

13 Isaiah 1:17.

14 Talmud Avoth 1.2.

15 Talmud Sanhedrin 56a–b.

16 Exodus 34:6–7.

17 Genesis 1:27.

18 Isaiah 49:6.

19 Talmud Makkot 24a.

20 Micah 6:8; Isaiah 56:1; Habakkuk 2:4.

21 Talmud Shabbat 31a; see also Tobit 4:15.

22 The preferred rabbinic term is *Aseret ha-Dibrot*, which literally means "The Ten Sayings."

23 Talmud Berakoth 12a.

24 Exodus 20:1–17; Deuteronomy 5:6–21.

25 Genesis 18:1–5.

26 Mark 12:28–31.

27 Deuteronomy 6:4–5.

28 Leviticus 19:18.

29 Romans 2:14–15.

30 Mark 10:19.

31 The Exodus version lists the house first and the wife second, while the Deuteronomic version has the wife at the head of the list of the neighbor's "possessions."

32 Matthew 5:17.

33 Matthew 5:21–2, 27–8, 38–9, 43–4.

34 For example, see 1 Corinthians 13.

35 John 13:34.

36 Matthew 7:12.

37 Matthew 25:40.

38 Influential Christian theologians and writers from the period 100–800 CE.

39 The Forty Hadith of An-Nawawi, n.13.

40 Qur'an 91:1, 7–10.

41 Qur'an 25:1.

42 Qur'an 17:23–38; see also 6:151–3.

43 Qur'an 33:21.

44 Qur'an 69:40–7.

Chapter 4

BIRTH

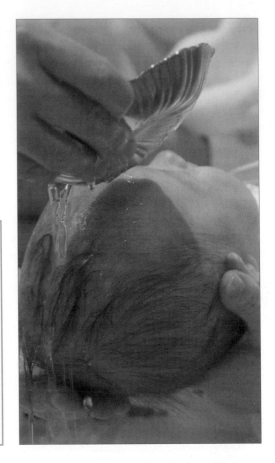

CONTENTS

 Baptism

 B'rit Milah

 Aqiqah

 Birth Samskaras

 The Buddhist Exception

Introduction

In addition to its ethical dimension, religion also sheds meaning on the journey of life, and especially important milestones along the way such as birth, marriage, and death. Over the next three chapters we will examine the life-cycle rituals associated with these three key moments, commencing in this chapter with the ways in which the five world religions celebrate and interpret the beginning of human life. What are the birth ceremonies in each of the five religions? What primary symbols and gestures are used and why? How do they convey notions of identity and membership of the faith community?

✝ Baptism

All four canonical **gospels** agree that the public ministry of Jesus commenced somewhere on the banks of the river **Jordan** where curious crowds gathered to witness an enigmatic religious figure named **John**. In the classical prophetic tradition, John's message was directed at the contemporary generation of Jews, beckoning them to acknowledge their failings and recommit themselves to the **Torah**. It was essentially a call to repentance. Moreover, like the **prophets** of old, John used a visual symbolic action to highlight the meaning of his words. He invited his audience to immerse themselves in the waters of the river as a powerful expression of their desire to be washed of their guilt and start afresh with a clean heart.

We are told that **Jesus** was among those who gathered at the Jordan but something unusual occurred when he entered the water. A voice from heaven declared him to be "my Son" and the Spirit of God descended like a dove and hovered over him. One of the few explicit references to the **Trinity** in the gospel account, this marks the anointing of Jesus as the long-awaited **Messiah**. The gospels differ slightly in regard to who precisely hears the heavenly voice: Jesus alone, John alone, or everyone present.[1] However there is no dispute that this is a key turning point in the life of Jesus, akin to Prince Siddhartha's first encounter with the world outside his palace and Muhammad's first vision in the cave near Mecca. In hindsight, Christians see John as the Messiah's precursor – a figure akin to the prophet **Elijah**[2] who will herald the coming of God's chosen one at the start of the messianic age. History remembers John as "the **Baptist**" and the symbolic action of washing in water, which is the basis for his famous epithet, was adopted by the Church as the definitive rite by which a person becomes a Christian – **baptism**.

The term *baptism* is derived from a Greek verb meaning "to immerse, to dip or to bathe." In fact John's use of water baptism was not without precedent in the Jewish world. The Torah prescribes a purifying bath (**mikveh**) for those who have become spiritually contaminated, for example women during menstruation or someone who has been in contact with a corpse.[3] Moreover, conversion to Judaism requires the mikveh which symbolizes a total cleansing from past sinfulness and a new beginning as a member of the chosen people of God. However, the baptismal rite quickly became identified with initiation into Christianity. It seems to have been used as the gateway to the new faith from the very earliest generations. Initially baptism was celebrated for adult converts from either Jewish or pagan background, but as Christianity eventually became the majority religion within the Roman Empire, the ritual was increasingly performed for the newborn children of Christian families. Even today, while it is the official means to mark adult conversion into the Church, baptism is more commonly experienced in Christian societies and cultures as the ritual associated with human birth.

Not all Christian churches agree with the practice of infant baptism. For **Baptists**, Pentecostals, Seventh-Day Adventists, Jehovah's Witnesses, and Mormons, the informed and conscious choice of the recipient is absolutely necessary for baptism. It is not as if these groups **liturgically** ignore the wonderful moment of childbirth, since most have a dedication service of some sort during which the congregation gives thanks for the birth of a new life and prays for the child. But in such churches, the appropriate age of baptism is when the person is aware of what is entailed and freely embraces the Christian faith. This can vary from 8 years among Mormons, who stress moral responsibility, to the threshold of adulthood in other communities. The fundamental birth imagery is carried forward since the person who is baptized at an older age is often described as being "born again."[4]

In contrast, infant baptism is common practice in the **Orthodox**, **Catholic**, **Lutheran**, and **Anglican** Churches. There are several arguments proffered in justification. For some, especially the Catholic Church, a key motivation is the deep-seated concern for the fate of a baby who dies unbaptized, since only baptism can wash away original sin.[5] More prevalent today is the argument based on parental responsibility. Advocates point out that religious upbringing is one of many legitimate decisions taken by parents on behalf of a baby, along with food, clothing, shelter, and education. Furthermore, the child is always free to ratify or reject the parents' choice when he or she reaches adulthood.[6]

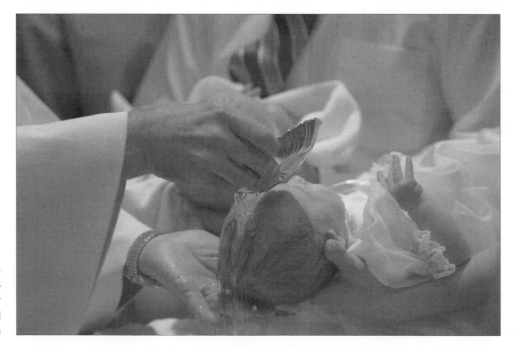

Figure 4.1
A priest pours holy water over a baby's head during a baptism

So what happens during a baptism ceremony? Naturally, the central symbol is the water-bath, although the precise manner in which this occurs varies from full immersion to sprinkling (aspersion) or pouring (infusion) of the water over the head of the child. Most churches tend to agree that immersion is a more powerful and effective symbol, but many adopt the latter methods for convenience particularly where tiny babies are involved. Baptisms may take place at rivers, lakes, and other natural bodies of water, and many Christian pilgrims are baptized in the river Jordan itself. However the majority of denominations perform baptisms inside the church building, usually over a special font or in a pool. The water itself is blessed, often with references to relevant biblical passages that stress the life-giving and saving powers of water: God's Spirit hovering over the waters of creation; **Noah**'s ark with the kernel of a new human family surviving the Great Flood; and the miraculous crossing of the sea by **Moses** and the Israelites (see box 4.1).[7]

The action is always accompanied by words. Some churches prefer to baptize "in the name of Jesus," which may have been the original formula used in the early Church.[8] However, the traditional practice is to use the Trinitarian formula that appears at the conclusion of Matthew's gospel: "in the name of the Father and of the Son and of the Holy Spirit."[9] Sometimes the Trinitarian dimension is reinforced by a triple pouring or immersion.

Churches that advocate infant baptism agree that the ceremony must involve an expression of belief. Given that the baby is unable to speak for itself, the task of declaring the faith falls to the parents and godparents. In practice the latter are often close

---

PRAYER OVER THE BAPTISMAL FONT (CATHOLIC RITE)

Box 4.1

Father, you give us grace through sacramental signs, which tell us of the wonders of your unseen power. In baptism we use your gift of water, which you have made a rich symbol of the grace you give us in this sacrament. At the very dawn of creation your Spirit breathed on the waters, making them the wellspring of all holiness. Your Son willed that water and blood should flow from his side as he hung upon the cross. And after his resurrection Christ told his disciples: "Go out and teach all nations, baptizing them in the name of the Father, and of the Son, and of the Holy Spirit." Father, look now with love upon your Church, and unseal for them the fountain of baptism. By the power of the Spirit give to the water of this font the grace of your Son. You created us in your own likeness: cleanse us from sin in a new birth to innocence by water and the Spirit. We ask you, Father, with your daughter/son, to send the Holy Spirit upon the water of this font. May all who are buried with Christ in the death of baptism, rise also with him to newness of life. We ask this through Christ our Lord. Amen.

relatives or family friends, but in theory they should also be models for the child's moral and religious upbringing. The profession of faith is usually based on ancient Christian creeds and commonly takes the form of question and answer such as:

MINISTER: Do you believe in God, the Father almighty, creator of heaven and earth?
PARENTS AND GODPARENTS: We do.
MINISTER: Do you believe in Jesus Christ, his only Son, our Lord, who was born of the Virgin Mary, was crucified, died and was buried, rose from the dead and is now seated at the right hand of the Father?
PARENTS AND GODPARENTS: We do.
MINISTER: Do you believe in the Holy Spirit, the holy catholic Church, the communion of saints, the forgiveness of sins, the resurrection of the body, and life everlasting?
PARENTS AND GODPARENTS: We do.

There is also a specific renunciation of **Satan** or evil.

The baptismal ceremony is frequently called a "christening" which today also carries the broader secular meaning of naming a person or object. Indeed, it is during baptism that a child is officially given his or her name, usually at the very moment of the water-bath itself. For generations in Western society, the individual "Christian" name along with the family surname designated social identity. Baptism is understood to "christen" the child, thus bestowing religious identity. Traditionally, the names of Christian saints or Old Testament figures were preferred, although secular influence rather than religious piety tends to determine the most popular names today.

The term *christening* is derived from "**Christ**," which literally means "anointed one," and many churches actually include an anointing in the ceremony. The substance used is called "chrism" (Greek for "anointing") and is usually olive oil scented with a sweet perfume such as balsam and blessed by the local bishop at a special ceremony during Holy Week. The anointing itself symbolizes the gift of the Holy Spirit and is called "chrismation" in the Orthodox tradition. While Anglicans and Catholics anoint the baby during baptism, they also celebrate a second anointing ceremony later, when the person is mature enough to ratify the original decision of their parents to have their child baptized. The ceremony is appropriately named **confirmation** and is the converse of the dedication ceremony for infants in churches that postpone baptism until a later age.

Thus, the fundamental meaning of baptism is initiation into the faith and the beginning of the Christian life. As the gateway into the Church, baptismal fonts are often located near the entrances of church buildings and baptism itself is understood as the first of the Christian life-cycle rituals known as **sacraments** (see box 4.2). Moreover, what this implies is that one is not automatically considered a Christian by virtue of being born into a Christian family. Christian identity is conferred by baptism, hence the traditional statement that Christians are "made, not born."

The use of water has several layers of meaning. As the most common cleansing agent on earth, it clearly evokes the idea of washing. The figurative dirt that is washed away in baptism is sin – for adults past personal sins and for the newborn child original sin. But Christians also see water as a symbol of the tomb – an idea that is much more effectively expressed when full immersion is practiced. As the person enters the pool and then emerges from it,

THE SEVEN SACRAMENTS	Box 4.2
1 Baptism	
2 Confirmation	
3 Eucharist	
4 Matrimony	
5 Holy Orders	
6 Reconciliation	
7 Anointing of the sick	

they figuratively join Christ in his death and emerge with him to new life. The idea of union with the dying and rising Lord is also captured in other ritual elements such as making the sign of the cross on the child, the Orthodox practice of cutting a cross-shaped tonsure in the baby's hair, the giving of a candle (which represents the light of Christ), and clothing the baby in white to reflect its new dignity as a member of Christ's body, the Church.[10]

The decision of the early Church to use water baptism as its initiation rite was made against the backdrop of Christianity's gradual dissociation from its Jewish provenance. Although the process took several centuries, a key moment in the parting of the ways was the ruling that pagan male converts were not obliged to undergo the ancient ritual that, both spiritually and physically, indicated membership of God's chosen people – circumcision.[11]

B'rit Milah

Eight days after the birth of a Jewish boy, family and friends gather together at the home or in the local **synagogue** to celebrate one of Judaism's most ancient and distinctive rites. The ceremony begins when the kvatter (a couple chosen for the occasion) bring the infant into the room while the guests stand. The baby is then placed on a highly ornate seat known as the Chair of Elijah, named after the ninth-century BCE prophet who defended the covenant against pagan influence and who is believed to be present at every **circumcision** ritual. The child is then placed in the lap of the sandek (godfather) and is given a formal Hebrew name. A prayer is offered expressing the community's hope for the child's future: "Just as he has been brought into the covenant, so may he enter Torah, the canopy of marriage, and the performance of good deeds." It is a great honor to be chosen as a sandek, and in many Jewish families the grandfather fulfills this role. Not unlike a Christian godparent, the sandek has a duty to insure a proper religious upbringing for the infant, especially in the event of the death of the parents.

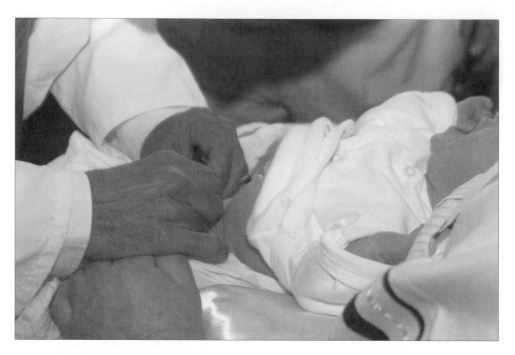

Figure 4.2 A mohel prepares a child for circumcision

The climax of the ritual is when the surgeon (**mohel**) performs the actual circumcision with a special double-edged knife. He then takes a cup of wine and places a few drops on the lips of the child, which may originally have served as a mild form of anesthetic. The mohel then removes any blood from the wound and hands the infant back to its mother, after which those present celebrate the occasion with a festive meal (**seudat mitzvah**). The mohel is not necessarily a medical doctor, but he must have official certification indicating that he is capable of determining beforehand whether it is safe to proceed, and if so that he is also competent to perform the physical operation. Jews often stress that the circumcision ritual is essentially a religious event and not merely a medical procedure. Thus, a mohel is more than a physician; he must be a person of devout faith though not necessarily a rabbi.[12] If a male mohel is not available, then Jewish law allows for a female to perform the circumcision based on the precedent of Moses's wife Zipporah who circumcised their son.[13]

In **Ashkenazi** Jewish communities, the circumcision rite begins on the first Friday after the child is born with a simple ceremony known as shalom zakhar. Thanksgiving is offered for the successful birth and the infant is consoled for having forgotten everything he had learned while in his mother's womb. The next event is the vachnacht [night of the guard] on the eve of the eighth day. The mohel, the sandek, family

---

PRAYER FROM A JEWISH CIRCUMCISION RITE   **Box 4.3**

Blessed are You, King of the universe, who sanctified your loved one from birth and established your law with his descendants giving them the sign of the holy covenant. By this merit our living God, you commanded to save your loved one from the abyss, because of the covenant made in the flesh. Blessed are You, the maker of the covenant. Our God and God of our fathers, let this child grow up with his parents, and let his name be called [*name*]. Let the father be happy with his progeny and the mother with her offspring.

---

relations, and friends watch over the child until midnight, reciting prayers to ward off evil spirits who seek to obstruct the fulfillment of the commandment to circumcise (see box 4.3). A **Tanach** or other religious book may be placed under the pillow or mattress, symbolizing the hope that the baby will grow into a person of faith and wisdom. At this point the mohel may also examine the child to ascertain if there are any health risks to the operation the next day.

The practice of circumcision is far from unique to Judaism. Archeological evidence from artwork and tombs indicates that the Egyptians practiced circumcision as early as the Sixth Dynasty (c.2340–2180 BCE) and it seems to have been common among Semitic peoples by the first millennium BCE. However, it was so vehemently discouraged in the Greek and Roman Empires that it had essentially become associated with Jews and Jewish Christians by the beginning of the Common Era.[14] Circumcision is also found among certain African and Australasian indigenous peoples as well as throughout the Islamic world.

The purpose of the circumcision rite varies according to the socio-religious context. Reasons often cited for circumcising include its being an aid to hygiene, a means to suppress or enhance sexual desire, a sign of social status, a passage to adulthood, and even a symbol of castration.[15] In the case of Judaism, there are quite specific religious interpretations involved. Primarily, circumcision is an act of trusting obedience to the divine command. Jews circumcise their male children because it is God's will. Circumcision is one of the earliest of the 613 **commandments** of the Torah, appearing for the first time in **Genesis** where Abraham is told by God:

This is my covenant, which you shall keep, between me and you and your offspring after you: Every male among you shall be circumcised. You shall circumcise the flesh of your foreskins, and it shall be a sign of the covenant between me and you. Throughout your generations every male among you shall be circumcised when he is eight days old.[16]

The text states that circumcision is a sign of the sacred pact between God and his people. Appositely, the Hebrew name of the ceremony, **b'rit milah**, means "covenant of circumcision."[17]

Circumcision does not make a newborn child Jewish in the way that baptism makes a child Christian. For one thing, that would disenfranchise half of the community since there is no female circumcision in Judaism. Jewish identity is conferred on both male and female by birth, not by ritual. Traditionally a child is considered Jewish if he or she is born of a Jewish woman, although there are some liberal groups today that regard those who have a Jewish father and a non-Jewish mother as Jewish. However, as the main Jewish ceremony associated with childbirth, circumcision powerfully expresses ideas of membership and belonging. The permanent mark left on the male body as a result of the act of circumcision carries strong connotations of identity. The circumcised look physically different from the uncircumcised, underlining the idea that the soul of Judaism, like the bodies of its male members, is unique.[18] Rabbinic commentators speak of the appropriateness of having the identifying sign on the male procreative organ since the sacred covenant is a priceless gift passed on from generation to generation. Membership of the covenant comes at a price, however. Physical circumcision has exposed Jews to considerable risk of persecution and death under oppressive regimes from the ancient Romans to the Nazis more recently. Despite the dangers, Jews have courageously continued to fulfill the divine commandment and declare their Jewishness in an unambiguous physical manner down through the ages.

The theme of Jewish identity is further highlighted by the bestowing of a formal Hebrew name during b'rit milah. Outside Israel, this means that Jews may have two names: a secular name for everyday business and a Hebrew name for religious events, such as being summoned to read the Torah in a synagogue service or when prayers are recited on the person's behalf. However, it is becoming increasingly popular for Jews to use their Hebrew name as their given name. Jewish naming customs vary but the most popular sources are the names of relatives, prominent biblical and historical figures, and foreign names translated into Hebrew.[19]

Another theme associated with b'rit milah is the idea of completion. According to some commentators, the foreskin is an unnecessary addition and its removal symbolizes the complete formation of a new human being. In other words, one must cooperate with the creator in fashioning the whole person in both the physical and the spiritual sense. Circumcision is a reminder that one is not born perfect, and the cutting away of selfishness and sinfulness is a lifelong process that requires human intent as well as divine assistance.

The Torah gives no explicit reason for the tradition of circumcising on the eighth day after birth. Neither does it specify the exact hour, although it is customary to celebrate b'rit milah in the morning, reflecting Abraham's enthusiasm to fulfill God's commandment as quickly as possible.[20] Although the hour is flexible, clearly the day is not. Jewish law states that the child must be circumcised on the eighth day, even when that day falls on a major festival such as **Yom Kippur** or on a **sabbath** when there are severe restrictions on what Jews can and cannot do. There are few Jewish institutions that take priority over the sabbath but b'rit milah is one of them, which is an indication of its extraordinary importance. Nevertheless, custom dictates that all preparatory work should be completed on the Friday and that the mohel should either stay overnight at the home or be within a sabbath's walk on the day itself. The only justification for postponing b'rit milah is the health of the child,[21] reaffirming the fundamental Jewish principle that human life has precedence over even the most binding ritual laws.

B'rit milah is not only one of the most ancient of Jewish practices but also one of the most universal. Nineteenth-century **Reform Judaism** initially opposed circumcision as blatantly sexist and medically unnecessary, but today many Reform Jewish communities have restored the ritual with pride. Even non-religious Jews often circumcise their male children as a confirmation of their birthright as members of the covenant people.

As mentioned above, female circumcision is not practiced in Judaism. Jewish girls usually receive their Hebrew name at synagogue on the first day of Torah-reading that the mother is able to attend after postnatal recovery. On that day, the girl's father is called forth to read the Torah, the cantor blesses the mother and baby, and the name is officially announced. The mother then says a prayer of thanksgiving in the presence of the congregation. Some have argued that women do not need to be circumcised since they carry within their ovaries the natural sign of the ongoing generative covenant. However Reform Jewish groups, sensitive to the gender imbalance, have developed a ceremony akin in wording to male circumcision called b'rit hahayyim [covenant of life]. The ritual contains the basic language of b'rit milah with its stress on covenant and membership, but there is no surgical procedure.

There are two other minor childhood rituals in Judaism, neither of which compares with the extensive practice and pre-eminent religious significance of circumcision. On the thirtieth day after birth, **Orthodox** and **Conservative** Jews celebrate pidyon ha ben [redemption of the firstborn]. This rite recalls the miraculous deliverance from the tenth plague of the Exodus which claimed the lives of all firstborn males in Egypt except those of the Israelites. According to Tanach, the spared sons were to be set aside as priests,[22] but they joined in the idolatrous worship of the golden calf in the wilderness and were replaced by **levites**. Consequently every firstborn male child is in need of redemption, which is provided through the pidyon ha ben ceremony. Basically the father of the child gives the equivalent of five shekels of silver to a **cohen** (a descendant of the ancient priestly tribe of Israel).[23] The child is thus ransomed, but one duty remains for the rest of his life: to fast on the eve of the annual feast of **Passover** in memory of the Egyptian sons who perished in the plague – a touching gesture of compassion for an ancient foe. If a boy's father fails to perform pidyon ha ben, then he is obliged to redeem himself before his coming of age. If the father is a cohen himself, he is exempt from the redemption rite.

In another ceremony at 3 years of age, Orthodox Jews celebrate upsherenish [cutting off] during which the child's hair is shaved and weighed, and the equivalent value is given to the poor.[24] Along with the key ritual of b'rit milah, these two secondary ceremonies enrich the way in which Jewish faith marks the birth of children. They also create strong resonances with another **Semitic religion**. Like Judaism, Islam also believes in membership by birth and marks the beginning of human life with circumcision, an official naming, a gesture of redemption, the cutting of hair and its weight value donated to the needy.

Aqiqah

The Qur'an has no specific instructions on how to celebrate the birth of a newborn child. Nevertheless, the official collections of **Muhammad's** teachings and actions (the **hadith**) provide the basis for a series of traditional Islamic birth rituals. There is some debate between Islamic legal schools as to whether each of these rituals is obligatory or merely recommended, and there are variations on some of the details concerning the timing, the procedure, and other aspects. Nevertheless, it is possible to identify three distinct moments in early infancy to which several ceremonies are linked.

The first occurs immediately after the birth of the child and consists of two simple symbolic actions. First, it is a widely held Islamic custom that the first and last sounds that every human person should hear in this world are those of the **adhan** – the brief call to prayer that is broadcast from minarets five times each day (see box 4.4). Before the fragile child is exposed to the cacophonous din of the world and even before its mind is able to comprehend the meaning of the sounds, its tiny ears will hear the pristine truth that lies at the heart of Islam: there is no god but God and Muhammad is his Prophet. According to tradition, Muhammad recited the adhan at the birth of his grandsons **Hasan** and Hussain, and today it is usually recited by one of the parents or a respected member of the community. The words are gently

---

Box 4.4

THE ADHAN (ISLAMIC CALL TO PRAYER)

God is most great.
I testify that there is no god except God.
I testify that Muhammad is the Messenger of God.
Come to prayer.
Come to salvation.
Prayer is better than sleep [*recited only at morning prayer*].
Come to the best of work [*added by Shi'ites*]
God is most great.
There is no god except God.

whispered so that the baby is not alarmed and it is often accompanied by the recitation of several verses from the **Qur'an**. Traditionally the adhan is spoken just once into the right ear of the child, but some Muslims also recite a similar phrase known as the iqamah[25] into the left ear as well.

The other ritual performed immediately after the birth is known as tahnik, in which the father or a person of good standing rubs a fresh date on the upper palate of the baby's mouth. Substitutes such as honey or some other sweet foodstuff can be used if dates are not available. The idea behind the action is that goodness and virtue will be transmitted from the adult to the child. Again, the gesture harks back to a custom of Muhammad who would chew a date and place it into the mouth of the newborn to convey a special blessing.[26]

The second moment comes approximately seven days after the birth when a series of rituals collectively known as **aqiqah** is celebrated. The precise timing of aqiqah is flexible, in contrast to Judaism's strict insistence that b'rit milah occur on the eighth day irrespective of sabbath or festival. There are three basic elements involved, although the exact order can vary. The term *aqiqah* itself literally means "to cut or to break" and, appropriately, the first element involves the cutting or shaving of the baby's hair. At one level, the shaving of scalp hair that has grown in the womb serves a hygienic purpose, especially if there are traces of blood. At another level, there are various moments in Islamic life where the cutting of hair carries the idea of detachment or transition, such as during the pilgrimage to Mecca.[27] In the case of aqiqah, the tradition states that the entire head must be shaved, not just part of it. The hair is wrapped in a piece of cloth and either buried or thrown into a river, but before it is discarded, it is weighed and the value of an equivalent quantity of silver is donated to charity. Affluent Muslims feel particularly obliged to maintain this custom, and those living in the West often send the money to their native country or to social welfare organizations in Islamic nations. Once again, the ritual is grounded in the example of Muhammad who shaved the heads of his two grandsons and ordered that the hair be weighed and the equivalent in silver be given to the poor.[28]

The second element of aqiqah is the formal naming of the child, which is a common thread in birth ceremonies in the religions discussed thus far. Traditionally the parents decide on the name, although they may invite another to do so in imitation of the companions of the Prophet who occasionally requested that Muhammad confer a name on their children. The hadith enjoins Muslims to choose wisely since each person will be called by their name on the day of resurrection.[29] Muhammad himself recommended religious names such as Abdullah (servant of God) or the names of the prophets.[30] Forbidden names include those that suggest service of someone or something other than God (such as Abd an-Nabi [servant of the prophet]), the enemies of Islam (such as Abu Lahab),[31] and even the titles of the chapters of the Qur'an. The fundamental Islamic disdain for idolatry is evident even in the naming of a child.

The third element of aqiqah is the sacrifice of an animal, usually a goat, a sheep, or a camel. The tradition does not specify the animal's gender[32] but requires that the animal be at least one year old and without blemish.[33] Some sources specify that two animals should be offered for a boy and one for a girl, while others state that one animal is sufficient for either gender.[34] There is also debate as to whether or not the bones may be broken, but all agree that the meat should be distributed in the same way as on the Feast of Sacrifices. At that great annual festival during the month of pilgrimage, Muslims around the world slaughter an animal and divide the meat into three parts: one-third for the family; one-third for neighbors; and one-third for the poor.

The purpose of the animal sacrifice is ostensibly a form of redemption, not unlike the pidyon ha ben ceremony of Judaism, although the form of payment is different: the life of an animal rather than an amount of money. The idea of ransoming the newborn stems from a saying of Muhammad that neatly sums up the three elements of aqiqah: "A boy is ransomed by his aqiqah. Sacrifice should be made for him on the seventh day. He should be given a name and his head should be shaved."[35] Islamic scholars have offered a number of interpretations regarding the precise nature of this ransom. Some propose that if the parents fail to offer the aqiqah sacrifice and the child dies prematurely, he or she will not intercede for his parents from heaven. Some see the sacrifice as a means of safeguarding the child from adversity and tribulation, while others see it simply as an act of thanksgiving to God for the birth of a new life. Whatever the meaning, it is clear that aqiqah is not an initiation rite that makes a child Muslim. As with Judaism, membership of the Islamic community is conferred by birth, although unlike Judaism it passes through the line of the father rather than the mother.

The final Islamic ceremony connected to birth is male circumcision which constitutes an important area of overlap with Judaism. However, there are significant differences. While the Jewish age is firmly set, the timing of Islamic circumcision can vary enormously. Some Muslims circumcise soon after birth while others wait until the child is old enough to recite the Qur'an or even until the threshold of adolescence. Thus in Islam, circumcision is a birth ritual for some groups and a rite of passage to adulthood for others. Moreover, in contrast to the strong biblical basis for Jewish b'rit milah, Islamic circumcision is not mentioned in the Qur'an and legal opinion differs as to its importance and necessity. The **Shafi'i** school considers circumcision obligatory while the **Maliki** and **Hanafi** schools categorize it as a recommended but not mandatory practice. In Islamic thinking, the main purpose of circumcision seems to be hygienic and its origin has more to do with a pre-Islamic Arabic custom than with the Jewish religious rite. In one hadith, it is compared to other forms of personal grooming such as trimming the moustache, cutting the nails, and cleaning the teeth.[36] For some, circumcision is necessary to insure purity during daily prayer, since there is less danger of clothes becoming contaminated from small amounts of urine trapped in the foreskin. It should also be noted that female circumcision, which is widely practiced in north African cultures and in parts of the Middle East, is neither required nor recommended by the Qur'an or Islamic tradition.

In summary, Islamic celebration of human birth is characterized by rites that are grounded in the example of the founder rather than obliged by law. Both Muslims and Jews officially name the child, perform a redemption ceremony, cut the hair and weigh it for alms, and circumcise male children. Yet in so far as Muslims also utter sacred words into the ear of the newborn child and offer it food, Islam resembles Hinduism with its elaborate series of sacramental rites stretching from the prenatal period into the first years of infancy.

🕉 Birth Samskaras

With over 40 ceremonies listed in its traditional manuals, Hinduism has one of the most extensive systems of life-cycle rituals among the religions that we are considering. These sacred rites of passage mark key moments in the human journey from conception to death and are collectively known as **samskaras**. In practice the full number was rarely celebrated and an abbreviated list of 16 ceremonies is most commonly cited (see box 4.5).[37] Today even the full 16 are seldom observed, despite the promotional efforts of the nineteenth-century reform movement, **Arya Samaj**, and its founder, Swami **Dayananda Saraswati**. Moreover, when the samskaras are celebrated, there is considerable variation depending on sect, region, **caste**, and gender. The immense variety of practice reminds us that Hinduism is a broad family of many diverse religious traditions which makes general descriptions difficult and dangerous. Yet the tradition of the samskaras is widely acknowledged as part of a common Hindu heritage and many life-cycle rituals today draw on their basic symbolism and form.

Although several samskaras mark important moments later in life such as adult initiation, marriage, and death, 9 of the 16 rites concern birth and infancy, indicating a heightened interest in the earliest years of human existence. The first samskara is aptly named garbhadhana [conception] since its primary purpose is to facilitate the fertility of the couple. Conceiving children, especially sons, is considered a binding sacred duty for a Hindu – the value of which stems not only from religious belief but also from a historical period when having large numbers of offspring provided economic security in old age. As with many events in Hindu life, the timing is crucial in a double sense. First, traditional wisdom dictates that garbhadhana be performed during the woman's fertile period, reckoned to occur between the fourth and the sixteenth day after menstruation. Second, it is widely believed that celestial events have a profound effect on human activity and, in this case, the actual date on which the child is conceived determines both its gender and its personality. For instance, an even

---

Box 4.5   ## THE TRADITIONAL HINDU SAMSKARAS

Prenatal
  Garbhadhana: conception
  Pumsavana: consecrating a male child in the womb
  Simantonnayana: parting the hair of a pregnant woman

Childhood
  Jatakarma: birth ceremony
  Namakarana: naming ceremony
  Niskramana: first outing
  Annaprasana: first solid meal
  Cudakarana: first tonsure
  Karnavedha: piercing of the ear lobes

Adolescence
  Upanayana and Vedarambha: thread ceremony and commencement of Vedic study
  Keshanta: first shaving of the beard
  Samavartana: end of studies and return home

Adulthood
  Vivaha: marriage
  Vanaprasthin: forest-dweller
  Sannyasin: ascetic
  Antyesti: funeral rites

---

date is supposed to result in a son while an odd date means a daughter. Moreover, the conception should occur at night rather than during the day since the latter will lead to an unhealthy and unlucky child. The ceremony itself consists of a simple offering of food to the gods and the chanting of appropriate **mantras** that speak of the creative energy unleashed by the conjunction of male and female forces.[38]

The second samskara is pumsavana [quickening of a male child] during which the couple express their preference for a boy. In one version, some drops of banyan juice are placed in the right nostril of the mother for her to inhale and she is given a mixture of yogurt and grains to consume. The gestures are intended to evoke the imagery of semen being implanted in the womb. Sometimes a special thread is also tied around her left wrist for protection. The ceremony is normally carried out between the second and fourth months of pregnancy, just before the fetus begins to move in the womb. According to popular belief, the moment of quickening is when the gender is finally determined. Although seldom celebrated today, pumsavana reflects the strong traditional Hindu preference for male children which is still prevalent in many parts of India, a bias that is essentially based on the concern to continue the family line, as daughters will eventually become members of their future husband's household.

The third and final prenatal samskara is simantonnayana [hair-parting] which is celebrated between the fifth and eighth month of the pregnancy. As the name implies, the husband parts his wife's hair three times from front to back using a special comb such as the quill of a porcupine. The ritual symbolizes the hope that the child will have a quick and incisive mind. The mantras contain themes such as the ripening of fruit and protection from evil spirits. From now on, the mother must adapt her lifestyle with her unborn child in mind. This usually means an appropriate diet, restricted physical activity, and the need to retain a calm and positive demeanor. Likewise the husband should refrain from certain actions such as haircuts, coitus, pilgrimage, and performing funeral rites.

The fourth samskara is performed immediately after the birth of the child and is known as jatakarma. Reminiscent of the Islamic practice of reciting the adhan and offering some sweet food, the father writes the sacred Sanskrit syllable **aum** (or **om**) on the baby's lips or tongue with a golden spoon dipped in honey, curds, and ghee.[39] The syllable *aum* (see figure 4.3) is considered by Hindus to be the fundamental sound of the universe and often prefaces sacred chanting. In written form, it is used as the identifying symbol for Hinduism in much the same way as the **Star of David** stands for Judaism and the cross for Christianity. The action marks the child as a new member of the Hindu world and also expresses the family's hope that it will use its organ of speech to express truth and wisdom. The father whispers into the infant's ear a secret name such as "Veda" or "Brahma" and hands the child to its mother. Just as Muslim babies enter the world to the sound of Islam's holy creed, the first sound heard by the Hindu infant is a sacred name that identifies him or her as part of the divine absolute itself. The father then bathes in the waters of a lake or river in order to redeem his debt to his ancestors. Traditionally the birth should occur in a darkened room in the southwest corner of the house. Elders often loosen knots in the house to symbolize the loosening of the mother's muscles in the act of giving birth.

After a 10- to 12-day period of ritual impurity has passed, the namakarana

Figure 4.3
The Hindu sacred sound *aum*

[naming] ceremony is performed.[40] The child is bathed, dressed in clean clothes, and handed to the father who sits before a sacred fire – a common feature in Hindu life ceremonies and worship. The head of the child should face north, since the realm of the dead is considered to lie in the south. Oblations of ghee are poured into the fire while appropriate mantras are chanted. An everyday name is then whispered into the ear of the child. Although the person will be known by this name in mundane affairs, it functions as a disguise for its secret name which was uttered at birth. To some extent the conferral of a double name parallels the Jewish custom, reminding the believer that they will live their life in both sacred and profane realms. There are various customs concerning Hindu names such as the tradition that male names should have an even number of syllables while female names should have an odd number. Astrological factors also play an important part in the actual choice of a name and a personal horoscope is usually drawn up and consulted for this purpose.

The final infancy samskaras mark various key moments in the early development of the child. At three to four months, the child is brought out of the house for the first time in a ceremony known as niskramana[41] – the first encounter with the sun and moon. Soon after dawn, the infant is bathed, dressed, and taken out into the sunlight, once again in front of a sacred fire, with the baby's head facing north and an appropriate mantra being recited. A similar ritual is performed in moonlight on the evening of the same day. The annaprasana [first feeding] is usually celebrated at

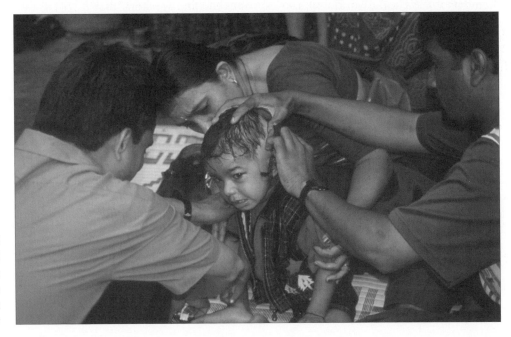

Figure 4.4
A Hindu child receives his first haircut in the cudakarana ceremony

approximately 6 months of age at the time of the child's first solid meal. The themes of the mantras emphasize good digestive powers, robust health, wholesome thoughts, and useful talents.[42]

Between 1 and 3 years of age, Hindus celebrate the eighth samskara, cudakarana [cutting of hair].[43] As in the case of Judaism and Islam, the literal cutting of the child's hair stands for a figurative cutting off from impurity and evil. The shaven head denotes spiritual cleanliness and selflessness, helping to mitigate the negative **karma** that may have built up in the previous life. The father combs some hair from the right side of the child's head, makes a loop with some blades of grass, and cuts the locks. The mixture of hair and grass is then placed in an earthenware container and buried in some remote location. A barber then shaves the child's head and the father rubs in some butter or other soothing substance, after which the child is bathed. Soon after the cutting of the hair ceremony, the final infancy samskara, karnavedha [ear-piercing], is performed.[44] Traditionally the physician begins with the right ear for a boy and the left ear for a girl. Karnavedha is not only about beauty and personal adornment, but it also represents the opening of the child's ears and mind to spiritual truth.

The term *samskara* itself is rich in meaning and can be translated in a number of ways that help to unpack its religious significance. First it can denote "purification" or "refinement." Indeed, many of the above rituals are concerned with cleansing the child from impurities carried over from its previous existence or from physical birth itself which, like death, is considered to be particularly contaminating. Celebrating the samskaras for a child at the appropriate time helps to shape and refine the person, just as cutting and polishing a rough stone transforms it into a precious gem. Samskara can also mean "construction" in the sense of the construction of the self within a particular socio-religious environment. The samskaras help to construct the spiritual setting in which the young person will grow and develop as an integrated member of Hindu society. Finally samskara can also mean an "imprint" in the sense of psychological impressions that shape the person's moral, emotional, and intellectual character from the earliest age. At this level, the Hindu samskaras function somewhat like Christian baptism which is said to leave an indelible but invisible mark on the soul. As life progresses, the remaining samskaras continue to mold and orient the person at key milestones on the journey such as adulthood, marriage, worldly renunciation, and finally death.

 ## The Buddhist Exception

In stark contrast to the elaborate Hindu system, Buddhism is remarkably devoid of life-cycle ceremonies. Neither the historical **Buddha** nor the fundamental scriptural texts set down any explicit guidelines in this regard. Buddhist religious life is not particularly characterized by rites of passage or sacraments, being more focused on themes such as personal enlightenment, ethical integrity, and liberation from undue attachment. Consequently, there is simply no universal Buddhist ceremony to mark the birth of a new child as in the other four major religions, making Buddhism an exception to the rule.

When seen in the context of Buddhism's cyclic view of human existence, birth can be interpreted as an unfortunate reminder that the person is still tied to the wheel of **reincarnation** and has not yet achieved complete liberation. Birth, understood as rebirth, is precisely what is not hoped for, signifying a delay in achieving one's ultimate purpose. Thus the moments of conception and birth are both listed among the 12 stages of life as outlined in the theory of paticca samuppada [dependent origination]. In this theory, each stage or moment is the cause of the next, therefore setting up a vicious circle of birth, suffering, death, and rebirth (see box 4.6).

BOX 4.6

THE 12 STAGES OF DEPENDENT ORIGINATION AND THEIR TRADITIONAL SYMBOLS (BUDDHISM)

1   Ignorance (blind person)
2   Intentional acts (potter's wheel)
3   Consciousness (monkey in tree)
4   Body and mind (passenger in vehicle)
5   The senses (house with windows)
6   Sense impressions (couple)
7   Feelings (arrow in eye)
8   Craving (sweet drink)
9   Clinging (gathering fruit)
10 Becoming (copulation)
11 Rebirth (childbirth)
12 Old age and death (corpse)

This is not to say that Buddhists fail to commemorate the crucial moment of childbirth altogether. They do. However, what one finds across the Buddhist world is an astounding variety in the ways birth is celebrated. Local custom plays a decisive factor in the form and content of such ceremonies. Moreover, in many Asian societies where Buddhism is the predominant religious belief, the rituals linked to the birth of a new child are often borrowed and adapted from Hindu practice. For example, in Sri Lanka, the Singhalese celebrate a series of birth rituals almost identical to the Hindu samskaras: the placing of milk and gold on the lips of the baby; the first solid meal; the first outing; the cutting of hair; and the piercing of the ears.[45]

Similarly, in Tibet there are a series of prenatal rites reminiscent of Hinduism such as ceremonies to help a woman conceive or to insure a safe pregnancy. These usually involve repetition of sacred Buddhist mantras, as well as **circumambulation** of and prostration before Buddha images. At birth, the sacred syllable dhih, symbolizing the celestial Buddha **Manjusri**, is painted on the baby's tongue in saffron powder or butter in the hope that the child will grow up to be wise. The child is then taken to the local monastery to receive a name. The father prostrates before the lama and makes a small offering of money wrapped in a special scarf known as a kata. The lama accepts the gift, blesses the scarf, and returns it to the family. Then, sitting in an upright position and concentrating on the baby, he cups his hands together and blows into a knotted cord that symbolizes protection for the child. The lama then bestows a name upon the baby and hands the cord to the father. A month later, on an auspicious day, the baby is taken outside for the first time, its nose blackened with ash to ward off demons.

In Thailand, the naming ceremony usually involves the local monks either at the parents' home or at the monastery. The monks are invited to chant the **Pancasila** – the five elemental moral principles of Buddhism – and other popular texts from Buddhist literature such as the Mangala Sutta, the Ratana Sutta, or the Metta Sutta. The child is then officially named, by either the father or the head monk. After the monks leave the house, a festive meal is celebrated. In Hindu fashion, Thai Buddhists also perform a head-shaving ceremony one month after the birth.

Amid the wide variety of practices generated by local custom, there is one common feature in Buddhist birth rituals that is of particular interest – the involvement of the monks. Buddhist monks are not primarily priests who preside at a range of sacramental rites such as in Christianity or Hinduism. Hence, the monks do not necessarily play a leading role in life-cycle ceremonies. However, their presence at such events is keenly desired. The reason lies in the monk's fundamental vocation to meditate on and apply the Buddha's teachings in a radical manner. In this way they build up a surplus of positive karma which not only facilitates their own personal advancement toward ultimate liberation but also constitutes a reservoir from which the laity might draw. On vital occasions such as childbirth, weddings, or funerals, it is positive karma that is in great demand. Basically, the monks provide the laity with the spiritual benefits of their stored karma, while the laity in turn provide the monks with material needs such as food and clothing.

This exchange of tangible support for intangible karma constitutes the fundamental covenant between the two main subdivisions of Buddhist society and underpins most Buddhist life-cycle ceremonies including birth rituals. Typically people will either bring their newborn child to the monastery temple or invite the monks to their home. As with other religions, the monks chant appropriate scriptural passages and other mantras aimed at bringing protection, health, and future success to the child. In return the family makes an offering to the monks. Significantly, the most common ritual action performed by the monks at birth ceremonies, as well as other life-cycle ceremonies, involves the pouring of water from one vessel to another. In one sense, the use of water takes us back to Christian baptism discussed at the start of the chapter. But while water represents the washing away of sin for the Christian, in the Buddhist rituals flowing water symbolizes the transfer of positive karma from the holy monk to the layperson whether they be a newborn infant, a bridal couple, or a deceased person lying on the bier.

SUMMARY

If one of religion's main functions is to provide ultimate meaning for existence, then the life-cycle rituals of the various faiths are prominent examples. Key moments of the human journey are given transcendent meaning via symbolic actions and words. This chapter has focused on the birth rituals of the five religions with an eye to the points of intersection.

The Christian ritual primarily associated with birth is baptism, although the Baptist tradition within Christianity defers the ritual until the person is old enough to make a free and informed decision for themselves. However in the majority of churches, infant baptism is practiced on the understanding that adults responsible for the child's upbringing – parents and godparents – may legitimately speak for him or her in terms of faith. Essentially the baptismal ritual involves a water bath symbolizing for some the washing away of original sin. More universally, it represents accompanying Christ into the tomb and beyond to risen life. As the gateway through which the child passes into Christianity, baptism is about initiation and religious membership. As the ceremony at which an official name is conferred on the child ("christening"), baptism is also about religious identity.

The baptismal rite was practiced from the very earliest moments in the Christian story, its inspiration and imagery drawn from the memory of Jesus's own baptism in the river Jordan at the hands of the prophetic figure known as **John the Baptist**. John's choice of immersion in water to symbolize repentance and a new beginning was based on the Jewish ritual bath known as mikveh, which is still required of converts today. Despite its Jewish provenance, baptism is a symbol of the divergence of Christianity and Judaism, for the Jewish ceremony associated with birth is not a water-bath but circumcision of newborn males, a rite abandoned by the early Christians.

The physical operation of circumcision is not unique to Judaism, and is found in many cultures both ancient and contemporary. However in the Jewish religious context it carries a specific and profound meaning – a sign of the covenant between God and Israel. As one of the positive commandments of the Torah, circumcision on the eighth day after birth carries the highest priority, taking precedence even over important institutions such as the sabbath and Yom Kippur. The only valid reason for postponement is concern for the child's health. As in the case of Christian baptism, adults such as the parents and godparents act on behalf of the infant during the ritual. However, unlike Christian baptism, circumcision does not make a child Jewish since the ritual is only performed on male children. In Judaism, religious membership traditionally comes via birth from a Jewish woman.

Themes of identity and change are also important aspects of circumcision as is the case in baptism. Like the Christian ritual, circumcision also involves the conferral of a name. Yet, unlike a water bath, circumcision leaves a very permanent, physical mark on the body, powerfully symbolizing the real and ongoing nature of religious identity. In terms of change, the waters of baptism represent the washing away of the old life and the commencement of a new life as a child of God. Similarly, the rabbinic tradition sees the cutting away of the foreskin as a symbol of the need to complete the birth process and shape the human person according to the divine will.

Judaism is not the only religion of the five to practice circumcision. There is a threefold intersection between Jews and Muslims when it comes to birth rituals. Both religions circumcise male children but they also have a redemption ceremony as well as the practice of cutting and weighing the child's hair, and donating an equivalent amount to the poor. Islamic birth rituals are somewhat more elaborate, based not so much on Qur'anic prescriptions but on the example of the Prophet. Immediately after birth, the child is given a sweet substance such as dates, and the Islamic call to prayer is whispered in its ear – food for both body and soul from the very first moment of life.

Approximately one week after birth the three aqiqah rituals are performed: a name is given according to traditional Islamic norms; the hair is cut and weighed and a donation given to the needy; and an animal is slaughtered as a gesture of redemption, although there is some debate as to its precise religious meaning. There are echoes here of the Jewish ritual of pidyon ha ben in which the firstborn male child is redeemed, although the symbolic ransom in the Jewish version involves the gift of coins to a priest rather than the gift of an animal to God. Finally, circumcision is performed but, unlike Judaism, the timing ranges from infancy to adolescence. Moreover Islamic circumcision is not Qur'anic and is more associated with purity and hygiene, whereas in Judaism it is a sign of the divine–human covenant.

Islamic birth rituals not only intersect with Jewish practice but display a surprising similarity to classical Hindu ceremonies. Hinduism has arguably the most elaborate and extensive series of life-cycle rituals among the five religions and a significant number of these are prenatal, birth, and infancy rites, suggesting a particular concern for purity and propriety in childhood. Although there is considerable variation in practice depending on geography, caste, and gender, the infancy samskaras are widely adapted across the myriad of Hindu sects. Prenatal rituals include simple ceremonies for various blessings at natural moments: prayers for fertility prior to conception; prayers for a male child at the quickening in the womb; prayers for a healthy birth toward the end of the pregnancy. Similarities with other religions become apparent in the post-natal rituals such as the writing of the sacred sound *aum* on the newborn's tongue with honey which resembles the Islamic custom of whispering the adhan. In both religions, the first forms of nourishment that the baby should receive are the most sacred sounds of all. As in Judaism, the naming ritual involves the conferral of a double name: one for spiritual and one for secular purposes. Similarly, the Jewish idea that circumcision symbolizes the cutting and shaping of the raw soul is also reflected in the Hindu term *samskara* which suggests a spiritual imprint, a refinement of the person, or the construction of the true self.

The fact that Buddhism has no specific birth ritual sets it apart from the other four faiths and serves as a reminder that the practical themes of this book are not necessarily relevant to all religions to the same degree. The religions have their own special character and cannot be forced into neat a priori categories. In one sense, Buddhism's lack of a common birth ritual reflects its understanding of human birth as the unfortunate return of a deceased spirit on the wheel of reincarnation. Birth is actually rebirth and the aim of Buddhism is to help people avoid being reborn into this world of enslaving desires. In another sense, ordinary Buddhist families rejoice in the birth of new children as people in all cultures do. In many cases, the birth is marked in cultural-religious fashion by borrowing from Hindu customs such as nourishment for the newborn, the first solid food, the first excursion outside the house, and so forth. One custom that is widely practiced as a Buddhist life-cycle ritual is the pouring of water from one vessel to another. Although the water theme takes us back to Christian baptism, the Buddhist rite is not about washing away guilt and sin, but rather the transfer of good karma from the monks.

Initiation and membership; naming and identity; refining, cleansing, and redeeming – these are some of the key themes that resonate across the birth rituals of the five religions. Furthermore, the notion of birth as unfortunate rebirth, which is shared by both Buddhism and Hinduism, leads naturally to life-cycle rituals that deal with the opposite end of life. The religious meaning of birth is inescapably tied up with the religious meaning of death.

DISCUSSION TOPICS

1 Are people born Hindu, Jewish, Islamic, Christian, or Buddhist?
2 How does someone convert to each of the five religions?
3 Explore the religious significance of naming a child in each religious tradition.
4 Examine the historical and religious reasons behind the practice of circumcision in Judaism and Islam.
5 Does Islam teach female circumcision? Where is female circumcision practiced today and why?
6 Examine the arguments for and against infant baptism.
7 Compare the Jewish and Christian "confirmation" rituals.
8 To what extent are the traditional samskaras celebrated today? What alternative rituals are used?
9 Why does Buddhism consider birth to be a sad event?

10   Examine Buddhist childhood rituals in places such as Sri Lanka, Japan, Tibet, or Thailand.

FURTHER READING

Cohn-Sherbok, Dan (2003). *Judaism: History, Belief and Practice*. London: Routledge, pp. 534–6.

Dessing, Nathal M. (2001). *Rituals of Birth, Circumcision, Marriage and Death among Muslims in the Netherlands*. Leuven: Peeters, chs. 2–3.

Hoffman, Lawrence A. (1996). *Covenant of Blood: Circumcision and Gender in Rabbinic Judaism*. Chicago: University of Chicago Press.

Johnson, Maxwell E. (1999). *The Rites of Christian Initiation: Their Evolution and Interpretation*. Collegeville, MN: Liturgical Press, ch. 1.

McGee, Mary (2004) "Samskara," in Sushil Mittal (ed.), *The Hindu World*. Abingdon: Routledge, ch. 15.

Michaels, Axel (2003). *Hinduism: Past and Present*. Princeton, NJ: Princeton University Press, pp. 71–89.

Segler, Franklin M., & Bradley, Randall (2006). *Christian Worship: Its Theology and Practice*. 3rd edn. Nashville: B & H Publishing Group, pp. 173–81.

White, James F. (2001). *Introduction to Christian Worship*. 3rd edn. Nashville: Abingdon Press, ch. 8.

NOTES

1   Compare Luke 3:21–2, Matthew 3:16, and John 1:32.
2   Like Elijah, John dresses in animal skin and a leather belt; see Mark 1:6; 2 Kings 1:8.
3   See Leviticus 12:2; Numbers 19:11.
4   See John 3:1–8.
5   Christian theologians describe original sin in many different ways but essentially it is a state of guilt and sinfulness associated with **Adam**'s first sin which is inherited by every human being at conception.
6   Orthodox Christianity cites Matthew 19:14 as justification: "Let the little children come to me, and do not stop them; for it is to such as these that the kingdom of heaven belongs."
7   See Genesis 1:1; 7:11–8:22; Exodus 14:21–30.
8   See Acts 2:38; 8:16; 10:48; 19:5.
9   The gospel ends with the Great Commission: "Go therefore and make disciples of all nations, baptizing them in the name of the Father and of the Son and of the Holy Spirit, and teaching them to obey everything that I have commanded you" (see Matthew 28:19–20).
10   See Colossians 3:10; Revelation 7:9.
11   See Acts 15:1–29. Paul would later argue that Christian baptism has replaced circumcision: "In him also you were circumcised with a spiritual circumcision, by putting off the body

of the flesh in the circumcision of Christ; when you were buried with him in baptism, you were also raised with him through faith in the power of God, who raised him from the dead" (Colossians 2:11–12). See also 1 Corinthians 7:19; Galatians 6:11–13; Philippians 3:2–3.

12 Shulhan Aruch, Yoreh Deah 264:1.

13 See Exodus 4:25.

14 Some Christian groups still circumcise today, such as the Copts and the Ethiopian Orthodox.

15 Jewish authors Philo and **Maimonides** argued that Jewish circumcision was intended to reduce the sexual urge; for example see Maimonides's *Guide for the Perplexed*, part III, ch. 49.

16 Genesis 17:10–12a; see also Leviticus 12:3.

17 *B'rit milah* is the Sephardic term while Ashkenazi Jews use the term *Bris milah*.

18 "Uncircumcised" is often used in Tanach as a metaphor for the **gentile** nations outside the covenant; see 1 Samuel 14:6, 31:4; 2 Samuel 1:20; Isaiah 52:1. It also refers to the unrepentant within Israel itself: see Jeremiah 9:25; Ezekiel 44:7, 9.

19 In general, Ashkenazi Jews tend to name their children after deceased relatives while Sephardic Jews prefer to choose names from living relatives.

20 Genesis 17:23–7.

21 Shulhan Aruch, Yoreh Deah 262:2; 263:1.

22 See Exodus 13:12–15; 22:29; 34:20; Numbers 3:45; 8:17; 18:16; Leviticus 12:2, 4.

23 See Numbers 3:47.

24 Some see a link with the biblical law that the fruit of a tree cannot be picked until the third year. See Leviticus 19:23.

25 The iqamah is a second call, which signals to the congregation that prayers are about to commence. It is almost identical to the adhan in content.

26 Sahih Bukhari 7.66.378; 2.24.578; Sahih Muslim 25.5340.

27 Pilgrims to Mecca cut their hair as a sign of leaving their mundane life and entering into a sacred state, albeit temporarily. The shaving of hair is also a traditional symbol of detachment in Buddhist and Christian monastic life.

28 Muwatta of Malik 26.1.2; 26.1.3.

29 Sunan Abu Dawud 4297.

30 Sunan Abu Dawud 4932.

31 An uncle of Mohammed and an early opponent of Islam during the Prophet's life (see Qur'an 111:1–5).

32 Sunan Abu Dawud 2829.

33 Muwatta of Malik 26.2.7.

34 Two animals for a boy are mentioned in Sahih Bukhari 7.66.380 and Sunan Abu Dawud 2828, 2829, 2830. However a single animal seems to be implied in Sunan Abu Dawud 2835 and Muwatta of Malik 26.2.4.

35 Sunan al-Tirmidhi 1522; Sunan Abu Dawud 2838.

36 See Sahih Bukhari 7.72.779: "I heard the Prophet saying: 'Five practices are characteristic of the Fitra: circumcision, shaving the pubic hair, cutting the moustaches short, clipping the nails, and depilating the hair of the armpits.'"

37 The 16 main rituals are collectively known as Shodasha Samskara.
38 See Rg Veda 10.85; Brhadaranyaka Upanishad 6.4.20; Chandogya Upanishad 1.6.
39 See Laws of Manu II.29; Brhadaranyaka Upanishad 6.4.24–28; Paraskara Grhyasutra 1.16.18; Asvalayana Grhyasutra 1.15.1–3.
40 See Laws of Manu II.30; Paraskara Grhyasutra 1.17.
41 See Laws of Manu II.34; Gobhila Grhyasutra 2.8.1; Paraskara Grhyasutra 1.17.
42 See Asvalayana Grhyasutra 1.16.1–5; Paraskara Grhyasutra 1.19.
43 See Laws of Manu II.35; Paraskara Grhyasutra 2.1; Gobhila Grhyasutra 2.8.10.
44 See Katyayana Grhyasutra 1.2; Rg Veda 1.89.8.
45 The ritual is known as the bali ceremony – a term that refers to the statuettes that represent the planetary deities.

Chapter 5

DEATH

CONTENTS

Introduction

A key element in religion's claim to provide an answer to the riddle of life is its insight into the meaning of death. The religious belief that a form of afterlife lies beyond the grave casts human existence in a completely new light. It opens up the possibility for definitive justice in a world where all too frequently the innocent suffer and die while the guilty go unrepentant and unpunished. It grounds the hope that love will not end and that dear ones may be seen again. It suggests that the desire to live forever, which is so deeply ingrained in the human spirit, is not in vain. But how does each of the five religions envisage the next world? What is the ultimate destiny of human beings? What is the significance of the physical body? What do the funeral rites of each religion tell us of these things?

⚙ The Wheel of Rebirth

One of the most common images in **Mahayana** Buddhist art is an elaborate six-spoked wheel held by the jaws, hands, and feet of a fearsome beast representing death. The six sections created by the spokes correspond to the six divisions of the universe: the realms of gods, titans, humans, hungry ghosts, animals, and hell. According to Mahayana belief, each time someone dies their spirit is reborn into one of these realms. At the top of the hierarchy, the realm of the gods, is a place of peace and happiness beyond the many distractions of this world. Technically it is further subdivided into many levels, some of which lie beyond the danger of rebirth. The realm of the titans (asuras) is inhabited by beings consumed with jealousy for the gods above, which thus deprives them of lasting joy. The human realm is our familiar world of sorrow and joy, pain and pleasure. The world of **hungry ghosts (pretas)** is considered lower again on the cosmic hierarchy where these spirits are constantly frustrated by the combination of small mouths and large appetites. The animal world is also considered inferior because such creatures do not have the level of intelligence, awareness, and freedom enjoyed by humans. Finally, as one would expect, hell is a state where inhabitants suffer a terrifying array of tortures, but only until bad karma is purged and the spirit is able to be reborn into one of the higher realms. In the center of the wheel, a rooster, a snake, and a pig chase each other in a tight loop, biting the tail of the preceding animal. The

Figure 5.1
Central section of the Buddhist wheel of life

three creatures symbolize greed, hatred, and ignorance, which together form a vicious circle that binds beings to the seemingly endless cycle of rebirth. Around the hub, white and black paths indicate the concurrent upward and downward movement of spirits through the various realms.[1]

The entire schema is not only a fascinating item of Buddhist art, but also a compact theological statement on life and death. For the Buddhist, human existence is essentially cyclic. Birth leads to death, which in turn leads to rebirth, and so on. Each lifetime is merely one stage in the epic journey of the individual involving hundreds or even thousands of rebirths. This process is commonly described in English as reincarnation, or transmigration of the soul. In both the Hindu and Buddhist traditions, it is known as **samsara** and constitutes one of their most distinctive features. The samsaric world view was originally inspired by the natural cycles of the agricultural world where trees and plants seem to die in winter and return to new life in spring each year. However, the wheel of samsara also functions as a sort of theodicy – an explanation for innocent suffering and the random way in which fortune and misfortune are experienced in this world with apparently no link to moral behavior. In the samsaric world view, the main reason why certain people are more fortunate than others in this life is because of a quality that has been carried over from their previous life – **karma**, which determines the particular cosmic realm into which one will be reborn after each death. For Buddhists, karma is measured by the extent to which one overcomes or fails to overcome the enslaving vices of greed, hatred, and ignorance. It is the force that drives the wheel of rebirth. For those who are advanced in the way of the Buddha, such as monks and nuns, there is a strong possibility that their good karma at death will elevate them into the realms of the gods or even enable them to attain final liberation. However, for the majority of laypersons who are not as wise or virtuous, the general expectation is rebirth into the world in some new form or some other realm.

Given the samsaric understanding of life and death, one can appreciate that each element of a Buddhist funeral is aimed at facilitating the journey of the deceased through the perilous process of death and rebirth. One way of providing the best passage for them is to insure the presence of those who have an abundance of good karma – the monks. As a result, Buddhist monks tend to be more involved in funerals than in any other life-cycle ritual. Prior to death, monks are often invited to the home to chant or recite **mantras** so that the final thoughts of the dying person are wholesome. Similarly, monks return to the house after the person has passed away to continue the chanting and recitation of appropriate sacred texts. They may also be invited to deliver a short talk on Buddhist teachings or to lead a session of meditation. In return for their spiritual service, families offer the monks food and clothing in the expectation that the merit gained through this gesture of generosity will benefit the deceased.[2] As at birth rituals, this is often accompanied by the act of pouring water from one vessel to another symbolizing the transfer of good karma. In some cultures, family members even become a monk or a nun for a short period in order to contribute to the provision of good karma.

The corpse is bathed and dressed in preparation for the funeral, which in Buddhist tradition does not have to take place immediately. A delay of several days is permitted, especially if it allows time for relatives and friends who reside at some distance to attend the ceremony. On the day of the funeral it is customary in many places to carry the body out of the home via a special door. If this is not possible, then the usual doorway is adorned in such a way as to mark the exceptional nature of this journey. Monks are invited to join the funeral procession and traditionally precede the coffin. In Thailand, they carry broad ribbons (bhusa yong) that extend to the coffin itself, again indicating the hope that good karma will pass into the spirit of the deceased at this critical moment of transition between worlds. The procession is often accompanied by cheerful rather than doleful music, aimed at consoling the bereaved so that more good karma can be generated.

It is a common practice in Buddhist cultures to cremate the body although there are exceptions. For instance, burial is common in Sri Lanka while Tibetan Buddhists, possibly because of the scarcity of wood, practice "sky burials," where the corpse is cut up and left for the vultures. The prevalence of cremation elsewhere in the Buddhist

---

BUDDHIST BARDO PRAYER (FOR THE DEAD)

Box 5.1

O Buddhas and Bodhisattvas abiding in all directions,
endowed with great compassion, foreknowledge and love,
affording protection to sentient beings,
come forth through the power of your great compassion,
please accept these offerings, those actually presented and those mentally created.
O Compassionate Ones, you who possess the wisdom of understanding,
the love of compassion, the power of doing divine deeds and protecting in incomprehensible measure,
[*Name of deceased*] is passing from this world to the next.
He/she is taking a great leap and the light of this world has faded.
He/she has entered solitude with karmic forces and has gone into a vast silence.
He/she is carried away by the great ocean of birth and death.
O Compassionate Ones, protect those who are defenseless.
Be to him/her like a mother and father.
O Compassionate Ones, let not the force of your compassion be weak, but aid him/her.
Let him/her not go into the miserable states of existence.
Forget not your ancient vows.

world is partly due to hygienic reasons in warm climates as well as the enduring influence of Hinduism. But another significant factor is that the historical **Buddha** himself requested that his body be cremated and stored in a monument. In order to avoid squabbling and jealousy over the location of such a holy site, the ashes were divided and stored in eight stupas in different kingdoms.

The **stupa** is one of the earliest forms of Buddhist monument designed to contain the remains of holy men and women. The earliest stupas were simple mounds of clay or cairns of rocks but they soon assumed an architectural pattern. In many cases, the stupa consists of basic geometric shapes each of which represents one of the five fundamental elements of the universe: a square base for earth; a hemispherical dome for water; a conical spire for fire; a crescent moon for air; and a disc at the very top for the ether. Buddhists also see in the hierarchical pattern a symbol of the various levels of enlightenment on the path to liberation. Some note that stupas also resemble the figure of Buddha sitting in meditation. In east Asia, the stupa evolved into the **pagoda**, which is pyramidal rather than bell-shaped, often with six stories representing the six cosmic realms.[3]

In one sense it is understandable that Buddhists felt the need to retain some tangible link with the historical founder and other holy figures via access to their mortal remains. Similarly, the ashes of ordinary folk are usually collected after cremation, placed in an urn, and stored in special columbaria within temple complexes or Buddhist cemeteries. Yet in another sense, the physical body carries no lasting significance in the samsaric world view. Given that this life is but one in a long series of births and rebirths in different forms and in different realms, the reduction of the corpse to ash via cremation makes theological sense: there is no further need of the body. But what happens to the part of the person that survives physical death and is reincarnated back into the wheel of life?

Buddhists differ in their beliefs about the time between death and the next reincarnation. In the **Theravada** tradition, there is a sense that rebirth is almost immediate, while Mahayana Buddhist mourning rituals suggest that there is an interval between death and rebirth. During this time, the living make offerings in order to earn good karma which is then transferred to the deceased in order to facilitate their next reincarnation.[4] A classical text on this intermediate period is the Tibetan Book of the Dead, which describes how the deceased moves through three stages or bardos (see box 5.2). In the first stage, the person is not aware that they have passed away: a brilliant light appears to which they will either be drawn, indicating final liberation, or from which they will flee, indicating that they must be reborn. In the second bardo, the person is aware that they are dead and they experience a review of life with its karmic consequences. At this point they begin to yearn for a new body. In the third bardo, their karma leads them to the appropriate realm in which they are conceived again in new form.[5]

THE SIX BARDOS OF TIBETAN BUDDHISM   **BOX**
                                                                             5.2

1 Bardo between birth and death (che shi): waking existence
2 Bardo of dreaming (mi lam): sleep
3 Bardo of meditative stability (sam ten): advanced state of meditation
   (samadhi)
4 Bardo of suffering (cho nyi): post-death unconsciousness
5 Bardo of becoming (si pa): reawakened consciousness
6 Bardo of gestation (che nay): consciousness unites with new embryo

---

The abiding challenge for Buddhism is to reconcile belief in the wheel of life, which underpins the popular funerary practices described above, with the Buddha's classical teaching known as *anatta* – that the concept of an enduring, substantial "soul" or "spiritual essence" is illusory. Exactly which part of the person, if any, survives death and undergoes reincarnation is an elusive notion and the subject of much debate. Metaphors such as a flame that passes from one candle to the next are commonly cited, but in the end Buddhism acknowledges the enigma that enshrouds not only death but also the concept of the self. Such humble agnosticism also flows over into Buddhist descriptions of **nirvana**. The term literally means "to extinguish" the fires of greed, hatred, and ignorance that bind us to the meaningless process of rebirth. However, it is unclear whether this means purifying the self from all egocentric desire so that it may enter an eternal state of perfect bliss or, more radically, the annihilation of the self which is ultimately a delusion and thus the real source of suffering and reincarnation. In the end, the Buddha recommended respectful silence before the greatest of life's mysteries, his preferred explanation being that the self neither exists nor does not exist.

In so far as Buddhism sees the ultimate goal of human existence as final liberation from the cycle of reincarnation, it bears an unmistakable resemblance to its mother faith. Similarly, the theological appropriateness of cremation as a means of bodily disposal and facilitation of a safe passage for the deceased spirit is a salient feature of Hinduism whose life-cycle rituals typically mark milestones in the human journey with the powerful symbol of fire.

The Last Sacrifice

Travelers in India experience a myriad of fascinating and memorable images. One of the more unsettling scenes they might encounter is the sight of a human corpse lying on a wooden pyre beside the waters of a river, slowly being consumed by flames as mourners watch in sadness. The exposed nature of the public cremation process forces upon the onlooker the starkness and finality of death. The physical body is revealed in all its impermanence and fragility while the **atman** (spiritual essence), with the assistance of Agni the god of fire, is released for the next stage in life's journey. The Hindu funeral is the last of many life-cycle ceremonies (**samskaras**) that mark milestones along the way. As with other samskaras, the details of the funeral rites vary considerably depending on region, **caste**, and gender. However, certain common elements can be identified across the Hindu world.

The manner and timing of death is particularly important for Hindus. A premature or violent passing, accompanied by vomit or urine and an anguished facial expression is considered to be a "bad death." In contrast, a "good death" occurs in old age after spiritual preparation and is manifest in a peaceful countenance. Once the person has passed away, it is customary in Hinduism to hold the funeral as quickly as possible. Coins are traditionally placed in the orifices of the body to stop the atman from escaping prematurely. Old clothes are replaced with new garments symbolizing the need for the deceased to surrender the old, obsolete body and dress in a new one. The corpse is placed on a bier adorned with flowers including roses, jasmine, and especially marigolds. The eldest son is considered the chief mourner and plays a crucial role in the following rituals for the happy release of the deceased, which is one of the

Figure 5.2
Lighting a Hindu funeral pyre on the banks of a river

main factors contributing to the intense socio-religious pressure on Hindu couples to have a boy. The body is carried feet first through a back or side door and then through the village or town along a special route symbolizing the unusual nature of this last journey. The bier is borne at the head of the procession, sometimes on a cart or a vehicle. Family and friends follow, traditionally with the oldest first. The names of a favorite deity, such as Hari or Rama, are repeatedly chanted along the way.

Cremation is the most common means of bodily disposal in Hinduism although there are some notable exceptions. Babies and children under the age of reason are often buried on the basis that they are still innocent, and thus do not require the purifying effect of the flames. Similarly, radical ascetics (**sannyasins**) are not cremated because they are considered to be already dead in the sense of being utterly detached from enslaving material desires. Such persons are so spiritually advanced that they are effectively already enjoying final liberation before their physical death.[6] Even the post-funeral rituals are not deemed necessary in such cases. Depending on their particular sect, a sannyasin may undergo a water burial or a ground burial. Burial is also common among lower-caste Hindus in southern India.

However, for the majority of Hindus who are neither children nor saints, cremation is considered the best way of reducing ritual impurity and facilitating the passage of the atman to the next phase of existence since it is believed that the spirit will linger as long as the physical body remains. The place of cremation (shmashana) is first purified by formulas designed to drive away demons, and the pyre is stacked with wood by a member of a special lower caste. The corpse is laid on the pyre with the feet facing south, toward the abode of Yama, the god of death. The cremation ground is usually located on the south side of villages and towns for the same reason. It is the duty of the eldest son to light the pyre with a torch. In doing so he walks around the body in a counter-clockwise direction – the opposite of normal clockwise **circumambulation** of sacred images designed to insure that the impure left side of the body is facing away.[7] Similarly, he wears his sacred thread over the right shoulder rather than the usual left, once again symbolizing the contrary nature of death. It is also his duty to sprinkle water onto the burning remains to ease the pain of the deceased.[8]

The cremation fire serves several religious purposes. First, it acts as a purifying agent, burning away the decaying cadaver which is a source of both hygienic and spiritual impurity. Second, fire is the common element in Hinduism's life-cycle rituals and daily worship. From the infancy and initiation samksaras to the wedding ceremony, offerings of food and drink are placed into the sacred fire for consumption by the gods. Now, at the end of life, the body itself is surrendered as a gift. Thus, cremation is rightly called antyesti – the final sacrifice. Third, the reduction of the physical body to a small mound of ashes is a powerful symbol of its transient nature. Only when the physical vessel is utterly destroyed by fire can the deceased begin to seek a new body and progress to the next plane of existence. In order to emphasize the need for the atman to depart from this temporary body, the eldest son performs the kapalakria, in which a hole is made in the skull with a bamboo rod.[9] The aim is to release the atman through the fontanel, which is known as the brahmarandhra [door of Brahma]. Alternatively a large clay pot full of water is broken to symbolize the crucial transition.

It is also customary for Hindus to restrain their grief because they believe that the tears of the living cause distress for the deceased.[10] Consequently, the mourners return home in procession without looking back, this time led by the youngest family members. After several days the chief mourner will return to the cremation site to collect the bones and ashes. Generally Hindus prefer to scatter the mortal remains in a river or lake rather than store them in an urn, again highlighting the transitory nature of the physical body and the avoidance of anything that may inhibit the passage of the atman to the next phase. For this reason Hindu cremation sites are often located on river banks (**ghats**). Some of the most famous cremation ghats in India are found in pilgrimage cities along the river Ganges such as Hardwar, Allahabad, and **Varanasi**. Those fortunate enough to have their ashes cast into sacred rivers are believed to pass directly into final liberation and escape from the wheel of rebirth.

While the cremation fire removes the impurities of the dead body itself, death has a spiritually polluting impact on members of the family, effectively cutting them off from ordinary life for a specific period of time. Typically the time of defilement lasts between 10 and 13 days depending on circumstances such as caste and local custom.[11] During this time all religious images are removed from the house and the sacred **Vedas** must not be read. Widows smash their bracelets, remove their jewelry, and erase the red mark (sindoor) on their head that symbolizes their married status. Family members must not shave or comb their hair, cut their beards, clip their nails, or wear shoes. They should sleep on the floor and cook their food on a separate fire. It is as if they too are dead until the deceased has moved to the next stage.

That vital transition is effected by a series of post-funeral offerings known as **shraddha**. In Hindu theology, the deceased person continues to exist as a preta or hungry ghost. As in the Buddhist scheme, pretas have thumb-sized spiritual bodies with large stomachs and tiny mouths, meaning that their basic desire for food and drink is constantly frustrated. Their only hope is that loved ones provide them with a fully developed spiritual body that will transform them from preta to pitri (ancestral spirit) and enable them to progress to the abode of the dead. Hence, the shraddha ritual involves offerings of special rice balls known as pindas. It is instructive to note that the term for a close relative is *sapinda* – someone bound by the duty of providing material support for a loved one when they pass away.

In Hindu tradition, a series of 16 pindas are offered over the span of 10 days. Six rice balls are placed in strategic places associated with the death: where the person died; where the corpse was laid; the first crossing during the procession; where the bier stopped; where the cremation occurred; where the ashes are scattered.[12] A pinda is also offered on each of 10 consecutive days in order to gradually create a new body for the deceased. According to Hindu tradition, the head is formed on the first day; the ears, nose, and eyes on the second day; the neck, shoulder, arms, and breasts on the third day; and so on until the new body is complete.[13]

On the tenth day, the chief mourner shaves, has a bath, and receives a new sacred thread. The long period of ritual defilement is ended and normality returns. On the eleventh day, in order to insure that the preta has now become a pitri and is capable of moving beyond post-death limbo, it is traditional to offer the gift of a cow which will assist the deceased to traverse the river of death and reach the land of the ancestors.[14] The cow is driven in a southward direction and allowed to run free. A further series of pindas are then offered to the gods over a period of time that can stretch up to one year. The rice balls are often given to the cows or even crows which, according to Hindu legend, drank from the nectar of immortality and thus never die.

The Hindu funeral rites described above are based on an ancient three-stage concept of the afterlife found in the Vedas. The purpose of the cremation and the post-funeral food offerings is to completely dispose of the old body as a source of pollution and to provide the preta with a new spiritual body, thus facilitating its transformation into a pitri. The deceased remains a pitri for three generations after which it joins the anonymous ranks of all ancestral spirits who abide in the mysterious realm of the dead. Many commentators have noted that this view is not fully consistent with the later idea of the wheel of reincarnation that first appeared in the Upanishads and developed into one of the most striking elements of the Hindu world view. There are some links to the samsaric world view in the traditional funeral rites such as the practice of not cremating holy ascetics who have already achieved final liberation, and the popular belief that scattering the ashes of the deceased in the Ganges and other holy rivers will guarantee release from the cycle of rebirth. There are also occasional references in the funeral prayers to ultimate liberation, but the central paradigm is reaching the land of the ancestors.

In one sense, Hinduism and Buddhism share a cyclic view of human existence based on the hope of ultimate liberation from the wheel of reincarnation and the unimportance of the physical body, which is thus cremated each time. In another sense, the Vedic-based Hindu funeral rites reflect a more corporeal, linear understanding of the afterlife where the deceased needs a new form of embodiment before it can become an ancestral spirit and reach the land of the forefathers from which it is not expected to return to the world. This is a view of the afterlife that is more reminiscent of the **Semitic religions**.

Resurrection of the Body

A common feature of many Jewish communities around the world is an organization of men and women dedicated to assisting fellow believers during the distressing time of death. The primary purpose of the hevra kadisha [holy society] is to insure that the bodies of deceased Jews are prepared for burial in a manner that accords with Jewish law. The caring work of the hevra kadisha is perceived as a genuine act of kindness not only toward the bereaved family but also for the benefit of the soul of the deceased.

Their main duty involves the tahara, or purification of the corpse, during which the body is thoroughly cleansed of dirt, fluids, and other impurities and then immersed in water. Following this the dead person is dressed in the tahrihim, or Jewish burial shrouds. These shrouds are a series of simple, white garments identical for all Jews, stressing the equality of all persons before God.[15] The pants have no pockets, emphasizing the total severance from the material world that is a consequence of death. Perhaps the most significant piece of tahrihim apparel is the **kittel** (jacket), which some Jewish men wear for the first time on their wedding day and thereafter at the feasts of New Year and **Yom Kippur**. On each of these occasions, as at death, the white kittel represents humble contrition for sin and the fervent hope of God's mercy.[16] The body is then wrapped in the **tallit** (prayer shawl) with one of its tassels cut to further symbolize the loss of life. Finally some dirt from Israel may be added as consolation for the fact that the person has died as an exile from the Holy Land.

The casket is then sealed, although not hermetically since it is Jewish belief that the body should have some contact with the earth in order to facilitate the natural process of decay. To this end, Jewish coffins are typically made of wood and sometimes holes are bored into the sides. In Israel itself, coffins are avoided; the corpse is wrapped in thick shrouds and is buried directly in the earth. There is usually no viewing of the body, or wake, in Jewish tradition, although members of the hevra kadisha may act as shomrin [watchers], traditionally for the purpose of insuring that the body is safe from desecration or theft until the funeral.

The vigil over the body does not last long since it is Jewish custom to bury the person as quickly as possible, preferably on the same day as their death. For many Jews this is a commandment of God, implied in a verse from Deuteronomy which declares of the executed criminal: "his corpse must not remain all night upon the tree; you shall bury him that same day, for anyone hung on a tree is under God's curse."[17] Apart from obedience to the divine command, a prompt burial also shows respect for the dead and provides psychological closure for the family. However, the haste to bury is counterbalanced by the practice of having the funeral procession stop seven times on the way to the grave site, acknowledging the natural unwillingness to lose a loved one.[18] At some stage before the actual burial, the mourners will perform kriah, where a piece of garment or a substitute ribbon is torn, symbolizing the emotional rendering caused by death.[19] The immediate family members usually make the tear on the left side, close to the heart.

In contrast to the Hindu–Buddhist tradition of cremation, traditional Judaism has always insisted on burial. Admittedly, **Reform** Jews have permitted cremation as an option since the nineteenth century and some **Orthodox** Jews allow the ashes of Jews who have been cremated to be placed in a Jewish cemetery. But in the eyes of Orthodoxy, cremation is strictly forbidden by God's law. There are two main texts usually cited in this respect. The first is Genesis 3:19 where the creator reminds **Adam**, the first human, of his material origin and destiny: "You are dust and to dust shall you return." The second text is the Deuteronomy verse quoted above where God explicitly uses the verb "to bury." For Jews, burial is an ancient custom dating back to the earliest biblical period, whereas burning is associated with capital punishment for serious sins.[20] Behind the weight of the divine imperative and age-old tradition, there are other reasons for the emphasis on burial. Some argue that natural decomposition is preferable to the artificial destruction of the body by fire, others that burial is a more reverent way of disposing of a sacred object, citing as example the Jewish practice of burying damaged Torah scrolls or prayer shawls. Cremation also has sinister connotations, because many Jews were burned to death during the medieval Inquisition and in Russian pogroms. Moreover the corpses of millions of Jews were incinerated in the death ovens of the Holocaust. But Jewish belief concerning the ultimate fate of the corpse is also an important factor. Unlike the Hindu–Buddhist world view of reincarnation and spiritual liberation, some streams of Jewish theology see human existence beyond death involving not only an immortal soul but also a resurrected body.

The term **resurrection** has become so strongly associated with Christianity that it is surprising for many to discover that it was actually a pre-existing Jewish concept. Although it can be interpreted in various ways including resuscitating a "dead" person back to earthly life, technically the term refers to the revitalization of the corpse after physical death – usually at the end of the world – with the result that the new transfigured body will never die again. At the time of Christianity's birth, there was disagreement among Jewish schools over the veracity of the concept. The Sadducee party maintained that it could not be a part of Jewish belief since resurrection is not explicitly mentioned in the **Torah**.[21] Their opponents, the Pharisees, accepted the notion on the basis of other biblical references, especially Daniel 12:2 which speaks of the last days: "Many of those who sleep in the dust of the earth shall awake, some to everlasting life, and some to shame and everlasting contempt."[22]

Scholars generally agree that the book of Daniel was written during the **Maccabean wars** (167–164 BCE) when the Jews fought a successful guerilla campaign against an oppressive Syrian overlord who had attempted to impose pagan **Hellenistic** customs on Israel. The non-canonical books of the Maccabees, dating from the same period, also explicitly mention the notion of God raising the bodies of the dead on the last day in order to reward the martyrs of the campaign and punish their murderers. In these works, bodily resurrection is connected to the final judgment. For this reason, it is thought that the concept originated in Persian **Zoroastrianism** which makes the same strong connection. Given that the innocent often die and the guilty go unpunished in this life, ultimate justice is possible only beyond death in the court of the divine judge. Moreover, the authors of these books presume that human existence is bodily whether in this life or in the next. The underlying anthropology so stresses the psychosomatic union of the human person that existence in the afterlife must involve some sort of body. In Jewish thinking, the human person is understood as an animated body rather than the embodied spirit of the Hindu–Buddhist world view.[23]

After the destruction of the **Temple** in 70 CE, the Pharisaic school prevailed and became the fountainhead for the new rabbinic form of Judaism. Thus most classical and medieval Jewish rabbis accepted the notion of bodily resurrection. For example, the Mishnah states: "All Jews have a portion in the world-to-come . . . But these do not have a portion in the world-to-come: one who says, 'Resurrection of the dead is not from the Torah.' "[24] The last of **Maimonides**'s famous Thirteen Principles includes the resurrection of the dead as a fundamental Jewish belief. Moreover, the second blessing of the **Amidah** (**Eighteen Benedictions**), one of the most important prayers in the thrice-daily **synagogue** service, praises God as one who "revives the dead." Consequently Orthodox Judaism emphasized the need to preserve the body for the final resurrection – or at least one part of the body, which the rabbis identified as the coccyx bone at the base of the spine. Today, Orthodox Jews disapprove of processes that compromise the integrity of the corpse such as autopsy, organ donation, and cremation. The practice of burial follows naturally from the doctrine of resurrection. However not all Jews accept the belief nor do they insist on the practice. The Reform movement rejects a literal understanding of bodily resurrection, ostensibly on scientific grounds, and has thus revised the second blessing prayer accordingly. Consequently, cremation is permitted in Reform communities.

Jewish mourning is divided into three distinct stages reflecting a gradual movement from intense sorrow to full resumption of a normal lifestyle, similar to Hindu post-mortem practice. Immediate family members are considered to be "official" mourners and carry special duties during this time.[25] The first stage is known as aninut and lasts from death to the burial, which is usually the same day. The mourners are exempt from religious duties such as daily prayer, but are obliged to abstain from meat, wine, and sexual activity. After the funeral is complete, the second phase commences and lasts for seven days, hence the name *shiv'ah*, meaning seven.[26] Upon returning home from the funeral, the hands are washed as a gesture of purification and a simple meal of consolation is served (seudat havra'ah). A range of normal activities are prohibited for the official mourners during this time: bathing and anointing; washing garments; cutting hair; wearing shoes; sexual intercourse; reading the Torah; and work in general. Forms of entertainment and parties should also be avoided, and in some Jewish cultures all mirrors in the house are covered as a further reminder that personal vanity is totally inappropriate at this time.[27] The common phrase "sitting shiv'ah" refers to the custom of family members sitting on low benches or even on the floor to express the depth of their sorrow and to accept condolence visits.

As the name implies, the third stage, or sheloshim [thirty], lasts until the thirtieth day after the funeral, except for the children of a deceased parent in which case it continues for one year. During sheloshim the official mourners may return to work and other normal activities, but they should still refrain from attending parties and functions with live music such as **bar mitzvahs** and weddings. Sheloshim is also the period during which mourners recite the beautiful **Kaddish** prayer for the deceased, although children of the deceased continue the practice for 11 months (see box 5.3). On the first anniversary of death (*yahrzeit* in Yiddish; *nohala* in Ladino), which is calculated according to the Hebrew calendar, it is customary to light a candle for 24 hours and recite Kaddish at all synagogue services that day. A headstone is sometimes unveiled at this time as a mark of respect and to fulfill what is considered a biblical commandment. The Jewish practice of placing stones on the grave is interpreted by some as a contribution to the construction of the headstone as well as a sign that the family has visited the cemetery.

The recitation of the Kaddish for a certain time after the funeral reflects the Jewish belief that the efforts of the living can benefit the dead. Although some liberal schools in Judaism suggest that the concept of an afterlife is unbiblical and unfounded, mainstream Jewish thinking holds that human life continues beyond death and that the final destiny of the human person is the olam haba, or the world to come. Olam haba is a state of spiritual perfection beyond human imagination, like the joy of **sabbath** multiplied a million times. At times it is described as *Gan Eden* [Garden of Eden], for

---

JEWISH KADDISH PRAYER

BOX 5.3

May His great Name grow exalted and sanctified in the world that He created as He willed.

May He give reign to His kingship in your lifetimes and in your days, and in the lifetimes of the entire Family of Israel, swiftly and soon. Amen.

May His great Name be blessed forever and ever.

Blessed, praised, glorified, exalted, extolled, upraised and lauded be the Name of the Holy One. Blessed is He beyond any blessing and song, praise and consolation that are uttered in the world. Amen.

May there be abundant peace from Heaven and life upon us and upon all Israel. Amen.

May He, who makes peace in His heights, make peace upon us and upon all Israel. Amen.

Figure 5.3
Memory stones on a Jewish grave

the rabbis believed that it is modeled on the pristine state of humanity. However, only the holiest of persons reach Gan Eden immediately after death. For most, the prerequisite is a purifying process that the soul undergoes in a place known as Gehinom. The term is derived from the name of a rubbish tip outside the walls of ancient Jerusalem where fires burned incessantly, aided by the occasional addition of brimstone (sulfur). It is said that pagans sacrificed children to their gods in the same valley, adding to its opprobrium. Gehinom is the origin of the Christian concept of hell, but the Jewish place is not eternal. According to tradition, the fiery purification of Gehinom lasts no longer than 11 months – precisely the period during which official mourners pray the Kaddish prayer for their loved one.

Gehinom functions within Judaism in much the same way as the cycle of samsara does in Hinduism and Buddhism. Both address the fact that most humans are spiritually and morally imperfect at the time of their death. Consequently both traditions agree that further refinement is necessary before the person is capable of attaining complete communion with the Absolute. In the samsaric world view, the residual bad karma is gradually erased over a series of reincarnations until final liberation is achieved. It should be noted that a similar notion exists in some streams of **Hasidic** Judaism that believe in gilgul – a reincarnation of the soul in various bodies over time until the required repentance is complete. However, in the predominant Jewish world view, the person lives and dies just once, with purification taking place at some point after death. Jews are not alone in such a linear **eschatology**. The equivalent of Gehinom and the garden of Eden can be found in Islam, along with the typically Semitic insistence on burial and its theological corollary, the resurrection of the body.

Salat al-Jenazah

According to Islamic belief, death ushers in the next stage of existence known as barzakh, or life in the grave. The immortal soul separates from the body and is interrogated by two angels, Nakir and Munkar, concerning the person's religious faith and the record of their moral behavior during life.[28] The answers to the angelic questions are of the utmost importance because they will determine the soul's eternal destiny at the end of the world. In the meantime, as the souls of all the dead await the last days, they experience the pressure of the grave pressing in on them, in proportion to the weight of their sins. Thus it is a common custom among Muslims to prepare the dying person for their encounter with the angels by whispering the **shahadah** (the single-sentence testimony of faith) into their ear. The last words heard by the deceased on earth will be one of the key answers sought by the heavenly messengers: there is one God and Muhammad is his Prophet. Similarly, in some cultures, the Qur'an is placed under the pillow of the deceased so that God's word is near them at the end.

The **Qur'an** does not contain many instructions for Islamic funeral rites, but this lack of detail is compensated by the example of the Prophet and the manuals of law. According to that tradition, the body is first washed and clothed in simple, white burial shrouds. The one exception is the case of martyrs who are buried in the clothing in which they died as a graphic testimony to the blood they shed for the faith. Modesty requires that those performing the bathing and shrouding are of the same gender as the deceased, except in the case of a parent or spouse. In accordance with Islamic dietary law, no alcohol is allowed in the scenting process and any form of embalming is strictly prohibited. Many Muslims use three sheets for a male, for the tradition states that the Prophet himself was buried in this manner.[29] Five sheets are commonly used for women – the extra two sheets consisting of a waist cloth and a head veil, reminiscent of the **hijab** that covered her hair in public during life.

Official prayers for the dead person are offered either in the home of the deceased, in a mosque, or even in an open courtyard which was the common practice in Muhammad's time (see box 5.4).[30] The one place where the prayers should not be recited is in the cemetery itself. The official prayer for the dead (salat al-jenazah) has the same basic structure as the standard **salat** (the five daily prayers). The service is led by an **imam** who stands beside the corpse with everyone facing Mecca.[31] However, there are differences that highlight the special nature of this particular service. For example, most of the formulas are said silently rather than aloud, and the usual bows and prostrations are omitted. Unlike daily salat, the timing of the funeral service is at the discretion of the mourners but it should not coincide precisely with sunrise, sunset, or noon in order to avoid any association with pagan sun worship.[32] The salat al-jenazah is said for all Muslims who have passed away, including infants who died at birth.

Muhammad once declared, "Hasten the funeral rites," out of respect for the deceased, and thus Muslims share with Hindus and Jews the preference for a quick burial.[33] The desire to avoid delays is one reason why Muslims usually bury the person close to where they died rather than transport the corpse to another place. The sense of haste is also evident in the custom of walking quickly during the funeral procession. Islamic funerals are characterized by moderation, simplicity, and a concern to avoid

> **Box 5.4** **A MUSLIM FUNERAL PRAYER**
>
> Glory be to You, O Allah and praise. Blessed is Your name and You are exalted. Your praise is glorified, and there is no god other than You.
>
> O Allah! Have Mercy on Muhammad and on those related to him, just as You have mercy and You send peace and blessings and have Compassion on Abraham and on those related to Abraham. Surely You are Praiseworthy, the Great!
>
> O Allah! Forgive those of us who are still living and those who are dead; those of us who are present and those who are absent, and our minors and our elders. O Allah! Let the one whom You keep alive from among us, live his life according to Islam, and let the one You cause to die from among us, die as a believer. Peace be upon you and Allah's Mercy.

idolatry of any kind. Extravagant expenditure on the funeral service itself and ostentatious structures over the grave are frowned upon,[34] even though the temptation is not always resisted. The placing of flowers, plants, food, drink, candles, or money around the grave is strongly discouraged because it is believed that such gifts are of no benefit to the dead.[35] The money should rather be spent on a worthy charity or used to pay any outstanding debts incurred by the deceased.

The emphasis on moderation also extends to mourning customs, for the Prophet explicitly forbade the excessive forms that were typical in the Arabian culture of his day such as prolonged wailing and shrieking, tearing the hair and clothing, slapping the face, beating the chest, and breaking objects. All of this only increases the pain of the deceased soul. According to Muhammad: "Truly the dead are punished in their graves by the wailing of their family over them."[36] Furthermore, Islam recommends only a brief mourning period of three days,[37] except for a widow who should grieve for four months and 10 days – a legal interval known as the *iddah*, during which time it is possible to ascertain whether or not she is pregnant.[38] The widow should not wear jewelry, move house, or marry during the iddah. Gatherings after a certain number of days or on anniversary dates are also downplayed because they are often a burden on the bereaved family and resemble pagan custom. Similarly, a visit to the grave is considered an honorable act but it should be carried out without wailing or screaming.

The means of bodily disposal in Islam is ground burial. As in Orthodox Judaism, there is a strict ban on cremation, although when a corpse is burned it does not preclude the soul from attaining Paradise. There are several reasons for the aversion to cremation in Islam. First, it is a popular belief that the dead person can feel the pain of the flames. Just as the soul can be distressed by excessive wailing of the mourners, so too can it acutely sense the destruction of its former body by fire. Second, Islam

Figure 5.4
Muslim women
visiting a
cemetery

considers incinerating the corpse or leaving it to be devoured by animals an act of sacrilege. This is because the body is seen as an integral part of the human person and not merely as a temporary or dispensable component. Such a corporeal anthropology is not unlike the Jewish conviction that the human person is a psychosomatic unity not just during earthly life but also in its post-mortem form. Although both religions embrace the notion of an immortal soul that survives physical death, they also sense that a disembodied person is somehow incomplete. Consequently, Islam also professes belief in the resurrection of the body at the end of time, when the complete person is restored, body and soul. As was noted with Judaism, such a belief is consistent with the practice of burial, through which the body is at least partly preserved, even if long-term decay and decomposition leave only the bones.

As the body of a deceased Muslim is lowered into the grave, supplication is offered reflecting the hope of eventual resurrection. The corpse is laid on its right side, with the head facing toward Mecca, sometimes supported by a small brick. For the entire duration of the barzakh, the Muslim will be oriented toward the holy city, as in official prayer. As the mourners sprinkle handfuls of dirt into the grave, appropriate verses from the Qur'an may be recited such as the following from Surah 36:

> And the trumpet shall be blown when, lo, from their graves they shall hasten on to their Lord. They shall say: O woe to us! who has raised us up from our sleeping-place? This is what the Beneficent God promised and the apostles told the truth. There would be naught but a single cry when lo! they shall all be brought before Us. So this day no soul shall be dealt with unjustly in the least, and you shall not be rewarded aught but that which you did.[39]

As noted above, the Qur'an may not contain much explicit material on funeral rites per se, but there is no shortage of verses pertaining to what Muslims call the Yawm al-Qiyamah [Day of Resurrection].[40] Eschatology is a key theme in **Muhammad's** message and it is considered to be one of the most important doctrinal principles of Islam. On the last day, the dead will be raised from their graves and will gather for final judgment by God. Unlike Jewish eschatology, two ultimate possibilities await each human person.

Those who have rejected the authentic revelation of the **prophets** such as Moses, **Jesus**, or **Muhammad**, converted from Islam to another religion, or lived wicked lives will be condemned to Jahannam (hell). The term is derived from the Hebrew *Gehinom* and is described in highly figurative language as an abyss of fire into which evil-doers fall as they attempt to cross the narrow bridge (the Sirat) that leads to eternal happiness. According to the Qur'an there are several levels in Jahannam, the lowest of which contains the bitter tree Zaqqum and a cauldron of fire and pitch.[41] The gravity of one's sin determines the level into which one is condemned. The Qur'an implies that although the most iniquitous souls are doomed to remain in Jahannam for eternity, others will be released after a time of purification, as with the Jewish Gehinom.

In contrast, the righteous are able to cross the bridge with consummate ease and enter heaven or Jannah. Once again the religious language used to describe the pleasures of Jannah is highly figurative and grounded in earthly experience. Jannah is described as a well-shaded, luxuriant garden whose inhabitants enjoy sumptuous food and drink, and an endless supply of obedient servants and pure companions (houri).[42] Muslims primarily, along with virtuous members of the **People of the Book** (Jews and Christians), are expected to reach Jannah. However, one of the most popular Islamic names for Allah is "The Merciful One" and Muslims are convinced that the Prophet himself will intercede for all humankind on the day of resurrection. Moreover, the family of each deceased soul is able to pray for their loved ones in the hope that God will exercise clemency.[43]

All in all, Islamic and Jewish eschatology share remarkable similarities: a preference for ground burial linked to the notion of the resurrection of the body; a linear view of human existence with one post-mortem judgment based on a single lifetime; and a temporary post-mortem punishment that prepares the person for final communion with God. The third Abrahamic faith also shares these elements but with one important difference: the claim that a single case of resurrection has already occurred, within history rather than at the end of time.

✝ First-Fruits

In no other world religion is so much theological weight placed on the ultimate fate of the founder as in Christianity. According to the **New Testament**, Jesus was crucified on a Friday afternoon and died after a few hours on the cross. His body was hastily buried before sundown in order to avoid breaking the rules of the sabbath. After respecting the day of rest, several female followers visited the tomb early on the Sunday morning only to discover that it was open and empty. The initial reaction of shock and consternation was soon transformed into a new religious faith when various groups of disciples claimed that Jesus had appeared to them in a partially recognizable bodily form. Given the Jewish background of the disciples, the inescapable conclusion was that the resurrection of the dead had begun and the world was about to end.[44] As time passed, Christian faith had to adjust to the obvious fact that the last days were not upon them, recasting the single resurrection of Jesus into a unique event within human history and not at its close.

The implications for Jesus's identity were enormous, eventually leading to the acceptance of his divine status. But it also had a considerable impact on the Christian understanding of death and the afterlife. Jesus's **resurrection** is seen as tangible proof of the veracity of the Pharisaic belief in the resurrection of the body – an item of faith that was incorporated into the earliest Christian creeds.[45] Moreover Jesus's resurrection was a foretaste of what was to come in the distant future: the "first fruits" of a harvest that would one day include all of humankind.[46] Given the centrality of the resurrection, it is to be expected that Christian funeral rites are dominated by the theme of Jesus's victory over death and the promise it holds for those who die with faith in him.

Spiritual care for the dying Christian varies from church to church but often involves prayers of comfort and appropriate scriptural readings. In the **Catholic** tradition, the priest performs a threefold ritual known as the "last rites" which comprises confession of sins, anointing with oil (formerly called extreme unction), and consumption of the sacred host known as viaticum, or food for the final journey. In all traditions the emphasis is on consolation and hope grounded in faith in the risen Lord who has conquered death and the fear associated with it.

Once death has occurred, there is no concern to bury quickly as in Judaism and Islam. In many cases the funeral is held after three or so days, reflecting the length of time that Jesus spent in the tomb.[47] During this period many Christian groups hold a simple vigil at which the mourners pray beside the coffin of the deceased either in a church or a funeral parlor. There is no prohibition in Christianity on viewing the body, and often the coffin is open for this purpose. Some Orthodox Christian churches have a continuous three-day vigil that symbolizes the unceasing praise of God by the angels and saints in heaven.[48] The recitation of the rosary is a common Catholic practice in this context. Akin to the Jewish concept of watchers, the traditional Irish wake involved someone keeping vigil beside the body of the deceased until the funeral, partly to insure that the person was genuinely dead and not simply unconscious. The tone of the wake was more festive than lugubrious, with food and drink in plenty, accompanied by stories celebrating the life of the departed one.

The funeral service itself is usually conducted in a church or cemetery chapel and presided over by a priest or minister. Occasionally a plain-colored cloth known as a pall is placed over the coffin to signify equality in death; hence the term *pallbearer* [one who carries the coffin]. The cross or crucifix is a common feature on coffins and graves, linking the deceased to the saving death of the founder. The service typically consists of readings from the Christian Bible, especially narratives of Jesus's resurrection and his teachings on eternal life.[49] The sermon expands on these themes, offering consolation and hope for the mourners. In Orthodox churches a small bowl of boiled wheat mixed with honey, sugar, or dried fruits (kolivo) is placed on a stand and mourners are invited to take some in remembrance of the words of Jesus: "Very truly, I tell you, unless a grain of wheat falls into the earth and dies, it remains just a single grain; but if it dies, it bears much fruit."[50] The contents of the Orthodox service resemble the official prayers for Holy Saturday – the day on which Christians commemorate Jesus lying in the tomb. It is common practice in Orthodox churches to open the coffin for a final time before burial and to place an icon of Christ in the hands of the deceased and a wreath on the forehead. Other denominations place wreaths of flowers on the coffin itself, symbolizing Jesus's victory over death and the crown of life that he shares with his own followers.[51]

Gestures and objects associated with the baptismal ceremony often reappear as part of the funeral service, forming a sacramental link between birth and death. The sprinkling of holy water over the coffin reminds mourners of the waters of **baptism** through which the deceased passed, entering the tomb with the crucified Christ in the hope of exiting the tomb with the risen Christ. The large **Easter** candle, which is used at baptisms, is kindled again at the funeral in the hope that the soul of the deceased now dwells in the brilliant light of God's presence. The use of incense is a sign of reverence for the physical body which is considered to be a temple of the Holy Spirit who dwells in the baptized person.

The committal service occurs at the cemetery where family and friends express their final farewell to the departed. Most services consist primarily of prayers that commend the soul of the deceased into the merciful hands of God while the body is committed to the earth. Given Christianity's Jewish provenance and its traditional belief in the resurrection of the body, for most of Christian history burial has been the preferred form of disposal. Even today the Orthodox churches are adamantly opposed to cremation which is seen as a denial of both the lasting significance of the body and the reality of resurrection. Moreover burial is considered to be a more faithful imitation of Jesus's own experience. However Catholic and Protestant churches have allowed their members the option of cremation in recent times.[52] In their thinking, the burning of the corpse no longer implies an attack on the notion of resurrection. Moreover, contemporary theology has tended to downplay the literal link between the physical remains and the utterly new form of embodiment involved in resurrection.

Although all Christian churches agree that the hope of everlasting life springs from belief in Jesus's resurrection, there is debate as to whether the prayers of the living can benefit the dead in any way. The question is linked to the nature of the afterlife itself, especially what is known as the intermediate state between a particular individual's death and the general resurrection of the dead at the end of time. According to the Catholic tradition, most virtuous souls still require further cleansing before they are worthy, indeed capable, of living in the presence of God. The post-death process in which the remnants of sin and selfishness are purged away is aptly known as purgatory.[53] Although the most common metaphor for purgatory is a painful but purifying fire, its flames are often confused with hell, the state of eternal damnation. Purgatory is actually good news, for it is a temporary process that guarantees eventual access to heaven. There is always a tendency to apply spatio-temporal language literally when discussing the afterlife and purgatory is a prime example. In popular Catholic imagination, purgatory was understood to be a place where souls spent a

Figure 5.5
Cross and flowers on a Christian grave

certain number of days, months, or years depending on the degree of purification required. The theological principle that prayers of the living could aid them was thus often expressed in terms of shortening their stay. Despite the inherent limitations of the language, the justification for the principle is that death has been conquered and thus cannot totally separate the living and the dead. The Church cannot be sundered. Just as the saints in heaven can help those on earth, so too those on earth can pray for and genuinely assist those in purgatory. Catholic theology finds scriptural backing in the second book of Maccabees where prayers and sacrifice are offered on behalf of the dead so that their sins might be forgiven.[54] Hence Catholics are encouraged to offer masses and rosaries for the souls in purgatory. Moreover, the second day in November each year is set aside precisely for the purpose of praying for the deceased in order to expedite their passage to heaven: it is known as All Souls' Day.[55]

It is also common practice in Christian Orthodox churches to pray for the dead, especially on days of special significance such as the fortieth day after burial, drawing on the belief that Jesus ascended to heaven 40 days after his resurrection. Apart from the anniversary of death for each individual, Orthodox Christians also set aside the eve of **Pentecost** to remember all the faithful departed. Yet despite such practices, the Orthodox churches do not profess a doctrine of purgatory and the dominant metaphor for the intermediate state is "sleeping in the Lord." In fact, the term *cemetery* is derived from a Greek word meaning a place to sleep; the deceased are envisaged peacefully resting in their graves as they await the general resurrection. The analogy is also present in the Catholic tradition where a requiem mass literally means prayers offered so that the deceased may *rest* in peace.

Protestant Christianity is even less enthusiastic about praying for the dead and generally rejects the concept of purgatory for a number of reasons. Martin Luther's initial protest against Rome was triggered by his outrage that indulgences, which guaranteed the shortening of a soul's term in purgatory, were being sold to raise ecclesiastical funds. Apart from the simony attached to the practice, there are two more profound theological reasons for his position. First, the Protestant tradition does not recognize the books of the Maccabees as part of their Bible since they are not part of the Jewish **Tanach**.[56] Consequently Protestant churches argue that there is no scriptural foundation for the Catholic practice of praying for the dead.[57] Second, and more importantly, Protestant theology considers that praying for the dead implies that Jesus's sacrifice on the cross is insufficient to save souls and requires the supplementation of human works. Protestant Christians agree that most souls need further cleansing before they are able to enter heaven but the intermediate state is usually understood to be a painful but instantaneous purification wrought by God's grace and not human prayers.

What awaits the purified soul once it is reunited with its resurrected body is an eternal existence in the presence of the creator and all other virtuous beings in a state known as heaven. Numerous metaphors from biblical and traditional sources are employed to describe the wonders of the Christian heaven. These include: the festive wedding banquet of Jesus's parables; the garden of Eden, or Paradise, echoing Jewish and Islamic themes; the heavenly Jerusalem illuminated solely by the light of God; and the beatific vision in which the creature gazes in ecstatic wonder at the divine countenance. In stark contrast, mainstream Christianity also admits a terrible alternative fate for unrepentant perpetrators of evil – hell. The dominant image of hell that emerges from the **gospels** is an underworld of darkness and unquenchable fires where there is "weeping and gnashing of teeth."[58] Unlike the Jewish Gehinom, the Christian hell is a state of total and eternal alienation from God. As in Dante's epic, *The Divine Comedy*, the sign over the gates of this dreaded place sums up the horror of its never-ending nature: "Abandon all hope ye who enter here."[59] Not surprisingly, the fear of unending damnation has served as a powerful motivation in Christian preaching over the centuries. Moreover, the torments of hell have been graphically depicted in sermon, book, and art. Despite its horrific and frightening nature, Christian churches are reluctant to declare officially that any particular person is in hell, even the most despicable figures of human history. In contrast, there is a long-standing tradition of confident formal declarations that outstanding examples of virtue and faith populate heaven: the saints.

SUMMARY

If religion is about recasting key moments of human life in the light of belief in transcendent being, there is perhaps no more pertinent moment than physical death. The religious claim that there is a dimension of reality beyond time and space becomes immensely relevant as the person passes away. Each of the five major religions has developed funeral and mourning practices that not only provide pastoral support for the believer, but also reveal each religion's fundamental beliefs about the mystery of death. What emerges from a comparative study of the funeral rituals of the five religions is a reinforcement of the classical division between the two Oriental religions on the one hand and the three Semitic religions on the other.

The Hindu–Buddhist world view considers human existence to be fundamentally cyclic. Birth leads to death, which is followed by rebirth into this world, and so forth. This particular life is only one in a long series of reincarnations aptly symbolized by the image of the wheel. The universe itself is hierarchical and the spiritual essence of the individual re-enters it at a different level each time, depending on the amount of good or bad karma that has been accumulated in each reincarnation. In both Buddhist and Hindu thinking, good karma is generated by behavior in accordance with specific ethical, social, and religious norms. In this sense, the wheel of reincarnation and the law of karma function as a compelling moral incentive as well as an explanation for the apparent inequalities in the world. One's actions in this life determine one's reincarnated form in the next.

In contrast, the **Abrahamic religions** display a more linear view of human existence which entails being born and dying just once before judgment that determines one's eternal fate. There is no wheel of reincarnation – just a line from birth through death to everlasting life. However, it must be acknowledged that this neat division between the cyclic Oriental world view and the linear Semitic world view is broad and far from absolute. The Hindu shraddha ritual, which is aimed at providing a new body for the deceased who can then proceed directly to the land of the ancestors, suggests a more linear, corporeal notion of the afterlife. Conversely, the Jewish gilgul tradition, which envisages a series of reincarnations until the soul is purified, echoes the Hindu–Buddhist wheel of samsara.

Perhaps the most salient feature of funeral rituals that reflects the contrast between the cyclic and linear world views is the means of bodily disposal. One consequence of the Hindu and Buddhist samsaric understanding is that the physical body has only limited importance since it is merely one particular form in a long series of lives. Moreover none of the physical forms will play any part in final liberation. Thus, the general custom of cremation among Hindus and Buddhists makes theological sense. The situation is quite different in the Semitic religions where the physical body carries much more significance. The absence of a cycle of reincarnation means that each person only ever has one body which constitutes an integral part of their identity. This is true not only during earthly life but also beyond the grave. Embodiment of some sort or other is understood as an essential aspect of being human. The classical doctrine of the afterlife that expresses such strong psychosomatic anthropology is that of the resurrection of the body. The central idea is that the remains of the person will be raised up at the end of time and transformed into a new, spiritual body for all eternity. The notion first appears explicitly in the Maccabean period of Jewish history and may have its origins in Persian Zoroastrianism. Eventually it became a part of classical Jewish, Christian, and Islamic faith, although there are differences of opinion today as to whether it should be taken literally or metaphorically. The importance of the physical body in the Semitic religions is reflected in their traditional preference for ground burial as a means of bodily disposal, although cremation has been permitted in sections of Judaism and Christianity in recent times. What sets Christianity apart from Judaism and Islam, therefore, is not belief in the resurrection of the body but the unique claim that one resurrection has already occurred within history, which carries immense implications for the identity of the one who was raised.

All five religions teach that the final destiny of the human person lies in a transcendent world beyond death. In Hinduism and Buddhism, this destiny is best described as liberation. Both religions agree that the wheel of reincarnation is a source of frustration and suffering. The physical world is an attractive and seductive place which causes its inhabitants to desire transient things that cannot bring ultimate satisfaction. The final goal of all beings is to escape from the wheel once and for all, as indicated by both the Hindu concept of moksa and the Buddhist concept of nirvana. Both traditions also agree that liberation can take a considerable amount of time and that most human deaths will lead to rebirth. Only those who are extremely advanced in the ways of spiritual progress can hope to find liberation when they pass away. For the rest, the general hope is reincarnation at a higher level on the hierarchy. However, there is a considerable degree of debate and ambiguity as to the precise nature of liberation and the final fate of the self in both religions. Some Hindu schools speak of absorption of the self back into the all-embracing Brahman while others envisage a continuing purified self in perfect harmony with Brahman. Buddhism, following the lead of its founder, is reluctant to describe nirvana in positive terms, preferring to stress that it is the extinguishing of suffering and desire, but leaving the fate of the self in some doubt.

In contrast, the three Semitic religions link the ultimate fate of the person to a post-death judgment in which they are held accountable for their earthly actions. One possible outcome in Christian and Islamic traditions is a state of eternal damnation and punishment for the most evil individuals. However, all three religions also teach a post-death process of purification and refinement after which the person is capable and worthy of living forever in the divine presence. This process acknowledges that most persons are not perfect at death. In this sense, it parallels the function of the Hindu–Buddhist cycle of reincarnation which also aims at the eventual purification of the individual prior to ultimate fulfillment. What takes many reincarnations in the Hindu and Buddhist world views occurs during an intermediate period after death in the Jewish, Christian, and Islamic world views. Moreover, these religions have less ambiguity about the survival of the self than in Hinduism and Buddhism. For Judaism, Christianity, and Islam, the final destiny of the individual soul is not absorption or extinction but ongoing communion with a personal God and other virtuous beings in a state of supreme happiness. Although the exact nature of Jewish Gan Eden, Islamic Jannah, and Christian heaven is beyond human imagination, a prevalent image is that of a luxurious garden, echoing the pristine environment of newly created humankind in the Jewish book of **Genesis**.

The post-death process of purification also has ramifications for those who remain on earth. The mourning rituals not only provide an outlet for emotional grief, but also reflect a common feature that cuts across all five religions: the idea that the actions of the living can bring some benefit to the dead. The 10 days of Hindu shraddha food offerings contribute to the construction of a new body for the deceased person. Gifts to Buddhist monks generate good karma that can be transferred to the dead who seek rebirth in an appropriate form. The Jewish recitation of Kaddish for 11 months after death coincides with the period during which the soul is purified in Gehinom. The

Islamic salat al-jenazah and private prayers include petitions to God for mercy toward the deceased. Catholic Christian prayers for the souls in purgatory are said to help the soul move more swiftly through the fires of purification and into heaven. Despite the significant differences concerning cyclic and linear world views, reincarnation and resurrection, cremation and burial, all religions offer their followers hope and meaning beyond the grave. They also provide opportunities for the bereaved to express grief in their loss and to assist the deceased in the next stage of their spiritual journey.

DISCUSSION TOPICS

1 Compare how the living can assist the dead according to each religious tradition.
2 How does each religion offer consolation for mourners who have lost loved ones?
3 Examine the details of the Buddhist wheel of life and its six realms. Are there other realms in the Buddhist system?
4 Is Hindu moksa the same as Buddhist nirvana?
5 Does the resurrection of the body make sense? What problems are associated with the concept?
6 Why do some religions ban cremation and organ donation?
7 Why did most Christian churches eventually lift the ban on cremation?
8 Compare Jewish, Christian, and Islamic images of heaven? How should such language be interpreted?
9 What are the arguments for and against the Islamic and Christian belief that some people deserve to remain in hell for eternity?
10 Explore the origins and significance of the Jewish tradition of reincarnation (gilgul). How does it relate to mainstream Jewish beliefs about death?

FURTHER READING

Bhaskarananda, Swami (2002). *The Essentials of Hinduism*. 2nd edn. Seattle: Viveka, pp. 92–6.

Coward, Harold (ed.) (1997). *Life after Death in World Religions*. Maryknoll, NY: Orbis.

Davies, Douglas James (2002). *Death, Ritual and Belief: The Rhetoric of Funeral Rites*. London: Continuum.

De Lange, Nicholas (2000). *Introduction to Judaism*. Cambridge: Cambridge University Press.

Dessing, Nathal M. (2001). *Rituals of Birth, Circumcision, Marriage and Death among Muslims in the Netherlands*. Leuven: Peeters, ch. 5.

Gordon, Matthew S. (2002). *Understanding Islam*. London: Duncan Baird, pp. 90–7.

Harris, Elizabeth (1999). *What Buddhists Believe*. Oxford: Oneworld, ch. 2.

Keown, Damien (2000). *Buddhism: A Very Short Introduction*. Oxford and New York: Oxford University Press, ch. 3.

Marcus, Ivan G. (2004). *The Jewish Life Cycle: Rites of Passage from Biblical to Modern Times*. Seattle: University of Washington Press, ch. 4.

Michaels, Axel (2003). *Hinduism: Past and Present*. Princeton, NJ: Princeton University Press, pp. 131–58.

Obayashi, Hiroshi (1991). *Death and Afterlife: Perspectives of World Religions*. New York: Praeger.

Renard, John (1996). *Seven Doors to Islam: Spirituality and the Religious Life of Muslims*. Berkeley and Los Angeles: University of California Press, pp. 59–63.

Reynolds, Frank E., & Carbine, Jason A. (eds.) (2000). *The Life of Buddhism*. Berkeley and Los Angeles: University of California Press, chs. 9, 14.

Rutherford, Richard (1990). *Death of a Christian: The Order of Christian Funerals*. Collegeville, MN: Liturgical Press.

NOTES

1   The wheel is a common motif in Buddhist art and architecture. An eight-spoked wheel represents the Eightfold Path to enlightenment and liberation. Moreover, the Buddha's First Sermon, which was delivered to his five original companions soon after his Enlightenment and which outlines the eightfold path, is often described as the "turning of the wheel."

2   For example, in Thailand the mataka-bhatta and mataka-vastra-puja are offerings of food and clothing respectively for the benefit of the deceased (mataka).

3   The stupa is known by various terms in different cultures: *pagoda* in Thailand; *chörten* in Tibet and Bhutan; *dagoba* in Sri Lanka; *caitya* in Nepal; *candi* in Indonesia.

4   The period varies from three days to several years, although 49 days is widely practiced.

5   The Tibetan Book of the Dead, or Bardo Thodol, also speaks of three other bardos during life: ordinary consciousness; meditation; and dreams. Thus in the broader context, there are various states of consciousness both before and after death that are all merely transitional stages on the way to final liberation (see box 5.2).

6   Sannyasins often burn an effigy of themselves signifying their death to the material world and its pleasures.

7   The left hand is associated with impure bodily functions such as going to the toilet. The prejudice against the left side of the body is not absent from the Western tradition: consider, for example the negative connotations of the Latin word for left, *sinister*.

8   Garuda Purana Uttarakhanda 24.12.

9   Garuda Purana Sarodhara 1.33.

10 For example, in the classical Hindu epic the Mahabharata, the hero Yudhisthira is reprimanded by the holy teacher Vyasa for grieving his nephew's death.

11 According to tradition, the defilement period differs according to class: 10 days for a brahmin, 12 days for a kshatria; 15 days for a **vaishya**; and one month for a **shudra**. The death of a child causes little pollution and the period of impurity is only a few nights.

12 Garuda Purana Sarodhara 10.9ff.; 12.57–9.

13 Garuda Purana Sarodhara 1.50–4.

14 Garuda Purana Sarodhara 1.56ff.

15 A similar stress on this democracy in death is reflected in the traditions of avoiding ornate decorations on coffins, and the preference for charitable donations rather than money spent on lavish flower arrangements.

16 The white of the kittel also symbolizes cleansing from sin as expressed in the text from Isaiah 1:18: "Though your sins are like scarlet, they shall be like snow." The kittel is also worn by the head of the family at the Passover **seder**.

17 Deuteronomy 21:23. Jewish tradition considers that the commandment to bury on the same day applies not just to victims of capital punishment but to all members of the Jewish people.

18 Traditionally psalms of consolation such as Psalm 91 are read at these pauses.

19 Tearing of clothing is a common sign of grief in the Jewish Bible. For example, see Genesis 37:34 where Jacob mourns for Joseph whom he thinks is dead.

20 The **patriarchs** of Israel and their wives were buried in the ground or in caves; see Genesis 25:9; 35:8; 47:29–30; 48:7; 49:29–31; 50:5. Perpetrators of incest, priests' daughters who commit prostitution, and persons in possession of certain banned objects are to be burnt to death according to Leviticus 20:14, 21:9, and Joshua 7:15.

21 According to most of the Tanach, the souls of the dead go to a shadowy subterranean world known as *sheol*, not unlike the Greek Hades. For example, see Genesis 37:35; 42:38; 1 Samuel 2:6; Psalm 6:5; Proverbs 1:12; 7:27; and Job 7:9.

22 Other biblical verses that are sometimes interpreted to refer to bodily resurrection include 1 Samuel 2:6; Job 19:26; Isaiah 26:19; Ezekiel 37:12.

23 A similar contrast can be seen between the anthropologies of the Greek philosophers, Aristotle and Plato respectively.

24 Talmud Sanhedrin 90a.

25 Jewish law specifies the following categories as "official mourners": father, mother, son, daughter, brother, sister, and spouse. See Leviticus 21:2–4.

26 There are several explanations for the origins of the seven-day mourning period. According to the Talmud, seven days of mourning were observed even before the Flood (see Talmud Sanhedrin 108b). Others claim that it is a reversal of the seven days of celebration during the **Passover** and **Sukkoth** festivals, citing Amos 8:10: "I will turn your feasts into mourning." There are also specific rules on how to count the seven days if a sabbath or festival falls within the period.

27 Some traditions suggest that the mirrors are covered so that the spirit of the deceased does not see itself and become traumatized.

28 See Qur'an 79:1–2.

29 According to the hadith, the Prophet was shrouded in three white sheets from Yemen: Sahih Bukhari 2.23.354.

30 Sahih Bukhari 2.23.337; Sahih Muslim 4.2077.

31 Sunan Abu Dawud 3188.

32 Sahih Muslim 4.1811.

33 Sahih Bukhari 2.23.401; Sahih Muslim 4.2059.

34   Sahih Muslim 4.2116.

35   The hadith records one exceptional occasion when Muhammad placed a palm leaf on a grave (Sahih Bukhari 2.23.443).

36   Sahih Bukhari 2.23.379; Sahih Muslim 4.2015.

37   Sahih Bukhari 7.63.254; Sahih Muslim 9.3552; Sunan Abu Dawud 4180.

38   Qur'an 2:234.

39   Qur'an 36:51–4.

40   Qur'anic references to the day of resurrection are numerous. Surah 75 of the Qur'an is even entitled "Al-Qiyamah: The Resurrection."

41   Qur'an 44:43–6.

42   Qur'an 3:185; 4:57; 9:72; 64:9.

43   Qur'an 59:10; Sahih Muslim 35.6590.

44   Paul's earliest letters reflect the overriding sense that time was short and that Christ would return very soon to usher in the final judgment of humankind. See 1 Thessalonians 4:13–5:7; 2 Thessalonians 2:1–12; 1 Corinthians 7:25–31. The gospel of Matthew hints at the general resurrection when it describes how the tombs of many holy men and women were opened on the day Jesus died and their occupants were subsequently seen in the holy city (Matthew 27:51–3).

45   For example, the final segment of the Apostles' Creed, which dates from the second century, states: "I believe in the Holy Spirit, the holy catholic church, the communion of saints, the forgiveness of sins, the resurrection of the body and life everlasting."

46   Paul uses this metaphor in 1 Corinthians 15:20–3.

47   The statement that Jesus was raised "on the third day" is found in the earliest Christian creeds and picks up a recurrent theme in the Jewish Tanach: the day on which God acts in a decisive manner. In the case of Jesus it is linked to the discovery of the empty tomb on the Sunday morning – the first day of the week in the Jewish calendar but the third day after his death if one follows the ancient custom and counts Friday as the first day.

48   See Revelation 4:8.

49   For example John 11:24–27; 14:1–4. Another popular biblical text is Psalm 23, which commences with the well-known verse "The Lord is my shepherd."

50   John 12:24.

51   See 1 Corinthians 9:24–6; Revelation 2:10.

52   The Vatican lifted the ban on cremation for Catholics in 1963. In 1997 it allowed Catholics to hold a prayer service with the cremated remains of the deceased.

53   The term first appears in the eleventh century but the concept of post-death cleansing is evident in the works of Church Fathers such as Tertullian, Cyprian, and Origen.

54   See 2 Maccabees 12:41–5.

55   It follows immediately after All Saints' Day (or All Hallows) on November 1 when Catholics recognize the vast number of anonymous holy men and women down through the ages who have not been officially declared saints by the Church. The date was probably chosen on the basis of a pre-Christian Celtic festival on October 31 known as Samhain [Summer's End] which honored the dead. Under Christianity the name was changed to *Halloween* (All Hallows Eve).

56   The Protestant **Old Testament** coincides precisely with the Jewish Tanach but Catholic and Orthodox Bibles also include a number of Greek texts that were part of the ancient Greek version of Tanach known as the Septuagint. Thus these works are called **apocryphal** by Protestant Christians and deutero-canonical by Catholic and Orthodox Christians. They consist of 1 and 2 Maccabees, Judith, Tobit, Ecclesiasticus (or Ben Sirach), The Wisdom of Solomon, Baruch, and parts of Daniel. The Orthodox churches also add 1 Esdras, 3 and 4 Maccabees, and Psalm 151.

57   See Martin Luther, Small Catechism (expanded), question 211; The Thirty-Nine Articles, article 22.

58   See Matthew 5:22, 29–30; 8:12; 22:13; 25:41–6; Luke 16:19–28.

59   Dante Alighieri, *The Divine Comedy*, Inferno, canto III.

Chapter 6

MARRIAGE

CONTENTS

   Nikah

   Under the Huppah

   Householder and Forest-
Dweller

   Bride of Christ

   The Renunciation

Introduction

Alongside birth and death, the third rite of passage that is commonly invested with religious meaning and celebrated with religious ritual is marriage. For many faiths, the formal union of husband and wife is not merely a vital social institution in which children are conceived but also a serious religious duty, a means of worship, and an earthly symbol of a transcendent reality. How does each of the five world religions understand the meaning of marriage? What are its primary ends? How does this understanding affect practical issues such as interfaith marriages, the number of partners, and the conditions of divorce and remarriage? How is this meaning expressed in the symbolism of the wedding ceremony? What is the attitude of each religion to celibacy as an alternative lifestyle? What impact has the example of the founder had on belief and practice?

☾ Nikah

When **Muhammad** was approximately 25 years of age he married a woman named **Khadijah** who was his employer and about 15 years his senior. Khadijah bore Muhammad four daughters[1] and was one of the first believers in his prophetic claim. Her constant support as loving wife and faithful disciple was a crucial factor during the difficult early years of Muhammad's preaching in **Mecca**. So respected and valued was Khadijah that the year of her death in 619 CE is described as the "year of sorrow."[2] Muhammad eventually married another 11 women before his own death in 632 CE, including two from Jewish and Christian backgrounds respectively. For Muslims, the wives of Muhammad are known as the "mothers of the faithful," shining examples of religious belief and spousal devotion (see box 6.1). Moreover, the example and teaching of the Prophet who was both husband and father is a key element in the Islamic understanding of marriage.

Marriage is considered to be of the utmost importance in Islam and there is extensive material in both the **Qur'an** and the **hadith** on the vital role it plays in the life of faith. It is often described as having both a vertical and a horizontal dimension. On

---

THE WIVES OF MUHAMMAD		**Box 6.1**
Khadijah	Widow and Muhammad's employer who bore him four daughters and two sons but only the girls survived infancy	
Sawda	Widow and early convert to Islam	
Aisha	Daughter of Abu Bakr	
Hafsa	Widowed daughter of Umar	
Zainab bint Khuzayama	Widow from the battle of Badr	
Umm Salama Hind	Widow from the battle of Uhud	
Zainab bint Jahsh	Widow who married then divorced Muhammad's adopted son, Zaid bin Harith	
Juwairiya	Daughter of the leader of the Mustaliq tribe	
Ramalah	Widowed daughter of Abu Sufyan, leader of the Quraish tribe in Mecca	
Safiyah	Daughter of the leader of the Jewish Nadir tribe	
Maymunah	Widow from a leading Quraish family and stepsister of Zainab bint Khuzayama	
Maria al-Qibtiyah	Coptic Christian sent as a slave to Muhammad who bore him a son who died in infancy	

the vertical plane, marriage is understood as an act of worship in that it is pleasing to **Allah** and fulfills the divine plan. According to tradition, Muhammad declared that no institution is more loved by Allah. Moreover, when a person marries he has completed "half of his religious obligations."[3] On the horizontal plane, marriage is a legal contract between two individuals. In this sense, it requires the usual elements of any contract: mutual consent between the parties, specified conditions, and public witness.

As in many cultures, Islamic marriages have been arranged for much of history and this is still common practice today. The involvement of parents and family in the selection of a suitable partner is based on the principle that marital success cannot be founded on romantic love alone. Long-term compatibility is an essential factor that includes considerations such as moral character and religious faith. Marriage is seen as not only the union of two individuals but also the joining of two families, and thus broader interests must be taken into account. However, an arranged marriage is not a forced marriage and Islamic law stipulates that the free consent of both parties is necessary for its validity, even if the bride acts through her official guardian, or wali.

The Islamic marriage contract specifies certain conditions as binding on both parties. In terms of financial responsibility, it is the husband's duty to provide for his wife and children irrespective of her personal wealth, which she is entitled to retain for her own purposes. Moreover, a dowry, or mahr, must be paid to the wife in order for the marriage to be valid. The mahr can be in the form of money, some other asset, or even an intangible gift such as education. The mahr becomes part of the wife's personal property and remains thus even in the case of divorce. Often only part of the mahr is paid at the time of the wedding on the understanding that the remainder is due in the event of divorce – a deterrent to a husband who may be considering a divorce without good reason. It is relatively simple for a husband to obtain an Islamic divorce since all that is required is that he inform his wife of his intentions on three separate occasions over a period of three months. Conversely, a woman needs to establish grounds for divorce. One possible option for a woman is to return her mahr and obtain a "no fault," or khula, divorce. In practice many women use the mahr to support their families but the law does not oblige them to do so.[4] The duties of a wife toward her husband include an acknowledgment of his authority in the house which can be interpreted in diverse ways depending on the particular Islamic society or culture in question. There is considerable debate within Islam itself regarding the extent to which a husband may impose restrictions on his wife's activities and freedom, and the manner in which this is done.

Islamic weddings vary enormously according to local culture but typically there are two stages. The first is the signing of the marriage contract, or nikah – the common term for marriage in Islam which suggests that commitment to the marriage covenant is the heart of the matter. It is often a simple ceremony involving the two parties and official witnesses. The bride does not even have to be present but can act through her wali, who is usually her father or guardian. There is no special religious ritual as such, although nikah is performed in the presence of an Islamic religious official (**imam**) with appropriate readings from the Qur'an and a short sermon. The second stage of the ceremony is the walima, or wedding banquet, during which the couple and their families and friends celebrate the joyous event. The walima serves to express the public dimension of the marriage, although its actual timing can vary from immediately after the signing of the contract to some time after the consummation of the relationship.

One of the more striking features of Islamic marriage is the existence of a limited form of **polygyny** based on the Qur'anic text:

> And if you fear that you cannot act equitably towards orphans, then marry such women as seem good to you, two and three and four; but if you fear that you will not do justice (between them), then (marry) only one or what your right hands possess.[5]

The verse has traditionally been understood as granting permission for Muslim men to take up to four wives concurrently.[6] The revelation should be considered in the original context of pre-Islamic Arabia where there was no limit to the number of wives a man could have at the same time. As with many Qur'anic teachings regarding marriage, the intent is to improve the lot of women. This underlying principle is further evident in the strict condition that applies to Islamic polygyny. The Muslim husband must be able to support all of his wives and treat them with equality. This means parity not only in terms of material support, but also in all aspects of the marriage including emotional and sexual relationships. Basically, the husband cannot indulge in favoritism. Some Muslims argue that the Qur'an itself implies that this is extremely difficult and thus its spirit is one of discouragement rather than encouragement:

> And you have it not in your power to do justice between wives, even though you may wish (it), but be not disinclined (from one) with total disinclination, so that you leave her as it were in suspense.[7]

The inference is that polygyny is really only appropriate in exceptional circumstances such as a severe scarcity of males in time of war.[8] Indeed this was the situation during Muhammad's lifetime when many of his own wives and those of his companions were women who had lost their husbands in the series of battles between Mecca and **Medina**.[9] In reality, polygyny is rare in the Muslim world today, and is more or less restricted to wealthy men in countries whose civil law codes allow the practice such as Saudi Arabia, the United Arab Emirates, and parts of west Africa. Moreover, marriage contracts sometimes include a clause requiring the husband to obtain permission from the first wife before he is able to marry a second.

There is a strong expectation in Islam that both partners are Muslim. Marrying a non-believer is explicitly prohibited by the Qur'an unless he or she converts:

> And do not marry the idolatresses until they believe, and certainly a believing maid is better than an idolatress woman, even though she should please you; and do not give (believing women) in marriage to idolaters until they believe, and certainly a believing servant is better than an idolater, even though he should please you.[10]

An exception is made in theory for Muslim men who may marry women "of the Book": in other words, Jewish and Christian women who share with Islam the revealed truth of God's oneness.[11] However in practice it is often so restricted by certain conditions that it is almost impossible.[12] The rule is based on the principle that the faith of the children is paramount and the presumption that the husband of any household has the final say concerning their religious education. Thus a Muslim woman is not allowed to marry a non-Muslim man, even if he is a Jew or Christian, since she cannot guarantee that the children will be raised as Muslims.

Islamic marriage is understood to have two primary objectives. The first is the mutual support and companionship of the spouses. When referring to marriage the Qur'an often uses the term *zawj* which means partner or friend. It is part of Allah's design that a husband and wife find joy and comfort in each other's company: "And one of His signs is that He created mates for you from yourselves that you may find rest in them, and He put between you love and compassion."[13] The second objective of marriage is procreation. The intimate sexual union of man and woman not only powerfully expresses their conjugal relationship but also has the potential to generate new life. In the divine plan, marriage is the sacred context in which children are conceived.[14] The Qur'an describes marriage as a "fortress" of chastity where the powerful sexual drive can be safely channeled and controlled for the good of the offspring and society in general. Extra-marital sex is considered to be a serious breach of the marriage covenant and a grave sin.[15] Yet sexual activity in itself is understood as part of God's good creation and an essential element of the conjugal relationship. Failure to provide sexual satisfaction to one's partner by either can be cited as grounds for divorce.

Although there are set times for abstaining from sexual intercourse such as during the **Ramadan** fast and menstruation,[16] Islam does not perceive voluntary celibacy as a means of spiritual advancement or a higher form of religious life. There are cases of celibacy among the mystical **Sufis** but these are exceptional.[17] Islamic law places marriage in the category of what is recommended, even obligatory, for those with a strong sexual drive. Muhammad himself is reported to have declared that "there is no celibacy in Islam" and his own example, as well as that of the **prophets** of old, testifies to the idea that marriage is the divine preference.[18] The same emphatic insistence on marriage as a fundamental part of God's plan and a binding religious duty, the example of the prophets, and a general suspicion of celibacy can also be found in Judaism.

Under the Huppah

The first book of the Jewish scriptures opens with two accounts of the creation of the world. In the first chapter of **Genesis**, God shapes the cosmos over six working days and rests on the seventh. At the climax of the process, God creates male and female human beings "in his image" and immediately instructs them: "Be fruitful and multiply, and fill the earth and subdue it."[19] The very first explicit divine commandment in the **Torah** is the duty to procreate. In the second chapter of Genesis an older version of creation describes how God first fashions a man (adam) from clay (adamah) and places him in a garden as cultivator and keeper. The creator acknowledges that it is not good that man should be alone and so he creates the animals as potential companions. But none of these satisfy the fundamental yearning of the solitary man for an equal, complementary partner. Thus, while the man sleeps at night, God takes one of his ribs and fashions woman. Upon seeing the new creature Adam joyously exclaims that "this at last is bone of my bones and flesh of my flesh."[20] Only when both male and female are joined together is the human person complete. The biblical author then adds a reference to marriage at the conclusion of the creation story: "Therefore a man leaves his father and his mother and clings to his wife, and they become one flesh."[21]

The two creation narratives powerfully highlight the twofold purpose of marriage in Judaism: companionship and procreation. Marriage is a divinely ordained partnership that fulfills the deep human need for intimacy and flows over into the generation of new human life. In Jewish theology, the relationship between husband and wife is described as kiddushin – a means of sanctifying each other in an exclusive and faithful bond of love in accordance with the will of God. This notion of the God-given partner who fills the gap in an individual's life is reflected in the long-standing Jewish tradition of seeking one's bashert [soul mate]. Moreover, the prophetic tradition of Israel added a third layer of meaning to marriage: the conjugal love between the groom and the bride is a symbol of the transcendent love of God for Israel. In one sense, God is married to his people.[22]

Such language presupposes monogamy as the ideal form of marriage, and this is reflected in contemporary Jewish law, although this was not always the case. The Torah and the **Talmud** allow a man to have more than one wife at the same time, and many prominent biblical characters such as **Abraham**, **Jacob**, **David**, and **Solomon** practiced polygyny and concubinage. The ban on polygyny is usually traced to the **Ashkenazi** Rabbi Gershom of Mainz (d. 1028 CE) who taught that a Jewish man should have only one wife, possibly as a result of pressure from the surrounding Christian culture.

In contrast, **Sephardic** Jews living in Islamic lands were allowed to have more than one wife in accordance with Muslim law.[23]

Clearly Judaism places much emphasis on marriage as a divinely ordained institution and the rich imagery of the traditional Jewish wedding ceremony expresses the depth of its religious significance. Timing is an important issue for Jews and there are certain days and dates on which a wedding is inappropriate. These are the **sabbath**, a day of mourning, or during the 50 days between **Passover** and **Shavuot** known as the Counting of the Omer, with the exception of the thirty-third day which is a popular choice for nuptials.[24] Tuesday is a considered to be an auspicious day since the Genesis creation account declares "it was good" twice on the third day (Tuesday). On the sabbath before the wedding in Ashkenazi synagogues, the groom is honored by being called up to read the Torah in what is known as an ufruf. The congregation may throw candy at the prospective bride and groom to symbolize the sweetness of the pending moment.

The themes of purification and a new start find practical expression as the bride attends the **mikveh** or ritual bath on the eve of the wedding. On the day itself, the couple fast until the ceremony is completed and confess their sins as all Jews do annually on **Yom Kippur** (Day of Atonement). She receives her guests while seated on an elegant throne in a custom known as Hakhnassat Kallah [Rejoicing of the Bride]. At the same time, but in a separate place, the Groom's Table is held. While guests partake of food and drink, the groom is expected to deliver a discourse on the Torah while his family and friends continually interrupt him in good humor. The groom is then taken to his bride for the bedeken, or veiling ritual, which is a remnant of the ancient year-long period of betrothal.[25]

A formal legal contract known as a ketubah is signed by the bride, groom, and two valid witnesses. The ketubah states the conditions of the marriage, especially the rights of the wife and the responsibilities of the husband. It usually specifies the amount to be paid to the wife in the event of divorce as well as the obligation of the husband to provide her with food, shelter, clothing, and sexual satisfaction.[26] As with the Islamic mahr, the primary purpose of the ketubah is to dissuade the husband from divorcing his wife without good reason.[27] The document itself is usually written in **Aramaic** which was the common language of the Jews during the first centuries of the Common Era. However, some schools of Judaism use modern **Hebrew** or the vernacular with more egalitarian adaptations of the traditional phraseology. Ketubah texts are often artistically rendered and adorn the homes of married couples.

The wedding ceremony is celebrated under an embroidered cloth canopy supported by four poles known as the huppah – a term that has become synonymous with "wedding." The huppah represents the new home that the couple will create out of their mutual love. Like Abraham's tent, which was visited by God disguised as a traveler, it is open on four sides as a sign of hospitality to all.[28] When the bride reaches the huppah, she circles the groom seven times. There are many explanations for this practice, including the staking out of a claim, in a similar way to how land was staked out in ancient times, or alternatively implying that her life now revolves around her husband.[29]

The wedding consists of two stages, the first of which is known as kiddushin [sanctification]. As a sign of their union, the couple drink from a cup of wine – a common element in Jewish life-cycle rituals – which is blessed by the officiating **rabbi**. The rabbi recites a blessing that praises God for the gift of marriage and the groom places a ring on the bride's right forefinger. Many Jewish weddings now include a double ring ceremony. The traditional Jewish wedding band is plain gold with no jewels or decorations except for engraving on the inside. The groom declares, "Behold, you are consecrated to me with this ring in accordance with the laws of Moses and Israel," after which the signed ketubah is read aloud.

The second stage is called nesuin [elevation] and consists of the sheva brachot, or the seven wedding blessings. This beautiful litany of prayers expresses sincere gratitude for such gifts as life, wine, and married love, and asks that God grant joy and peace to the couple as well as to all of Israel's children (see box 6.2). The symbolic number

---

THE SEVEN JEWISH WEDDING BLESSINGS   **BOX 6.2**

You are blessed, Lord our God, the sovereign of the world, who created everything for his glory.

You are blessed, Lord our God, the sovereign of the world, the creator of man.

You are blessed, Lord our God, the sovereign of the world, who created man in His image, in the pattern of His own likeness, and provided for the perpetuation of his kind. You are blessed, Lord, the creator of man.

Let the barren city be jubilantly happy at her joyous reunion with her children. You are blessed, Lord, who makes Zion rejoice with her children.

Let the loving couple be very happy, just as You made Your creation happy in the garden of Eden, so long ago. You are blessed, Lord, who makes the bridegroom and the bride happy.

You are blessed, Lord our God, the sovereign of the world, who created joy and celebration, bridegroom and bride, rejoicing, jubilation, pleasure and delight, love and brotherhood, peace and friendship. May there soon be heard, Lord our God, in the cities of Judea and in the streets of Jerusalem, the sound of joy and the sound of celebration, the voice of a bridegroom and the voice of a bride, the happy shouting of bridegrooms from their weddings and of young men from their feasts of song. You are blessed, Lord, who makes the bridegroom and the bride rejoice together.

You are blessed, Lord our God, the sovereign of the world, creator of the fruit of the vine.

Figure 6.1
Traditional breaking of the glass at a Jewish wedding

seven, frequently used in both ritual and calendar, is linked to the seven days of the Jewish week and the seven days of creation, signifying completeness and newness.

The couple drink from the cup of wine for a second time and the groom breaks a glass with his foot – a gesture that carries a number of meanings. According to the Talmud, it signifies the need for decorum and sobriety even in the most joyous of moments.[30] For many it is a reminder that marriage involves not only happiness and pleasure but also heartbreak and sacrifice. The shattered glass also recalls the destruction of the First and Second **Temples**.[31] The couple are then escorted to a private room for a short period known as the yihud, during which they end their pre-nuptial fast with a brief meal and share their first moments alone together as husband and wife. Traditionally this was understood as an opportunity for the new couple to consummate their marriage. Finally they rejoin their family and friends for the seudat mitzvah – a festive meal that marks the fulfillment of a divine commandment such as circumcision, bar mitzvah, or marriage.

Given the significance of marriage in Judaism, the choice of a partner is a serious consideration not only in terms of social and economic issues but also in terms of religion. Traditionally a matchmaker, or shadchan, would identify a prospective spouse and arrange a series of meetings to ascertain whether the couple was compatible. The shadchan might be a family member, a rabbi, or even a professional hired for the purpose. Arranged marriages still require the free consent of both partners and Judaism insists that a couple must at least have seen each other before the wedding.[32] Some argue that the derivation of the term *shadchan* is "calm," suggesting that the main purpose of the matchmaking process is to enable the young persons to settle down successfully.

As with Islam, **Orthodox** Judaism insists that the married couple share the same Jewish faith in accordance with the explicit biblical prohibition on marriage to certain **gentile** nations.[33] In this view, the kiddushin ceremony has little meaning if one of the partners is non-Jewish and such a marriage does not enjoy religious legitimacy. Nevertheless, the frequency of interfaith marriages today is steadily growing among Jews in the Western world. **Reform** rabbis will often allow such a marriage provided the children are educated in the Jewish faith.

Despite its lofty ideals, Judaism has acknowledged from earliest times that marriages can fail and has thus allowed for divorce and remarriage. The religious document of divorce is known as a get, which derives from the Torah instruction that the husband must issue his wife with a "bill of divorce."[34] Without a get, neither party can marry again in the eyes of Jewish law. However the divorce requires the consent of both parties which raises the problem of the recalcitrant spouse. Such a scenario is difficult for either party if they choose to remarry, but the situation of the woman is worse because her second marriage would be considered as adulterous whereas the husband's would be "merely" polygamous. Women in such a position, as well as those whose husband's death cannot be incontrovertibly established, are effectively blocked from remarrying and are known as agunot [anchored]. A common solution to the dilemma of the agunah seeking divorce is to include a clause in the ketubah that requires the husband to attend a religious court or pay an exorbitant amount of money if he refuses to cooperate.[35]

As one of the first positive biblical commandments, marriage is seen as a fundamental duty for all Jews. In a sense, an unmarried person is considered incomplete. As with the Muslim world view, religious celibacy has had little relevance in Jewish belief and practice. Traditionally, leadership positions in the Jewish community were expected to be occupied by married persons. Talmudic literature frequently endorses marriage and raises questions about celibacy.[36] Exceptions to the general rule exist such as the prophet Jeremiah who was commanded by God not to marry, but scholars point out that this was because of the impending doom that threatened **Jerusalem** as a result of the invasion of the Babylonian army.[37] According to the first-century CE historian **Josephus**, some members of the Essene sect were celibate.[38] Similarly Philo of Alexandria refers to the celibate members of the Therapeutae community.[39] But these are exceptions and both examples possibly reflect the influence of **Hellenism** which is characterized by more suspicious attitudes to sex and marriage.

Somewhat surprisingly, the sacred canopy, circling movements, and a sevenfold blessing are also features of Hindu wedding ceremonies. Moreover, the Jewish and Islamic understanding of marriage and procreation as a fundamental sacred duty is also a salient feature of the Vedic tradition within Hinduism. However, the life stage of the married Hindu householder is complemented by other life stages where celibate renunciation takes on a more positive value than for Jews and Muslims.

Householder and Forest-Dweller

Most Hindu life-cycle rituals are sensuous events but perhaps none more so than a wedding with its exuberant atmosphere, stunning imagery, and rich symbolism. As with the Hindu religion itself, there is enormous variety of wedding traditions across the subcontinent. Nevertheless common elements can be identified, many of which are drawn from the classical Vedic literature.

The physical appearance of bride and groom is vitally important since on this special day they represent incarnations of **Vishnu** and his consort **Lakshmi**. On the morning of the wedding, bride and groom bathe and anoint their bodies with substances associated with fertility such as turmeric, sandalwood paste, and oil. One of the most distinctive customs associated with Indian weddings is **mehendi**, or the painting of intricate patterns on the bride's hands and feet with red and brown henna.[40] The term *mehendi* is often used as a synonym for marriage in much the same way as *huppah* in Judaism and *nikah* in Islam. The atmosphere is light-hearted as female relatives and friends play humorous games and tease the bride. Her dress is customarily a shade of red or pink which is considered an auspicious color. She also wears as much jewelry as possible, such as necklaces, earrings, bangles, rings, nose-ring, anklets, and toe-rings, in the same way as statues of the goddess Lakshmi are lavishly adorned out of respect and honor.

As with most events, the ceremonies commence with prayers to **Ganesha**, the elephant-headed god who removes obstacles and brings good fortune. The bride's family welcomes the groom with gestures such as the application of the **tilak** to his forehead, the circular movement of five lights known as arati, the showering with flower petals, or the sprinkling of perfumed water. The traditional venue is the home of the bride although today weddings can be held in parks, hotels, and special halls. When the bride arrives she is escorted to the center of the hall where a mandap has been constructed. Like the Jewish huppah, the mandap is a canopy of cloth with poles draped in flowers, symbolizing the protection of the gods and the new household about to be created.

In Indian culture, marriage means that the daughter will leave her own family and become a member of her husband's kin. Thus one of the most poignant moments early in the wedding ceremony is the kanya dan when the bride's father hands over responsibility for his daughter to the groom. Her husband promises to care for her in terms of **dharma** [duty], artha [prosperity], and kama [pleasure].

As with most Hindu life-cycle ceremonies, the central rites of marriage are performed before a fire which symbolizes **Agni**, the god of fire and chief witness to the proceedings. After offering some rice or other food to Agni, the couple walk around the fire seven times during which they declare their wedding vows.[41] The groom then ties a piece of their clothing together in a knot and the bound couple take seven steps (saptapadi) together, each of which symbolizes a particular blessing: food, strength, prosperity, happiness, progeny, longevity, and friendship. According to Indian civil law, the marriage is finalized at the end of the seventh step.[42] In southern India, the ritual emphasis is placed on the "tying of the knot," usually symbolized by a garland or neck-lace known as mangalsutra that is placed around the bride's neck. The mangalsutra is one of the most precious objects that a woman wears and indicates her married status like the wedding ring in the West. The equivalent sign in northern India is the line of vermilion sindoor powder that the groom marks along the parting of her hair.

The stars play an important part in the planning of all important events for Hindus and weddings are no exception. The couple's horoscopes are initially consulted in order to fix the most auspicious date for the wedding, and the heavens also figure in the traditional ceremony itself. If the wedding occurs in the evening, the couple will be invited by the priest to step outside and turn their eyes toward the Pole Star (known in Sanskrit as Dhruva). This star remains perfectly stationary as the nocturnal sky revolves around it, symbolizing the steadfastness and trust that will be the axis of the couple's

Figure 6.2
A Hindu wedding
with canopy
(mandap) and
sacred fire

new life together.[43] If the wedding occurs during the day, the couple face the sun and meditate on it as the utterly reliable source of life and warmth.[44] The husband and wife worship for the first time as a couple by placing food offerings in the sacred fire. After seeking blessings from their parents they leave the mandap and the grand wedding feast begins.

In order to understand the significance of Hindu marriage it is necessary to set it in the context of the classical teaching concerning the **ashramas** or life stages (see box 3.1 on p. 89). According to Vedic tradition, there are four stages in the life of an upper-caste Hindu man. The first stage is that of the **brahmacarin**, or student. It begins with the last of the childhood rituals – the conferring of the sacred thread – and ends when the young man marries. Thus the wedding ceremony marks the passage from the first to the second stage, that of the **grihasthin**, or householder. In many ways this is the most important of the ashramas since it supports the others, and the wedding ceremony that ushers it in is the most intensely celebrated of the many **samskaras** (life-cycle rituals). In the Vedic world view, it is a holy duty to marry once a person reaches a certain age. Marriage is a part of the cosmic dharma that is incumbent upon all who are physically and mentally capable.

Although polygamy is condoned in the ancient **Laws of Manu**, most contemporary Hindu sects see monogamy as the ideal form of marriage. Wedlock is often compared to the union of primal complementary forces that give rise to the cosmos. Moreover, marriage is a mirror of the transcendent. The human love of bride and groom reflects the love between divine couples such as Vishnu and Lakshmi, **Shiva** and **Parvati**, **Rama** and **Sita**. Marriage reflects the mysterious unity of the male and female within the ultimate mystery itself. In this sense, the grihasthin life stage is a holy reality, and within its sacred context spouses are free to savor the pleasures (kama) of married life including sexual enjoyment.[45]

But the grihasthin life stage also involves dharma or religious duty. The householder is expected to honor and support his wife, earn a respectable living, have children, care for aged family members, offer hospitality to the stranger, and assist the needy. The obligation to beget children, especially sons, is very strong. Not only do male children carry on the family name but a son is essential for the proper performance of the funeral rites by which the deceased person is assisted in their journey to the land of their ancestors.

The stress on the union of the couple has been so emphatic, especially among upper-caste Hindus, that remarriage has been almost impossible for widows who are expected to remain faithful to their husband even after death. The extreme case of such ongoing devotion is the practice of **sati** which involves the widow lying on her husband's funeral pyre and being cremated with him. There is some debate as to the actual frequency of sati in times past, but it occurs only rarely today. It was definitively outlawed by the British in 1829 as a result of persistent efforts to ban it by the prominent nineteenth-century reformer **Ram Mohan Roy**.[46] The ideal of eternal marriage that reflects a divine reality naturally leaves little room for divorce. Indian civil law allows for divorce based on a range of legitimate grounds but many devout couples, especially among the upper castes, will not take such a step for fear of public humiliation and social disapproval.

As with Judaism and Islam, Hindu marriages have traditionally been arranged by the parents, with the consent of the young persons (at least theoretically). Key considerations in partner selection include **caste**, family background, financial status, appearance, and character. Although secular Indian law allows marriages across castes and religious affiliations, there are still powerful socio-religious forces in place that mean ostracism and even injury or death when couples defy conventions. The general trend in southern India is to strengthen existing kin relations and thus partners are sought among cousins and other family members. This means that the bride will be reasonably familiar with her future in-laws. In northern India, village exogamy is the norm and thus a daughter will typically marry into a family that has no kinship relation to hers and may even live some distance away. In such cases, the kanya dan [giving away of the daughter] is particularly poignant and the expressions of sorrow by the bride and her family as she departs for her new home on her wedding day are often based on a genuine sense of apprehension and loss.

An important aspect of the premarital arrangements is the question of the dowry which is an amount of money given by the family of the bride to the family of the groom. The gift is intended as compensation for the cost of the groom's education necessary to secure his future earnings. Abuse of the dowry system by unscrupulous parents-in-law has sometimes resulted in the "accidental" death of the wife and thus the opportunity to seek a new daughter-in-law along with her dowry. Although Indian law has banned the practice, unfortunately it still occurs from time to time, especially in certain regions and among upper-caste Hindus.[47]

Not surprisingly, most Hindus fulfill the grihasthin life-stage duties by marrying and having a family. In this respect, Hinduism shares with Judaism and Islam the belief that the married state is sanctioned by divine law and thus constitutes a serious duty that should not be ignored. In the ashrama system it is an important step on the way to ultimate liberation. However, where Hinduism begins to depart from the **Semitic religions** is the existence of two more life stages beyond that of the householder in which celibacy is seen as the higher way.

In fact, the first stage of the brahmacarin or student requires self-restraint and celibacy (although this is also the expectation of Judaism and Islam in regard to young single persons). It is interesting to note that the term *brahmacarin* has now become synonymous with celibacy. However, what is more noteworthy is that the third stage, which follows the householder, is known as **vanaprasthin** – the forest-dweller. According to the Laws of Manu, when a householder sees "his skin wrinkled, his hair white and the sons of his sons"[48] he should leave behind the familiar world of society and assume the lifestyle of the religious ascetic. Now that his duties as householder are complete, in that his sons have married and he has seen the birth of his grandchildren, he should abandon the material world for the world of the spirit. His dwelling place is no longer in the family home but in the solitude and silence of the forest. According to tradition, his wife was permitted to accompany him during the third ashrama, but the expectation was that their relationship would be celibate. In Hindu spirituality, sexual abstinence is seen as a means to facilitate meditation. Sexual energy is rechanneled up through the spine and into the mind where it activates higher levels of consciousness. In practice, very few Hindus progress to this demanding ashrama since most remain in the householder stage as husbands, fathers, and grandfathers.

Those who do undertake the arduous lifestyle of the forest-dweller are essentially preparing themselves for the fourth and final ashrama: the **sannyasin**, or ascetic. There is really only a difference of degree between the third and fourth ashramas. The forest-dweller is permitted to maintain some contact with society. He may continue to use fire to cook his meals and may enjoy the company of his wife albeit in a platonic relationship. However the fourth stage requires absolute renunciation. A sannyasin no longer uses fire for cooking but must rely entirely on natural food or begging. Setting aside his name and family, a sannyasin will often burn an effigy of himself to symbolize the utter severance of all ties with his past and the material world. Such persons are considered to be already liberated from the wheel of **reincarnation**. They have died to the world and have achieved **moksa** (liberation), even though they still live. They are considered so holy that when they die their corpses are not cremated but simply placed in a river or lake.

Thus, for Hinduism there is an appropriate time for marriage and sexual activity (the householder stage), and for celibacy (the forest-dweller and ascetic stages). At a certain age, there is a divine duty to marry and have children, and at another age the spiritually advanced should move beyond material concerns and earthly passions to embrace the life of abstinence and renunciation. The ideal that the same adult person should adopt both states of life at different phases of the journey is unique among the five world religions. However, the acknowledgment that both marriage and celibacy serve a purpose and possess genuine value is similar to the other Semitic religion that considers matrimony to be part of the divine plan and a symbol of a heavenly reality, but whose founder never married.

Bride of Christ

According to the gospel of **John**, Jesus's first miracle was performed at a wedding feast in the village of Cana, where he turned six large jars of water into wine. Moreover, one of most common images in his parables is the wedding banquet which functions as a familiar symbol for the more abstract notion of the Kingdom of God.[49] The choice of a wedding as the venue for his first public sign and as a prominent pedagogical theme in his teaching is an apt one given that the preacher and his audience were Jewish. **Jesus** and his listeners would have appreciated the high-spirited joy of wedding celebrations and have shared the Jewish understanding of marriage as an integral part of God's plan. The Christian theology of marriage has inherited much from the Jewish tradition, including the classical expression of its threefold purpose found in the books of Genesis and Hosea.

Christian churches frequently teach that the first purpose of marriage is lifelong partnership between two persons, as expressed in Genesis chapter 2. The human individual is essentially a relational being and the most intensive, intimate form of relationship is the unique love that finds its fulfillment in wedlock. Thus Christianity stresses the exclusivity of such love and views adultery as a grave offense against one's partner and God. The second purpose of married life is the generation of children which flows naturally from the conjugal love of husband and wife. In the spirit of Genesis chapter 1, fertility is a gift from God who invites humans to cooperate with him in the ongoing creation of the world. Thus churches often insist that married couples explicitly declare their willingness to have children before the marriage can be blessed. As in other religions, Christians share the belief that marriage is the ideal social institution in which children should be conceived and raised. Marriage channels the powerful sexual drive and safeguards against sexual sins.[50]

The third purpose of marriage takes up the theme, expressed by the Jewish prophet Hosea, that God is married to the people of Israel. However in the Christian version it is applied to the relationship between Christ and the Church. **Paul**'s letter to the Ephesians provides its classical expression:

> In the same way, husbands should love their wives as they do their own bodies. He who loves his wife loves himself. For no one ever hates his own body, but he nourishes and tenderly cares for it, just as Christ does for the church, because we are members of his body. "For this reason a man will leave his father and mother and be joined to his wife, and the two will become one flesh." This is a great mystery, and I am applying it to Christ and the church.[51]

In other words, Christian marriage not only formalizes the exclusive, fruitful love between two human persons, but also mirrors a more profound transcendent reality: the love of the risen Christ for the community of the faithful. Actually, two metaphors are intertwined here: the Church as the body of Christ and the Church as the bride of Christ. The body of Christian believers is seen both as Christ's physical presence in the world and as his beloved spouse.

For this reason the **Orthodox** and **Catholic** traditions include matrimony as one of the seven **sacraments** (see box 4.1) – official ecclesiastic rituals that mark specific moments in Christian life and confer God's special grace in particular ways. As a channel of God's love and a mirror of a higher divine reality, Christian marriage is thus a sacred reality that commands the highest respect. Although most **Protestant** churches admit only two sacraments (**baptism** and the **Eucharist**), they agree on the importance and nobility of marriage, often describing it as one of the divine "ordinances" by which God's favor is shown to us. In Christian denominations, marriage is seen as part of God's design and as a means of sanctification.

As in other religious traditions, the rich theology of marriage is manifest in the wedding ceremony itself. As a public declaration of love, Christian weddings are usually conducted in a place of worship, in the presence of the Church's representative (the minister), official witnesses (groomsmen and bridesmaids), and the believing community itself. The ceremony can vary considerably depending on denomination and culture but usually there is a selection of pertinent scriptural readings such as references to prominent Old Testament couples, the gospel story of Cana, a parable of the wedding feast, or the passage from Ephesians mentioned above. The minister may then deliver a sermon on the joys and duties of marriage. The central part of the rite involves the wedding vows which are essentially solemn public promises by the bride and groom that they will love and honor each other for the remainder of their days. Rings are blessed and exchanged and the couple is declared husband and wife. The register is signed, the bride and groom are blessed, and the new union is celebrated by family and friends at the wedding reception. Today many churches symbolize the union of the two groups of kin by having the couple light a single candle from two family

---

PRAYER FROM AN EASTERN ORTHODOX WEDDING RITE   Box 6.3

O Lord our God, who didst accompany the servant of the patriarch Abraham into Mesopotamia, when he was sent to espouse a wife for his lord Isaac, and who, by means of the drawing of water, didst reveal unto him that he should betroth Rebecca: Do Thou, the same Lord, bless also the betrothal of these thy servants, [*names*], and confirm the word which they have spoken. Establish them in the holy union which is from Thee. For Thou, in the beginning, didst make them male and female, and by Thee is woman joined unto the man as a helpmate, and for the procreation of the human race. Wherefore, O Lord our God, who hast sent forth Thy truth upon Thine inheritance, and Thy covenant unto Thy servants our fathers, even Thine elect, from generation to generation: Look Thou upon Thy servant [*name*], and upon Thy handmaid [*name*], and establish and make stable their betrothal in faith, and in oneness of mind, in truth and in love.

candles. In the Orthodox tradition, the priest places a crown (stephana) on the head of the bride and groom, signifying the new "kingdom," or household, that will be established by the couple. The stephana also evokes the image of the martyr's victory, indicating that a successful marriage will require self-sacrifice by both parties.[52]

There are also gestures that are reminiscent of Jewish and Hindu practices which express the union of the couple. In Orthodox Christianity, the bride and groom encircle the wedding table several times while the priest holds a Bible indicating that the word of God is their guide and that their love is endless like the circle in which they walk. In many denominations the wedding ceremony also includes the consumption of consecrated bread and wine as a sign of their communion with each other and with Christ. In a similar vein, the priest or minister will sometimes wrap the hands of the bride and groom in his own vestments as a symbol of how their lives are now interwoven as one.

Traditionally Christians have been encouraged to marry other baptized persons, in many cases members of the same denomination. Although interdenominational and interfaith marriages are now very common in Western society, Catholic canon law still officially describes such a situation as an "impediment" that requires the permission of the local bishop (usually given as a matter of course). Moreover, a marriage between a Christian and a non-Christian, while valid, is not considered a sacrament,

Figure 6.3
A Christian bride
and groom take
their vows before
the altar

and the Catholic partner must promise to do all that is reasonable to insure that the children are raised in the Catholic faith. Statistically, marriage has been a source of many conversions to Catholicism by the non-Catholic partner. The Orthodox tradition is even stricter on such matters. While a church wedding is possible for an Orthodox Christian who marries another baptized Christian, it is not permitted for marriage with a non-Christian.

The Christian ideal is that marriage is a permanent relationship and that divorce is contrary to the divine will, based on the explicit teaching of Jesus:

> Some Pharisees came to him, and to test him they asked, "Is it lawful for a man to divorce his wife for any cause?" He answered, "Have you not read that the one who made them at the beginning 'made them male and female', and said, 'For this reason a man shall leave his father and mother and be joined to his wife, and the two shall become one flesh?' So they are no longer two, but one flesh. Therefore what God has joined together, let no one separate." They said to him, "Why then did Moses command us to give a certificate of dismissal and to divorce her?" He said to them, "It was because you were so hard-hearted that Moses allowed you to divorce your wives, but at the beginning it was not so. And I say to you, whoever divorces his wife, except for unchastity, and marries another commits adultery."[53]

Despite the firm teaching of the founder, most Christian churches accept the reality of marriage breakdown and allow divorce and remarriage for pastoral reasons. The Orthodox tradition permits remarriage a second and even a third time but it is no longer considered a sacrament and the tenor of the ceremony is more restrained. The Protestant tradition likewise stresses the ideal of permanence but allows for divorce and remarriage within the Church. Even the Catholic Church, which is strictest in its interpretation of the permanence of marriage, has developed a process of annulment whereby a Catholic may remarry within the Church if it can be established that an element was lacking in the original marriage that prevented it from being considered a sacrament: for example, psychological maturity or the willingness to have children. Otherwise, Catholics who remarry outside the Church may not participate in Holy Communion until the situation is rectified.[54]

There is also some debate as to whether the permanence of marriage extends beyond death and into eternity. Mormons and some Orthodox Christians believe that marriage continues in heaven and thus is not automatically dissolved by the death of a partner. However the mainstream Christian position is that marriage lasts "until death do us part" and thus a person is free to remarry if their spouse dies. The key basis for this position is Jesus's response to a question regarding the true husband of a widow who remarries several times. His answer is instructive because it not only implies that marriage is restricted to this world, but it also alludes to the classical alternative to the married state and the reason why Jesus himself never married: "For in the resurrection they neither marry nor are given in marriage, but are like angels in heaven."[55] In other words, while married love is divinely ordained and a sacrament of the love of Christ for his bride, the Church, there is an even higher form of love that is an anticipation of the life of heaven itself: celibacy.

Given the Jewish view of marriage as a divine commandment, it would have been quite unusual for someone like Jesus to be still unmarried in his thirties. One gospel passage hints at the possibility that he may even have been ridiculed as a eunuch by his opponents, but it also reveals that his choice of the celibate life was a result of his absolute commitment to his vocation:

> For there are eunuchs who have been so from birth, and there are eunuchs who have been made eunuchs by others, and there are eunuchs who have made themselves eunuchs for the sake of the kingdom of heaven. Let anyone accept this who can.[56]

Although some Christians interpreted the passage in a literal sense,[57] the analogy of a "eunuch for the kingdom" of course refers to a spiritual castration: the free choice of celibacy for a higher purpose, classically expressed in the Christian monastic life. In the Catholic and Orthodox traditions, celibacy is seen as a more radical imitation of the founder, a sign of the world to come and a practical lifestyle that frees the person from the duties of family life for apostolic service to the Church and community. In this respect the nuptial image was applied to nuns who were known as "brides of Christ" and whose vows ceremony was modeled on a wedding in which she "married" the Lord. Monks and nuns, who renounced marriage and family, were traditionally seen to have chosen "the better way"[58] although the Protestant Reformation vigorously challenged this bias. Recent Catholic theology has also adopted a more balanced approach and acknowledges the intrinsic value of both states of life.

Compulsory celibacy has also been a condition of the clerical state in certain churches. Catholic priests are still required to be celibate by canon law although some exceptions exist.[59] Orthodox priests are allowed to be married, but the marriage must have taken place before ordination. However, Orthodox bishops are usually chosen from among the celibate monks or they must assume a celibate life if they are a married priest. The **Anglican Church** has no restrictions on the marriage of bishops and priests and most Protestant churches encourage their ministers to marry and raise a family.[60]

Thus Christianity shares with Judaism, Islam, and Hinduism a positive understanding of marriage as part of the divine dispensation. However the unmarried state of Jesus and the traditional Catholic and Orthodox leaning toward celibacy as a higher path not only resembles the Hindu forest-dweller tradition but also finds strong resonance in Buddhism where the founder was a husband and father who renounced married life for a more advanced path to liberation.

✳ The Renunciation

When the historical **Buddha** was born, a sage predicted that the young prince **Siddhartha** would grow up to become either a great ruler or a holy man. Intent on insuring that the boy assumed the throne after him, his father, the local ruler of the Sakya people, raised the boy in the artificial environment of the palace, immune from the distractions of a wider, darker world. When Siddhartha was about 16 years of age, he was married to a cousin named Yasodhara, who gave birth to a son, Rahula. As the years went by it seemed that Siddhartha's career would be a political one in accord-ance with his father's strategic plans. However, something happened one day that changed everything – it was the crucial turning point in his life, akin to the baptism of Jesus in the Jordan and Muhammad's first encounter with Gabriel in the Meccan hills. Despite his privileged existence, Prince Siddhartha was constantly troubled by a deep unease and curiosity. On that fateful day he asked his charioteer to take him outside the palace walls for a short excursion. Along the way he saw what Buddhists call the Four Sights: a sick person; an aging person; a corpse being carried in a funeral procession; and a holy ascetic (sannyasin). Disturbed by his first experience of illness, old age, and death, Siddhartha eventually made the most important decision of his career. He would leave his comfortable, privileged existence and embark on a spiritual quest for the ultimate meaning of life. It was a quest that ended one night under a tree at **Bodhgaya** when the prince gained supreme **Enlightenment** and became the Buddha. The moment of his departure from the palace is known in Buddhist tradition as the Renunciation, symbolized by the image of Siddhartha cutting his hair. To this day, Buddhist monks still shave their heads as a sign of complete detachment from ordinary, mundane life.

Figure 6.4
A new Buddhist novice with shaven head and robes

As we have already seen, the life and example of the founder has a profound influence on the way in which a religion understands the place of marriage and celibacy in life. Like Muhammad, and unlike Jesus, Siddhartha experienced marriage and parenthood first-hand. However, unlike Muhammad, and like Jesus, Siddhartha renounced the life of the householder for a higher path. The Renunciation of the Buddha definitively sets up monastic celibacy as the more advanced road to liberation in Buddhism. It is interesting to note that the name of Buddha's son, Rahula, is usually translated as "fetter" or "chain" – an implication that family responsibility was an obstacle to his true destiny. This is not to say that Buddhism condones abandonment of marital and parental responsibilities. The decision of the Buddha to leave behind his spouse and son is a very special circumstance, taken for the good of humankind. Moreover, in Buddhist tradition, Siddhartha returned home after some years and was recognized by his family as the Buddha, an acknowledgment that his Renunciation had been the correct decision in the bigger picture. As a further endorsement of this, his stepmother became the first Buddhist nun while Rahula, although still a minor, assumed the life of the itinerant monk with his father.[61]

Given the example set by Siddhartha, where does marriage fit into the Buddhist world view? Certainly there is no suggestion in Buddhism that married life is an evil to be avoided at all costs. The vast majority of Buddhists in the world are married with families, and Siddhartha's own treatment of his wife and child during the years of his marriage is considered to be exemplary in terms of lovingkindness. The Buddha's teachings contain a legacy of practical advice for spouses on the values and virtues needed to live happy and fulfilling married lives.[62] Marital fidelity is also implied by the third of the five fundamental Buddhist moral precepts, the **Pancasila**, which states that all Buddhists, not just monks, should refrain from improper sexual activity such as adultery and fornication.

However, in comparison to other world religions, Buddhism is less concerned with marriage in theory and less engaged with marriage in practice. Marriage is not understood by Buddhists to be an earthly symbol or sacrament of a divine–human relationship, neither is it seen as a sacred duty incumbent upon humans. There is no specific set of laws or instructions from the Buddha himself or the tradition with regard to issues such as interfaith marriage, polygamy, divorce, and remarriage. Neither is there any Buddhist wedding ceremony as such. In fact the involvement of the monks is minimal. In many Buddhist cultures, it was considered inauspicious to have monks attend a wedding ceremony partly because it was thought that their vow of celibacy could cause infertility, and partly because monks are primarily associated with the funeral service. According to the **Theravada** tradition, the **Vinaya Pitaka** prohibits a monk from being involved in any activity that might lead to a romantic relationship or marriage:

> Should any **bhikkhu** engage in conveying a man's intentions to a woman or a woman's intentions to a man, proposing marriage or paramourage – even if only for a momentary liaison – it entails initial and subsequent meetings of the Community.[63]

In practice, many Buddhist couples seek the blessing of monks at some stage before or after the wedding by visiting a Buddhist temple or inviting monks to the family home. This visit usually involves reverencing Buddha images, the recitation of **mantras**, and a short sermon by a monk. As on other occasions in life, material gifts such as food and clothing are offered to the monks in return for the transfer of good **karma**. Sometimes this is symbolized in some tangible way such as the pouring of water or the Thai custom of a string or ribbon connecting the couple to the monks, much the same as in funeral services. Monks are also consulted for astrological advice as to the most auspicious date for a wedding. However the wedding ceremony itself is usually a purely civil affair or is celebrated with non-Buddhist elements from the local culture. For example, in China, the wedding of a Buddhist couple is often performed with Confucian features, while in Japan the ceremony is usually carried out in a **Shinto** temple. In recent times, especially in **Mahayana** Buddhism, the traditional taboo on monastic involvement has been relaxed and weddings are now sometimes held in Buddhist temples with the blessing of the monks who are also able to issue the legal marriage certificate.[64]

Underpinning this general lack of involvement, even deliberate distancing, of monks from weddings is the fundamental principle expressed by the Buddha's own renunciation: celibacy is the more advanced spiritual path that brings one closer to **nirvana**. Although not inherently evil, the sexual desires and activity that constitute such a significant part of married life are seen as transient cravings that can impede our progress toward ultimate liberation. As the Sutta Pitaka states:

> This body comes into being through sexual intercourse. Sexual intercourse is to be abandoned. With regard to sexual intercourse, the Buddha declares the cutting off of the bridge.[65]

To reinforce the point, marital scenes are sometimes depicted on artistic renditions of the wheel of life, indicating that marriage can bind us to the cycle of reincarnation and postpone our final goal. Detachment from all sensual desires is the necessary means by which true inner peace can be found:

> Always, always, he sleeps in ease: the **brahman** totally unbound who doesn't adhere to sensual pleasures, who is without acquisitions and cooled. Having cut all ties and subdued fear in the heart, calmed, he sleeps in ease, having reached peace of awareness.[66]

The preference for sexual abstinence is also reflected in the common belief that only a celibate is really capable of becoming an **arhat**, someone who is so spiritually advanced that they will reach nirvana after death. The best that the married lay person can realistically hope for is that they are reincarnated as a monk or a nun in their next life.

For those who are ordained, celibacy is a serious matter. The classical scriptural text that outlines the rules for monastic life, the Vinaya Pitaka, is replete with material aimed at protecting the vow of celibacy. Engaging in sexual intercourse is one of the most serious infringements possible and an offending member is instantly expelled from the community. However, the Vinaya explicitly identifies and warns against a host of other situations that could **cause** a monk's thoughts or actions to be sexually compromised. For example, a monk should not travel alone with a woman or allow a woman to sew him special robes or have physical contact with a woman.[67]

It should be stressed that although monastic celibacy involves a substantial degree of self-control, it is a lifestyle that should be undertaken freely and without compulsion. Celibacy should flow naturally from the perspicacious mind that understands the illusory nature of the self and the unsatisfying nature of sensual pleasure. Furthermore, those who become Buddhist monks or nuns are not usually bound by lifelong vows and are thus free to leave at any stage. In some cultures, such as in Thailand, many young men join a monastic community for a short period of time, especially during the wet season. Even a brief period of such radical detachment earns good karma for the young man and his family. In Laos and Burma men occasionally return to the monastery for a temporary period after being married, provided that they obtain their wives' permission.

There are also exceptions to the general rule of celibacy for Buddhist monks and nuns such as the Nying-ma (Red Hat) sect in Tibet and certain groups in Korea. But perhaps the most striking example is Japanese Buddhism where the majority of monks are married with families. As long ago as the thirteenth century, the Japanese Buddhist reformer Shinran (d. 1262), founder of the **Jodo-Shin** school, radically advocated the marriage of monks. Shinran himself was married and had children. In his view celibacy implied a lack of faith in the Buddha **Amitabha** and unnecessarily alienated the monk from the experience of the ordinary layperson. Several centuries later, in the nineteenth century, the Meiji government strongly encouraged monks to marry. However, these are exceptions that prove the rule. Celibacy is still the norm in most Buddhist monastic traditions where the idea of a married monk is a contradiction in terms and a sign of the fading of the dharma as predicted by the Buddha.

SUMMARY

As a prominent rite of passage and a fundamental social institution in most cultures, marriage often constitutes an important element of religious practice. With the exception of Buddhism, the major religions have developed extensive theological interpretations of marriage in general and have profoundly shaped the wedding ceremony in particular. A comparison of the main elements across the religions reveals not only distinguishing differences in belief and practice, but also considerable overlap in terms of the meaning, purpose, and symbolism of marriage.

In their own way, each of the religions acknowledges that marriage is the formalization of a special union between two persons. Much of the symbolism associated with the wedding ceremony is about binding the couple and their families into a new relationship of mutual support and companionship. The exchange of promises, rings, wine, crowns, and garlands, which often constitutes the heart of the ceremony in the different traditions, symbolizes the coming together of two individuals and the establishment of a unique, permanent, and potentially fruitful relationship. The Judeo-Christian tradition draws on the biblical image of man and woman being essentially one flesh, while Hinduism tends to depict the conjugal bond as a reflection of complementary cosmic forces. The idea that marriage involves the creation of a new home is physically signified by the traditions of the Jewish huppah and the Hindu mandap.

The legal dimension of marriage is highlighted by some religious traditions more than others. The Islamic wedding ceremony is usually quite simple, focusing on the signing of the contract which implies rights and duties for both parties. A similar stress on the contractual aspect of marriage is reflected in the Jewish ketubah, which is solemnly read at the wedding and proudly displayed in the home. The public nature of the marriage contract is reflected in the roles of the official witnesses such as the best man and chief bridesmaid at Christian weddings. In the Hindu tradition the fire itself symbolizes the silent divine witness that blesses and validates the ceremony.

If the first purpose of marriage is spousal companionship, the second is procreation. Most religions welcome the birth of children, and traditionally teach that the proper place for their conception is within the parameters of married life. Thus premarital and extramarital sexual intercourse are considered to be serious infringements of the social and moral order. The duty to procreate is perhaps most strongly experienced in Judaism and Hinduism. For Jews, the first positive commandment in Tanach is to increase the human family. Similarly, classical Hinduism sees the conception of children, especially sons, as a sacred duty for a young man in the householder stage of life – an expectation reinforced by the desire to have one's funeral rites performed properly in order to insure safe passage to the next phase of existence.

Apart from its twofold purpose on the horizontal plane, marriage is also given religious significance on the vertical plane. Muslims see marriage as an act of obedience to God and thus as a genuine form of worship. Judaism and Christianity also see marriage as an earthly symbol of the mystical relationship between the divine and the human. God is Israel's faithful spouse, and the Church is the bride of Christ. Hinduism also acknowledges a transcendent dimension to marriage: the couple are mirrors of the love between divine partners such as Vishnu and Lakshmi, or Shiva and Parvati, as symbolized by the lavishness of Hindu wedding attire and bodily adornment.

The idea that marriage reflects the pure, exclusive love of the divine tends to lend itself more naturally to monogamy as the ideal form. Indeed this is the case in the majority of the five religions today although various forms of polygamy were practiced in past periods such as biblical and Vedic times. The obvious exception is Islam where a conditional form of polygyny is allowed – a tradition that stems from a social context in which widowhood was tantamount to penury and unmarried women faced a precarious existence. Islamic law limits the number of concurrent wives to four and the Qur'an insists that all wives must be treated fairly and equally.

All five religions consider marriage to be permanent, ideally, but also acknowledge that the ideal is often not achieved in reality. Jewish and Islamic law allow for religious divorce and remarriage. Despite the explicit teaching of Jesus against divorce, most Christian churches also have processes in place to enable divorced believers to remarry in a religious ceremony. Arguably Hinduism sets the highest expectations in this regard, especially for upper-caste women where remarriage after the death of the husband was traditionally frowned upon and the practice of sati was an extreme expression of such unconditional fidelity and companionship.

The religious affiliation of the spouse has also been an important consideration in most traditions where marriage to a non-believer has been either discouraged or even prohibited. Muslim men are permitted to marry Jewish and Christian women on the basis that the People of the Book share with Muslims a fundamental belief in monotheism. The converse is not allowed on the presumption that the faith of the children is determined by the father. Similarly, Jews and Christians have traditionally been expected to marry within the faith, or even within one's specific denomination in the case of Christianity. Such limitations have now been eroded by contemporary social and cultural forces in most Christian and more liberal Jewish communities. However, the choice of partner is still a serious matter within the Hindu world, not only in terms of religious belief but also in terms of caste, family background, and financial status.

Finally, attitudes to celibacy vis-à-vis marriage differ quite sharply across the five religions and, understandably, the example of the historical founder has considerable impact. At one end of the spectrum, Judaism and Islam concur that marriage is an integral part of God's plan for humankind and a basic duty for all believers. Consequently voluntary celibacy is seen as a failure to fulfill the divine command to marry and procreate. Muhammad's own life is a resounding endorsement of marriage – a long, monogamous relationship with his first wife, Khadijah, and subsequent marriage to 11 other women many of whom were widows and all of whom are considered to be highly respected "mothers of the faithful." The prophets of Jewish tradition were also married men and a rabbi is generally expected to take a wife and raise a family in order to gain full respect and authority.

Hinduism is more nuanced on the celibacy issue in that its classical system of four ashramas (life stages) allows for both lifestyles at different times. In the householder stage of young adulthood to middle age, there is a strong obligation on the Hindu believer to marry and have children. However, in later years, the ideal is a turning to the celibate life as "forest-dweller," where ordinary existence is abandoned and sexual energy channeled into spiritual enlightenment. Although few Hindus actually take such a radical step, those who do so are regarded as holy persons on the verge of final liberation from the cycle of rebirth. Christianity is similarly nuanced, although not in the Hindu sense of different lifestyles for different phases of life. Although Christianity sprang from a Jewish context, Jesus embraced a celibate life and thus set an abiding example that tilted the scales away from marriage for much of Christian history. Marriage is still a holy sacrament or ordinance that was sanctioned by God and considered to be the appropriate lifestyle for most Christians. But the radical imitation of Christ undertaken by the celibate monk and nun has been traditionally seen as the higher way, at least in Catholic and Orthodox traditions. Along with its suspicion of divine images, the Protestant downplaying of monastic celibacy places it closer to the Jewish and Islamic positions.

Vindication of the celibate life is even more powerfully epitomized in the life of Siddhartha who left his wife and child for a more advanced spiritual path. That crucial moment, known as the Renunciation, established monastic celibacy as the nobler pathway to nirvana, and much of the Vinaya Pitaka is devoted to protecting the monk and the nun from situations in which their vows might be compromised. Consequently, of the five religions Buddhism is the strongest endorser of celibacy and the least interested in marriage. As with birth rituals, there is really no such thing as a Buddhist wedding ceremony as such, and the involvement of the monks has traditionally been discouraged. Buddhism's primary focus on liberation from distracting earthly desires has meant the avoidance of anything that might bind one to the wheel of reincarnation, including the sexual desire that lies at the heart of the conjugal relationship. Although the Buddha left a legacy of wise advice on what is required for a successful marriage, his own example and the thrust of his philosophy point to the higher path of sexual abstinence.

DISCUSSION TOPICS

1   Is celibacy a more spiritual lifestyle than marriage? What are the advantages and disadvantages of religious celibacy?
2   Why does the Catholic Church still insist on a celibate priesthood?
3   Compare the lifestyle and role of Buddhist and Christian nuns.
4   Compare the Jewish Song of Songs and the Hindu Krishna–Radha stories. Is it appropriate to apply sexual or erotic imagery to the divine?
5   Why do feminists criticize traditional religious views about the roles of husband and wife? How far does this critique apply to each religion?
6   What does each religion teach about sexual activity outside of marriage?
7   What does each religion teach about contraception?
8   What does each religion teach about homosexuality?

9   Why does Islam allow polygamy? What are the arguments for and against the practice?
10   Is it easy or difficult to obtain a divorce in each religion?

FURTHER READING

Bhaskarananda, Swami (2002). *The Essentials of Hinduism.* 2nd edn. Seattle: Viveka, pp. 35–46.

Browning, Don S., Green, M. Christian, & Witte, John Jr. (eds.) (2006). *Sex, Marriage and Family in World Religions.* New York: Columbia University Press.

De Lange, Nicholas (2000). *Introduction to Judaism.* Cambridge: Cambridge University Press, pp. 107–14.

Dessing, Nathal M. (2001). *Rituals of Birth, Circumcision, Marriage and Death among Muslims in the Netherlands.* Leuven: Peeters, ch. 4.

Kaelber, Walter O. (2004). "Ashrama," in Sushil Mittal (ed.), *The Hindu World.* Abingdon: Routledge, ch. 17.

Madan, T. N. (2003). "The Householder Tradition in Hindu Society," in Gavin Flood (ed.), *The Blackwell Companion to Hinduism.* Oxford: Blackwell, pp. 288–305.

Marcus, Ivan G. (2004). *The Jewish Life Cycle: Rites of Passage from Biblical to Modern Times.* Seattle: University of Washington Press, ch. 3.

Michaels, Axel (2003). *Hinduism: Past and Present.* Princeton, NJ: Princeton University Press, pp. 111–30.

Neusner, Jacob, et al. (eds.) (2000). *Judaism and Islam in Practice.* London: Routledge, part II.

Olivelle, Patrick (2003). "The Renouncer Tradition," in Gavin Flood (ed.), *The Blackwell Companion to Hinduism.* Oxford: Blackwell, pp. 271–88.

Ramon, Einat (2001). "Tradition and Innovation in the Marriage Ceremony," in Harvey E. Goldberg (ed.), *The Life of Judaism.* Berkeley and Los Angeles: University of California Press, ch. 8.

Segler, Franklin M., & Bradley, Randall (2006). *Christian Worship: Its Theology and Practice.* 3rd edn. Nashville: B & H Publishing Group, pp. 246–52.

Solomon, Norman (1996). *Judaism: A Very Short Introduction.* New York: Oxford University Press, pp. 91–6.

White, James F. (2001). *Introduction to Christian Worship.* 3rd edn. Nashville: Abingdon Press, pp. 276–95.

Wijayaratna, Mohan (1990). *Buddhist Monastic Life: According to the Texts of the Theravada Tradition.* Cambridge: Cambridge University Press, ch. 6.

NOTES

1   Zainab, Ruqayyah, Umm Kulthum, and Fatima. Shi'ite Muslims claim that only Fatima was Muhammad's daughter, the other three being children of Khadijah from an earlier marriage or her nieces. Khadijah also gave birth to two sons who died in infancy.

2 Muhammad's uncle, Abu Talib, who had effectively raised him and whose social and political influence provided much-needed protection, also died in the same year. The two deaths and the ongoing rejection of his message led to Muhammad's eventual decision to leave Mecca and establish himself in Medina.

3 Wasa'il al-Shiah, vol. 5.

4 Qur'an 4:4: "And give women their dowries as a free gift, but if they of themselves be pleased to give up to you a portion of it, then eat it with enjoyment and with wholesome result."

5 Qur'an 4:3.

6 When the revelation of the limit of four wives was revealed, Muhammad did not marry again. However he did not divorce any to reduce the number of wives to four since this would mean exposing them to further difficulties given their limited prospect of remarriage.

7 Qur'an 4:129.

8 For example, in 2006 the government of Chechnya considered changing marriage laws to allow Muslim men to take more than one wife as a response to the serious lack of men due to the war in that country.

9 Eight of Muhammad wives were widows: Khadijah, Sawda, Hafsa, Zainab bint Khuzayama, Umm Salama Hind, Zainab bint Jahsh, Ramalah, and Maymunah.

10 Qur'an 2:221.

11 Qur'an 5:5.

12 In **Shafi'i** law, the permission to marry Christian or Jewish women applies only to those living under Islamic law.

13 Qur'an 30:21.

14 See Qur'an 16:72.

15 See Qur'an 17:32; 24:1–3.

16 See Qur'an 2:187, 222.

17 There are rare cases of Muslim mystics living as celibates such as Rabi'a of Basra (d. 801) and Lalla Zaynab (d. 1904).

18 See Qur'an 13:38: "And certainly We sent apostles before you and gave them wives and children, and it is not in (the power of) an apostle to bring a sign except by Allah's permission; for every term there is an appointment."

19 Genesis 1:28.

20 Genesis 2:23.

21 Genesis 2:24.

22 See Hosea 2:14–16; Song of Songs, *passim*.

23 Even today many elderly Yemenite and Ethiopian Jews are polygamous and those who migrated to Israel in the 1940s and 1950s were allowed to retain their wives under a special dispensation.

24 Mourning days include Tishri 3 (the Fast of Gedaliah), Tevet 10, Tammuz 17, Av 9, and Adar 13 (the Fast of Esther).

25 It also serves to ensure that the groom is marrying the correct girl, recalling the story of Jacob who is fooled by his father-in-law into marrying Leah, the sister of his intended bride since he could not see her face. See Genesis 29:20–30.

26   Exodus 21:10; Talmud Ketubot 61b.

27   Talmud Yevamot 89a.

28   See Genesis 18:1–8. The theme of hospitality is also prominent at the Passover meal where a cup is set aside for the unexpected visitor who may turn out to be the prophet **Elijah**.

29   Some interpret this custom in terms of Joshua and the Israelite army circling the walls of Jericho seven times before they miraculously collapsed. In the case of marriage, the walls that divide the couple will fall and their souls be united. In more progressive communities, the groom also circles the bride.

30   Talmud Berakhot 31a.

31   See Psalm 137:5. **Kabbalist** Judaism sees the breaking of the glass as a symbol of the broken fragments of creation which is in need of spiritual repair.

32   This is based on the biblical injunction to "Love your neighbor [*re'acha*] as yourself" (See Leviticus 19:18) where "neighbor" can also be understood as "spouse."

33   Deuteronomy 7:3. Some have described the increasing rates of marriage to non-Jews as the "silent holocaust." See also Ezra 9:10–15.

34   Deuteronomy 24:1.

35   This is known as the Lieberman clause in **Conservative** Judaism.

36   Talmud Yevamot 62b, 63a. Marriage was so important that if finances were at stake, one should sell a Torah scroll in order to marry (see Talmud Megillah 27a). According to the Shulhan Aruch, only one who is married should lead the congregation in worship, just as the High Priest was required to be married in biblical times (Shulhan Aruch, Orach Hayim 581:1).

37   Jeremiah 16:1–4.

38   The Essene community lived a monastic life at Qumran on the shores of the Dead Sea. Their writings were discovered in the mid twentieth century and are known as the **Dead Sea Scrolls**.

39   See Philo, *De Vita Contemplativa*, 68, 21–39. The Therapeutae were a monastic community of Hellenized Jews living beside Lake Mareotis near the city of Alexandria.

40   Henna is a tropical shrub whose leaves, when dried and ground into a paste, give out a rusty-red pigment. It possesses a cooling property and has no side effects on the skin.

41   The circumambulation of the fire is known by various names throughout India, including Pratigna-Karan, Parikrama, Pradakshina, Mangal Fera, and Pheras.

42   See Section 7(2) of the Hindu Marriage Act 1955.

43   Sometimes the couple are also asked to look at the bright star Vasistha in the constellation of Ursa Major and its close companion Arundhati. These twin stars (known in Western astronomy as Mizar and Alcor) represent a faithful couple from Hindu legend.

44   See Rg Veda 10.173.4; 7.66.16. The ideals of fidelity and reliability are also expressed in another Hindu wedding custom known as the Shila Arohan, or Ascending the Stone. The bride steps onto a stone slab or millstone as a symbol of steadfast faithfulness to her husband.

45   This is the appropriate context for the well-known Hindu text on the art of sexual love, the Kama Sutra.

46   The term *sati* is derived from the name of a goddess who burned herself alive because of her father's objections to her love for Shiva. Some of the socio-religious factors that

contributed to the practice include: the belief that a widow could expect little of life after her husband's death, especially if she was childless; the halo of respect associated with the sacrifice; the sense that a widow was a drain on the family's resources; and the taboos associated with a widow as a source of impurity and misfortune.

47 The converse practice of a bride-price or payment by the groom to the family of the bride is more common in lower castes. The reason for the inversion is that lower-caste women are expected to engage in manual wage-earning work and thus contribute to the family income whereas the upper-caste wife is often seen as a non-income-earning financial burden.

48 Laws of Manu VI.2.

49 For example see Matthew 9:15–16; 22:1–15; 25:1–13; Luke 14:8–14.

50 See 1 Corinthians 7:9.

51 Ephesians 5:28–32.

52 The first Christian martyr was Stephen whose name is derived from the Greek term for crown. See Acts 7:55–60.

53 Matthew 19:3–9.

54 See Catechism of the Catholic Church 1665.

55 Matthew 22:30.

56 Matthew 19:12.

57 For example, the third-century Christian scholar Origen is said to have castrated himself on the basis of a literal reading of this passage.

58 A reference to the gospel episode where Jesus visits the home of two sisters, Mary and Martha. Jesus remarks that Mary has chosen the better part by sitting and listening to him, rather than her sister Martha who is busy preparing the food. Christian tradition has seen the two women as symbols of the monastic and married life respectively. See Luke 10:39–42; Matthew 19:29.

59 For example, Anglican priests who converted to Catholicism and were ordained have been allowed to remain married. Also certain Eastern Catholic rites, such as the Lebanese Maronite rite, have married priests.

60 The Protestant Reformers felt that the oath of celibacy undermined the holiness of marriage and was a key reason for widespread sexual misconduct by the clergy at the time. See Calvin, *Institutes of the Christian Religion*, IV.12.23–8.

61 Rahula asks Siddhartha for his inheritance, and the Buddha answers that he is heir to the greatest treasure of all – the **dharma**, or Buddha-truth.

62 For example see Anguttara Nikaya 8.54.

63 Suttavibhanga, Sanghadisesa 5.117.

64 The Mahayana tradition tends to interpret the Vinaya rule cited above in a different manner, namely, as a prohibition on a monk facilitating an immoral sexual relationship between two persons. Thus Mahayana monks are more likely to be registered as marriage celebrants and to perform the wedding ceremony in a temple.

65 Anguttara Nikaya 4.159.

66 Anguttara Nikaya 3.34.

67 See Suttavibhanga, Sandhadisesa 1.90; 2.100; 4.115; Suttavibhanga, Parajika 1.45; Suttavibhanga, Nissaggiya Pacittiya 4.182; 17.214; Suttavibhanga, Pacittiya 7.280; 22.323; 27.329.

Chapter 7

FOOD

CONTENTS

Introduction

It is generally acknowledged that the two most basic physical necessities of human existence are food and clothing. As corporeal beings in time and space, our bodies need inner nourishment and external protection. These two ordinary aspects of daily life also constitute an important part of religious practice and are thus invested with extraordinary meaning. In this chapter we focus on religious practices involving food, drink, and meals. What types of food does faith favor or forbid? What principles lie behind traditional food taboos? How does food reflect the relationship between fellow believers, and between the believer and divine reality? What role does food play in worship and the quest for salvation or liberation?

⚙ Ahimsa and Samadhi

Soon after the young **Siddhartha Gautama** renounced the comfortable, protected life of the palace in search of a higher spiritual truth, he joined a small group of wandering ascetics. For several years he adopted their radical lifestyle of utter detachment from material pleasures including a severe regime of fasting and self-discipline. Although such extreme measures were meant to liberate the spirit from the enslaving passions of the body, Siddhartha eventually came to the realization that these practices led to emaciation rather than emancipation. He was simply becoming seriously ill. Thus, one day, to the utter consternation of his companions, he decided to break the strict fast and take a meal. It was to be a prelude to the fateful moment when, now strengthened by the nourishment, Siddhartha spent an entire night under the bodhi tree in meditation and became the **Buddha**. It is for this reason that Buddhism often describes itself as "the middle way." For the Buddha, truth lies between two extremes and this applies also to the most basic of human needs – food. Neither indulgent hedonism nor excessive mortification benefits the mind's search for enlightenment and liberation. The body should be neither pampered nor neglected. Hence Buddhist monks and nuns have always eaten responsibly, but they also fast on a daily basis by not taking any food after the midday meal.

Apart from the daily monastic fast, are there other customs regarding what Buddhists should or should not eat? Does Buddhism have any food laws? The answer lies in the set of fundamental moral principles known as the **Pancasila**, or Five Precepts (see box 3.3 on p. 94). In particular, the first and fifth of these basic ethical norms have repercussions for the Buddhist diet, especially in terms of meat and alcohol.

The first precept of the Pancasila states that the believer must refrain from taking life. The intrinsic value of innocent human life is a common feature in most religious and moral systems, but the first precept is not limited to human beings in its application. Its scope is broader and neatly summed up by the term **ahimsa**, or unwillingness to harm. Ideally, all forms of life should be respected and violence in any form is to be avoided. In Buddhist thinking, violence begets violence and ultimately brings negative karmic consequences on the perpetrators themselves. The principle of ahimsa, which was eventually incorporated into Hinduism, was originally championed by the two influential ascetic religious movements of the fifth century BCE: Jainism and Buddhism. A more radical form of ahimsa is found in **Jainism** where the prohibition on killing applies to all forms of life including plants. Jains are famous for wearing masks over their mouths and padded sandals on their feet to avoid destroying the smallest of insects. Forbidden occupations include not only the slaying of animals but also the deliberate harvesting of crops for food. Thus they advocate the consumption of fruit that falls naturally to the ground. However, Buddhism tends to interpret ahimsa in terms of creatures with breath, namely animal life. Thus most Buddhists have no qualms about harvesting grains or picking fruits and vegetables. However, the question is whether the first precept of the Pancasila requires that a Buddhist refrain from eating meat.

There is some disagreement within Buddhism on this issue. Even those who are most committed to the middle way, the monks and nuns, are not always strict vegetarians. For example, Tibetan Buddhism does not practice total avoidance of meat partly because vegetables are difficult to grow in its poor soil and cold climate, and partly because its unorthodox **tantric** form of practice places less importance on abstinence from forbidden substances. However, red meat is preferred, where a single large animal is killed to feed many people thus minimizing the contravention of the ahimsa principle. Similarly, Japanese Buddhist sects such as Shingon and Tendai have also downplayed the need to avoid meat. On the other hand, Chinese and Vietnamese monks are generally expected to refrain from meat altogether, as well as certain pungent spices such as garlic, onion, and leek because these are considered to stimulate sexual desire if eaten cooked or to provoke anger if eaten raw.[1]

Buddhists who profess strict vegetarianism naturally base their argument on the principle of ahimsa. The eating of meat necessarily involves the slaying of animals in contravention of the first precept. Not only is there suffering on the part of the slaughtered beast, but its spirit is forced to begin the painful process of rebirth again. Although there is little scriptural support for strict vegetarianism in the **Theravada** Pali Canon, a number of later **Mahayana** writings explicitly condemn the consumption of meat.[2] One prominent example is the Mahaparinirvana Sutra. On the eve of his death, the Buddha orders his followers to abstain from meat on the basis that it undermines the compassion expected of a **bodhisattva**. The text also declares that monks should not consume meat even if it is given to them during the alms round (see box 7.1).[3] Similarly, the Lankavatara Sutra lists over 20 arguments in favor of vegetarianism[4] including: animals are reincarnations of fellow spirits on the wheel of **reincarnation**; meat is essentially impure and unhygienic; meat-eating spreads terror among animals; and human beings are not naturally carnivorous.[5]

However, according to the **Tipitaka, Sakyamuni** was not an absolutely strict vegetarian himself and his teaching on the issue is nuanced. In Buddhaghosa's account, the Buddha's last meal was tainted pork which purportedly caused his death, although Mahayana versions claim it was truffles. The Pali Canon suggests that there were occasions when he ate meat and even recommended certain types as a cure for particular illnesses. The incident most often quoted in this regard is the story of the conversion of General Siha who prepared a meal for the Buddha and his companions at which meat was served.[6] In this context the Buddha revealed his threefold guideline for monks: "Do not eat meat knowing that it has been killed specially for your use. I allow the

---

THE BUDDHA'S TEACHING ON EATING MEAT

Box 7.1

"This indeed is how the Bodhisattvas, custodians of my doctrine, should understand. Son of my lineage, even those who keep close company with me, must not eat meat. Even if, in a gesture of faith, almsgivers provide them with meat, they must shrink from it as they would shrink from the flesh of their own children." Then the Bodhisattva Kashyapa asked the Buddha, "But why indeed, O Lord and Tathagata, do you forbid the consumption of meat?" "Son of my lineage!" the Lord replied. "Eating meat destroys the attitude of great compassion." "But in the past, O Lord," asked Kashyapa, "did you not allow the eating of meat found suitable after it has been examined in three ways?" "Yes," the Buddha said. "I allowed the eating of meat found suitable after threefold examination, in order to assist those who were striving to overcome their habit of eating meat." (Mahaparinirvana Sutra)

---

use of fish and meat blameless in three ways, unseen, unheard and unsuspected."[7] Later, toward the end of Siddhartha's life, the monk Devadatta requested that he revise the rules concerning monastic diet and impose a total ban on meat-eating. The Buddha refused and reiterated the threefold rule.[8]

Thus Theravada Buddhism distinguishes between two kinds of meat: uddissakata-masa (blameful) and pavattamasa (blameless). Only the latter may be consumed by monks in good conscience. What constitutes "blameless" meat? The Buddha refers to three criteria: that the monk has not actually witnessed the killing of the animal; that the monk has not been told that the meat had been prepared specially for him; and that the monk does not suspect that such a meal was being prepared. This position acknowledges that there can be degrees of involvement in the killing of the animal. Direct involvement brings negative **karma** and hence the meat trade is listed among occupations that are inappropriate for Buddhists: "Business in weapons, business in human beings, *business in meat*, business in intoxicants, and business in poison."[9] But less direct involvement opens up the possibility that other factors be taken into account such as courtesy toward a host who offers food. Thus the principle of ahimsa is not necessarily violated provided the monk is adequately distanced from the negative karma associated with the animal's death. This is achieved by insuring that the meal has not been prepared specifically for him. Although the teaching is addressed to monks and nuns, it is often understood as an ideal toward which the laity should also strive.

Some argue that the threefold guideline applies only to monks who receive food on their alms round and thus have no say over what they are given. However, if monks purchase food from the marketplace then, like the slaughterer and the vendor, they too must accept the karmic implications. The stricter vegetarian position of the later Mahayana texts may reflect the fact that many Mahayana monasteries owned their own cultivated fields which enabled them to avoid reliance on donated food. In contrast, there has always been a stress in Theravada Buddhism on the alms round and thus humble acceptance of whatever is placed in the bowl including meat or even rotten food. The practice has been part of the daily routine of the Buddhist monk since the earliest times, although not all communities still practice it today. Many Buddha images depict the Enlightened One in the act of holding the alms bowl in his hands, just as the hand postures might also depict him teaching, meditating, or resisting temptation. The term for monk, **bhikkhu**, literally means one who begs, and the bowl was traditionally one of only five items the monk was allowed to possess.[10] Senior monks often pass their bowl on to a new generation of junior monks as a sign of succession within the community. Unlike Western society, which considers begging to be a pitiful sign of utter destitution, for Buddhists the practice is a symbol of the mutual relationship of support between monk and laity. The monk depends on the laity for material support while the laity depend on the monks for the provision of good karma and spiritual assistance.

The fifth precept of the Pancasila also impacts on Buddhist dietary practices. Whereas the first precept condemns violence and thus implies vegetarianism, the fifth condemns the use of any intoxicating substance and thus implies abstinence from alcohol and other mind-transforming drugs. Such a position is understandable given that the Buddhist Eightfold Path to **nirvana** is based on clear-minded wisdom and responsible moral action. The Buddha's last words stress the importance of awareness: "Behold, O monks, this is my last advice to you. All component things in the world are changeable. They are not lasting. Strive with clarity of mind to gain your liberation." According to the Buddha's final injunction, the quest for liberation requires **samadhi** – the intense mental concentration that enables one to enter into deep states of meditation and enlightenment. While alcohol and drugs can alter one's mental state, Buddhism traditionally sees their effects as negative and in direct opposition to samadhi. Although most Buddhist cultures have not prohibited alcoholic drinks, monks and nuns are expected to embrace total abstinence.

A well-known Mongolian folk story makes the point. A Buddhist lama was on a journey among the nomadic tribes who gave him food and accommodation in exchange for his advice and good karma. One night he was offered lodging by a young single woman on condition that he would do one of three things: sacrifice a goat; sleep

Figure 7.1
Buddhist monks carrying bowls on their daily alms round

with the woman; or drink alcohol. After pondering his dilemma, the monk decided that the third option was the least harmful. However, after several hours he became drunk. In his intoxicated state, the sound of the goat annoyed him so much that he killed it, and when he woke up the next morning he found that he had slept with his hostess.

The fifth precept does not imply that alcohol in itself is evil, but rather warns against its inebriating effects which cloud judgment, reduce self-control, and undermine the other four precepts. Similarly, the first precept does not imply that meat in itself is evil, but rather that the process by which meat is obtained involves the violent death of animals which undermines the principle of ahimsa. Buddhist dietary practice suggests that it is moral attitude and action that render one impure rather than the food or drink that one consumes.[11] Buddhist concerns about meat and alcohol are not focused on the substances themselves but on their potential to bind one to the wheel of **samsara** and thus postpone nirvana. This intrinsic link between food and liberation from samsara is also a strong theme in Hinduism where diet affects spiritual purity and devotees eat the blessed leftovers of food offerings to the gods.

Blessed Leftovers

Hinduism places such great emphasis on the role of food that it has been appositely called "the kitchen religion." The regular social greeting "Have you eaten?" carries the same meaning as "How are you?" in Western cultures, hinting not only at the importance of physical nourishment but its socio-religious significance as well. As with most things Hindu, there is enormous diversity. Many culinary customs stem from the ancient **dharmashastras** but vary from region to region, depending on factors such as climate, geography, and culture. However, the link between food and spiritual purity is a common feature across the many sects, and general patterns can be identified.

Like Buddhism, Hinduism sees a fundamental connection between the food that is consumed and the quest for liberation from the cycle of reincarnation. Eating and drinking are relevant to the **atman**'s search for **moksa**, since these fundamental human activities have the potential to generate significant amounts of good or bad karma, thus facilitating or impeding its progress. Whereas Buddhist restrictions regarding meat and alcohol are essentially based on the principles of non-violence (ahimsa) and clarity of mind (samadhi) respectively, the more extensive Hindu food taboos are primarily aimed at protecting the believer from spiritual pollution. Insuring that one eats the correct food types that have been prepared in the correct manner and consumed in the correct company is a lifelong concern for devout Hindus.

One aspect of Hindu life in which food and dining are particularly pertinent is **jati**, or **caste**. The English term is derived from the Portuguese *casta*, meaning pure, and is related to the word *chastity*. It correctly implies that the complex caste laws are essentially about avoiding contamination. Disregarding these rules is to risk becoming impure. All Hindus should abide by their caste duties if they are to make progress toward liberation, but the danger of pollution is most felt by those at the top of the hierarchy for whom food laws are the most restrictive. Consequently, caste boundaries are rigorously defined and enforced in a number of ways such as physical segregation, restrictions on marriage partners, and especially meals.

There are many factors that directly affect the purity of a meal including how the food is prepared, who prepares it, and with whom one dines. In terms of preparation, it is vital that the cooking is performed in an unpolluted environment. Although it may come as a surprise to Western ears, the kitchen is therefore the purest room in the house, so much so that Hindus feel comfortable storing their household images (**murti**) there. Access to a Hindu kitchen is usually designed so that strangers, lower-caste persons, animals, and restless spirits cannot enter. For example, in Nepal many kitchens are located on the first floor of the house. The kitchen is often cleaned and purified every day and those engaged in cooking bathe beforehand and wear clean clothing.

The person preparing the food must also be unpolluted because it is widely believed that the consciousness of the cook enters the food and influences the mind of the consumer. Cooked food in particular is vulnerable to the essence of the person preparing it. Thus the caste of the cook is an important consideration and upper-caste cooks and waiters, if they are available, have traditionally been in high demand in restaurants and temples, although such customs are gradually being eroded in contemporary urban life. Conversely, members of the upper caste endeavor not to accept food cooked or offered to them by members of lower castes.

Purity is also contingent upon those with whom one eats. Sharing a meal is not simply a question of eating and drinking at the same time and in the same place. Dining with another person carries rich layers of social implications in all human cultures. In Hinduism, where food itself is particularly sensitive to pollution, there is heightened concern for purity at mealtimes. Caste laws generally require that a person dines only with members of the same caste or those just above or below. Thus Hindus are careful about whom they invite to dinner and are cautious about taking food communally.

Food and purity are linked in terms not only of caste distinction but also of individual spiritual advancement. In the Hindu world view, the food that one consumes has a profound influence on the spirit as well as the body. As the Chandogya **Upanishad** declares: "Of curd when it is churned, that which is its subtle part rises upward and that becomes clarified butter. In this very way, of food when it is eaten, that which is the subtle part, that rises upward, and that becomes mind."[12] We are what we eat in more than just the physical sense and thus a proper diet is essential for progress on the path to moksa.

Such a diet would include food types that purify and exclude those which pollute. An entire section of the **Laws of Manu** is dedicated to this topic,[13] although in practice there is considerable variation from place to place. Many food customs are based on elements such as whether the food is raw or cooked, boiled or fried, grown above ground or below, prepared at home or elsewhere. As in Buddhism, pungent substances such as onions and garlic are often thought to stimulate improper desires and thus inhibit moral behavior. Similarly many Hindus abstain from alcohol although there is no absolute ban on intoxicants as in Buddhism. In fact, the Vedic texts make frequent positive reference to a ritual drink known as soma whose intoxicating effects induced altered states of mind.[14] Some foods are innately pure such as the products of the cow including milk, yogurt, and especially clarified butter known as ghee. Moreover food that is fried in ghee is considered purer and safer than food that is prepared in water, which is more susceptible to polluting influences. Thus fried foods are categorized as pukka, or preferred, and can be eaten outside of the home and even across caste boundaries to some extent. In contrast, boiled foods are described as katcha, or poor quality, and must be prepared in the purity of one's own kitchen.[15]

Of the various Hindu sects, **Vaishnavism** possesses a developed theology of food that places edibles into three categories based on the **gunas**, or fundamental qualities that shape the universe and all beings within it.[16] The first and highest guna is sattva, which refers to superior qualities such as wisdom, compassion, tranquillity, and nobility. According to the **Bhagavad Gita**, sattvic food is tasty, "soothing and nourishing."[17] It is purifying to the mind and healthy for the body. It facilitates meditation and generates energy and vitality. Sattvic foods include vegetables, fruits, nuts, and dairy products. The second guna is rajas, which describes personal qualities such as courage, decisiveness, passion, and strength. The Gita tells us that rajasic foods are "acid and sharp, and salty and dry."[18] Such food excites the emotions and generates actions and passions but it also distracts the mind from higher spiritual things. Rajasic foods include meat, fish, eggs, spices, onions, tea, coffee, and tobacco. The third guna is tamas, which refers to negative qualities such as lethargy, dullness, ignorance, and inertia. Thus tamasic foods are stale, tasteless, juiceless, and impure such as leftovers, half-cooked or overcooked foods.[19]

Meat is sometimes listed as a tamasic food and is thus something to be avoided. Indeed, there is a strong tradition of vegetarianism in Hinduism, especially among members of the **brahmin** class which is associated with sattvic qualities and carries higher expectations than in other classes. Even for those who eat meat, beef is usually forbidden and pork often restricted. As with Buddhism, the principal motivation behind Hindu vegetarianism is ahimsa or non-violence. The Laws of Manu warn of the karmic consequences of eating meat: "Meat can never be obtained without injury to living creatures, and injury to sentient beings is detrimental to (the attainment of) heavenly bliss; let him therefore shun (the use of) meat."[20] However, the specific ban on beef is linked to the special status given to the cow in Hinduism as a result of several factors. First, the cow plays an important role in India's economy. The Hindi word for cow, *aghnaya*, literally means "not to be killed." In ancient times, cattle rather than cash was the primary indicator of a person's wealth and the shift from nomadic pastoralism to settled agriculture meant that the cow became an even more vital asset on the farm. It made sound economic sense to protect the cow rather than slaughter it for its meat which was difficult to preserve in a tropical climate anyway. After 1000 BCE it became an offense to eat beef and those who worked with leather were considered outcastes. Second, the cow was even more revered as it became the sign of religious and national identity. Converts to Islam and Christianity were often given a meal of beef to signify their complete abjuration of the Hindu faith. At the same time, leaders like **Dayananda Saraswati** and Mahatma **Gandhi** promoted the cow as the symbol of Indian independence and Hindu faith during the years of British colonial occupation. Third, the cow is seen by Hindus as a supreme example of generosity because it provides so many beneficial products and asks nothing in return except a grassy paddock. Not surprisingly, dairy products are considered to be inherently auspicious and capable of purifying other foods as well.

Figure 7.2
A cow on an Indian street

Thus far we have seen how food helps to safeguard against impurity by defining and reinforcing Hindu caste boundaries. Moreover different foods are categorized as beneficial or detrimental to a Hindu's spiritual well-being and are thus recommended or avoided accordingly. However, there is a third important link between food and faith in Hinduism that involves the consumption of food offered to the gods. The standard form of daily Hindu worship known as **puja** comprises simple acts of reverence and hospitality to the deity who is portrayed via the sacred image or murti. In most instances, the murti is bathed, clothed, adorned, and offered nourishment just as one would honor and respect an important guest. A range of foodstuffs such as rice, fruit, ghee, sugar, and sweets are set before the image according to certain specific rules, such as placing cooked food on the right and uncooked food on the left. It is believed that the divine guest consumes the invisible essence of the food, or bhogya. What remains are merely the physical leftovers known as **prasad** – a term that literally means mercy, compassion, or generosity.[21] Unlike Buddhists, who tend to distribute the leftovers from worship to beggars and animals, prasad is in great demand among Hindu believers because it is no longer ordinary food: it has become blessed leftovers.

As a key element of Hindu worship, prasad is rich in religious meaning. First, it reminds Hindus of the need to purify all daily meals by first offering it to the gods at the domestic shrine. As the Bhagavad Gita states: "The devotees of the Lord are released from all kinds of sin because they eat food which is offered first in sacrifice. Others, who prepare food for personal sense enjoyment, verily eat only sin."[22] But prasad is not confined to worship at home. Gaining an audience (**darshana**) with the deity through the sacred image and obtaining the blessed leftovers are major motivations for participation in temple worship. Temples throughout India freely distribute prasad on a regular basis after puja, especially among Vaishnavite and **Shakti** sects. Moreover the leftovers are usually distributed to all believers irrespective of caste or gender. Thus the second, and somewhat paradoxical, meaning of prasad is a meal that reflects the fundamental equality of all Hindus rather than reinforcing hierarchical and caste differences as meals usually do. Third, if prasad conveys equality among believers on the horizontal plane, then it is because all believers are utterly subordinate to the deity on the vertical plane. Just as the wife eats only after her husband and sons in the traditional Hindu home, so the believer dines on leftovers only after the deity has been satisfied.

Because prasad has passed the lips of the gods, it has been sanctified in some respect. Although these are leftovers, they are from the divine table and thus consumption of them brings the believer closer to the deity in a very physical sense. Although the wife eats after her husband, there is still a conjugal bond between the two who eat under the same roof and in the same household. Thus a fourth level of meaning arises for prasad: communion between the believer and their Lord. The double potential of Hindu prasad to symbolize not only the fundamental unity among believers on the horizontal plane but also intimate union between the divine and the human on the vertical plane, finds strong a resonance in Christianity where the central ritual involves a meal of bread and wine that is understood as a holy communion.

Bread and Wine

One of the most important features in many Christian churches is a piece of furniture that usually occupies central position either in the very middle or at the far end of the congregational seating. Variously described as an altar or a table, it is the place at which the principal Christian ritual is performed – the **Eucharist**. Over the centuries, the Eucharist has evolved into a variety of forms, ranging from casual gatherings to grandiose ceremonies. It has been interpreted in differing ways that have provoked some of the deepest divisions among Christians. But despite the many layers of **liturgical** accretions and theological controversies, it remains in essence a meal of bread and wine. As in Hinduism, at the heart of Christian worship one finds food and drink.

One of the earliest names for the Eucharist was the "breaking of the bread" and it was already common practice among the very first generation of Christians.[23] According to the **New Testament**, the ritual originated in certain words and actions of the founder during his final meal with his followers. We are told that, at his **Last Supper**, **Jesus** took some bread, broke it, and handed it to those present, declaring "Take, eat; this is my body." Similarly, he passed around a cup of wine with the words, "Drink from it, all of you; for this is my blood."[24] Scholars speculate that the occasion may have been a Jewish Passover meal which would have included unleavened bread and wine among other symbolic foods. Alternatively, some believe it was more likely a sabbath meal. Whatever the actual context, Jesus's unforgettable gesture was understood by the first Christians as the institution of a new rite, which the founder intended to be celebrated in his memory.

As noted above, the manner in which the Eucharist is celebrated today varies considerably across Christian denominations, but there are identifiable common features. The Eucharist is usually a communal event involving a gathering of believers who are led in prayer and ritual action by a president. **Catholic** and **Orthodox** Churches insist that the Eucharistic president must be an ordained male priest because they take on the role of Jesus at the Last Supper. Other Christian denominations allow women to preside because they do not consider masculinity to be as essential for the part.

The Eucharist typically involves readings from the Christian Bible accompanied by a sermon and other prayers including petitions for a variety of needs. Many churches organize the biblical readings around annual cycles so that a selection of holy text is proclaimed and pedagogically expounded over a specific period of time. For many Christians, especially in the **Protestant** tradition, this is considered at least as important as the meal that follows in terms of spiritual nourishment. Consequently, the pulpit or stand, from which the readings are proclaimed and the sermon delivered, is often positioned more centrally and referred to as the "table of the word."

The bread and wine are prepared beforehand on the altar/table or, in some churches, brought to it in a formal procession. The president prays over the bread and wine, using a formula that incorporates the words of Jesus from the Last Supper (see box 7.2). At the sound of those words, Christians believe that the Holy Spirit descends upon the food and consecrates it. After further prayers, the sanctified bread and wine are then distributed to the congregation for consumption, although in some churches, especially in the Catholic tradition, only the bread is given for practical reasons. Many churches use a form of unleavened bread on the presumption that this is what would have been used at the Last Supper if it was a Passover meal. However, Orthodox churches and some Protestant Christians prefer to use leavened bread. Similarly, most churches use alcoholic wine as in the Jewish tradition, although many Protestant congregations prefer non-alcoholic grape juice because of their commitment to temperance. There is also debate today as to whether Christians from cultures in which wheat is a foreign grain should use their own traditional staple food for the Eucharistic "bread." The issue is one that surfaces often in religion where a choice has to be made between fidelity to the historical tradition and relevance to a new contemporary situation.

There are also differences between churches concerning the preferred name of the ritual, its frequency, and the appropriate age of reception. Orthodox Christians refer to it as "the divine liturgy"; Catholics speak of "**the Mass**," while Protestant communities

---

Prayer from an Anglican Rite of the Eucharist

Box 7.2

CELEBRANT: On the night he was handed over to suffering and death, Our Lord Jesus Christ took bread; and when he had given thanks to you, he broke it, and gave it to his disciples, and said, "Take, eat: This is my Body, which is given for you. Do this for the remembrance of me." After supper he took the cup of wine; and when he had given thanks, he gave it to them, and said, "Drink this, all of you: This is my Blood of the new Covenant, which is shed for you and for many for the forgiveness of sins. Whenever you drink it, do this for the remembrance of me." . . . We celebrate the memorial of our redemption, O Father, in this sacrifice of praise and thanksgiving. Recalling his death, resurrection, and ascension, we offer you these gifts. Sanctify them by your Holy Spirit to be for your people the Body and Blood of your Son, the holy food and drink of new and unending life in him. Sanctify us also that we may faithfully receive this holy Sacrament, and serve you in unity, constancy, and peace; and at the last day bring us with all your saints into the joy of your eternal kingdom. (Rite Two of the US Book of Common Prayer, 1979)

often use terms such as "communion service," "the Lord's Supper," and the biblical "breaking of bread." The frequency of celebration varies from a daily event in Catholic churches to occasional or even annual celebrations in certain Protestant traditions. The age at which children are allowed to start receiving Eucharist also varies from infancy in Orthodox churches to "first communion" at the age of reason in Anglican and Catholic traditions.

Given its strong links with Jesus's last explicit wish and its pride of place in Christian practice, it is not surprising that the Eucharist carries a rich array of theological meanings. The term *Eucharist* itself was in use by the end of the first century and literally means thanksgiving.[25] It possibly stems from the Jewish practice of giving thanks to God at meals for daily nourishment, but the gratitude expressed by Christians is for more than the gift of ordinary food and drink. As mentioned above, the central piece of furniture is described not only as a table around which the sacred meal is consumed but also as an altar on which a sacrifice is commemorated. The language of "body and blood" naturally evokes images of death, and clearly the dramatic words and actions of Jesus at the Last Supper were intended to shed light on the events of the following day. For Christians, his bloody crucifixion on Good Friday can only be properly understood in the light of Holy Thursday – not as a tragic death but as the unique and supreme self-sacrifice that brings definitive nourishment to a hungry world and thus renders all other forms of sacrifice (animal or otherwise) redundant.[26]

The "body" language of the Eucharist also evokes the important theme of **communion**. On the vertical plane, communion refers to the spiritual union established between the individual and Christ via the act of consuming the sacred bread and wine that are now understood to be his body and blood in some manner. In this sense, the

Eucharist has a strong hint of theophagy (the eating of one's God) which echoes to some extent the Hindu idea that food is Brahman and Brahman is food. Theophagy was characteristic of the mystery religions of the Roman Empire at the time Christianity emerged. Thus some have speculated that this is the real source of the Christian Eucharist since it seems unlikely that Jesus, as a Jew, would have commanded others to drink blood even in a symbolic sense. However, Eucharistic practice is found in the very earliest stages of Christianity when it was still predominantly Jewish, suggesting that the idea of eating his body and drinking his blood did originate with Jesus himself.[27] Irrespective of its precise origins, Christians today understand that the consumption of the consecrated bread and wine establishes an extraordinary and intimate communion between the believer and Christ. The physical appropriation of the man-God makes the Christian more godlike. As in Hinduism, we become what we eat.

Figure 7.3
Bread and wine used in a Christian Eucharist

Communion also operates on the horizontal plane between Christians themselves. The "body of Christ" refers not only to the consecrated bread used during the rite, but can also mean the body of believers, the Church.[28] The act of breaking a single loaf of bread and sharing a single chalice of wine signifies the fellowship among believers gathered around the table of the Lord.[29] Sadly, this communion has been broken by acrimonious theological disputes and shattering ecclesiastical divisions. Ironically, the great sacrament of Christian fellowship is actually a stumbling block to Christian unity today. For instance, although most churches welcome members of other Christian denominations at their Eucharistic celebrations, not all churches feel free to offer the sacred bread and wine to their guests. Catholic and Orthodox churches believe that until the differences in belief are resolved it is hypocritical to share the bread and wine as if there were complete unity. Protestant churches take a different approach, arguing that such reunification is possible only if the different denominations begin sharing the bread. For the Catholic Church, a Eucharist at which all Christians would receive the bread and wine is the goal of ecumenical discussions, whereas for Protestants, sharing the bread is the means toward the desired reunification of a fragmented Christianity.

One significant cause of these divisions is the conflicting ideas about what actually happens to the bread and wine during Eucharist. Most Christians accept the notion of a "real presence" of Christ in the sanctified bread and wine. However, Catholic and Orthodox theology have traditionally understood Jesus's phrase "this is my body" in a literal and permanent sense. In other words, for them the bread and wine actually become the body and blood of Christ, even though there is no change in their outward appearance. The classical theological formulation of this position is the medieval doctrine of transubstantiation which borrows the Aristotelian philosophical categories of "substance" and "accident" to explain the religious mystery. What is visible to the senses (accidents) does not change. What "stands beneath" these and constitutes the reality of a thing (substance) is miraculously transformed. It is ultimately a question of faith since nothing empirical could ever be observed or proven. But in the eye of the believer, what is consumed is no longer bread or wine but the real flesh and blood of the Savior.[30] High Anglican and Lutheran traditions profess a more nuanced approach in which the consecrated host is simultaneously bread and Christ's body.[31] The further one moves along the Protestant spectrum, the less literal and more symbolic the interpretation becomes.[32]

A direct consequence of the belief in transubstantiation is the practice of "reserving" remaining bread after the ceremony. In the Catholic Church, the consecrated wafers are placed in a receptacle known as a **tabernacle** [tent]. A lit candle burning beside the tabernacle indicates the presence of the sacred host, one of which is occasionally brought out and placed in an ornate container for viewing and prayerful adoration by the believers. Processions of the host are often held on the Catholic feast of Corpus Christi [Body of Christ] which was established precisely to reinforce belief in the real presence.[33] While most Protestant Christians do not reserve the sacred bread after the Eucharist has ended, many Christians agree that they may be set aside provided that the reason is to take them to the sick who are unable to attend the communion service.[34]

Apart from the significant role that food plays in its central ritual, Christianity does not have the sort of dietary restrictions that typify Buddhism and Hinduism. Christians fast and abstain from certain foodstuffs such as meat or sweets during the season of **Lent** (see chapter 10), and some churches promote the total avoidance of alcohol in a manner akin to the fifth precept of Buddhism. But otherwise there are few, if any, specifically Christian food laws. The reason for this lies in both the teaching of the founder himself and a key decision taken by the early Christian community. Mark's gospel reports Jesus's attitude to existing food customs: "'Do you not see that whatever goes into a person from outside cannot defile, since it enters, not the heart but the stomach, and goes out into the sewer?' (Thus he declared all foods clean)."[35] Furthermore, the Acts of the Apostles describes a vision experienced by Peter in which God declares all foods fit for consumption.[36] The context of both texts is the increasing admission of non-Jewish converts into the nascent community and the question of what precisely should be required of them. Just as Christianity no longer insisted on circumcision for its new members from pagan background, so too it further differentiated itself from its parent religion by abandoning the extensive system of Jewish food laws.

✡ Kosher

If Hinduism is sometimes called the "kitchen religion" because of its strong links between food and spiritual liberation, then Judaism could equally qualify for such a title given the considerable impact of its food laws on the dietary habits of its members. The generic term that gathers together the complex network of Jewish food rules and regulations is *kashrut*, from which the common term **kosher** (fitting or proper) is derived. In the broad sense, kosher can apply to a range of religious objects and processes, but in its narrow sense it refers to food that is fit for consumption according to Jewish law. In contrast, forbidden food is designated as treifah, which literally means torn.[37] The basis on which foods are categorized as kosher or treifah is the will of God, expressed in the **Torah**, elaborated in the **Talmud** and codified in classics such as the **Shulhan Aruch** [The Well-Set Table]. So which foods are kosher and which treifah? Before delving into the intricacies of kashrut, it is important to note that food is not rendered kosher by blessing prayers, even though the recitation of prayer at mealtimes is a vital part of Jewish practice and an expression of profound gratitude to the creator.

Similarly, although restaurants sometimes advertise "kosher-style" cooking, the manner of preparation is not relevant as it in Hinduism where fried foods are traditionally preferred over boiled foods. The definition of kosher food can be summed up in seven fundamental principles.

First, animal type is vitally important. The popular image that Jews cannot eat pork is true but its prominence is based on the fact that pork was popular in Europe and an important source of protein. There are in fact many other meats that are also banned by kashrut. According to the Torah, the only land animals that may be eaten are those that have a divided hoof and chew the cud. Thus meat from sheep, cattle, goats, and deer is kosher whereas meat from pigs, rabbits, horses, camels, and so forth is treifah.[38] The prohibition also extends to the organs, eggs, milk, and fat of forbidden animals. The Torah further specifies that the only marine animals that may be consumed are those with fins and scales.[39] Thus shark, eel, shellfish, lobster, oyster, and crab, among others, are forbidden.[40] The Torah also provides a list of unclean birds from which the rabbinic tradition inferred that all predatory and scavenger birds are treifah, whereas domestic fowl such as chickens, geese, turkeys, and ducks are kosher.[41]

Second, the manner of death is relevant, at least for land animals and birds. Animals that die of natural causes or are killed by other animals or as part of hunting sports are treifah.[42] The animal is kosher only if it has been slaughtered according to the proper method, or shehitah. This involves a qualified ritual slaughterer (shohet)[43] making a swift cut across the throat with a perfectly sharp knife. Kosher laws specify that the blade of the knife must have no burrs or nicks, that there must not be any hesitation or delay while drawing the knife, and that there not be any chopping, burrowing, or tearing motion. The principle behind such detailed requirements is the minimization of the animal's distress and pain. In other words, although the method may sound archaic and brutal to modern ears, the point of the entire operation is to reduce suffering on the part of the animal by rendering it unconscious as quickly as possible.[44] Modern methods such as electric shock, stunning, or anesthesia are rejected since the traditional law demands that the animal must be conscious when killed so that the slaughterer and consumer are aware that life is being taken. Contemporary animal rights groups have criticized Jewish and Islamic slaughtering methods as cruel but traditional religious authorities usually respond by insisting on the effectiveness of the method when properly implemented. Once killed, the carcass is then inspected for any disease or flaws, especially in the lungs. If there are no problems the animal is declared glatt [smooth].

Third, the Torah expressly forbids the consumption of blood which is regarded as a creature's life source and thus properly belongs to the creator. For this reason, the next step in the slaughtering process is to hang the carcass so that as much blood as possible can be drained.[45] Other methods are also utilized such as soaking, salting, and grilling. Eggs with spots of blood are avoided for the same reason.

Fourth, certain parts of the animal are prohibited, in particular the hind quarters that surround the sciatic nerve and fat around vital organs such as the kidney and spleen.[46] The ban on meat from the hind quarters stems from the biblical story of Jacob who wrestled with an angel of God one night at the river Jabbok. The angel struck him on the sciatic nerve to gain the ascendancy but the injured Jacob was rewarded for his resilience and thus was renamed Israel.[47] In other words, the ban on the hind quarters of an animal is a constant reminder to the Jewish people that their very existence springs from the acknowledgment of God's primacy by a recalcitrant Jacob.

The fifth principle originates from an enigmatic Torah passage that states: "Do not boil a kid in its mother's milk."[48] The command probably refers to an ancient pagan custom that Israel is warned to eschew. However, the rabbinic tradition has interpreted it to mean that the meat of land mammals and birds must never be consumed at the same time as dairy products.[49] For some, the separation of the two food types symbolizes the fundamental distinction between life (dairy) and death (meat). Foods are thus designated by the Yiddish terms fleishig (meat), milchig (dairy), and pareve (neutral). Kosher laws specify that three to six hours should transpire after the consumption of fleishig food before one should take milchig food since particles of meat can remain in the mouth for a considerable time. The reverse order (milchig followed by fleishig) usually requires only rinsing the mouth and eating some neutral food such as bread. Because of the need for constant vigilance in this regard, many Jews have adopted vegetarianism as a convenient way of compliance with the meat–dairy rule, taking inspiration from the biblical creation account which portrays God's original plan for humankind as vegetarian.[50] Jewish advocates of vegetarianism also argue that abstinence from meat helps to usher in the messianic age in which the world will revert to the pristine state of Eden. However, there is also a strong Jewish tradition that meat should be eaten on the **sabbath** and major festivals as a sign of celebration and joy.

The sixth kosher principle is a direct consequence of the fifth principle in that the separation of meat and dairy also applies to the kitchenware used to cook both food types. Ideally, a separate set of utensils, dishes, towels, and tablecloths should be used for meat and dairy foodstuffs. Thus Jews who follow kosher laws strictly often have two entire sets of utensils and even two kitchens if they can afford it.

The seventh and final principle is the ban on grape products, such as wine or grape juice, that have been produced by non-Jewish sources. Wine itself is seen as a precious gift of the creator and plays an important symbolic role in many Jewish religious ceremonies such as **circumcision**, sabbath meals, **bar mitzvah**, weddings, as well as key festivals such as Passover and Purim. However, the seventh kosher principle stems from the biblical concern that the pagans often used wine and other forms of alcohol in their religious rituals. Thus the aim of the law is once again to distinguish Israel from its **polytheistic** neighbors and their idolatrous practices. Consequently, a kosher certificate is normally required for such products.

The theological explanation of the rationale for kashrut appeals to a number of ideas. The biblical texts themselves do not always provide a clear-cut reason for the specific food laws. Consequently rabbinic commentators have argued that the true purpose is hidden in the mystery of God's unfathomable wisdom. They are hukkim commandments which require unquestioning, trusting obedience from the believer. However, others maintain that God always has a reason for his commandments and thus it is possible and legitimate to speculate on God's rationale for imposing kosher laws. Leviticus suggests that one important factor is purity and holiness. The Hebrew term for "holy" (kadosh) is etymologically related to the idea of distinction and separation. God is the epitome of holiness because God is utterly unique, unrivalled, *sui generis*. Similarly, many of the biblical kosher laws appear to reinforce the difference between Israel and other peoples. The people of God are a holy nation in an unholy world, and the food laws emphasize their unique status and calling, setting them apart from the rest. Just as Hindu food laws often serve to reinforce the internal boundaries between castes, Jewish food laws serve to reinforce the external boundary between Israel itself and the world.

Jewish commentators also point out that the kosher laws challenge the believer to exercise the virtues of discipline and self control. They strengthen one's ability to make difficult moral choices, curb dangerous basic appetites, and help the mind to channel desire in correct directions.[51] In this sense they are part of the call to moral goodness. Others point out that many of the ancient kosher laws reflect a historical concern to avoid what were perceived as dangerous or unhealthy dietary practices at the time. In other words, hygiene and health are the real issue, for example, the separation of meat from dairy in order to minimize cross-contamination; the inspection of the lungs of the slaughtered animal for various diseases; the ban on eating carrion or animals that have died of natural causes; the avoidance of shellfish and other animals that feed on the seabed; and the prohibition of pork which is a common source of trichinosis when not properly cooked. It could be argued that religious dietary law has been built on ancient dietary prudence.

The level of adherence to the food laws varies considerably across Judaism. **Orthodox** and **Conservative** Jews are more likely to practice kosher meticulously, while more liberal Jews tend to see it as less relevant. But there are other food customs that mark Jewish practice, in particular the association of certain foods with various festivals on the religious calendar that gives each a distinctive flavor. Thus Jewish New Year is marked by honey, apples, and, for **Ashkenazi** Jews, a casserole known as tzimmes which symbolizes the sweetness of a new beginning. Similarly, the circular shaped hallah bread signifies the cycle of the seasons.[52] The feast of **Hanukkah**, which commemorates the miracle of the Temple oil cruse that lasted eight days, is appositely characterized by foods fried in oil such as potato pancakes (latkes) and doughnuts (sufganiyot). At **Purim**, when Jews remember the victory by the heroine Esther over

Figure 7.4
Jewish Passover
plate with
symbolic foods

the evil Haman, a triangular pastry known as "Haman's pocket" and dumpling (kreplach) are widely eaten, and copious amounts of wine drunk to the point of inebriation.[53] At **Shavuot** (Pentecost), which celebrates the gift of the Torah on Mount Sinai, dairy foods such as ice cream, cheesecake, and cheese-filled blintzes are served based on the description of the Torah as "milk and honey" under one's tongue.[54]

Arguably the most concentrated use of symbolic foods occurs at the **seder** meal on the feast of **Pesah** (**Passover**) which celebrates the escape of the Hebrew slaves from Egypt under the leadership of **Moses**. As a symbol of the haste with which the refugees fled the land of their captors, all leaven (hametz) is forbidden during the eight days of the festival and only unleavened bread (matzah) may be eaten.[55] At the Passover meal a range of foodstuffs are placed on the table, each signifying an aspect of the Exodus experience: horseradish (maror) and bitter herbs (hazeret) for the bitterness of slavery; salt water for tears of sorrow; a mixture of nuts, apples, and wine (haroset) representing the mortar used by the Hebrews as slave laborers; the shankbone of a lamb (zeroah) symbolizing God's outstretched arm which signaled to the angel of death to "pass over" the Hebrew homes during the final plague; a green vegetable (karpas) such as celery or parsley for the new life of spring; a burnt egg (beitzah) representing the temple sacrifice; and four cups of wine symbolizing the stages toward liberation or four different words for "freedom."

As noted above, there is a strong possibility that Jesus's Last Supper was in fact a seder meal although some argue that it may have been a sabbath meal where bread and wine are prominent features. With Christianity's decision to abandon the elaborate kosher laws of Judaism, the historical and symbolic link between the Jewish Passover or sabbath meal and the Christian Eucharist became the principal intersection between these two religions concerning food. In contrast, the third Abrahamic faith adopted most of the Jewish kosher laws with some modifications and one striking exception.

☾ Halal

One of the most common signs posted on the front of butcher shops in cities and towns around the globe is the word **halal**. For over 1 billion Muslims in the world, the term indicates that the meat sold in these shops is in accordance with Islamic law as expressed in the **Qur'an**, the **hadith** and the legal tradition. As with *kosher*, the term *halal* can have both a general and a particular sense. Its broad meaning refers to a range of items or activities that are appropriate such as certain behavior, speech, or dress. Its more technical meaning pertains to the food laws of Islam. But it is not only the terms that are similar. There is an unmistakable resemblance between Islamic halal and Jewish kosher. Both are based on the conviction that certain foods have been prohibited by God and that obeying these laws is a vital aspect of religious practice. Moreover, many of the details of the two systems have much in common, although there are also important differences.

Islam divides comestibles into three basic categories: halal (fitting); mushbooh (uncertain); and haram (forbidden). The basic presumption is that all foods are halal except for those that are explicitly identified otherwise. The Qur'an declares: "O you who believe! eat of the good things that We have provided you with, and give thanks to Allah if Him it is that you serve."[56] For Muslims, the plants and animals of the earth are part of the bountiful providence of the creator. So which foods in particular are considered **haram**?

As in Judaism, there is a strong focus on meat in Islamic food laws. With regard to marine life, Islam teaches that all sea creatures are halal provided that they live in the water all the time: "Lawful to you is the game of the sea and its food, a provision for you and for the travellers."[57] Thus the Muslim diet is less restrictive than Judaism when it comes to seafood, although some Muslims avoid crustaceans such as lobsters, oysters, and prawns. Amphibious animals that do not fit neatly into either aquatic or terrestrial categories are considered haram. A similar pattern can be seen with land

Figure 7.5 An Islamic butcher shop in Leeds, England

animals. The Islamic position is once again more liberal than the Jewish since there is no equivalent of the kosher requirement that the animal have cloven hooves and chew the cud. Thus Muslims are not banned from eating camel, horse, and rabbit as Jews are. However there are some limitations which are stated in a key Qur'anic text from the second surah ("The Cow"): "He has only forbidden you what dies of itself, and blood, and flesh of swine, and that over which any other (name) than (that of) Allah has been invoked; but whoever is driven to necessity, not desiring, nor exceeding the limit, no sin shall be upon him; surely Allah is Forgiving, Merciful."[58] The hadith adds animals with fangs, birds of prey, pests, and poisonous animals to the list[59] but the Qur'anic focus is on the three main items of pork, blood, and carrion – all of which are also features of kosher law.

It is well known that Muslims, like Jews, are not permitted to consume pork, ham, bacon, and other related products. Many foods are categorized as mushbooh precisely because it is suspected that they contain derivatives of pork such as emulsifiers, gelatine, and certain enzymes. Like the Torah, the Qur'an does not provide an explicit reason for the need to avoid pig flesh, suggesting that the divine reason is hidden from our minds and ultimately is not as important as trusting obedience. One hadith tradition suggests that Allah turns a deaf ear to the Muslim who eats haram food, implying that failure to respect proper dietary practice cannot be isolated from other aspects of religious life including the efficacy of personal prayer.[60] Again in a manner reminiscent of Judaism, Muslim writers also appeal to health and hygiene as the underlying purpose, pointing out that porcine flesh is more liable to disease in warm climates than other types of meat. Allah's commandment to avoid pork is ultimately aimed at protecting believers from serious illness. Moreover, pigs are considered filthy animals in popular Islamic culture and many believe that eating pork contributes to moral laxness. As in Hinduism and Christianity, we become what we eat.

The ban on consuming blood also echoes both Jewish practice and the Jewish justification. The blood of an animal is its life source which belongs exclusively to Allah, the ultimate source of all life. Consequently animal carcasses must be thoroughly drained and hung before being prepared for sale. But the parallel with Judaism continues in the Islamic concern with the manner of the death as well. According to the Qur'an, carrion is also taboo. Animals that have died of natural causes or that have been killed by other animals are haram. The animal must be slaughtered in the proper way to be halal. Just as Judaism prescribes shehitah, so the proper Islamic method of slaughter is known as zabihah, which applies to land animals and birds but not seafood.

Zabihah requires that the slaughterer be a mature, committed Muslim who understands the method and is approved by the religious authorities. Prior to the killing, the animal's eyes and ears should be checked to insure that it is fit for consumption, in the same way as the Jewish shohet pronounces an animal glatt. As in Judaism, there is a general concern to minimize the animal's suffering. It should be given some water to drink beforehand in order to quench its thirst. Moreover it is forbidden to sharpen the knife in front of the animal which only increases its distress. The knife itself must be non-serrated and perfectly sharp. A single swift stroke should be made across the throat in order to render the animal unconscious as quickly and painlessly as possible. Islam also agrees with Judaism that it must be killed while still conscious and so anesthesia or stunning is disallowed. As one hadith states: "Two are the things which I remember Allah's Messenger (may peace be upon him) having said: Verily Allah has enjoined goodness to everything; so when you kill, kill in a good way and when you slaughter, slaughter in a good way. So every one of you should sharpen his knife, and let the slaughtered animal die comfortably."[61]

A blessing such as "Bismillah Allah-u-Akbar" [In the name of God, God is Great], or at least the name of Allah, must be uttered before or during the slaughtering as an acknowledgment that the creator is the one who gives life and takes it back:

> Therefore eat of that on which Allah's name has been mentioned if you are believers in His communications . . . And do not eat of that on which Allah's name has not been mentioned, and that is most surely a transgression; and most surely the Shaitans suggest to their friends that they should contend with you; and if you obey them, you shall most surely be polytheists.[62]

The interval between the recitation of the divine name and the slaughtering must not be excessive. Furthermore, it is imperative that the abattoir premises, the machinery, and all equipment, including the knife, are regularly cleaned.[63]

The significant similarity between Jewish and Islamic food laws raises the issue of whether Muslims may eat kosher meat, especially when halal meat is not available. Some note that the Qur'an implies an affirmative answer when it states: "This day (all) the good things are allowed to you; and the food of those who have been given the Book is lawful for you and your food is lawful for them."[64] Others disagree, claiming that a Jewish slaughterer would not satisfy the requirement that the name of Allah be uttered over the animal as expressly stated in the quotation from the Qur'an in the previous paragraph. A related question is why Islamic food laws are not as restrictive as kashrut. One traditional answer is that the more demanding Jewish system was a punishment for the sins of Israel and so did not apply to Muslims. An alternative approach, suggested by the Qur'an itself, is that many of the kosher laws are human additions to the divine law, such as the separation of meat and dairy and the exclusion of important desert food sources such as the camel.[65] For this reason, Islam has discarded these as an unnecessary burden, in much the same way as Christianity rejected the entire system of kosher laws.

If Judaism is more restrictive than Islam when it comes to meat taboos, the converse is the case with regard to alcohol. As noted above, wine is a common feature of Jewish ritual and a much treasured gift from the creator. In contrast, a noticeable aspect of Islamic practice is the total ban on alcohol and any other form of intoxicant. There is evidence in the Qur'an that **Muhammad** and his young community only gradually came to such a belief. Initially the Qur'an simply states the fact that certain plants are the source of both fruit and intoxicating drink: "And of the fruits of the palms and the grapes – you obtain from them intoxication and goodly provision; most surely there is a sign in this for a people who ponder."[66] At a subsequent point the Qur'an warns that alcohol can lead to intoxication which has the potential to undermine daily prayer: "O you who believe! Do not go near prayer when you are Intoxicated until you know (well) what you say."[67] Alcohol is also linked to gambling and thus is seen as a possible source of vice:

> They ask you about intoxicants and games of chance. Say: In both of them there is a great sin and means of profit for men, and their sin is greater than their profit. And they ask you as to what they should spend. Say: What you can spare. Thus does Allah make clear to you the communications that you may ponder.[68]

The point is made even more strongly in another Qur'anic verse where alcohol and gambling are described as "Satan's works" which must be shunned totally.[69] Muslims understand this evolution of thought as part of God's educative process, whereby he patiently reveals the true nature of alcohol and steadily weans the community off a long-established pre-Islamic habit.

The ban on alcohol extends to all intoxicating substances including narcotics and, in some opinions, even caffeinated beverages such as coffee. Muslims should not only abstain from alcoholic drinks but should also avoid foodstuffs that contain alcohol as well as any commercial transactions involving it. For some Muslims even medicines and mouthwashes that contain small amounts of alcohol are haram, especially if non-alcoholic alternatives can be found. It is not alcohol per se but the deleterious effects of intoxication that are the problem, including immorality and the neglect of daily prayer. Thus the Islamic vision of heaven includes an abundance of wine but it does not muddle the mind.[70] If there is significant common ground between Islam and Judaism on the question of meat, Islam clearly moves away from its Semitic cousin on the question of alcohol. In fact, it has much more in common with the religion of Sakyamuni with which this chapter opened. Islam's concern that abuse of alcohol undermines mental clarity, moral responsibility, and spiritual health brings us full circle, resonating with the sentiments expressed in the fifth precept of the Buddhist Pancasila.

SUMMARY

As the most basic of human needs, food plays an important role in religious ritual and practice. The ordinary reality of eating and drinking is taken up and given a new, extraordinary significance through the eyes of faith. A meal can provide access to ultimate reality and become a channel of transcendent meaning. Food is linked to spiritual purity and holiness, religious identity and membership. For a range of reasons, certain foods are prescribed while others are proscribed. Each major religion uses food in a rich variety of ways that reflect both the distinctiveness of each tradition and the fascinating intersections between them.

Many of the food customs of the five religions concern the consumption of meat. Vegetarianism is widely considered to be mandatory for Buddhists, or at least Buddhist monks, given the fundamental importance of the principle of non-violence (ahimsa). The first of the five Buddhist moral principles known as the Pancasila prohibits the taking of animal life. However, the historical Buddha's own example and teaching admit that there may be exceptional circumstances when strict vegetarianism is not possible, such as when meat is offered during the alms rounds. The general principle in Theravada Buddhism has been that a monk may consume meat when offered it provided it was not prepared specifically for him. The link between the monk and the actual act of slaughter must be minimal. Ahimsa is also a principle highly valued in the Hindu tradition where the higher the caste the greater the expectations. Upper-caste Hindus have traditionally practiced vegetarianism for this reason. Although vegetarianism is not as pronounced in Judaism and Islam, the required method of slaughter in both Semitic traditions reflects a concern to reduce the suffering of the animal in the spirit of ahimsa. Shehitah and zabihah both require that the animal be killed by a swift cut to the throat so that unconsciousness is instantaneous and pain is minimized.

Jewish and Islamic food laws are also quite specific about the type of meat that the believer may eat. Jewish kosher law allows only marine animals with scales and fins, and terrestrial animals that have cloven hoof and chew the cud. This means that many types of foods are prohibited for Jews including crustaceans as well as common meats such as horse, rabbit, and pork. Islam is less restrictive in that it singles out pork as the main form of prohibited meat and allows most seafood. Both Semitic traditions prohibit the consumption of blood and carrion. Blood symbolizes the life force in all animals, and its avoidance is an expression of respect for the creator's dominion over life. The ban on carrion reflects a concern for the manner of the animal's death that is related to the rules of slaughter. Jews and Muslims accept this set of restrictions as part of the divine will, although both religions admit that hygienic reasons may also be part of the overall rationale. Pork is particularly prone to contamination; carrion is likely to be diseased or flawed; and crustaceans are filter-feeders that live on the muddy seabed and are considered impure. If kosher and halal laws partly reflect this fundamental link between diet and bodily health, then the food customs of Hinduism are also based on the same premise: we are what we eat, both spiritually and physically. Thus the traditional Hindu classification of foods into pukka and katcha, or into the three gunas in the Vaishnavite tradition, rests on the notion that certain types of food are more spiritually uplifting than others.

Alcohol is also given prominence in religious food customs, albeit in quite contrasting ways. The fifth precept of the Buddhist Pancasila specifies that the believer should refrain from taking anything that reduces the capacity to think and behave responsibly. Clarity of mind is considered essential for concentrated meditation (samadhi) and moral propriety. Thus the devout Buddhist will avoid not only alcoholic drink but any form of intoxicant or drug that compromises this standard. Among the other major religions, it is Islam that most prominently shares Buddhism's stress on the negative effects of alcohol and drugs. The Qur'an reflects a gradual educative process whereby Allah slowly brings the young Islamic community to the point of abjuring existing customs and accepting a total ban on alcoholic beverages. In contrast, Judaism and Christianity not only allow the responsible consumption of alcohol but have incorporated wine into their holy ritual. The central Christian rite of the Eucharist is essentially a sacred meal of bread and wine that originated in Jesus's Last Supper. For many, the Last Supper was probably a Jewish Passover or sabbath meal during which wine is drunk to symbolize salvation and blessing. Although some Protestant Christian churches use non-alcoholic grape juice at the Eucharist and preach total abstinence from alcohol, mainstream Catholic, Orthodox, Anglican, and Lutheran Christians share a positive attitude toward wine that is more typical of Judaism. Jewish life-cycle ceremonies such as circumcision, bar mitzvah, and weddings use wine as a symbol of human happiness and abundant divine blessing. Wine is also an important part of many Jewish festivals including Purim when the rabbinic tradition actually encourages the believer to become inebriated for the sheer joy of God's liberating power.

Food laws are also linked to notions of membership and identity. In Hinduism, where fulfillment of caste duties is a means to ultimate liberation, meals function as a reinforcement of caste boundaries in much the same way as marriage. Hindu caste expectations not only determine whom one can marry but also with whom one should eat. In this way purity is maintained and liberation from the wheel of reincarnation is a step closer. Even the well-known ban on eating beef became a proud badge of Hindu Indian identity under British rule. Jewish kosher laws also function in a similar way. Unlike Hinduism where the differentiation is internal and between castes, Jewish food customs set Israel apart from the other nations and ground its special call to holiness (otherness) in an unholy world. The Christian Eucharistic meal is also understood as a symbol of unity among fellow believers who gather around the table of the Lord and celebrate their fellowship as the "body" of Christ. Sadly, the great rite of Christian unity has actually become a focal point of Christian division. Catholic and Orthodox churches believe that, until theological differences are resolved, there can be no meaningful sharing of the bread and wine with members of other Christian denominations.

Finally, religious food customs also concern communion with the transcendent. The Christian Eucharist not only symbolizes a horizontal union among fellow believers but also a vertical union with the incarnate God who offers himself as nourishment to the communicant. Although there is debate among Christian churches over whether the focus should be on the bread and wine itself or the act of eating and drinking, all Christians acknowledge a "real presence" of Christ in the Eucharist in some sense. Whether the words are taken literally or metaphorically, somehow the bread and wine become the body and blood of Christ, which are real nourishment for body and soul. On this point, there is a discernible intersection with the Hindu practice of prasad in which the believer and the deity share a meal. In Hindu worship, where the deity is symbolized in physical terms by the murti (statue) and treated like a royal guest, food offerings naturally play a vital role. The divine visitor eats the essence of the food and the human host consumes the leftovers that not only symbolize subordination but also a loving communion that is the goal of the bhakti tradition of Hindu devotion.

DISCUSSION TOPICS

1   Why is the pig so prominent in religious food taboos, especially in Judaism and Islam?
2   Do Hindus worship cows? Explore the religious significance of the cow for Hindus.
3   Is alcohol inherently good or evil? Compare attitudes to alcohol in the five religions.
4   For what religious reasons do some people espouse vegetarianism?
5   Compare Jewish, Islamic, and Christian attitudes to the consumption of blood.
6   Why are Jewish and Islamic food laws so similar? Are they essentially a question of hygiene?
7   Examine how caste affects cooking and eating habits in Hindu society.
8   Compare the Hindu prasad and the Christian Eucharist.
9   Examine how Jewish Passover themes are applied to the Christian Eucharist.
10   Explore the practice of fasting in each religion.
11   How important is the alms round for Buddhist monks from different cultures?

FURTHER READING

Bhaskarananda, Swami (2002). *The Essentials of Hinduism*. 2nd edn. Seattle: Viveka, pp. 59–63.

Cohn-Sherbok, Dan (2003). *Judaism: History, Belief and Practice*. London: Routledge, pp. 554–8.

Cooper, John (1994). *Eat and Be Satisfied: A Social History of Jewish Food*. Lanham, MD: Jason Aronson.

De Lange, Nicholas (2000). *Introduction to Judaism*. Cambridge: Cambridge University Press, pp. 89–91.

Esposito, John (2002). *What Everyone Needs to Know about Islam*. Oxford and New York: Oxford University Press, pp. 110–12.

Hertzberg, Arthur (ed.) (1998). *Judaism*. New York: Free Press, pp. 141–4.

Michaels, Axel (2003). *Hinduism: Past and Present*. Princeton, NJ: Princeton University Press, pp. 175–85.

Saeed, Abdullah (2003). *Islam in Australia*. St Leonards, NSW: Allen & Unwin, ch. 10.

Segler, Franklin M., & Bradley, Randall (2006). *Christian Worship: Its Theology and Practice*. 3rd edn. Nashville: B & H Publishing Group, pp. 173–86.

Solomon, Norman (1996). *Judaism: A Very Short Introduction*. New York: Oxford University Press, pp. 89–91.

Vajda, Georges (2006) "Fasting in Islam and Judaism," in G. R. Hawting (ed.), *The Development of Islamic Ritual*. Aldershot: Ashgate, ch. 8.

White, James F. (2001). *Introduction to Christian Worship*. 3rd edn. Nashville: Abingdon Press, ch. 9.

Wijayaratna, Mohan (1990). *Buddhist Monastic Life: According to the Texts of the Theravada Tradition*. Cambridge: Cambridge University Press, ch. 4.

NOTES

1   Shurangama Sutra 6.
2   Shurangama Sutra 6.20–3; Brahma Net Sutra 6.3; Lankavatara Sutra 8.
3   Mahaparinirvana Sutra 7.3–5.
4   Lankavatara Sutra 8.
5   The Shurangama Sutra also argues that animals and humans are kindred spirits in a samsaric universe and so meat-eating entails a form of cannibalism (see Shurangama Sutra 7).
6   Khandhaka, Mahavagga 6.31–2.
7   Khandhaka, Mahavagga 6.233.
8   The Vinaya Pitaka lists 10 types of flesh that should not be consumed by monks: human, elephant, horse, dog, snake, lion, tiger, leopard, bear, and hyena. The implication may be that other meats are permissible (Suttavibhanga, Pacittiya 8.4).
9   Anguttara Nikaya 5.177.
10   The five items were a set of robes, a needle, a razor, a bowl, and a water-strainer.
11   Khuddaka Nikaya, Sutta Nipata 245: "The Buddha said: 'Anger, arrogance, inflexibility, hostility, deception, envy, pride, conceit, bad company, these are impure foods, not meat.'"
12   Chandogya Upanishad 6.6.1–2.
13   See Laws of Manu, ch. V.
14   Soma was a ritual drink used during the Vedic period for its intoxicating qualities.
15   In contemporary India, inferior housing is categorized as katcha (constructed from mud and leaves) or pukka (constructed from burnt bricks or other superior forms of building materials).

16 The three gunas are features of the Samkhya philosophical school in Hinduism. In contrast to the Vaishnavite tradition, **Shaivite** Hindus observe fewer dietary restrictions and Shakta followers of the Mother Goddess are more inclined to eat meat which is traditionally obtained from animal sacrifice.

17 Bhagavad Gita 17:7–8.

18 Bhagavad Gita 17:9.

19 Bhagavad Gita 17:10.

20 Laws of Manu V.48. A few verses later Manu acknowledges that meat-eating, along with alcohol and sexual intercourse, are natural activities, albeit ones that should be minimized as far as possible: "There is no sin in eating meat, in (drinking) spirituous liquor, and in carnal intercourse, for that is the natural way of created beings, but abstention brings great rewards" (Laws of Manu V.56).

21 In Vedic literature *prasad* also means a mental state experienced by gods, sages, and other powerful beings marked by spontaneous generosity. Later texts, such as the Shiva Purana, begin to apply the term to the material food offered to the deity in worship and subsequently consumed by the believer.

22 Bhagavad Gita 3:13; see also 9:27.

23 See Acts 2:42, 46; 20:7.

24 See Matthew 26:26–8; Mark 14:22–4; Luke 22:17–20; 1 Corinthians 11:23–5.

25 See Didache 9; Ignatius, *Letter to the Philadelphians*, 4.

26 WCC Faith and Order Paper 111: Baptism, Eucharist, Ministry: Eucharist, E8.

27 The language of **John**'s gospel is particularly insistent on this point: see John 6:55–6.

28 See 1 Corinthians 12:12–27; Ephesians 5:23–32.

29 See 1 Corinthians 10:16–17: "The cup of blessing which we bless, is it not a participation in the blood of Christ? The bread which we break, is it not a participation in the body of Christ? Because there is one bread, we who are many are one body, for we all partake of the one bread."

30 Council of Trent (1551), DS 1642; see Catechism of the Catholic Church (1992), 1376.

31 Augsburg Confession, article 10.

32 **Calvinism** accepts the notion of Christ's "real presence" but emphasizes the believer's faith rather than any real change in the bread and wine. See Westminster Confession of Faith, ch. 19. **Baptist** and other Protestant Christian groups follow the position of Zwingli who stressed the symbolic nature of the meal and rejected any miraculous change in the bread and wine.

33 Corpus Christi is traditionally celebrated on the second Sunday after Pentecost.

34 WCC Faith and Order Paper 111: Baptism, Eucharist, Ministry: Eucharist, E32.

35 Mark 7:18–19.

36 Acts 10:1–17.

37 The term is derived from the biblical ban on eating animals that have been killed (torn) by other beasts. See Exodus 22:31.

38 Leviticus 11:3–4; Deuteronomy 14:4–8.

39 Leviticus 11:9–10; Deuteronomy 14:9–10.

40 The swordfish is an interesting case in point since it has scales when young but sheds these in adulthood.

41 Leviticus 11:13–19; Deuteronomy 14:11–18. The Leviticus text goes on to forbid rodents, reptiles, amphibians, and most insects.

42 Exodus 22:31; Deuteronomy 12:21.

43 The shohet is not merely a butcher but must also be a person of faith, familiar with kashrut and officially authorized by a recognized rabbinic authority.

44 A related law disallows the killing of the offspring and parent on the same day out of compassion. See Leviticus 22:28.

45 Leviticus 7:26; 17:10–14; Genesis 9:4. The ban on blood does not apply to marine animals.

46 Leviticus 7:23–5.

47 Genesis 32:22–32.

48 Exodus 23:19; 34:26; Deuteronomy 14:21.

49 Talmud Hullin 8.1–3.

50 Genesis 1:29: "God said, "See, I have given you every plant yielding seed that is upon the face of all the earth, and every tree with seed in its fruit; you shall have them for food."

51 See Maimonides, *Guide for the Perplexed*, 3.48.

52 The **Sephardic** tradition has an elaborate food ceremony similar to the Passover seder, including a whole fish, dates, and pomegranates.

53 Talmud Megilla 7b. Traditionally a Jew is encouraged to drink wine on Purim until he can no longer distinguish between the phrases *arur Haman* [cursed is Haman] and *baruch Mordechai* [blessed is Mordechai]. See also Shulhan Aruch, Orach Hayim 695.

54 Song of Songs 4:11. Another explanation states that the gift of the Torah meant that kosher rules came into effect. Because the Israelites had not slaughtered their meat legally on that first day of the new law, they ate dairy foods instead.

55 Exodus 12:15–20; 13:7. The "hametz hunt" is usually held on the night before the festival starts.

56 Qur'an 2:172.

57 Qur'an 5:96.

58 Qur'an 2:173. See also 16:115; 5:3.

59 Sahih Bukhari 7.67.438.

60 Sahih Muslim 5.2214.

61 Sahih Muslim 21.4810.

62 Qur'an 6:118, 121.

63 The same principles apply to animals killed as a result of hunting. The meat may be eaten provided the name of God was uttered when the arrow was released or the hound set. See Sahih Bukhari 7.67.387.

64 Qur'an 5:5.

65 Qur'an 3:93; 22:36.

66 Qur'an 16:67.

67 Qur'an 4:43.

68 Qur'an 2:219.

69 Qur'an 5:91–2. See also Sahih Bukhari 7.69.481–543.

70 Qur'an 56:18–21.

Chapter 8

CLOTHING

CONTENTS

 The Veil of Modesty

 Kippah, Tefillin, and Tallit

 The Thread and the Mark

 Vestments and Habits

 The Three Robes

Introduction

Along with food, clothing is one of the most fundamental of human physical needs. Apart from the basic function of providing protection for the body from the elements, the clothes that we wear also carry an array of social meanings. Different styles of apparel can be used to maintain levels of modesty, indicate particular occupations and roles, and signify membership of socio-cultural groups. In some respects, the old adage has a point: "Clothes maketh the man." Religious practice is also characterized by the inherent potential in ordinary clothing to convey deeper theological values. This chapter will explore the most prominent forms of religious attire in each of the five religions. In what specifically religious ways do believers dress and fashion their appearance? Do such customs apply to all believers or only certain members of the faith? Are they linked to daily life or special circumstances? Most importantly, what religious meanings do they signify?

The Veil of Modesty

In late 1989, three female Muslim students were suspended from a secondary school in Creil, France for refusing to remove their veils in the classroom. The incident sparked a controversial national debate that has lasted for nearly two decades, involving more than 100 cases and capturing the attention of the world's media. At stake is the secular nature of the French public school system versus the right of all citizens to freedom of religious expression. Coupled with increasing Western criticism of Muslim dress customs as symptomatic of the suppression of women, there is little doubt that the veil is currently the most striking and controversial aspect of clothing in Islam.

The requirement that women cover the whole or certain parts of their bodies in public is not unique to Islam. Women have been expected to wear veils in cultures as diverse as ancient Greek, Byzantine, Persian, and Indian societies. Historians argue that the obligation for Muslim women to cover their heads emerged only gradually, several generations after the death of **Muhammad**. Moreover, there is evidence that those who first wore the veil were from the upper classes and that the practice reflected elevated social status rather than oppression and subjugation. Wealthy urban women would wear the veil while their less affluent rural sisters went about bare-headed. In time, Islamic law came to interpret certain Qur'anic passages as commanding all female believers to dress in a certain way. The two key texts state:

> And say to the believing women that they cast down their looks and guard their private parts and do not display their ornaments except what appears thereof, and let them wear their head-coverings over their bosoms, and not display their ornaments except to their husbands or their fathers, or the fathers of their husbands, or their sons, or the sons of their husbands, or their brothers, or their brothers' sons, or their sisters' sons, or their women, or those whom their right hands possess, or the male servants not having need (of women), or the children who have not attained knowledge of what is hidden of women; and let them not strike their feet so that what they hide of their ornaments may be known; and turn to Allah all of you, O believers! so that you may be successful.[1]

> Prophet! Say to your wives and your daughters and the women of the believers that they let down upon them their over-garments; this will be more proper, that they may be known, and thus they will not be given trouble; and Allah is Forgiving, Merciful.[2]

The two passages clearly call for women to behave and dress modestly in public but it should be noted that the Qur'an makes the same basic demand upon men: "Say to the believing men that they cast down their looks and guard their private parts; that is purer for them; surely Allah is aware of what they do."[3] The central issue for both genders is what Islamic scholars call the arwah: those parts of the body that should be concealed in public. The main legal schools agree that the arwah for men extends from the navel to below the knees, although the **Maliki** school allows for the knees to be uncovered. Moreover, men are prohibited from wearing silk clothing and gold or silver ornaments because such items are associated with worldly splendor and ostentation.[4]

In contrast, women are allowed to adorn themselves in fine clothes and jewelry in order to enhance their physical beauty, provided this is not done with the intention of stimulating sexual desire in men other than their husbands. Indeed, it is precisely the concern to control sexual arousal that constitutes the rationale for the more rigorous dress requirements that apply to women. Thus the dress code does not come into effect until the age of puberty when sexual temptation becomes a factor. Furthermore, it does not apply when a woman is only in the company of her husband, young boys, or close male relatives with whom marriage is forbidden. In general, Islamic tradition prescribes that female clothing be sufficiently loose and thick to hide the shape of the body and the color of the skin. Nevertheless, the garments should be sufficiently different from male apparel so as to reflect her femininity.

What this means in practice varies since there is considerable difference of opinion within Islam as to the precise extent of the arwah for women. The Qur'anic text itself is somewhat ambiguous in that it speaks of drawing a head-covering over the bosom and not displaying beauty "except what appears thereof." This enigmatic phrase has consequently given rise to different interpretations which in turn give rise to different degrees of sartorial concealment. Most positions agree that at least the hair, the arms, and the legs must be covered but not necessarily the face. According to one relevant hadith, the Prophet himself specified:

> Asma, daughter of Abu Bakr, entered upon the Apostle of Allah (peace be upon him) wearing thin clothes. The Apostle of Allah (peace be upon him) turned his attention from her. He said: "O Asma, when a woman reaches the age of menstruation, it does not suit her that she displays her parts of the body except this and this" and he pointed to her face and hands.[5]

Thus many Muslim women believe that by wearing the **hijab** they are fulfilling the divine commandment. The term literally means a partition or barrier, but in the context of religious clothing it refers to a simple scarf that covers the hair and neck but leaves the face visible. There is no prohibition on the color and style, and thus the hijab does not have to be drab. A common sight in many Islamic communities is the rich variety of attractive, fashionable scarves that enhance appearance. A more formal variation of the hijab is the khimar, a semi-circular flair of fabric with an opening for the face, somewhat resembling the wimple of a Catholic nun.

However there are Islamic leaders who adopt a stricter interpretation of the arwah and insist that not even the face should be exposed in public. This theological

Figure 8.1
Islamic women
in the hijab

position is reflected in a form of dress that is more concealing than the hijab. One version of such a garment is the Iranian chador which is a loose-fitting, full-length robe covering the entire body including the head. Typically there is a narrow slit for the eyes but the face is covered by a niqab, or face veil. A similar form of covering is the burqa, common in places such as Saudi Arabia and Afghanistan, which covers the entire face including the eyes.

As mentioned earlier, many Western critics see the female dress code as indicative of an allegedly oppressive attitude toward women in Islamic societies. Religiously sanctioned restrictions on a woman's ability to participate in public life and the underlying presumption that a woman's God-given role is limited to the domestic sphere are serious issues that affect all religions founded in ancient patriarchal societies. Some even see in the hijab and the chador an implicit declaration of the Islamic requirement that Muslim women not mix with, and thus not marry, non-Muslim men, as required in Islamic law. Yet Islamic voices, many of them female, point to the positive meanings signified by the veil. First, the Qur'an makes it clear that the dress code is basically an assertion of the importance of sexual modesty. In fact, many Muslim women argue that their Western sisters are the ones who are really enslaved by the pressures of a superficial popular culture in which a woman's value is essentially based on her physical attractiveness. The hijab and the chador are a silent protest against the exploitation of woman via the cult of beauty. Second, many Muslim women point out that, paradoxically, the dress code actually allows them to leave their homes and participate in social, economic, and political life protected from sexual harassment and abuse to a greater degree than in the West. Finally, Islamic dress, especially when worn in multicultural Western societies, is an unambiguous statement about religious identity. A woman who wears the hijab or the chador is making a declaration not only about modesty and the need to see beyond physical beauty but also about her Islamic faith. She is proudly declaring that she is Muslim by the very apparel in which she is clothed.

The status of the hijab as arguably the most recognizable form of Muslim religious dress is highlighted by the fact that no special attire is required for official communal worship. Shoes must be removed before entering a **mosque** so as not to defile the sacred space and in some cases men are encouraged to wear a head-covering such as a cap or turban. Women would naturally wear a hijab or chador since the prayers are in the public arena. One hadith confirms the connection between covering the head and prayer: "The Prophet (peace be upon him) said: 'Allah does not accept the prayer of a woman who has reached puberty unless she wears a veil.'"[6]

The prominence of the everyday hijab is further reinforced by the fact that Islam has no priesthood and thus no special garb to differentiate the cleric from the layperson. The **imams** who lead Islamic prayer services in mosques do not customarily dress any differently from the congregation itself although in some traditions a colored turban indicates such a role. **Shi'ite** religious leaders prefer to wear black as a sign of mourning for **Ali**, the cousin and son-in-law of Muhammad. A black turban may also indicate that the wearer is a sayyid or sharif – a descendant of the Prophet through his daughter **Fatima** and her husband Ali. Where one does find special symbolic apparel is among the mystical brotherhoods whose garments reflect their individual spirituality. The term **Sufi**, which refers to Islamic mystical sects whose members traditionally wore a simple robe of white wool, is derived from the Arabic word for "wool." Sometimes the habit of the brotherhood has a deeper meaning. For example, the Turkish Mawlawiyah order, better known as the "whirling dervishes," wear somber black garments and tall hats symbolic of the grave and headstone. However when they commence their famous twirling dance of meditation, they remove their doleful outer layers to reveal stunning white garments symbolic of the resurrection.

Perhaps the best example of a special Islamic dress associated with a particular religious practice is the garment worn by pilgrims to **Mecca**. Upon arrival in the holy city, the visitor dons a simple, two-piece white garment known as the **ihram**. Irrespective of their social or financial status, all pilgrims wear the same uniform and stand before Allah as equals in both external appearance and inner reality, as they will on the day of judgment. Muslims also interpret the ihram as the dress of the beggar who comes before the Almighty: humble, empty-handed and utterly dependent. Many pilgrims retain their ihram and some request that they be buried in the garment which symbolizes a state of purity and consecration. While male pilgrims must, out of respect, keep their heads bare during the pilgrimage, women wear a simple white dress or their own native costume, with the ever-important veil.

Apart from the Qur'anic emphasis on clothing (especially female clothing) as a means to insure modesty of thought and action between the sexes in social settings, Muslim women also use their attire as a statement of true feminine worth and religious affiliation. The function of clothing as a badge of identity and differentiation can also be found in the religion of Moses where, at least for men, the covering of the head with a small skullcap is both an act of reverence before God and an unambiguous public profession of Jewish belief.

Kippah, Tefillin, and Tallit

At some stage during the first millennium CE, a tradition emerged in Judaism that drew its inspiration from the head-covering that the priests in ancient Israel always wore while serving in the **Temple**.[7] In the treatise on the **sabbath**, the **Talmud** commands the believer: "Cover your head in order that the fear of heaven may be upon you."[8] Elsewhere the Talmud relates how Rabbi Huna, the son of Rabbi Joshua, never walked more than four cubits (about two yards) with his head uncovered as a sign of his faith that the divine presence was always over him.[9] Thus began the custom of men wearing the distinctive **kippah** which has become one of the most recognizable signs of Jewish identity today.

The kippah is typically a thin, slightly rounded cloth skullcap that is worn on the crown of the head. Rabbinic commentators teach that it should be large enough to be called a head-covering and visible from all sides, but it has evolved into a small, lightweight cap probably as a result of practical convenience. The color and style of the kippah can also be indicative of religious or political persuasion within Judaism. For example, a blue or brown crocheted kippah is often associated with Zionism; a black velvet kippah is popular among yeshiva-style Jews; and the younger people often wear a smaller kippah as a sign of polite protest against tradition.

According to **Maimonides**, the kippah should be worn by Jewish men during prayer times[10] and thus many Jews don their kippah when attending **synagogue**, praying privately, studying the **Torah**, performing a ritual, and during meals because these are accompanied by blessings. However, **Orthodox** Jews usually abide by the **Shulhan Aruch** which teaches that it should be worn always on the basis of Rabbi Huna's example quoted above. The kippah may be removed if etiquette requires, such as in courtrooms, or when it is impractical to wear, such as while swimming or bathing.

As expressed in the **Talmud**, the primary meaning of the kippah is that the believer stands under the authority and power of the Almighty. The Hebrew term *kippah* literally means "dome" and the one who wears this dome acknowledges the constant divine presence that covers them. Some argue that the **Yiddish** term for the skullcap, *yarmulke*, connotes the same idea since it derives from an **Aramaic** phrase that means "in awe of the King." Thus wearing the kippah is first and foremost an act of humility and an affirmation of the sovereignty of God in all aspects of life. Like the Temple priests of old, the believer covers the crown of the head, the highest point on the human body, in reverence and submission before a higher being.[11] The kippah is also an aid to concentration during prayer, especially when it is not worn at other times, and thus it accentuates the sacred nature of the exercise. For the Jewish men who wear the kippah at all times, it functions as a public statement of religious identity just as the hijab is a badge of faith for Islamic women.

But what of Jewish women? Traditionally the kippah was restricted to male Jews, although some **Reform** Jewish women now wear it. In Orthodox circles, married Jewish women wear a scarf, hat, or snood to synagogue and there is also a general expectation that a woman will cover her hair in the presence of men other than her husband for modesty's sake. Some ultra-orthodox women fulfill the requirements of a head-covering without actually wearing one by shaving their head and wearing a wig, although some rabbis argue that this is against the spirit of the law. In this respect, the aim of the head-covering has shifted from a head-covering signifying reverence before God to concealment of the hair in accordance with the demands of modesty, as in Islam.

In some **Hasidic** and **Sephardic** communities, the wig is not sufficient and women are required to wear some other covering as well.

Hair is also an issue for Jewish men. The book of **Leviticus** states: "You shall not round off the hair on your temples or mar the edges of your beard."[12] The rabbinic tradition has interpreted this commandment to mean that Jews are not to use a razor to shave their beard or their sideburns.[13] For those who prefer to be clean-shaven, scissors, electric razors (which are deemed to operate like scissors rather than a razor blade), and depilatory powder are permitted. However many Jews traditionally grow a small beard that they keep trimmed. Hasidic Jews often allow their beards and sideburns (peyot) to grow long in obedience to the commandment, curling the sideburns or tucking them behind the ears or into the kippah. The Torah does not specify the reason for the prohibition on the use of the razor although some suggest that it was a practice among pagan priests and thus the Jewish ban is a statement against **polytheism** and idolatry. Others point to a connection with a verse in the same section of Leviticus that commands farmers not to harvest the corners of their fields but to leave these for "the poor and the stranger."[14] Under this interpretation, trimmed beards and long sideburns are a reminder that all things belong to the creator, from the crops in the field to the very hairs on one's head.

If the kippah, the wig, the beard, and the peyot are aspects of everyday Jewish appearance and attire, there are also clothing traditions that are associated with explicitly religious activity. As with Islam, there is little emphasis in Judaism on distinctive garments for the leaders of official prayer ceremonies. The **rabbi** and the cantor in a synagogue service do not function as a cultic priesthood presiding over a sacrificial ritual. Simple gowns similar to those used in the Protestant Christian tradition tend to be the norm. However, there is one traditional piece of apparel worn by Jewish laymen that links sacred moments across an entire lifespan: the simple white robe known as the **kittel**. A man will wear the kittel for the first time at his wedding and for the last time as his grave clothes. In between those two crucial moments, it is donned each year by the leader of the **Passover** meal and by married men in attendance. The kittel is also worn for the two High Holy Days (New Year and **Yom Kippur**) at which penitence is a major theme. The kittel's white hue symbolizes the purity that results from the forgiveness of sin.[15]

There are two other prominent Jewish dress customs that are directly based on the Torah and provide rich layers of meaning for the act of prayer. The first is the tefillin, two small black boxes made of kosher animal skin with straps attached. Each box contains four texts from the Torah inscribed on special parchment:

1   Deuteronomy 6:4–9, which declares the oneness of God and the fundamental commandment to all Jews to love God with their whole being;
2   Deuteronomy 11:13–21, which outlines the rewards and blessings that are bestowed on those who keep the commandments;

3 Exodus 13:1–10, which recalls the miraculous escape of the Israelite people from slavery in Egypt;

4 Exodus 13:11–16, which explains that the deliverance from Egypt was brought about by the death of the first-born in the land.

In each of these texts there is a commandment to "bind" these words on the forehead and the hand as a reminder of the liberating acts of God in Israel's history and the concomitant obligation to follow his will. Thus, the tefillin are a literal fulfillment of that command. The sacred words are placed inside the container and strapped to the body. One tefilla (shel rosh) is strapped around the head so that the box sits in the middle of the forehead. The second tefilla (shel yad) is strapped around the left arm so that the container rests on the inside of the bicep, near the heart.[16] The strap is started on the middle finger and wrapped around the arm seven times. The process of donning the tefillin is accompanied by the recitation of special prayers (see box 8.1). The tefillin are sacred objects and the user normally stands when removing them, kissing them as he does so. They are worn by adult Jews, especially of the Orthodox tradition, during weekday morning prayer services, but not on sabbath or festivals since it is felt there is less distraction to spiritual concentration on such occasions. Jewish law does not require women to wear the tefillin, although there are some congregations in which it is permitted.

The tefillin are often described as phylacteries, or charms to ward off evil influences, in much the same manner as a talisman or amulet. Some point out that the idea of strapping and knotting suggests a prophylactic function such as protection from demons. But the fundamental meaning of the tefillin is relatively self-evident. The texts inside them are statements of Jewish faith that the believer must keep in mind and apply to action at all times. The literal binding of these words to the head and the arm is a powerful symbol that all thoughts and deeds should be guided by the divine

---

PRAYERS ON DONNING THE TEFILLIN

Box 8.1

[*As the hand tefilla is placed on the left arm*] Blessed are you, Lord, our God, sovereign of the universe, Who has sanctified us with His commandments and commanded us to put on tefillin.

[*As the head tefilla is fitted*] Blessed are you, Lord, our God, sovereign of the universe Who has sanctified us with His commandments and commanded us about the mitzvah of tefillin. Blessed be the Name of His glorious kingdom for ever and ever.

[*As the strap is wrapped around the hand*] I will betroth you to me forever; I will betroth you to me in righteousness and in justice and in kindness and in mercy; I will betroth you to me in faithfulness and you will know the Lord.

will. As the four texts themselves suggest, the tefillin are worn so that believer will not forget. They are essentially reminders of the covenant.

The second important item of Jewish apparel associated with official prayer is the **tallit**, or prayer shawl. The term literally means cloak and it is probable that the tallit evolved from a garment originally used during outdoor prayers. The relevant biblical text is found in the book of **Numbers**:

> Speak to the Israelites, and tell them to make fringes on the corners of their garments throughout their generations and to put a blue cord on the fringe at each corner. You have the fringe so that, when you see it, you will remember all the commandments of the Lord and do them, and not follow the lust of your own heart and your own eyes. So you shall remember and do all my commandments, and you shall be holy to your God.[17]

Given that most garments in the ancient world were rectangular in shape, the intention of the original commandment was that everyday clothes were to have fringes added to the corners as a reminder of the divine law. As fashion evolved and four-cornered garments became less common, the commandment was deemed to be fulfilled by wearing the specially designed shawl. Thus a tallit is a rectangular piece of cloth large enough to cover the shoulders as well as the neck so that it qualifies as a garment. Twisted strings are inserted into a hole at each corner and then twirled and knotted in intricate patterns to form the tassel or tzitzit. The tallit may be made of any material provided it is not a combination of wool and linen which is forbidden by the Torah.[18] In general practice, wool is the most common choice.

Figure 8.2
Jewish boy wearing kippah, tallit, and tefillin

The background color is traditionally white but the Numbers text states that a "blue cord" should be added to each tassel. In time, blue parallel stripes were added along the sides of the shawl in place of the blue cords specified, creating the well-known pattern reflected in the design of the Israeli flag. At some stage during the sixth or seventh centuries CE, the precise formula for producing the blue dye was lost, in particular the identity of the animal that was traditionally used in the process. The Talmud refers to it as a chilazon and informs us that it was an expensive shelled sea-creature whose body was the same color as the ocean.[19] Experts hypothesize that the chilazon may be a form of cuttlefish or sea-snail. Because of the doubt surrounding the source of the dye, white stripes were added in a different weave to avoid breaking the commandment by using the wrong shade of blue. In addition, black stripes were used as a sign of mourning for the lost formula. Many shawls have an artistic motif known as an atarah (crown) sewn along the edge that is worn against the neck.

Some Orthodox Jews wear a tallit katan [small tallit], also known as an arba kanfot, underneath their daily clothes but not directly on the skin. However, the most common form of the prayer shawl is the tallit gadol, or "large tallit," which is worn over the shoulders during weekday morning services. Unlike the tefillin, it is also worn on the sabbath and holy days. Many synagogues have spare shawls available for Jewish visitors or those who may have forgotten to bring their own.

Along with the kittel, the tallit is also linked to key moments in the journey of life. A Sephardic boy usually receives his tallit at **bar mitzvah** when he has come of age and is now obliged to fulfill the commandments as an adult. For this reason, a tallit is frequently one of the most precious bar mitzvah gifts. In contrast, Ashkenazi Jews often commence wearing the tallit when they are married, although some rabbis are concerned that this postpones the fulfillment of an important commandment that should apply from the age of 13. The tallit is worn by many Jews on their wedding day and is sometimes used to form the wedding canopy itself, drawing on the theme of protection. Outside of Israel, a deceased Jew is clothed in the kittel and the tallit with one of the tzitzit cut off as a symbol of the loss that death entails. In Israel itself, where caskets are not the norm, the kittel and tallit are used as coverings for the corpse. The person enters the shadow of the grave with the great symbols of their prayer life draped about them.

The obligation to wear the tallit applies only to male Jews but many rabbinic authorities through the ages, including Rashi and Maimonides, have taught that there is no legal impediment to women wearing it. Consequently liberal Jewish communities now permit women to use the shawl but the practice is still discouraged in Orthodox Judaism.[20] Today, Jewish women's movements often use the tallit as a symbol of their struggle for religious equality.

At one level, the kippah, the tefillin, and the tallit all function as reminders of the fundamental covenantal relationship between God and the believer. The covering of the crown of the head, the words strapped to the forehead and the arm, and the shawl worn over the shoulder with its intricate tassels and distinctive blue stripes are all designed to keep in mind the faith and its obligations. In Judaism, religious clothing is designed to prompt memory and recall basic truths. Attire is about remembering the commandments, but there are also other layers of significance at work. As in Islam, the wearing of the skullcap in public is a declaration of faith and a badge of identity. Moreover, the prayer shawl, first received at bar mitzvah and ultimately taken by the believer to the grave itself, is also associated with initiation into adult faith life with its greater obligations and its ultimate goal of communion with the divine. Such connections can also be seen in other major religions, including Hinduism, where marks on the forehead serve as a public statement of religious affiliation and a special thread worn over the shoulder is given when one comes of age spiritually.

The Thread and the Mark

One of the most important of the many Hindu life-cycle rituals is the **Upanayana** ceremony – a term that literally means to bring someone into sight of the truth. It is an apposite title, for the ritual marks the end of childhood and the beginning of the first of the four classical life stages (**ashramas**): the **brahmacarin**, or student, during which spiritual truths are learned. At the heart of the ceremony, the young man is presented with an item of clothing that will serve as a permanent sign of his Hindu faith, his **caste**, and his newly acquired adult status. So important is the symbolic piece of apparel that the alternative name for the entire ritual is derived from it: the ceremony of the sacred thread.

According to ancient texts, the ceremony is best performed in the morning after a period of fasting. The young man's head is shaved and he is bathed for purification. The Upanayana is essentially a clothing ceremony with each item carrying particular religious meaning. The traditional deerskin loincloth is replaced today by a yellow cotton garment with some deerskin threads attached. It symbolizes the detached and pure lifestyle of the student who seeks life-giving wisdom. A simple girdle holds the loincloth in place and represents how the sacred **Vedas** will encircle the boy's understanding and outlook. A wooden staff evokes the image of support on life's journey that the Vedas will provide. But the most important sartorial symbol is the upavita,[21] or sacred thread, that constitutes the climax of the ritual. The guru places the thread over the left shoulder and under the right armpit so that it wraps diagonally around the body. The thread is a permanent item of clothing, never to be removed, even when bathing or going to the toilet. In this sense, it becomes part of the person. During inauspicious ceremonies such as funerals, its position is reversed so that it sits on the right shoulder, reflecting the contrary nature of the event. Threads are usually changed each year at a specific date, sometimes linked to the festival of **Rakhi Bandan** in July or August. Even then, the new thread is put on before the old one is removed.

The thread itself is highly symbolic, consisting of three strands folded three times over each other and knotted in a particular manner.[22] Custom requires that the thread be 96 times the breadth of four fingers, which is supposedly equal to a man's height. The reference to the four fingers is sometimes interpreted to symbolize the four states of mind: waking; dreaming; dreamless sleep, and complete enlightenment. The three strands have many numerological interpretations: the **Trimurti**, or three chief deities (**Vishnu**, **Shiva**, and **Brahma**); the three primal forces (**gunas**) of the universe (sattva, rajas, and tamas); the threefold debt to one's ancestors, the ancient sages, and the gods; or the three syllables of the sacred sound **aum**. The physical intertwining of three strands into one thread captures the common Hindu theme of the interplay between the one and the many within the created universe and within ultimate being itself.

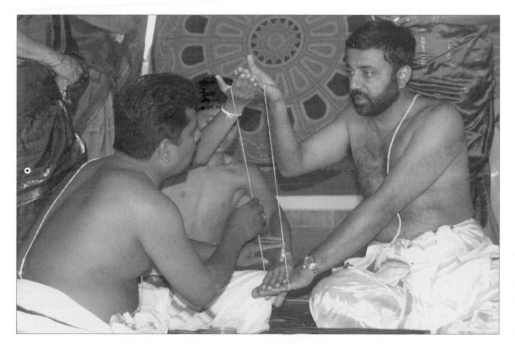

Figure 8.3
A young man receives the sacred thread during an Upanayana ceremony

The simple thread that a boy carries on his upper body is a succinct statement of a fundamental aspect of the Hindu world view.

According to the **Laws of Manu**, the Upanayana ceremony was performed only for male children of the upper three classes: the **brahmin** (priestly class), the **kshatria** (warrior class), and the **vaishya** (merchant class). The ceremony rendered the person **twice-born** in the sense that a new stage of the spiritual journey had begun. The boy received a new religious name and looked upon his teacher as his new father and the **Gayatri Mantra** as his new mother. The Gayatri Mantra, arguably the most popular in Hinduism, is recited by upper-class Hindus on a daily basis. It is imparted to the boy by his father and the ceremony leader as they huddle under a cover in secret. One possible translation of the mantra reads: "Almighty Supreme Sun, enlighten us with your divine brilliance so we may attain a noble understanding of reality."[23] The basic theme of enlightenment is reflected in the part of the Upanayana ceremony when the young man is asked to look at the sun and learn unswerving duty and resolute discipline from it. The boy then stands on a stone, implying that he will be steadfast in his faith and his studies.

The Laws of Manu specify the ideal ages at which upper-class boys should receive their sacred thread: 8 years for brahmins; 11 years for kshatrias; and 12 years for vaishyas (see box 8.2).[24] However, in contemporary Hinduism, the Upanayana has become almost

---

**BOX
8.2**

THE UPANAYANA CEREMONY

In the eighth year after conception, one should perform the initiation of a Brahman, in the eleventh year after conception that of a Kshatria, but in the twelfth year that of a Vaishya. Let students, according to the order of their castes, wear (as upper garments) the skins of black antelopes, spotted deer, and he-goats, and lower garments made of hemp, flax or wool. The sacrificial string of a Brahman shall be made of cotton, twisted to the right and consisting of three threads; that of a Kshatria of hempen threads; and that of a Vaishya of woollen threads. A Brahman shall carry, according to the sacred law, a staff of Bilwa or Palasa; a Kshatriya, of Vata or Khadira; and a Vaisya, of Pilu or Udumbara. Having taken a staff according to his choice, having worshipped the sun and walked round the fire, turning his right hand towards it, the pupil should beg alms according to the prescribed rule. (Laws of Manu, chapter II)

---

exclusively associated with the brahmin class. Moreover, most thread ceremonies are something of a formality, performed in a perfunctory manner just prior to a young man's wedding, when it is considered to be the last opportunity to carry out the ancient rite. The ideal was that the bestowal of the thread ushered in the life stage of the celibate pupil who served his guru in humble obedience. Today, at the conclusion of the ceremony, the initiate takes a short walk to a nearby house, symbolizing his journey to the holy city of **Varanasi**. However, he immediately turns around and returns to his own home, signifying the end of the student phase. Sometimes male members of his family entice him back by referring to his forthcoming wedding. Thus the classical ceremony of initiation into adulthood has become a premarital ritual. However, the thread continues to be worn by many Hindus today and remains a highly treasured symbol of religious faith. After marriage, which ushers in the second life-cycle phase of the householder, a man will wear a second thread representing the added responsibility of his wife and family.

As with the Jewish tallit and tefillin which are also traditionally restricted to male believers, the sacred thread has attracted criticism on the basis of its implied gender and class discrimination. Advocates of women's religious rights point out that girls received the thread during Vedic times but were subsequently excluded from the mainstream life-cycle rituals by the Laws of Manu. Their initiation into spiritual adulthood is marked either at the commencement of menstruation or at their wedding. Thus the thread is often symbolic of the debate between conservative and liberal forces within Hinduism. Many reform movements, such as the **Arya Samaj**, teach that both genders and all classes and castes should be allowed to receive the sacred thread as a public sign of spiritual maturity.

Apart from the sacred thread for the twice-born of the upper classes, there are few items of clothing that are specifically Hindu. Indian women often wear the sari, which can be used to cover the hair in public, not unlike the Islamic hijab, but it is not necessarily a religious garment. Men's fashions vary according to local custom although the simple loincloth known as the dhoti is a common sight, especially for temple worship. Paradoxically, one of the most striking examples of Hindu religious dress is precisely a lack of dress. When a person reaches the final ashrama and embraces the ascetical life of the **sannyasin**, they have no further regard for the physical body and its appearance. Thus the sannyasin is usually seen with unkempt, matted hair (jata) and dressed in the barest of rags or even naked ("sky-clad").

There is another important sign "worn" by the Hindu that carries a range of theological meanings, even though it is not a piece of clothing as such. The tradition of marking the forehead with a colored paste can be traced back to Vedic times and has become an important element in most Hindu ceremonies. The most common form is a single tiny dot in the center of the forehead known as a **tilak**, from the Sanskrit for "seed."[25] Various substances can be used to create the paste, including sandalwood, ashes, clay, and sindoor powder, all of which are reputed to have a cooling effect on both the body and the spirit. In contemporary India, many people, including non-Hindus, wear a tilak purely as a form of decoration with no explicitly religious intention. Nevertheless, for many who do have the sacred dot applied to their body, it is a profoundly religious sign.

Traditionally, the tilak is red or yellow in color which is understood as a symbol of the sun, the source of illumination and life. This is close to the more common interpretation of the tilak as the "third eye." Just as the two natural eyes are the organs of physical sight, so in Hindu theology the third eye is the means of seeing on the spiritual plane. Sometimes the tilak is actually painted in the shape of an eye. In Hindu art, Shiva and other gods are frequently depicted with the tilak between their brows. The position of the third eye corresponds to the sixth of the seven traditional cakras or energy points in the human body that stretch from the base of the spine to the crown of the head (see table 8.1). The sixth cakra (anja cakra) is associated with intuition, extra-sensory perception, and high-level mental activity. The tilak functions both as a symbol and a constant reminder of the transcendental dimension of the universe that is the domain of religious belief. The spiritual eye of faith enables the human person to see beyond the confines of ordinary time and space. But the tilak is also a constant reminder to the wearer of that faith. In this sense, it resembles the Jewish kippah, tefillin, and tallit which also call to mind the existence of the holy other.

A second highly significant bodily mark is the red line traced along the parting in the hair of a married woman. The name *sindoor* derives from the type of powder commonly used. The sindoor functions as a sign of a woman's married state in much the same way as the wedding ring does in the West. The groom applies the sindoor

Table 8.1   The seven cakras

Cakra	Location	Color	Element
sahasrara	top of head	white	the Absolute
anja	forehead	gold	universal mind
vishuddha	throat	indigo	ether
anahata	heart	blue	air
manipura	navel	red	fire
svadhisthana	genitals	silver	water
muladhara	pelvis	ochre	earth

for the first time during the actual wedding ceremony, and thereafter it is a part of her daily routine of adornment. The sindoor is removed when a women is widowed. Finally, naamam, or caste markings, on the head can indicate an association with a particular tradition within Hinduism. **Shaivites** usually mark their foreheads with three parallel horizontal lines, representing the same range of spiritual notions that are also linked to the triple-stranded sacred thread. **Vaishnavites** draw two vertical lines on the forehead roughly in the shape of a U or a V. There is also a tradition of painting the names of Vishnu on the 12 main parts of the body.

As in Islam and Judaism, Hindu clothing can function as a badge of religious identity. The thread and mark are both quite visible to the public eye and thus constitute unmistakable statements that the wearer is an adherent of the sanatana dharma. The tilak, which symbolizes the third eye, is a declaration that the religious vision provides a more profound and penetrating perception of existence than is otherwise possible. Other forms of head markings can indicate marital status or association with a particular Hindu deity such as Shiva or Vishnu. The sacred thread itself is traditionally worn only by the twice-born males of the upper three classes who are considered closest to ultimate liberation from the wheel of reincarnation. On this level, the links to a second spiritual birth and a privileged male class pertains not only to Hindu but also to certain Christian clothing customs.

Vestments and Habits

During a **Catholic** ordination ceremony, immediately after they have been consecrated by the bishop, the new priests are vested in garments indicative of their sacerdotal role. The clothing of the candidates at the high point of the ritual marks their special status in the Christian community. It also calls to mind the initiation of their faith life many years earlier when, as infants, they were baptized in holy water and clothed in white garments as a sign of their Christian dignity. In both ceremonies, the act of putting on physical garments carries the deeper symbolic meaning of clothing oneself in Christ – a metaphor used on several occasions in the writings of Saint Paul.[26] The clothing dimension of both rituals powerfully captures the notion that the baptized baby and the ordained adult are somehow wrapped up in a new relationship with Christ.

In practice, the special garments of baptism are worn only on that day. Few Christian churches require their members, children or adults, to wear anything distinctive in public or even at worship, such as the Jewish skullcap or the Hindu tilak. If there is a mark of baptism it is an invisible one on the soul rather than something visible on the body. The common sartorial phrase "Sunday best" refers to a time when Christians dressed up for the weekly service and it was considered improper for a woman not to wear a hat or head scarf when inside a church.[27] But many of these customs have been relaxed or discarded in recent decades. A cross hanging from a necklace today is often a secular item of fashion rather than a sign of Christian faith. This is not to say that Christianity has no clothing customs. It does, but they pertain more to special positions within the Christian community rather than to the ordinary lay member: in particular, the cleric and the monk.

Historical records suggest that Christian clergy did not use a distinctive form of clothing in the early centuries of the Church. However, after the collapse of the Roman Empire in the sixth century, priests and bishops began to dress differently from the laity. By the time of the Middle Ages, a tradition of clerical dress was well established and even sanctioned by canon law in both the **Eastern** and **Western** Churches. Despite changes in fashion over time and variations based on local culture, many denominations are still characterized by a form of attire that sets the ordained minister apart from the rest. One of the most well-known forms of everyday clerical apparel is the cassock, an ankle-length black robe probably based on the tunic worn under the toga in Roman times. Black has been the traditional color of the general clergy across the Christian spectrum, although more colorful styles have appeared since the late twentieth century. Color has an important hierarchical significance in this context. In the Western Church, purple usually denotes the rank of bishop and red the rank of cardinal, while white is reserved for the Pope. A colored skullcap or zucchetto, which is a derivation of the Jewish kippah, is also used by higher-ranking ecclesiastics.

However, it is during official ceremonies that the symbolism of sacred clothing reaches its fullest potential, especially in denominations that stress the sacramental, ritual dimension of Christianity such as the **Orthodox, Catholic,** and **Anglican Churches**. During official prayer services, especially the **Eucharist**, the priest dresses in an elaborate set of garments known as vestments whose design is based on the standard fashion of late antiquity.

The most common **liturgical** undergarment is a long robe held around the waist with a girdle. In Western Christianity it is called an alb, from the Latin for white, while in the Eastern Churches it is known as the sticharion. For both traditions it represents the garment worn at baptism, which is the commencement of Christian life and the foundation for all other spiritual developments. Just as this hidden vestment sits underneath the other more elaborate and visible items, so too baptism underpins the dignity of the priestly vocation.

Over the alb the priest wears a number of garments, the most important of which are presented to them on the day of their ordination. The first is a long, narrow strip of colored cloth that is draped around the neck and hung down the front of the body or crossed over the chest. Variously called the stole in Western Christianity and the epitrachelion [over the neck] in Eastern Christianity,[28] it is the primary symbol of the Christian priesthood. The imagery is taken from a well-known saying of **Jesus:**

> Come to me, all you that are weary and are carrying heavy burdens, and I will give you rest. Take my yoke upon you, and learn from me; for I am gentle and humble in heart, and you will find rest for your souls; for my yoke is easy, and my burden is light.[29]

A yoke is a bar of wood or metal placed across the back of a farm animal, such as an ox or cow, so that it can easily be controlled and steered for plowing and other chores.

Figure 8.4
Image of
St Patrick in
episcopal dress
with miter and
crozier

In the context of spirituality, the term is both etymologically and metaphorically linked to the great Hindu tradition of yoga, which is essentially about yoking or disciplining the body and mind in order to attain sublime levels of meditation. In the Christian tradition, the "yoke of the Kingdom" is the burden that any follower of Christ must shoulder as a consequence of following his way. For the Christian, the yoke becomes the cross that Jesus carried on his shoulders to his death at **Calvary**. Paradoxically it is a "light" weight, carried out of love for God and in service of others. Although the image applies to all followers of the Nazarene, the yoke-inspired stole/epitrachelion is a specific reminder to priests that they carry the special responsibility of Christian leadership in both prayer and life.

The other important vestment worn by the Christian priest when he presides at the Eucharist is a colored sleeveless outer garment known as the chasuble in the West and the phelonion in the East.[30] The chasuble is a large round or rectangular piece of cloth with a hole in the center through which the head passes. Thus it sits over all other vestments like a poncho or a small house (*casula*) from which its Western name derives. Some traditions interpret the chasuble/phelonion as the yoke of Christ in the same sense as the stole. But the more common meaning is taken from the Pauline clothing metaphor:

> As God's chosen ones, holy and beloved, clothe yourselves with compassion, kindness, humility, meekness, and patience. Bear with one another and, if anyone has a complaint against another, forgive each other; just as the Lord has forgiven you, so you also must forgive. Above all, clothe yourselves with love, which binds everything together in perfect harmony.[31]

Thus the visible outer priestly garment represents Christian love which covers all things and binds them together.

In the Catholic and Anglican traditions, the color of the chasuble and stole symbolizes the liturgical season. Purple, the somber color of penitence and self-denial, is worn during the seasons of **Advent** and **Lent**. Crimson is used in some Anglican churches for the final week of Lent as its climax approaches. In contrast, white, the color of joy and purity, is used for the seasons of **Christmas** and **Easter** as well as feasts of Christ and the saints. It is the traditional color for weddings and, in recent times, for funerals as well, reflecting a shift of emphasis toward new life and resurrection and away from mortality and judgment (once symbolized by black vestments). Red, the color of blood, is worn on Good Friday and the feasts of martyrs who sacrificed their lives for the faith. Red is also worn at **Pentecost**, representing the fire of the Holy Spirit that descended on the first believers according to the Christian scriptures. Blue is sometimes used in the Catholic and Anglican traditions for feasts of Mary, the mother of Jesus. For ordinary days outside of the main seasons, chasubles and stoles are green, the color of springtime and hope. In contrast, the phelonion in Orthodox Christianity is lavish but its colors do not usually indicate a liturgical season.

The use of symbolic colored vestments for church ceremonies is not widely practiced in the Protestant tradition where the stress is more on the verbal rather than the visual. In fact, the appropriateness of liturgical garb was the central issue in the Vestments Controversy which broke out in England during the reigns of Edward VI and Elizabeth I. What was at stake was not just the question of liturgical dress itself but the deeper theological principles symbolized by the garments and the context in which they were worn. Consistent with the emphasis on teaching and preaching rather than sacramental rites, the attire of ministers in many Protestant communities today tends to be modeled on academic garb: gown, scarf, and hood.

Like everyday clerical dress, liturgical vestments also reflect ecclesiastical rank. While bishops in the Western tradition wear the zucchetto for everyday affairs, they don a more elaborate head-dress known as a miter (from the Greek for turban) during sacramental ceremonies. The Western miter, a tall, pointed, two-sided folding cap, evolved from hats worn by Byzantine court officials. Eastern bishops also wear a miter but their version is more rounded, reminiscent of the imperial crown itself. The implication is clear. The miter symbolizes the privileged status and authority of the bishop as teacher and leader of the believing community. This pedagogical dimension of the bishop's role is complemented by a more pastoral symbol that is carried during ceremonies. The crosier is shaped like a shepherd's staff and stands for the guidance and protection offered by one who stands in the place of Christ, the Good Shepherd.

In striking contrast to the ceremonial vestments are the robes of the Christian monk and nun. The traditional monastic habit consists of a large gown, a girdle, a hood, and a sleeveless coat known as a scapular, after the Latin for shoulder. The girdle traditionally has three knots representing the religious vows of poverty, chastity, and obedience. The habit signifies a radically different lifestyle and a special place in the Christian world, but also serves to differentiate different monastic orders, often by their color. This has given rise to three well-known monastic synonyms: "Whitefriars" for the Carmelites; "Blackfriars" for the Dominicans; and "Greyfriars" for the Franciscans (although most wear brown habits today). Until recently most nuns' habits were very similar, with a wimple and head-veil in place of the hood, although many orders have relaxed their dress codes since **Vatican II**. Black is a common color for monks in the Eastern churches whose garments also reflect grade or seniority.

While the liturgical vestments are colorful, ornate, and elaborate, depicting the beauty and splendor of ceremonial Christianity, the monastic habit is traditionally sober and modest, depicting a life of humble service and material simplicity. Where one type of garb is reminiscent of the prince, the other is evocative of the pauper. Just as the new priest receives the stole and chasuble on the day of ordination, the novice monk or nun enters the community by means of an investiture ceremony. The newly professed cast away their old apparel and dress themselves in a different set of clothes to symbolize their passage from secular daily life to the spiritual world of the monastery. A traditional part of that passage was the tonsure, or shaving of some hair from the crown of the head to signify severance from the past life. Moreover it is no coincidence that the monastic uniform is called a habit, for the person is expected to adopt a new mindset and a new style of behavior, literally becoming what their clothing signifies.

Christian liturgical dress customs have echoes in the other religions discussed above, even if they are faint at times. In the sense that the Christian stole/epitrachelion is worn over the shoulders and signifies initiation into the priestly class, it is reminiscent of the Hindu sacred thread which is also worn over the shoulder and promotes a young man into the adult echelons of the upper classes. In some cases within both religions, the rites of passage, with their clothing symbolism that was once the monopoly of the male, are now being extended to female members. Similarly, the donning of special clothing to symbolize entry into the sacred time of official prayer is reflected in both the Christian priestly garb and the Jewish tallit and tefillin customs, although in one case it is the prayer leader alone while in the other it applies to all worshipers. In addition, both Christian and Hindu clothing traditions point to the radical lifestyle of the ascetic. In Hinduism the sannyasin dresses in rags or even discards all clothing and allows the hair to grow wildly as a sign of utter renunciation. Similarly, Christian monks and nuns both literally and figuratively adopt a new habit as a sign of their radical commitment to their faith. Such renunciation is also at the heart of the fifth religion which is centered on a monastic lifestyle symbolized by the cutting of hair and an investiture in "beggar's" robes.

The Three Robes

A few weeks after the end of the wet season, Buddhist communities around Asia celebrate a ceremony known as **Kathina**. The term comes from an ancient **Pali** word meaning a wooden frame for sewing clothes. As the name suggests, Kathina concerns the gift of clothing by the lay community to members of the local monastery. On the day of the festival, visitors arrive at the monastery and enjoy a meal together. On behalf of the entire **sangha**, two monks are chosen to receive the gift of new cloth from the lay community. The spokesperson for the laity says something along these lines:

> May we, Venerable Sirs, present these robes together with the other requisites to the Sangha. So, Venerable Sirs, please accept these robes and the other requisites from us, for our long-lasting welfare and happiness.

The monks then formally announce the name of the community member who will benefit from the gift. That night, the monks prepare, cut, and sew the cloth so that a new set of robes is ready before dawn the next day for the chosen monk to wear. The ceremony reflects the mutual dependence of monastics and laity. While the former offer an abundance of good **karma**, the latter provide material necessities, especially food and clothing. The Buddhist scriptures relate how the laity were delighted when the **Buddha** gave monks permission to receive robes since they realized that their gifts would bring karmic benefits.[32] While there are many occasions during the year when such an exchange takes place – such as naming ceremonies, weddings, and funerals – Kathina is a formal annual acknowledgment of its importance. Moreover, it is also indicative of the important symbolic value placed on the clothing worn by the monks.

Although there is no particular dress or marking worn by lay Buddhists to indicate their religious affiliation, one of the most striking features of the Buddhist monk is their distinctive robe. The robe is one of just five items a monk is allowed to possess ideally, the other four being a bowl, a water-strainer, a razor, and a needle. In reality, monks today have access to a range of basic commodities beyond these rudimentary objects. Nevertheless, the principle enshrined in the ideal is absolute detachment which is the key to ultimate liberation. A monk will rely on others for his food; he will strain small creatures from his drink out of respect for life; he will shave his head regularly as an ongoing sign of renunciation; he will mend his own clothes; and his entire wardrobe will consist of a single set of robes that are still based on the pattern set by the historical Buddha himself.[33]

The **Vinaya Pitaka** [Basket of Discipline], which contains the rules of Buddhist monastic life, dedicates a number of sections to the question of the monk's clothing. The traditional monastic habit is known as the tricivara and consists of three basic garments: an inner robe, sometimes described as a sarong; a thick waistband or girdle to secure the sarong; and an outer garment or mantle that can be worn over the shoulders. When a monk leaves the monastery, he should insure that he is wearing all three robes and that the mantle covers both shoulders: "One should not enter a village with just an upper and under robe. Whoever does so commits an offense of wrong-doing."[34] However, while inside the monastery he should leave the right shoulder uncovered. Many statues of the Buddha depict him dressed in the tricivara with his right shoulder bare as prescribed in the rule. The reason for this is probably practical rather than theological. Ancient garments were large, loose pieces of cloth draped over or wrapped around the body like the Roman toga. In order to facilitate movement, it was more convenient to leave one arm free of encumbrance. Since the left hand is associated with polluting activities such as going to the toilet, the natural choice was to have the right arm free. In colder climates, the monk often covers both shoulders with the inner robe but drapes the outer garment over the left shoulder nevertheless.

The religious symbolism of the tricivara is essentially one of material simplicity. Buddhist tradition speaks of four basic "resources" available to the monk: living on alms; dwelling at the foot of a tree for shelter; using only cow's urine as medicine; and dressing in rags. As with the five possessions of the monk mentioned earlier, the imagery here conjures up a life of utter detachment from the ordinary forms of food, shelter, medicine, and clothing. For the monk, there is little if any inherent value in the material things of life and the robes themselves should convey this ideal of complete indifference to physical comfort and pleasure. Thus, the very cloth from which the robes are made is symbolic. Apart from fabric that is donated by the laity, monks were instructed to obtain cloth by collecting rags from the local rubbish heap and cemeteries: "I allow householder robe-cloth. Whoever wishes, may be a rag-robe man. Whoever wishes may consent to householder robe-cloth. And I commend contentment with whatever is readily available."[35] The rags were then stitched together in a rough patchwork style reminiscent of Asia's paddy fields. According to the tradition, **Sakyamuni** asked his close companion **Ananda** to create a design for the outer garment. Looking out over the countryside, he noticed the chessboard appearance of the rice fields and proposed this as the pattern, which was accepted. The rule specifies six types of fabric permissible for making the robe: linen, cotton, silk, wool, hemp, and canvas.[36] It is also the individual monk's duty to insure that his robes are mended when necessary.

When people today think of the robes of a Buddhist monk, they often imagine the saffron-colored garments widely used throughout southeast Asia. Although the bright orange of saffron may suggest royalty and opulence, the intention is actually the very opposite. The choice of saffron originated in the desire to insure that all monks' robes were uniform in color, thus denoting a fundamental equality beyond caste. Monks simply dyed the rags and cloths in the cheapest and most readily available substances such as saffron and ochre. The result was a bland brownish-yellow hue that was meant to be unpretentious rather than ostentatious. Some see a deeper symbolism in the autumnal colors. Just as the red, yellow, and brown leaves drop from trees during the autumn, so too the monk must avoid clinging to the things of this earth that bind one to the wheel of **reincarnation**. As Buddhism expanded to the north along the Silk Road and eventually west again into Tibet, the standard colors of the robes evolved as cultural influences set in. Dark red is a common inexpensive dye color in Tibet and thus the Tibetan robes are often a deep maroon or crimson. In the Far East, dull blue, gray, and black are more common in compliance with the principle to avoid strong primary colors.

Figure 8.5
Thai Buddhist monks in their traditional saffron robes

As in Christianity, the entry into Buddhist monastic life is symbolized by an investiture ceremony in which the candidates receive a form of tonsure and replace their ordinary clothes with the new garments of holiness and self-discipline. While the tonsure for Christian monks involved cutting a portion of the hair on the crown of the head, Buddhist monks have their entire scalp and eyebrows shaved. The gesture echoes the decisive moment in the life of Sakyamuni when he left the palace and his princely life for a higher path, marking the moment by cutting off his long hair. Today, Buddhist monks and nuns have their heads shaved on a regular basis as a sign of their religious commitment. After the shaving, the newly professed Buddhist monks, like their Christian counterparts, put on the garments of their new state. They confirm their commitment to the **Pancasila** and profess five special promises pertaining exclusively to monastic life.

The presentation of the cloths to the monks at the Kathina ceremony each year draws on a rich array of history and symbolism. At a general level, the robes function as badges of religious identity like other garments in Islam, Judaism, Hinduism, and Christianity. To be seen in public with shaven head and saffron robes is an unambiguous statement of one's Buddhist faith. But not all Buddhists are monks and thus the robes also symbolize a special type of believer within the tradition – one who has taken an extra step and embraced a community lifestyle of radical renunciation. The fundamental equality of the members of the sangha is symbolized in the uniform shape and color of the robes. But ultimately the most powerful message conveyed by the tricivara is detachment from the material world. The shaved head, rag-like cloth, rough sewing patterns, and subdued bland color all speak of frugality and austerity. Ultimately the three robes worn by the Buddhist monk symbolize in graphic manner the core of Sakyamuni's teaching that clinging to a transient world cannot bring ultimate satisfaction or freedom.

SUMMARY

Each of the five religions has its various forms of clothing traditions and although these are undeniably unique to each faith, nevertheless interesting points of connection are discernible. One of the most basic functions of clothing is to ensure appropriate levels of modesty in society, although this can vary enormously across human cultures due to variable factors such as geography and climate. In general, each of the five religions endorses respect for the human body and appropriate covering in public with a view to controlling sexual arousal. The most striking example of this principle among the five religions is the Islamic hijab. Although the Qur'an requires modest dress for both male and female, women's clothing has been the subject of more extensive theological and legal interpretation over time. The hijab is not worn by all Islamic women, but when it is, the custom varies from a simple veil covering the hair to the full burqa concealing the entire body, including the face and the eyes. On one hand, many in the West see the hijab as symptomatic of an entrenched prejudice against women which limits their role to domestic duties. On the other hand, the hijab is interpreted by many Muslim women themselves as a protest against a demeaning attitude to women in Western fashion which implies that they are ultimately sexual objects whose worth is primarily grounded in physical attractiveness.

However, most forms of religious clothing customs are more concerned with identity than modesty. The hijab itself is not only a means of safeguarding respectability in public but it is also an unambiguous statement of a woman's Islamic faith. In this sense religious garments can function as a badge of membership. The Jewish kippah (for men at least) and the Hindu tilak are similar examples. Moreover, the style and appearance of these items can further signify the type of membership within Islam, Judaism, and Hinduism. The grades of hijab from the simple veil to the full burqa reflect different ways in which Muslims apply Qur'anic principles. The size, stitch, and color of the Jewish kippah can imply liberal or conservative stances. In Hinduism, vertical or V-shaped marking on the forehead indicate a follower of Vishnu while three horizontal lines are the sign of a devotee of Shiva.

Clothes are also used to symbolize a special stage or position within a religious tradition, especially via official investiture ceremonies. The sacred thread ceremony of Hinduism is one of the most important of the classical life-cycle rituals, celebrating adult initiation for males of the upper three classes, although today it is mainly confined to Brahmins just prior to marriage. The thread itself, which is worn every day of one's life, signifies the harmony of the one and the many at various levels within the cosmos. It renders the recipient "twice born": a child of the Vedas. There are echoes in the Jewish bar mitzvah ceremony which also marks the coming of age of a young Jew. Although bar mitzvah is essentially about reading the Torah in synagogue for the first time, it is often the occasion on which a young man receives his tallit or prayer shawl. The tallit and the tefillin are worn at certain prayer services in fulfillment of the biblical injunction. Like the thread for the Hindu twice-born, the shawl and the black boxes remind the Jew of their covenantal relationship with God which is the key to their identity.

Baptismal rites often include special garments, symbolizing the "second birth" of a Christian child or adult, although these are not worn every day or even at prayer as in the case of Hinduism and Judaism. In many churches, greater emphasis is placed on the link between investiture and the role of the cleric or the monk. Many Christian clerics dress in distinctive garb in every day life as a sign of their special ministry. Clothing also indicates the various ranks within the clergy, mainly by the specific colors associated with priests, bishops, cardinals, and popes. But it is in the role of the president of official ritual that Christian clothing customs find their most elaborate expression. The liturgical vestments are based on the fashion of late antiquity and are typically ornate in style, reflecting the importance of the occasion. The two most prominent items worn by Eucharistic presidents in Catholic, Anglican, and Orthodox traditions

– the stole/epitrachelion and the chasuble/phelonion – signify the yoke of obedience and the mantle of love respectively. The colors of these garments also follow the cycle of Christian liturgical seasons. In many Protestant churches, where the verbal nature of the ceremony and the didactic role of the ministry are emphasized, the president's garb is more reminiscent of academic dress.

In contrast, the Christian monastic habit is more sombre and austere in color and design, symbolizing renunciation of the material world. The phrase "taking the habit" not only means the clothing ceremony at the commencement of one's monastic life, but also the very lifestyle itself characterized by poverty, chastity, and obedience. This is the most obvious point of contact with Buddhism, given its central stress on radical detachment from worldly pleasures personified by the monk or nun. The traditional three-fold monastic robes of the Buddhist monk are traceable to Sakyamuni's own example and instructions. The robes themselves were traditionally made from rags, sewn roughly together and dyed in a simple, uniform color. Moreover, the cutting of hair in both Christian and Buddhist monastic traditions adds to the symbolism of severance from the norm. Conversely, the radical world-renouncers of Hinduism allow their hair to grow long and unkempt, but the same principle is at stake: letting go of that which hinders spiritual progress. In its most radical form, the sannyasin transcends clothing altogether and goes about "sky-clad."

DISCUSSION TOPICS

1   List the different types of Islamic female dress. Do they represent suppression or liberation for Islamic women?
2   Should believers be allowed to wear religious dress in public schools?
3   Compare the meaning attached to growing or shaving hair in different religions.
4   Examine the use and meaning of the sacred thread for Hindus today.
5   Why do Hindus paint markings on their bodies?
6   Why do some Jews wear the tallit, kippah, and tefillin while others do not?
7   How and why do Hasidic Jews dress in a distinctive manner?
8   Outline in detail the symbolism of ecclesiastical vestments in a particular Christian tradition.
9   Compare the design and symbolism of monastic robes in Buddhism, Christianity, and other religious traditions.

FURTHER READING

Corrigan, John, et al. (1997). *Jews, Christians, Muslims: A Comparative Introduction to Monotheistic Religions*. Upper Saddle River, NJ: Prentice Hall, pp. 341–418.

Esposito, John (2002). *What Everyone Needs to Know about Islam*. Oxford and New York: Oxford University Press, pp. 95–101.

Fadwa El Guindi (2003). *Veil: Modesty, Privacy and Resistance*. Oxford: Berg.

Kuhns, Elizabeth (2003). *The Habit: A History of the Clothing of Catholic Nuns*. New York: Doubleday.

Michaels, Axel (2003). *Hinduism: Past and Present*. Princeton, NJ: Princeton University Press, pp. 92–107.

Shirazi, Faegheh (2003). *The Veil Unveiled: The Hijab in Modern Culture*. Gainesville, FL: University Press of Florida.

Tarlo, Emma (1996). *Clothing Matters: Dress and Identity in India*. Chicago: University of Chicago Press.

Wijayaratna, Mohan (1990). *Buddhist Monastic Life: According to the Texts of the Theravada Tradition*. Cambridge: Cambridge University Press, ch. 3.

NOTES

1 Qur'an 24:31. See also Sahih Bukhari 6.60.282; Sunan Abu Dawud 4091.
2 Qur'an 33:59. See also Sunan Abu Dawud 4090.
3 Qur'an 24:30.
4 The Qur'an is silent but there are many hadith on this issue, e.g. Sahih Bukhari 7.69.536–9.
5 Sunan Abu Dawud 4092.
6 Sunan Abu Dawud 641.
7 Exodus 28:4.
8 Talmud Shabbat 156b.
9 See Talmud Shabbat 199b; Talmud Kiddushin 31a.
10 Mishneh Torah, Ahavah, Hilkhot Tefilah 5:5.
11 Shulhan Aruch, Orach Hayim 2:6.
12 Leviticus 19:27.
13 Shulhan Aruch, Yoreh Deah 181:10.
14 Leviticus 19:9.
15 See Isaiah 1:18.
16 The hand tefilla has one compartment which contains the four texts written upon a single piece of parchment in four parallel columns. The head tefilla has four compartments each of which contains one piece of parchment. See Talmud Berachot 13b; Talmud Eruvin 95b; Talmud Kiddushin 36a.
17 Numbers 15:38–9. See also Deuteronomy 22:12.
18 Leviticus 19:19; Deuteronomy 22:9–11.
19 Talmud Menachot 44a. See also Megillah 6a; Berachot 9b; Menachot 42b, 43b.
20 See Shulhan Aruch, Orach Hayim 17:2.
21 The thread is also referred to as *yajnopavita*.
22 The Laws of Manu specify that a different fabric be used for the different castes: cotton for brahmins; hemp for kshatrias; wool for vaishyas. See Laws of Manu II.44. Similarly

the recommended season varies for each caste: brahmins in spring, representing moderation; kshatrias in summer, indicating fervor; and Vaishyas in autumn, when commerce recommences after the wet season. See Shatpath Brahmana 2.13.5.

23 See Rg Veda 3.62.10.
24 Laws of Manu II.36.
25 Other terms include *pottu* in Tamil, *bindi* in Hindi, *bottu* in Telugu, and *teep* in Bengali.
26 See Galatians 3:27–9; Romans 13:14; Ephesians 6:10–17.
27 See 1 Corinthians 11:3–10.
28 There are three types of stole in Eastern Christianity: the orarion for deacons; the epitrachelion for priests; and the omophorion for bishops.
29 Matthew 11:28–30.
30 Eastern bishops usually wear a sakkos or tunic with half-sleeves and a distinctive pattern.
31 Colossians 3:12–14.
32 Khandhaka, Mahavagga 8.1.35.
33 For rules concerning an extra robe see Khandhaka, Mahavagga 8.13.6–8.
34 Khandhaka, Mahavagga 8.23.1.
35 Khandhaka, Mahavagga 8.1.34.
36 Khandhaka, Mahavagga 8.3.1.

Part III

TIME AND SPACE

Chapter 9

DAY

CONTENTS

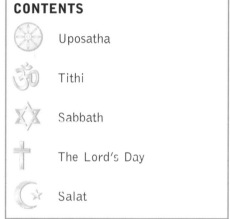

Uposatha

Tithi

Sabbath

The Lord's Day

Salat

Introduction

Human existence is played out in a four-dimensional cosmos, shaped by the fundamental categories of time and space. The very fabric of our being and all aspects of our world are intrinsically spatio-temporal by nature. Even religion, which points beyond time and space toward transcendent reality, is nevertheless rooted in this world of now and then, here and there. As with other aspects of daily life, these basic categories are taken up and transformed by religious understanding. Time and space are recast through the eyes of faith and given a more profound, holy meaning. The next two chapters focus on this temporal aspect of reality. In particular, the focus is on how the five religions sanctify time itself, commencing in this chapter with themes connected with the notion of the "day." Do the religions celebrate a regular holy day? Is it based on the cycle of the week or the month? What is its religious significance? What practices are associated with it? Are other weekdays sanctified in particular ways?

Uposatha

The Buddhist scriptures relate an episode in the life of **Sakyamuni** in which the mother of one of his disciples joined him in meditation while he was staying at her residence. When the **Buddha** asks her why she has come out in the middle of the day, she replies that she is "keeping uposatha." At this point, the Enlightened One proceeds to deliver a discourse known as "The Roots of Uposatha," outlining its incalculable value. During the treatise Buddha declares that observing **uposatha** in the correct manner is worth more than even the most precious gemstones:

> The moon and sun, both fair to see, shed radiance wherever they go, scattering darkness as they move through space, brightening the sky, illuminating the quarters. Within their range is found wealth: pearl, crystal, beryl, platinum, raw gold, and refined gold. Yet they, like the light of all stars when compared with the moon, are not worth one sixteenth of the eight-factored uposatha.[1]

So, what is uposatha and how does one "keep" it so that it takes on immeasurable value? The answer lies in the reference to the moon and the sun at the opening of the quotation. In the ancient world in which Buddhism first emerged, the most fundamental of clocks was the sky itself and the celestial objects whose movements produced natural units of time. Sunrise and sunset defined the day; the passage of the sun through the zodiacal constellations gave rise to the seasons and the year; and the $29^{1}/_{2}$-day cycle of the moon's phases was the basis of the month. The last of these had particular significance. In pre-Buddhist India, it was already an established tradition among various ascetic groups to consecrate certain days in the monthly cycle for special religious purposes. The most obvious choices were the new moon, the full moon, and the two half-moon days. Brahmanical Hindus would retire to the seclusion of the forest at these times, in order to perform Vedic rituals away from the distractions of ordinary social life. **Jain** ascetics also marked these days with more intense self-renunciation and meditation. As with many aspects of its calendar, early Buddhism adapted existing customs to its own purpose. Sakyamuni himself endorsed the practice during his own lifetime by encouraging the monks to set aside the four special lunar days each month to deepen their commitment to the Noble Eightfold Path. Thus the tradition of uposatha was born.

In Buddhist monasteries today, especially in the **Theravada** school, uposatha days are observed on a regular basis. In some instances only the full moon and new moon are involved – the former enjoying greater significance since it is said that the Buddha's birth, **Enlightenment**, and death all occurred under a full moon.[2] In other instances, half-moon days are also included. In other words, uposatha represents a regular lunar-based weekly or fortnightly holy day dedicated to more concentrated spiritual activity.[3]

Uposatha is primarily geared toward the monk and the nun, and thus constitutes an important element in the rhythm of monastic life. On an uposatha day, those in vows engage in a number of activities designed to deepen their understanding of the Buddha's teachings and strengthen their resolve to follow his example. Fasting is a common practice. Even though Buddhist monks traditionally fast every day from the midday meal to the following morning, many reduce their intake to just one meal at uposatha. Sometimes monks refrain from sleeping, spending the entire night sitting, standing, or walking in meditation. Physical labor is often reduced to allow more time for reflection and study.

However, the most salient feature of uposatha is the focus on the 227 rules of monastic life known as the Patimokkha.[4] Often, members of the community gather on the evening of uposatha and listen to each other recite sections or even the entire collection by heart. The practice of committing the rule to memory is ultimately a means whereby the monk interiorizes and appropriates its underlying principles. Monks also gather in small groups to confess transgressions against the rule. The purpose of the exercise is not to dwell on shortcomings per se, but to heighten each monk's awareness of the importance of the rule and the constant need for discipline in order to remain faithful to the fundamental values it enshrines.

Although it is essentially a time of self-examination and renewal for monks, Buddhist laity also partake in the spirit and observance of uposatha. Lay persons often stay overnight in a monastery and take this opportunity to deepen their own commitment to the way of the Buddha. A common practice is to promise to take particular care in keeping the five fundamental ethical precepts known as the **Pancasila** (see chapter 3), which are binding on all Buddhists:

I promise to refrain from:

1   harming living beings;
2   taking things not freely given;
3   sexual misconduct;
4   false speech;
5   intoxicating drinks and drugs causing heedlessness.

Thus on uposatha day, lay persons will typically abstain from sexual intercourse with their spouse, avoid alcohol, and be careful not to harm even the tiniest of creatures.

In addition to the Pancasila, Buddhist monks and nuns are also required to embrace five extra ideals that, together with the Pancasila, form the "Ten Precepts":[5]

I promise to refrain from:

6   taking untimely meals;
7   dancing, singing, and music;

8   wearing garlands, perfumes, and cosmetics;
9   sleeping in a high or large bed;
10   accepting gold or silver.

These encapsulate for the monk the fundamental notion of renunciation that lies at the heart of the Buddha's teaching on liberation from the wheel of **reincarnation**. Although they are reserved for monks and nuns, the special precepts are often embraced by lay persons on uposatha day. Thus many of the laity join the monks in fasting (avoiding untimely meals) or abstaining from meat. They may participate with the monks in all-night meditation, listen to a talk from an expert on the Buddha's teachings, or pay homage before Buddha images in the shrine room. The laity often make a donation of food or clothing to the community on uposatha as a gesture of generosity, which brings good karma to the benefactor. For both monk and layperson, uposatha is a constant reminder of the importance of understanding the wisdom imparted by the Buddha and implementing it via daily virtuous action. As the lunar cycle progresses through its phases, the four key moments provide a holy time of renewal for the followers of the one who gained Enlightenment under a full moon.

The importance of the monthly lunar cycle did not mean that Buddhism lacked a concept of the week. The earliest scriptures indicate that the religion of Sakyamuni also inherited the seven-day week from its context within Indian culture. However, seven days do not fit neatly into the $29\frac{1}{2}$-day cycle of the moon. With the priority given to the lunar-based uposatha in Buddhism, the week consequently possessed little religious significance, although weekdays are used in the **Vinaya Pitaka** as convenient measurements of time. The preference was to identify days by the number that had passed since the last uposatha, giving rise to the idea of the two fortnights: one while the moon is waxing and the second while it is waning. In this regard, Buddhism followed the patterns of its mother faith, Hinduism, which also links holy days to the lunar phases and counts time by the cycle of a dark and a light fortnight.

Tithi

One of the most important steps in planning a religious festival or a family event in India is to consider the alignment of the heavens in order to guarantee a favorable time. Whether it be a religious ceremony, a wedding, a journey, or a business enterprise, it is vital to insure that the day eventually chosen is an auspicious one. It often comes as something of a shock to the Western mind to discover such an intrinsic connection between astrology and religion, but in the Hindu world view the cyclic movements of the sun, the moon, and the stars are part of the greater cosmic order in which all things have their proper place and time. Thus, millions seek advice from experts who are able to read a pancanga – a Hindu almanac that provides detailed tables and statistics on the position of the relevant celestial objects. Casting and interpreting a pancanga requires considerable mathematical skill and profound spiritual expertise. More importantly, the pancanga is an important key to unlocking the ways in which Hinduism understands and consecrates time.

The term *pancanga* literally means "five limbs," reflecting the process of determining the auspicious time which involves consideration of five astronomical factors. The five factors are: vara (weekday); tithi [lunar day]; nakshatra (the constellation in which the moon resides); yoga (the angular relationship between the sun and the moon); karana (progression of the angular relationship between the sun and the moon). The last three are somewhat arcane and not particularly relevant here, but the first two are noteworthy.

The seven-day week that Buddhism inherited from its mother faith, Hinduism, is thought by scholars to have originated in ancient **Mesopotamian** culture and to have been exported to a host of subsequent civilizations including Egyptian, Persian, Greek, Roman, and Aryan. Unlike the day, the month, and the year, the seven-day week is not based on any natural cycle. The original choice was inspired by the seven visible celestial objects that "move" among the stars. The Mesopotamians dedicated each day of their week to one of these "gods" and the tradition is still clearly discernible in the names of most of the weekdays in Romance languages such as French, Spanish, and Italian.[6] Hinduism is no different and its weekdays are also based on the Sanskrit names of the same set of celestial bodies (see table 9.1).

As in Buddhism, there is no particular Hindu weekday that is universally accepted as a pre-eminent holy day, although different sects often associate a certain day with their particular deity. Moreover, the character of each weekday is determined by its ruling planet, rendering certain activities appropriate and others inappropriate on that day. Thus, Chandravar (Monday), named after the ever-changing moon, is a popular day of fasting and silence for followers of **Shiva**. Budhvar (Wednesday) is dedicated

Table 9.1 Weekday names

Celestial object	English	French	Sanskrit
Sun	Sunday	dimanche	Itvar
Moon	Monday	lundi	Chandravar
Mars	Tuesday	mardi	Mangalvar
Mercury	Wednesday	mercredi	Budhvar
Jupiter	Thursday	jeudi	Guruvar
Venus	Friday	vendredi	Shukravar
Saturn	Saturday	samedi	Shanivar

to Mercury and the elephant-headed god **Ganesha**, who removes obstacles and blesses new enterprises. Guruvar (Thursday), the day of Jupiter, is considered auspicious for almost all ventures, especially financial and educational initiatives. Shukravar (Friday) is a particularly popular choice for weddings, parties, new purchases, and visiting temples because of its connection with **Lakshmi**, the goddess of prosperity. In contrast, Mangalvar (Tuesday) and Shanivar (Saturday) are darker days ruled by Mars and Saturn respectively, thus requiring greater caution. Many pray to **Hanuman**, the warrior monkey-god of the **Ramayana**, to counter the negative effects of Tuesday which is associated with war and bloodshed. Saturdays are extremely inauspicious and many of the above activities are completely avoided. Itvar (Sunday) is an ambivalent day often dedicated to the Mother Goddess.

Despite the significance attached to the weekday as such, the second factor of the Hindu pancanga, the **tithi**, has proven to be even more important in determining the dates of festivals and the appropriate timing for a variety of religious and social events. Technically a tithi is the time it takes for the angle between the moon and the sun to increase by 12 degrees.[7] Because there are 360 degrees in a full circle, this means that there are 30 tithis in every lunar cycle. So a tithi is a sort of "lunar day" – a thirtieth of each "lunar month." Moreover, unlike the months of the Western calendar which no longer have any connection to the moon as such, a Hindu month corresponds to the complete cycle of lunar phases: from new moon to quarter moon, to full moon, to quarter moon, and back to new moon again.

The tithi dating system also takes note of the natural fact that the moon waxes for about 15 days and then wanes for about 15 days. This gave rise to the concept of the two fortnights. The waxing phase (from new moon to full moon) is designated the shukla paksha or "light" fortnight; the waning phase (from full moon to new moon) is known as the krishna paksha or "dark" fortnight. Because the time between new moons is actually about 29$\frac{1}{2}$ days, occasionally a day has to be dropped to keep the tithis synchronized with the moon. The Hindu calendar is further complicated by the use of two different systems. In southern India, where the amanta system is in force, a new month commences with a new moon and thus the light fortnight precedes the dark fortnight. In this system, the first tithi of the month will always be a new moon and the fifteenth corresponds to the full moon. In contrast, the full moon is the first day of each month in the purnimanta system that is prevalent in northern India. Thus, the dark fortnight precedes the light fortnight and the first day of the month will always be a full moon while the fifteenth will be a new moon.

Consequently, Hindu dates usually consist of the tithi, the fortnight, and the month. For example the birthday of Rama is the ninth day after the new moon (bright fortnight) of the month of Chaitra. The system not only provides reference for major feast days but also sets parameters for every day in the cycle. As with the seven weekdays, each of the 15 tithis in a fortnight is traditionally associated with a

Table 9.2   Hindu lunar dates (tithi)

	Tithi	*Auspicious activities*
1	Pratipat	Religious ceremonies
2	Dvitiya	Laying foundations of buildings
3	Tritiya	Shaving and cutting hair and nails
4	Caturthi	Removal of obstacles and combat
5	Panchami	Medicine and surgery
6	Shashti	Coronations and festivities
7	Saptami	Journeys and dealing with things of a movable nature
8	Ashtami	Building defences and fortifications
9	Navami	Combatting enemies and violence
10	Dasami	Acts of virtue, spiritual practices, and pious activities
11	Ekadasi	Fasting and devotional activities
12	Dvadasi	Religious ceremonies
13	Trayodasi	Forming friendships, sensual pleasures, and festivities
14	Caturdasi	Administering poison and summoning the spirits
15	Purnima (full moon) or Mavashya (new moon)	Duties to ancestors

particular god and a series of appropriate activities. For example, the fourth, ninth, and fourteenth days are dark days linked to violence and combat; the second is a good day for building, the seventh for commencing a journey, and the tenth and twelfth for religious ceremonies (see table 9.2). The new moon is traditionally set aside for paying one's respects to deceased family members. Fasting and abstinence are widely practiced, travel is avoided, and offerings are made to the ancestors. Similarly the full moon is considered to be extremely auspicious for spiritual exercises such as meditation, prayer, and fasting. Many of the major Hindu festivals fall on either the new moon or the full moon (see chapter 10).

Apart from the new moon and the full moon, **Vaishnavite** schools in particular single out one day in each fortnight as a special day of spiritual exercise and self-discipline. On the eleventh day, appropriately named ekadasi (eleventh), followers of Vishnu are urged to observe a strict fast commencing on the sunset of the eve of ekadasi until sunrise of the following day. Some gurus recommend a total fast of all food and drink including water. Others suggest that the believer eat only one meal. Yet others advocate abstinence at least from solid food or certain foodstuffs such as grains, honey, beans, or other vegetables. The fast is meant for all devotees and not just ascetics who have committed themselves to a more radical form of the spiritual life. Study, chanting, and meditation are also common practices on ekadasi.

There are a number of explanations for the choice of the number 11. One interpretation appeals to the yoga tradition which speaks of **cakras** or energy centers within the body. The mind moves through these cakras over the course of a month in a way that is analogous to ocean tides. According to the tradition, the eleventh day of the two fortnights is when the mind is located in the cakra of the forehead and in the cakra of the heart respectively. In both places, it is "at home" and the ability to meditate is considered to be greatly enhanced. Fasting on ekadasi is thus understood to increase the capacity to channel energy and facilitate higher states of meditation. Another explanation is that the mind can be understood as the eleventh organ, following the five sense organs (eyes, ears, nose, tongue, skin) and the five motor organs (hands, feet, mouth, reproduction, and excretion). Thus ekadasi is a symbolic reminder of the pre-eminence of the mind relative to the body. It is a day when the body is disciplined through fasting and the mind elevated through spiritual exercises.

The prevalence given to the moon's phases in determining the religious significance of certain days is a salient feature of the Hindu and Buddhist calendars. Both religions utilize the seven-day week and Hindu almanacs consider the weekday to be a vital factor in defining sacred time, but it is the lunar cycle that is more influential. The converse is true in the **Abrahamic religions**. Although some major festivals are celebrated on new moons and full moons, the regular holy day is linked to the seven-day week rather than the monthly cycle – perhaps not surprising given that Abraham originated in the land of Mesopotamia.

Sabbath

The first chapter of the book of **Genesis** graphically describes the progressive creation of the universe from a single eruption of light in the primal void to a marvelous world abounding in life forms, in which the human species stands as the apex. The author sets the colossal activity of the creator against the backdrop of a working week. As evening and morning come and go, each new day sees another aspect of the cosmic masterpiece unfold. At the end of the sixth day of the epic project we are told:

> Thus the heavens and the earth were finished, and all their multitude. And on the seventh day God finished the work that he had done, and he rested on the seventh day from all the work that he had done. So God blessed the seventh day and hallowed it, because on it God rested from all the work that he had done in creation.[8]

Here, at the very beginning of the Jewish scriptures, is the biblical foundation for one of Judaism's most beloved and distinctive features – the weekly day of rest known as the **sabbath** (from the Hebrew *shabbat*). In Jewish thinking, the pattern established by the creator is to be emulated by his creatures. What happens in heaven should also be done on earth. Thus the concept of a regular respite from human labor is not simply a question of workers' rights but part of the divine plan itself. It is God's will that his people should rest from work on the seventh day.[9]

The question is what exactly does "work" mean? The rabbinic tradition created a list of 39 activities that must be avoided on the sabbath (see box 9.1). They are essentially daily tasks associated with farming, hunting, cooking, homecraft, and construction in the ancient world, although the Talmud also links them to the construction of the ancient Tabernacle.[10] However, Jewish tradition extends the prohibition to include other activities that are related to the 39 specified ones. Thus the ban on kindling a fire is interpreted by devout Jews today to include switching on an electric light or starting a car engine. The ramifications can be quite constraining for strict Jews. For example, cooked meals must be prepared on Friday and any heating on Saturday must be done by setting automatic timers. Travel by car is disallowed and so many Jews reside within walking distance of the **synagogue**. No commercial transactions may be

---

THE 39 PROHIBITED ACTIVITIES ON THE JEWISH SABBATH   **Box 9.1**

1	sowing	22	untying
2	plowing	23	sewing two stitches
3	reaping	24	tearing
4	binding sheaves	25	trapping
5	threshing	26	slaughtering
6	winnowing	27	flaying
7	selecting	28	salting meat
8	grinding	29	curing hide
9	sifting	30	scraping hide
10	kneading	31	cutting hide up
11	baking	32	writing two letters
12	shearing wool	33	erasing two letters
13	washing wool	34	building
14	beating wool	35	tearing down a building
15	dyeing wool	36	extinguishing a fire
16	spinning	37	kindling a fire
17	weaving	38	hitting with a hammer
18	making two loops	39	taking an object from a private to
19	weaving two threads		a public domain, or transporting
20	separating two threads		an object in the public domain
21	tying		

undertaken, including purchasing a newspaper or other items on the day. Basically, if something can be done before the sabbath then it is forbidden on the sabbath. But games and leisure activities are encouraged as well as Torah study and prayer. There are also interesting exceptions. As noted earlier, circumcision on the eighth day proceeds even if that day is a sabbath. Moreover the laws of sabbath are overridden whenever life is in danger.[11]

The importance of keeping the sabbath is reflected in that it is the only reference to sacred time mentioned in the **Decalogue** itself. The fourth commandment states:

> Remember the Sabbath day, and keep it holy. For six days you shall labor and do all your work. But the seventh day is a Sabbath to the Lord your God; you shall not do any work – you, your son or your daughter, your male or female slave, your livestock, or the alien resident in your towns. For in six days the Lord made heaven and earth, the sea, and all that is in them, but rested the seventh day; therefore the Lord blessed the Sabbath day and consecrated it.[12]

Thus the sabbath is a "holy day" as well as a "holiday," and Israel's propensity to neglect sabbath observance or downplay its importance is a constant target of criticism by the biblical **prophets**.[13] It is considered by many Jews to be the holiest day of the year despite the fact that it occurs every week. **Yom Kippur** is known as Shabbat Hashabbatot [Sabbath of Sabbaths] to emphasize that the holiness of this day emanates from its observance as a sabbath more than any other aspect of the day. On this point, rabbinic commentators have noted that the first use of the term *holy* or *made holy* in the scriptures is the Genesis text quoted above in reference to the sabbath. The theme of its special holiness is captured in the popular notion that one gains an extra soul (neshamah yeterah) on the sabbath, symbolizing the more intense spiritual nature of the day. It is also a time of joy and celebration, reflected in the traditional imagery of the arrival of a bride in all her beauty and splendor.[14]

As the seventh day of the week, the sabbath corresponds to Saturday in the Western calendar. However, the Jewish day commences and ends with sunset and thus observance begins on the Friday evening. The sabbath is ushered in by a simple ceremony in which the woman of the house lights two candles. The twin lights symbolize the two verbs used in the **Torah** in respect to sabbath duty: zachor [remember] in Exodus 20:8 and shamor [observe] in Deuteronomy 5:12. Commentators see in this the need for both mental awareness and practical application in fulfilling the divine commandment. Tradition recommends that the candles be lit at least 18 minutes before sunset since no flame can be kindled once the sabbath commences. The woman recites the blessing with her eyes closed, waving her hands over the flames in a gesture of gathering the light physically into her family.

The table is prepared with fine settings and wine which is used to sanctify the day. There is also a double portion of braided bread, in memory of how Israel was saved from starvation in the Sinai desert by the strange substance known as manna. According to the biblical account, the people would collect a day's supply for baking each morning, except on Friday when they gathered a double portion since any work, including gathering food, was forbidden on the sabbath.[15] Gathered around the table, the father recites the blessing over the children, hymns are sung, and the sabbath meal is celebrated in a family atmosphere of joy and thanksgiving.

Figure 9.1 A Jewish woman prays over the sabbath candles

Sabbath is also about gathering with the broader family of faith. Although official prayer services are held at synagogue every day, it is the sabbath service that is the main focus of Jewish congregational worship – generally Saturday morning for **Orthodox** Jews and Friday evening for **Reform** Jews. The special nature of the sabbath service is reflected in the practice of reading a section from the Torah each week so that all five books are covered in the course of one year. Moreover, seven persons are invited to come forward for the Torah readings – more than on other weekdays. Traditionally a **cohen** and a **levite** are the first two readers. It is in this context that a boy who has just celebrated his thirteenth birthday comes forward to read for the first time and becomes a **bar mitzvah** [son of the commandment]. The sabbath readings are followed by a learned exposition or sermon (drasha) by the **rabbi**. The service usually ends with blessings over refreshments in the context of a fraternal gathering.

The sabbath ends at sunset on Saturday – or rather, about 40 minutes after sunset to insure that it is not inadvertently cut short. The customary sign that sabbath is over is when three stars are visible in the evening sky. Its conclusion is marked by a simple home ritual known as havdalah. Blessings are recited over three symbolic objects. The first is a cup of wine, a common element in Jewish ceremonies, representing joy in God's good creation. The second is a box of aromatic spices whose sweet fragrance eases the sadness at the loss of the extra soul and the ending of the sabbath. The third item is a special multi-wicked candle whose kindling symbolizes the return to work. The final blessing expresses the key theme of separation which is the literal meaning of havdalah:

> Blessed are You, Lord our God, King of the universe, who makes a distinction between sacred and profane, between light and darkness, between Israel and the nations, between the Seventh day and the six work days. Blessed are You Lord, who makes a distinction between sacred and profane.

In other words, the distinctiveness of the Sabbath vis-à-vis other weekdays is a reminder of the distinctiveness of Israel vis-à-vis the other nations. The sabbath is a day of rest and spiritual renewal but it is also a statement of the uniqueness of Judaism and its special covenantal relationship with the creator.

Although sabbath is the main day for congregational worship and spiritual activity, it is not the only day on which Jews gather in synagogue as a praying community. Official synagogue services are usually held three times on every day of the week, reminding the believer that all time belongs to God. Attendance levels vary at weekday services depending on the size of the local community and the personal faith of the individual. Sometimes numbers are important because, in some schools of Judaism, certain prayers during the service cannot be said unless there is a traditional quorum of 10 adults (**minyan**).

Since the day commences with sunset, evening prayer (ma'ariv) is the first of the three daily services. Ma'ariv is traditionally connected with the biblical scene in which **Jacob**, Abraham's grandson, camps one night during a journey and dreams of a ladder stretching from earth to heaven.[16] Themes include thanksgiving for the day and prayers for a peaceful sleep. The morning service (shacharit) can be offered at any time between dawn and noon. Shacharit is linked to the figure of **Abraham** who rose early in the morning to witness the destruction of Sodom and Gomorrah.[17] Shacharit expresses gratitude and praise for the gift of a new day. It is the longest of the daily services, and men wear the **tallit** and tefillin except on certain occasions.[18] The afternoon service (mincha) is offered between noon and sunset. It is associated with Abraham's son, **Isaac**, who was meditating in the fields in the late afternoon when he first met Rebecca, his bride-to-be.[19] The morning and afternoon services were traditionally considered the most important because it was at these times that sacrifices were offered in the ancient Temple. However, the evening service was gradually accepted as part of the obligation to sanctify the whole of each day: all time belongs to the creator. Moreover, tradition grounds the threefold sanctification of the day in the faith and example of Israel's three great **patriarchs**: Abraham, Isaac, and Jacob. Each service consists of blessings, scriptural readings, psalms, and other formal prayers that are chosen with various motifs in mind. One of the most important elements of all three services is the recitation of the **Amidah** [standing], otherwise known as the **Shemoneh Esrei [Eighteen Benedictions]**. As the name suggests, the congregation stands for the Amidah which is prayed silently with feet together, facing Jerusalem, and bowing at certain points.[20] Similarly, the Shema (see box 1.2 on p. 29) is prayed at evening and morning services, but not in the afternoon, on the basis of Deuteronomy 6:7.

The pre-eminence of the sabbath as the holiest of days underlines the dominance of the seven-day week as the basic structure of religious time in Judaism, in contrast to Hindu–Buddhist patterns. Admittedly, the full moon is significant in terms of annual Jewish festivals (see chapter 10), and the new moon (Rosh Hodesh), which was celebrated in biblical times, has been gradually transformed into a significant festival for women.[21] But it is perhaps not surprising that the concept of the week prevailed, particularly as its provenance is widely thought to be Mesopotamian culture whence Abraham himself originated. Consequently, seven is a richly symbolic number in Jewish belief and practice, representing wholeness and completeness. There are seven-branched candlesticks, a seven-day mourning period, seven-day festivals, seven weeks from **Passover** to **Shavuot**, seven wedding blessings, seven Torah readings on the sabbath, and so forth. The symbolism of seven, the sanctification of morning, afternoon, and evening, and a week-based holy day are not only characteristic of Judaism. Another religion applied the perfect number to many of its concepts, such as sacred rituals and deadly sins, and developed a system of official daily prayer consecrating different hours to God as in Judaism. Its earliest members also kept the sabbath, but in time shifted the focus from the seventh day to the first day of the week.

✝ The Lord's Day

The canonical account of the growth of early Christianity, known as the **Acts of the Apostles**, describes how **Saint Paul** frequently attended synagogue on the sabbath during his journeys.[22] This was a vital part of his missionary strategy but it also reflected the fact that Paul, like many early Christians, came from a Jewish background and naturally continued to keep a range of Jewish laws even after conversion. In many ways, Christianity looked very much like another new sect within the complex world of Judaism. However, as the new faith gradually spread throughout the Roman Empire and the proportion of pagan converts increased, Christianity slowly moved away from its mother faith. As with circumcision and **kosher** laws, the custom of gathering on the Jewish sabbath was slowly replaced by the Sunday assembly which has become a key feature of the religion.

The New Testament suggests that the first Christians started gathering on Sunday morning to break bread, to listen to Christian preaching, and to collect money for fellow believers in financial need.[23] Evidence suggests that by the end of the second century, most Christian communities had adopted Sunday as a weekly holy day, even though some Jewish Christian groups continued to observe Saturday as well. In 365 CE, the Council of Laodicea banned Christians from resting on sabbath according to Jewish custom, although various Christian movements throughout history have argued for its ongoing validity, such as the Seventh-Day Adventists in more recent times.

Various elements of Jewish sabbath practice were carried over into Christianity, including the term itself since some Protestant traditions regard Sunday as the true sabbath. However, most Christian churches acknowledge that the term more properly belongs to Saturday – a link reflected in languages such as Spanish and Portuguese (*Sabado*), Italian and Greek (*Sabbato*).[24] The same family of languages reveals the preferred

Figure 9.2
Sunday worship
in a Christian
church

designation for Sunday in mainstream Christian churches. It is *Kuriake* in Greek, *Domingo* in Spanish and Portuguese, *Domenica* in Italian, and *Dimanche* in French – all of which translate as "the Lord's Day."[25] The term is used by a number of early Christian authors in the context of believers gathering on Sunday for communal prayer and the ritual of breaking bread.[26]

The question arises as to why the early Christians chose Sunday as the natural replacement for the Saturday sabbath. The answer lies in the stories at the end of the four canonical gospels that testify that the discovery of **Jesus**'s empty tomb took place early on the morning of "the first day of the week," the day after the sabbath rest.[27] Moreover, the first appearances of the risen Lord are also said to have occurred on the same day.[28] Thus, Sunday came to be forever associated with Jesus's **resurrection**. In Christian practice the Roman "day of the sun" would now be known as the day of the Lord, and the first day of the Jewish working week would eventually eclipse the sabbath itself and become the new weekly holy day.

Based on the belief that Jesus rose from the dead into a new mode of human existence, Christian theology developed the idea of Sunday as the first day of a new world, analogous to the first day of creation itself.[29] The same theme is expressed in the concept of Sunday as the "eighth day," pointing beyond the seven days of a mundane week to timeless eternity. In Christian thinking, Jesus's resurrection completes God's original work of creation and raises humanity to a transcendent new level.[30]

There are two main practical aspects to the Christian holy day, both inherited from the Jewish sabbath. The first is congregational worship. Although many Christian denominations have services during the week, the main focus of official communal prayer is Sunday when there is a stronger expectation that members of the faith community will attend church. Just as Saturday is the most likely day for Jews to go to synagogue, Sunday is the day when larger numbers of Christians come together. Joining one's sisters and brothers in formal prayer highlights the collective dimension of Christian faith. It is also one way in which Christians consider that they continue to fulfill the fourth commandment of the Decalogue – to keep the sabbath holy. The **Catholic Church** is the most insistent in this respect, interpreting Sunday worship as a duty incumbent on all members. Its canon law states: "On Sundays and other holy days of obligation the faithful are bound to attend Mass."[31] Of course, these are ideals and the actual percentage of Catholics and other Christians who attend weekly Sunday service depends upon personal as well as socio-cultural factors.

The second practical aspect of Christian Sunday adapted from the Jewish sabbath is rest from labor. For the first few centuries of Christianity, Sunday was primarily seen as a day of common worship with little stress on the need to refrain from work, mainly because it was a working day. The situation changed in 321 CE when the emperor **Constantine** passed legislation declaring Sunday to be a day of rest, at least in an urban setting:

> On the venerable Day of the Sun let the magistrates and people residing in cities rest, and let all workshops be closed. In the country, however, persons engaged in agriculture may freely and lawfully continue their pursuits; because it often happens that another day is not so suitable for grain-sowing or for vine-planting; lest by neglecting the proper moment for such operations the bounty of heaven should be lost.[32]

The ancient Roman calendar was sprinkled with various holidays but this was the first time that a regular day of rest had been introduced into the rhythm of working life. The Jewish notion of the sabbath had found its way into the **gentile** calendar via Christianity.

In general, Christian belief accepts the need for a healthy balance between work and leisure, which also underpins the Jewish sabbath. However, Christian practice has never reflected the rigor that typifies Jewish sabbath restrictions, although there have been Christian groups that profess an extremely strict form of Sunday observance known as sabbatarianism. In modern times, the single day of rest eventually evolved into the two-day break known as the "weekend." Church leaders have occasionally expressed concern that increasing secularization and extended business hours in post-Christian Western society are threatening to undermine the uniqueness of Sunday within the week as both a holy day and a holiday.[33]

Christianity is indebted to Judaism not only for the concept of the weekly holy day. The Jewish practice of consecrating parts of the day via formal prayer was also taken up by the early Church whose members had first-hand experience of the morning and afternoon services in the Jerusalem Temple.[34] During the fourth century, the first Christian monks began to organize their day so that there was always at least one person praying at every hour, in literal fulfillment of Saint Paul's injunction to pray without ceasing.[35] In time, the tradition of the Office of the Hours emerged which involves recitation of official prayers at specific hours of the day (see box 9.2).

Box 9.2

TRADITIONAL PRAYER TIMES OF THE DIVINE OFFICE

Matins	pre-dawn
Lauds	dawn
Prime	early morning
Terce	mid-morning
Sext	noon
None	mid-afternoon
Vespers	sunset
Compline	before retiring

In the **Eastern** monastic tradition, the division of the day into official prayer times is known as the Orologion. It follows the Jewish pattern, commencing at sunset with evening prayer. This is followed by prayers at bedtime, midnight, dawn, and at three-hour intervals during the day. Appropriate themes characterize each time: death at bedtime; creation at dawn; the descent of the Spirit in the morning; and the death of Christ at mid-afternoon. In the **Western Church**, the hours are commonly known as the Divine Office and are prayed from a special book known as the breviary, so named because it was meant to be short and convenient to carry about. In the Catholic Church, priests, monks, and nuns are obliged to pray the office every day, while lay persons are encouraged to do so if they are able. The day begins with a set of special readings from the scriptures and classical Christian writers. Prayers are also said at morning, midday, evening, and bedtime. The Anglican Book of Common Prayer contains a very similar office. As in the East, each prayer has its own unique mood: praise in the morning; thanksgiving in the evening; examination of conscience and preparation for death at night. The actual prayers are a mixture of hymns, psalms, biblical readings, petitions, and blessings as well as the Lord's Prayer which is incorporated into the office so that it is prayed three times a day.

The spiritual rhythm of the Jewish day and week has had significant impact on the way in which Christians sanctify time. The Jewish practice of consecrating each part of the daily cycle via official prayer was taken up in the tradition of the Office of the Hours, although these prayers are recited mainly by monks and clerics rather than the laity. Furthermore, while Christianity eventually discarded sabbath observance, it retained the concept of a weekly holy day on which work is restricted and congregational worship expected. In similar ways, the third Abrahamic religion is also characterized by the division of the day into specific prayer times and the weekly gathering of believers. In the case of Islam, the traditional threefold daily prayer of the synagogue was expanded to a fivefold pattern, while the day before Saturday emerged as the regular day of community worship.

☾ Salat

It is said that one night during the year 621, **Muhammad** was miraculously transported on a winged creature from **Mecca** to Jerusalem and from there to heaven itself. The two parts of the mystical journey are known as **Isra and Mi'raj** respectively. During the journey, the Prophet is said to have met with several key religious figures including Abraham, Moses, and Jesus.[36] Finally Muhammad came into the presence of **Allah** himself who commanded him to instruct his followers that they pray 50 times a day. At Moses's instigation, Muhammad humbly requested that God reconsider and, after some negotiation, succeeded in reducing it to the more manageable number of five times a day. Thus was established, according to the popular tradition, the second of the five pillars of Islam – **salat**.[37]

While the Arabic term *du'a* refers to prayer in general, salat refers specifically to the five official daily prayers. Similar to the threefold Jewish synagogue services and the Christian Office of the Hours, salat is designed to punctuate the day with moments of sacredness both as a reminder of faith and as a means of sanctifying time itself. The chief difference between Islam and its fellow Abrahamic religions is that salat is considered a solemn obligation on all adult Muslims, male and female. Exception is made in the case of illness, but ideally the person should make up the lost prayer when they have recovered.

Although there is no single verse in the **Qur'an** that explicitly commands the believer to pray five times a day, there are references to prayer at morning, midday, evening, and nightfall.[38] Islamic law defines the times as indicated in box 9.3. In order to avoid any possible association with sun worship, Islamic tradition specifies that salat should never be prayed during the process of sunrise or sunset or precisely at noon. Nevertheless, salat should be prayed at some stage within the time intervals defined above.[39] One should never anticipate salat, although it can be delayed for a valid reason such as work shifts, sickness, and other extenuating circumstances. In such cases, two salats can be combined and abbreviated. The priority given to punctuality is reflected in the prohibition of alcohol which was linked to concerns that inebriation could interfere with the recitation of salat at the proper hour.[40] Moreover, the Qur'an often links salat to the third pillar of Islam, **zakat**, or the sacred tax. Together they are seen as the two dimensions of one's love of God: prayerful worship of Allah as the vertical axis and financial support for the needy as the horizontal axis.[41]

Box 9.3	**SALAT PRAYER TIMES**	
	fajr [dawn]	from pre-dawn light to the first moment of sunrise
	zuhr [midday]	after the sun has passed the zenith until mid-afternoon
	asr [afternoon]	when shadow length is equal to the height of the object until the start of sunset[42]
	maghrib [evening]	from sunset until the end of twilight
	isha [night]	from twilight to dawn

The faithful are alerted to the hour of salat by the haunting call to prayer known as the **adhan** (see box 4.4 on p. 124). Traditionally the adhan was chanted by the **muezzin** from a **mosque**'s **minaret** but today it is usually a taped version that is broadcast via loudspeakers. The words of the adhan, with the additional phrase "Prayer has begun" are repeated by the worshipers at the start of the actual prayer without pausing. In this form it is known as the iqamah.

A Muslim should be in a state of purity, both in a physical and spiritual sense, before entering into the sacred time of salat. This is achieved by ritual **ablutions** of which there are two basic forms, depending on the nature of the defilement. Minor impurity is the result of activities such as going to the toilet, passing wind, falling asleep, or touching the skin of an adult of the opposite sex who is not a close relative. In such cases, the wudu is performed which involves a threefold washing of the feet, hands, and head, including the face, ears, and hair. Major impurity arises as a consequence of sexual intercourse, menstruation, or contact with a corpse, and requires a full bath or shower known as a ghusl. Consequently, many mosques have washing facilities on site. If there is no water available, a tayammum, or dry wash, is performed with sand and the usual actions associated with wudu.

Timing and purity are not the only crucial aspects of salat: place and physical posture are also relevant. Although salat can be prayed anywhere, the ground beneath the worshiper must be clean. Thus Muslims must take off their shoes before entering a mosque, and inside the floor is usually covered with mats and carpets. If they pray salat outside a mosque, Muslims often lay out a special prayer mat. Furthermore, salat must be recited while facing toward the **Ka'bah** in Mecca. The term for the direction of official prayer is known as the **qibla** and it is usually marked by a niche in the wall of a mosque known as the **mihrab**. The original qibla was toward Jerusalem, but it was changed to Mecca soon after Muhammad arrived in **Medina**, reflecting the emerging distinction between the new religion and Judaism.

As with official prayer in many religions, Islamic salat involves a series of bodily movements that are meant to be a non-verbal complement to the spoken words. The

Figure 9.3
Muslims facing
the mihrab during
daily prayers

worshiper commences salat in a standing position, facing the qibla, hands at the side of the head with palms forwards, indicating submission and obedience to God. Still standing, but with hands by the side or crossed over the chest, the first chapter of the Qur'an (**Al-Fatiha**) is recited (see box 2.5 on p. 78). The worshiper then makes a deep bow, placing the hands on the knees. He or she then kneels down and prostrates him- or herself with the head touching the ground in a gesture of complete surrender to God. Each movement is accompanied by set Arabic prayer formulas. One complete series of such movements is known as a **raka**, and there are a stipulated number of rakas for each daily salat. In the **Sunni** tradition the number of obligatory rakas at each salat is two in the morning, four at noon, four in the afternoon, three in the evening, and four at night. Salat concludes with the person sitting back on their heels and offering a greeting of peace to those beside them. If they are praying alone, the custom is to greet their two guardian angels on either side.

The general principle that a Muslim may recite salat anywhere has one important exception. Adult male believers are obliged to pray the Friday noon salat in a mosque. The relevant verse in the Qur'an commands the believer to cease trading when the call to prayer comes on "the day of assembly" (yaum al-jum'ah), the Arabic term for Friday.[43] Some scholars interpret this as a reference to the custom of Jews gathering at the Medina marketplace on Friday afternoon in order to prepare for the sabbath.

Just as the tradition of Christian Sunday arose as a result of an event that occurred on the day after the sabbath, so it is possible that the special character of Friday noon prayer (salat al-jum'ah) in Islam is linked to a market day gathering on the eve of the Jewish holy day. Whatever the precise origins, Friday noon has become the Islamic day of congregational prayer, reminding believers that their faith has both a communal as well as a private dimension. Of course, a Muslim is allowed, and even encouraged, to pray other salats in a mosque during the week. According to the **hadith**, prayer performed with other believers is 25 times more effective than prayed alone.[44] Women are not duty bound to attend the Friday mosque service although many do. When the congregation is mixed, the tradition is that the two sexes are separated either by a curtain or barrier or simply by having the men stand in front of the women. The main reason for the segregation is that it is considered inappropriate and distracting for women to bow and prostrate in front of men.

The leader of congregational salat is known as the **imam**. An imam is not an ordained priest who intercedes to God on behalf of the people. Rather he is a layperson, albeit one who has a solid knowledge of Qur'an and Islamic teachings.[45] Theoretically any adult believer can act as the imam for salat, depending on the size and membership of the congregation. Even a woman may lead the prayers when there are no males present. The main feature of Friday noon prayers is the sermon or khutba, which is delivered from the **minbar** (pulpit) and is usually an exposition of a particular Qur'anic verse or theme. As with Jewish and Christian sermons, the style of the khutba depends on the preacher and can vary from scholarly dissertation to popular exhortation. The nature of Friday noon prayer places it alongside Saturday in Judaism and Sunday in Christianity as a special time dedicated to congregational worship and preaching. Although Friday is not a sabbatical day in the Jewish sense of avoidance of all activities that constitute work, in many Islamic cultures it is common for businesses to close down at noon for the remainder of the day.

SUMMARY

The concept of a regular holy day is a feature of all five religions although its form and meaning vary in each case. The natural rhythm set up by the lunar phases is given greater emphasis in the Hindu–Buddhist traditions. Although Buddhism is not a congregational faith with a weekly time dedicated to common worship, uposatha days mark key moments in the cycle of religious practice for both the layperson and the monk. The four uposatha days each month, corresponding to the new moon, the full moon, and the two quarter moons, are set aside as a special time to renew commitment to the way of the **Buddha**. Thus they are characterized by more intense spiritual activities. Monks undertake extra fasting coupled with more prolonged study and meditation. A central aspect of uposatha is the recitation of the Patimokkha rule which defines the monastic lifestyle and epitomizes the ideals of the Noble Eightfold Path. Mutual confession of transgressions against the rule is also an important custom, encouraging monks to identify areas of their life that require greater attention and discipline. The laity also often mark uposatha by visiting a monastery or undertaking the additional five monastic precepts.

Buddhism inherited its timekeeping from Hinduism which not only recognizes the importance of the lunar cycle but also regards it as an indispensable factor in selecting the appropriate occasion for religious and cultural events. The lunar month is divided into two fortnights that correspond to the waxing and waning of the moon. The lunar date (tithi) designates the number of days following a new moon or a full moon. The tithi forms an important part of the Hindu almanac (pancanga), which indicates the most auspicious time for activities such as a wedding, a journey or a religious ceremony. The new moon and the full moon are particularly auspicious for spiritual activities. In addition, Vaishnavite Hinduism singles out the eleventh day of each fortnight (ekadasi) as a special occasion for fasting. While the role of the moon dominates, Hinduism also uses the seven-day week in which the days are dedicated to the sun, the moon, and the five visible planets. Along with the tithi, the weekday (vara) is also vital in ascertaining whether or not a particular day is auspicious.

The seven-day week also found its way into Jewish culture where it has taken on greater religious significance than in the Hindu–Buddhist context. One of the most outstanding features of Jewish sacred time is the seventh day of the week. The sabbath is considered by many Jews to be the holiest of all days – a sacred interval during which one gains an extra soul. Theologically, the sabbath carries two fundamental meanings. First, as a day of rest the sabbath constitutes one of the oldest statements on the importance of a healthy balance between work and leisure. According to the first biblical creation narrative, even God rested on the seventh day after fashioning the world. In practice, keeping the sabbath for a devout Jew involves abstinence from anything that constitutes work, as defined by the 39 biblical categories. In no other religion is there such an elaborate framework to insure proper behavior on the holy day. Second, the sabbath is the weekday par excellence for community worship. Although there are synagogue services on every day of the week, Saturday is usually characterized by greater numbers of congregants and a more extended program of readings and prayers.

Because of their Jewish background, the earliest Christians kept the sabbath along with other customs. However, as Christianity began to differentiate itself more and more from its mother faith, the seventh day of the week was gradually eclipsed by the first day of the week in terms of communal worship and rest from labor. The choice of Sunday is grounded in its association with the finding of the empty tomb and the first appearances of the risen Jesus. It is the Lord's Day – the day of the resurrection. Although there are some Christian sects that still insist on the observance of the Saturday sabbath, Sunday became the main day on which Christians gather in churches to celebrate the weekly Eucharist. Most Christian churches also agree that unnecessary work should be avoided on a Sunday, but adherence to it has never been to the degree of strictness found in Judaism.

While the day after the sabbath was the natural choice for Christians, the day before the sabbath was adopted by the early Islamic community as a time for community prayer. In Islamic law, male adult Muslims are bound to pray their Friday noon prayers in the local mosque to emphasize the communal dimension of their faith. One of the key features of Friday noon prayers is the sermon which provides regular, ongoing religious instruction and encouragement for the believing community.

While the holy day is a prominent feature in the weekly cycle of the three Semitic faiths, ordinary days are also sanctified by the insertion of prayer at specific times. Jewish synagogues offer three services each day – evening, morning, and afternoon – a pattern inspired partly by the sacrificial system in the ancient Temple and symbolically linked to the biblical patriarchs Abraham, Isaac, and Jacob. Christianity adapted the Jewish practice and developed the Office of the Hours. In both Eastern and Western Christianity, official prayers are offered at certain times of the day on behalf of the Church and all humankind. The obligation to pray the hours is usually incumbent upon monks, nuns, and clerics, but many churches now encourage lay Christians to participate as well. While weekday attendance at synagogue and praying the hours are optional for most Jews and Christians, the second pillar of Islam requires that all adult Muslims, men and women, engage in ritual prayer five times a day, every day. As sacred time, salat requires purity of heart and mind, symbolized by the ablutions that precede its recitation. Salat is one of the most defining and unifying aspects of Islamic practice, punctuating every part of the day with a universal formula, articulated in a single holy language, expressed with the same bodily movements, and directed toward a common focal point in Mecca.

In its own unique way, each religion sets aside certain moments within natural cycles of time, consecrating them with special meaning and celebrating them with appropriate practices. Moreover, the observance of the holy day or the holy hour is an indirect declaration that all days and hours are an integral part of the religious world view. The lightening and darkening of the moon, the passage of the seven days, and the rising and setting of the sun are imbued with a transcendent significance. Of course, this sanctification of time is not confined to the hour, day, week, or month. The same principle is evident at the level of the year, where annual religious calendars are sprinkled with their own distinctive array of feasts, fasts, and sacred seasons.

DISCUSSION TOPICS

1   What are the origins of the seven-day week? Examine the meaning of the week-day names in various religions.
2   Why is Friday a special day for Muslims? How did the practice originate?
3   How do Jews apply the 39 traditional sabbath prohibitions in modern life?
4   What is Christian sabbatarianism? Should Christians keep Saturday or Sunday as their holy day?
5   Should commercial activities be limited on a Sunday in predominantly Christian nations?
6   Compare the official daily prayer routines of Judaism, Christianity, and Islam.
7   What happens during Islamic salat? Outline the main rules about how and when to pray salat.
8   Explore how different Buddhist communities keep uposatha.
9   Why do the religions prefer certain types of bodily gestures and postures during prayer – standing, kneeling, prostrating, bowing, swaying, circumambulating, and sitting?

FURTHER READING

Cohn-Sherbok, Dan (2003). *Judaism: History, Belief and Practice*. London: Routledge, pp. 494–500.

De Lange, Nicholas (2000). *Introduction to Judaism*. Cambridge: Cambridge University Press, pp. 92–7.

Eskenazi, Tamara, et al. (eds.) (1991). *The Sabbath in Jewish and Christian Traditions*. New York: Crossroad.

Goldziher, Ignaz (2006). "The Sabbath Institution in Islam," in G. R. Hawting (ed.), *The Development of Islamic Ritual*. Aldershot: Ashgate, ch. 3.

Hedayetullah, Muhammad (2002). *Dynamics of Islam: An Exposition*. Victoria, BC: Trafford, pp. 53–60.

Hertzberg, Arthur (ed.) (1998). *Judaism*. New York: Free Press, pp. 170–7.

Klostermaier, Klaus (1994). *A Survey of Hinduism*. 2nd edn. Albany, NY: SUNY Press, ch. 20.

Rubin, Uri (2006). "Morning and Evening Prayers in Early Islam," in G. R. Hawting (ed.), *The Development of Islamic Ritual*. Aldershot: Ashgate, ch. 7.

Zerubavel, Eviatar (1989). *The Seven Day Circle: The History and Meaning of the Week*. Chicago: University of Chicago Press.

NOTES

1   Anguttara Nikaya 3.70.
2   See the festival of Vesak in chapter 10.

3 These days are called poya in Sri Lanka and wan phra in Thailand.

4 There are traditionally 311 rules for nuns.

5 Sometimes the five monastic precepts are condensed to three, thus giving a total of Eight Precepts when combined with the Pancasila.

6 In certain Romance languages such as French, Saturday (samedi) and Sunday (dimanche) are the usual exceptions. The former derives from the Jewish *sabbath* and the latter from the Christian *Lord's Day*. In English, the weekday names are a mixture of Roman gods (Saturn, Sun, Moon) and Nordic gods (Tew, Woden, Thor, Freyja).

7 See Taittiriya Samhita 4.4.10.1–3; Atharva Veda 19.7.1.

8 Genesis 2:1–3.

9 See Leviticus 23:3.

10 See Exodus 25–30; Talmud Shabbat 49b.

11 Talmud Yoma 85b.

12 Exodus 20:8–11. See also Deuteronomy 5:12–15 where the significance of the sabbath is linked to the escape from Egypt rather than the six days of creation.

13 Isaiah 56:1–7; 58:13–14; Jeremiah 17:24–5; Nehemiah 13:15. Keeping the sabbath is considered as a sign of fidelity to the covenant in Exodus 31:16.

14 Talmud Shabbat 119a.

15 Exodus 16:13–30.

16 Genesis 28:10–22.

17 Genesis 19:27.

18 The tallit is worn at morning prayer on all days except the fast-day **Tisha B'Av**. The tefillin are worn at most morning prayers except for sabbath and major festivals.

19 Genesis 24:63.

20 The common Jewish practice of swaying forwards and backwards, or sometimes from side to side, is known as shokeling from the Yiddish word "to shake." Shokeling is not compulsory and emerged as a custom in the early medieval period, with the aim of increasing concentration and stimulating fervor. Some interpret the movement as symbolic of the soul's desire to leave the body.

21 See 2 Kings 4:23; Talmud Megillah 22b. Rosh Hodesh women's groups usually meet for shared prayer, study, and discussion of relevant issues.

22 See Acts 13:14, 44; 16:13; 18:4.

23 Acts 20:7; 1 Corinthians 16:2.

24 The pattern is evident even in Russian (суббота).

25 In languages such as English and German, where the word for the first day of the week refers to the sun, Christians nevertheless see a link with Christ as Light of the World.

26 Didache 14.1; Ignatius, *Letter to the Magnesians*, 9.

27 Mark 16:2, 9; Luke 24:1; Matthew 28:1; John 20:1.

28 John 20:11–23; Matthew 28:8–10; Luke 24:13–16, 33–7; Mark 16:9–11.

29 2 Corinthians 5:17; Colossians 1:15, 18.

30 Epistle of Barnabas 15:8–9.

31 Catholic Code of Canon Law, canon 1247.

32 *Codex Theodosianus*, II, tit. 8.1.

33 See Pope John Paul II, *Dies Domini*, Introduction, 4.

34 Act 3:1.

35 1 Thessalonians 5:17.

36 Sahih Bukhari 1.8.345. An alternative version is that Gabriel appeared to Muhammad five times on one day and recited salat each time (see Sahih Muslim 4.1268). Islamic tradition sees salat as originating ultimately with Abraham and the patriarchs (see Qur'an 14:35–40; 16:120–3; 19:54–5; 10:87).

37 Salat is also one of Ten Branches of Religion in the **Shi'ite** school.

38 Qur'an 2:238; 11:114; 17:78; 24:58; 30:18.

39 Qur'an 23:9; 70:34.

40 Qur'an 5:91.

41 Qur'an 21:73; 19:55.

42 The Hanafi legal school varies slightly in that it specifies that the afternoon salat commences when the shadow of an object is twice its height.

43 Qur'an 62:9–11.

44 Sahih Bukhari 1.8.466.

45 In large mosques the appointed imam is often a hafiz, one who has committed the Qur'an to memory.

Chapter 10

YEAR

Introduction

The sanctification of time by religion is not confined to the day, the week, and the month; it also touches on the broader scale of the year. Although they differ in detail, religious calendars all represent ways in which faith interprets the progress of the annual cycle through festivals and seasons. In this chapter we examine the calendar of each of the five major religions. What is its basic structure? How are the years counted? When do major festivals occur? What practices and meanings are associated with them? Are there specific periods or seasons inserted into the year and what do these signify?

† Four Seasons

An observer attending a **Catholic** or **Anglican Eucharist** at different times of the year would notice that the vestments worn by the priest as well as the cloths adorning the altar and tabernacle are not always the same. They would be purple during the months of December and March, white in January and May, green from June to November; and red on other occasions. The choice of color is far from arbitrary and is used to indicate an important aspect of the Christian religious life: the **liturgical** season. The term *season* here does not refer to the four natural seasons of spring, summer, autumn, and winter, but it does carry a similar meaning in the sense of a defined period of time with its own distinctive characteristics and motifs. Each color signals to the congregation that they are at a particular stage within the annual cycle of official worship, with its own unique set of readings, prayers, and practices. Although the tradition of ceremonial colors is not as prominent in **Orthodox** churches, the general pattern of the liturgical seasons is found across Eastern and Western mainstream Christianity.

The key to understanding the Christian seasons is that they hinge on the two greatest feasts, which celebrate the founder's birth and resurrection: Christmas Day and Easter Sunday. In each case, the feast is preceded by a time of preparation and followed by a time of celebration. Thus many Christians prepare for the birth of Christ during the season of **Advent** and celebrate the joyous occasion during the season of

Table 10.1 The Western Christian calendar

Season	Holy day	Time of year
Advent begins	First Sunday of Advent	Four Sundays before Christmas
Christmas begins	Christmas Day	25 December
	Epiphany	6 January
Lent begins	Ash Wednesday	40 days prior to Easter Sunday (omitting Sundays)
	Palm Sunday	Sunday before Easter Sunday
	Holy Thursday	Thursday before Easter Sunday
	Good Friday	Friday before Easter Sunday
Easter begins	Easter Sunday	Sunday following the first full moon after the March equinox
Easter ends	Pentecost Sunday	Seven weeks after Easter Sunday
	All Saints' Day	1 November

Christmas. Similarly, they prepare for the death of Christ during the season of **Lent** and celebrate his triumphant resurrection during the season of **Easter.**

In the **Western** Church, the season of Advent (Latin for "coming") commences four Sundays prior to Christmas Day, usually in late November or early December, and is traditionally regarded as the beginning of the Christian year. In contrast, the **Eastern** Church year commences in September but Orthodox Christians have a preparatory season for Christmas that is known as Winter Lent. As with the main season of Lent, this pre-Christmas period is traditionally a time of fasting and lasts for 40 days. The link with Lent is also visible in the Western tradition where the color of both seasons is purple, symbolizing sobriety and penance.[1]

The themes of Advent focus on keeping vigil for the coming of the **Messiah**. For Christians, this can have two meanings, past and future. First, it refers to Israel's long wait for the promised savior-king which, for Christians, was fulfilled in the historical birth of Christ at Bethlehem. Second, it refers to the present-day waiting for the second coming of Christ at the end of time.[2] In some traditions, the motif of waiting is symbolized by the Advent wreath which is placed in the sanctuary of the church with four candles attached. As each week of the season passes and Christmas draws ever closer, another candle is lit. Advent – or Winter Lent – concludes with the first of the great Christian festivals: Christmas Day. Both Western and Eastern Christians agree that the date of Christmas is December 25, but the celebrations are actually held on different days because the two traditions use different calendars. The Western churches follow the Gregorian calendar, named after Pope Gregory XIII who, in 1582, authorized a revision of the existing calendar to account for a 10-day lag that had arisen since its adoption under Julius Caesar.[3] However the Eastern Church continues to use the older Julian calendar to determine religious dates. Today, the difference between the calendars has increased to 13 days and thus December 25 in the Julian calendar actually falls on January 7 according to the Gregorian calendar.

The date of Christmas is itself an interesting historical tale given that the gospels do not provide any information regarding the precise timing of Christ's birth. The date of December 25 first appears in the third century CE and may be a consequence of the belief among some Christians that **Jesus** was conceived and died on the same date, 25 March.[4] However, the more popular explanation is that Christmas represents the "Christianizing" of an existing pagan feast associated with the northern winter solstice (December 21–2). In the Roman Empire, Saturnalia festivities lasted from December 17 to 23 and involved the closing of businesses as well as singing, gambling, and generally licentious behavior. In 274 CE, the emperor Aurelian chose December 25, a few days after the actual solstice, as the festival of Sol Invictus [The Unconquered Sun].[5] After the conversion of Constantine, the fourth-century Church was able to celebrate its festivals without fear of persecution, and it seemed a natural choice to transform the pagan solstice festival into the Christian feast of the Savior's birth.

The birth of Christ was also to become the key marker from which all Christian time would be measured. A monk named Dionysius Exiguus developed the new system in the sixth century by converting the old Roman year number to the new Christian designation Anno Domini [in the year of the Lord].[6] For the sake of convenience, this numbering system has been almost universally adopted by international organizations today, although the preferred phrase today is "Common Era" out of deference to non-Christians. Ironically, scholars point out that Dionysius made a small error in his calculations and it is likely that Jesus of Nazareth was actually born in the year 6 or 7 BCE. However, the original Christian system expresses the profound theological point that all cosmic time is divided into two great eras on either side of the momentous event of the **Incarnation**. Indeed it is the incarnation of the infinite God in human form that is the major theme of Christmas readings, sermons, and carols. Behind the charming gospel stories of the stable, the star, and the shepherds lies the fundamental claim best expressed in John's gospel: "And the word became flesh and lived among us."[7] The supreme, invisible God is made manifest in a fragile human baby. The focus on the birth of the Son of God is also reflected in traditions such as the nativity scene which adorns churches, homes, public squares, and even department stores in many societies.

Figure 10.1
Christmas
nativity scene

Christmas is a popular time for attending church services and numbers are usually at their highest, even though Christians argue that Easter is the more important feast. It is also a popular time for gift-giving, a tradition that has now overflowed into post-Christian secular society. The biblical inspiration for Christmas presents is Matthew's description of the mysterious "wise men" (**magi**) who follow a star from the East and discover the child Jesus at Bethlehem. There they present him with gifts traditionally identified as gold, frankincense, and myrrh.[8] The historical inspiration for the practice is Saint Nicholas, a fourth-century bishop from Asia Minor who gave gifts to poor children at Christmastide. Dutch settlers in New York brought with them the tradition of Sinterklass [Saint Nicholas] who was eventually refashioned by twentieth-century cartoonists and commercial advertisers into the contemporary myth of Santa Claus. The actual day of gift-giving can vary from culture to culture. In some places it is Saint Nicholas' Day (December 6); in others it is December 25 itself; in others it is January 6, the feast of the Epiphany which marks the arrival of the wise men in Bethlehem and sets up the traditional 12 days of Christmas (following Christmas day). In Western Christianity, the Christmas season lasts until one week after the Epiphany and the joyful color white is used in churches. However Eastern Christians set aside 40 days to celebrate the birthday of the Savior, taking the season to February 2 – the Purification of Mary,[9] or Candlemas when priests traditionally bless all candles for the coming year.

The second great annual Christian feast is Easter which is preceded by a period of preparation known as Lent (from the German for "springtime"). The more somber mood of Lent is signified by the liturgical color and avoidance of the word *alleluia* [praise be to God] in official services. Lent is the principal season of penitence and self-denial, a time when Christians are encouraged to seek forgiveness for sin and to subdue physical desires by fasting, abstinence, and more intensive spiritual activity. Forty days are set aside for Lent on the basis that Jesus fasted in the wilderness for that length of time at the commencement of his public ministry.[10] However, the method of calculating the 40 days varies. The days of Greater Lent, as it is known in the East (to distinguish it from the pre-Christmas period), are counted back from Palm Sunday (a week before Easter) which means that the season begins on what is called Clean Monday. In contrast, the Western Church counts back from Easter Sunday but does not include Sundays which are considered to be days of celebration rather than self-denial. Consequently, the Western Lent begins on Ash Wednesday, so named because ashes are placed on the foreheads of believers as a reminder of their mortality and need for continual repentance.

Most Christians practice some form of fasting or abstinence during Lent although the precise customs vary. For example, in Orthodox Christianity, the Sunday before Clean Monday is Cheesefare Sunday which is the last day to consume dairy foods until Easter. Similarly, the Sunday before this is Meatfare Sunday on which the last meat meals are eaten. The equivalent in the Western tradition is Mardi Gras [Fat Tuesday] – the day before Ash Wednesday and thus the final opportunity to enjoy food, drink, and other sensual pleasures before the austerities of Lent commence. Given its connection with the death of Christ, Friday is the preferred day for acts of self-denial in Western Christianity. But Lent is not only about giving up enjoyment. Many churches encourage believers to undertake positive actions such as spending more time in personal prayer and giving practical help to the poor via Lenten donation programs.

The final week of Lent is commonly referred to as Holy Week. It commences with Palm Sunday which commemorates Jesus's triumphant final entry into Jerusalem accompanied by his followers who enthusiastically waved palm branches in recognition of his messianic status. The season reaches its climax on the final three days: Holy Thursday (Jesus's Last Supper); **Good Friday** (Jesus's death); and Holy Saturday (Jesus's body lies in the tomb). Re-enactments of the **Last Supper** are a common feature of Holy Thursday ceremonies, including Jesus's gesture of washing his disciples' feet at the meal as a sign of leadership via service. Good Friday liturgies vary from denomination to denomination but the common theme is the death of Christ. The gospel description of his arrest, torture, and crucifixion (**the Passion**), is usually read in some form and many Christian groups perform the **Stations of the Cross**, a re-enactment of his final walk from Pontius Pilate's court to the hill of Calvary interspersed with prayerful pauses ("stations") with particular themes linked to his suffering and death (see box 10.1).

THE STATIONS OF THE CROSS ACCORDING TO THE CATHOLIC TRADITION
Box 10.1

1 Jesus is condemned to death
2 Jesus bears his cross
3 Jesus falls the first time
4 Jesus meets his mother
5 Simon helps Jesus carry the cross
6 Veronica wipes Jesus's face
7 Jesus falls the second time
8 Jesus meets the women of Jerusalem
9 Jesus falls the third time
10 Jesus is stripped of his clothing
11 Jesus is nailed to the cross
12 Jesus dies on the cross
13 Jesus is taken down from the cross
14 Jesus is laid in the tomb

As the sun sets on Holy Saturday, the sorrowful, penitential mood of Lent gives way to the exuberant joy of the Easter season which celebrates Christ's **resurrection** from the dead. The term **Easter** is derived from Eostre, the Old English word for April and possibly linked to a pre-Christian goddess of springtime. However, in the majority of European languages the name of the season is clearly derived from the Hebrew *Pesah* (**Passover**). This is significant because Christians consider Jesus's resurrection from the dead to be an even greater passover than the miracle that saved the Israelite nation from Egyptian slavery (see next section). Thus Easter is the "paschal" season. The connection was considered so important that parts of the early Church insisted on celebrating Easter on the same day as the Jewish Passover which, as a full moon feast, could be any day of the week. However other parts of the Church, including Rome, preferred the Sunday following the Passover moon in keeping with the emerging tradition concerning the first day of the week. In 325 the **Council of Nicea** adjudicated in favor of Sunday. As with Christmas, the use of the Julian calendar by Orthodox Christians means that their Easter is usually later than the West.[11]

Following the Jewish tradition of considering sunset as the start of the day, Easter ceremonies commence on the evening of Holy Saturday. Fire and light are the key elements used to express the theme of glory and triumph. A prominent symbol is the large paschal candle on which is inscribed the first and last letters of the Greek alphabet (alpha and omega) as well as the year number. The paschal candle stands in the sanctuary as a constant reminder to believers that the risen Christ is not only the Light of the World but also the Lord of Time.[12] The joyful atmosphere is also reflected in the change from purple to white vestments and the reappearance of "alleluia" in official services. The popular Easter egg itself is a religious symbol of Christ breaking free from the tomb. The season of Easter lasts for seven weeks and a day, ending on **Pentecost** Sunday when Christians commemorate the descent of the Holy Spirit on the apostles and the beginning of the Church's missionary outreach.

The remainder of the year, between Pentecost and the following Advent, is considered to be "ordinary time," during which green is the traditional color in the West. This period is sprinkled with a range of other feasts such as Trinity Sunday, the birthday of Mary, the Dormition (or Assumption) of Mary, and All Saints' Day, which is another example of a pre-existing pagan ritual being redefined and subsumed into the new religion's calendar. There is also a myriad of saints' anniversaries, but the overarching theme that shapes the entire Christian year is clearly the person of Christ. The calendar essentially traces his career from birth through adult ministry to death and resurrection. In none of the other four major religions is such extensive and overwhelming attention given to the founder in the cycle of festivals that mark the religious year. However, a similar focus on the key events in the life of the founder is evident in Buddhism where Sakyamuni, like Jesus, is considered to be the personification of eternal wisdom and the key figure of the age.

🌀 Full Moons and Monsoons

If a certain degree of diversity among churches typifies the Christian year, this is even more the case in Buddhism where no universally recognized calendar exists. For some Buddhists, a preoccupation with festivals may be an unhelpful distraction, for every day of the year should be dedicated to the **dharma**. Nevertheless, Buddhist cultures have developed annual cycles of celebrations. These can vary enormously since quite often they have incorporated local pre-Buddhist customs, but they also share a core of common festivals that celebrate key moments in the life of **Sakyamuni**.

The beginning of the year itself varies across Buddhism. In the **Theravada** tradition, it is linked to the full moon in April although only limited religious significance is attached to it. In Thailand the New Year festival is known as Songkran which is marked by the cleaning of houses and the playful throwing of perfumed water over each other. A popular custom is to gather fish from dried-out water holes and ponds and release them into a river in order to save their lives. In the **Mahayana** and Tibetan traditions, New Year is usually determined by the full moon in January or February, depending on local custom. The Tibetan New Year, or Losar, is a two-week festival stretching from new moon to full moon. Puppet shows and sculptures depict events from Sakyamuni's early life as an Indian prince. Processions of monks carrying large shapes made of butter known as tormas are said to purge away the bad **karma** of the previous year and provide believers with a fresh start.

The more important festivals from a religious perspective are connected to events in the life of the founder. In the Theravada tradition, three in particular are noteworthy, each of which occurs on a full moon and takes its title from the Hindu name of the lunar month in which it occurs. In one sense, these three festivals also correspond to the **Three Jewels** of Buddhism: the teacher (Buddha); the teaching (**dharma**); and the

Table 10.2   The Theravada Buddhist calendar

Holy day	Date
New Year	Full moon (Mar./Apr.)
Vesak	Full moon (Apr./May)
Asalha Puja	Full moon (June/July)
	Three-month Vassa period begins
Pavarana	Vassa ends
Kathina	Within one month of Vassa
Anapanasati	One month after Pavarana
Magha Puja	Full moon (Feb./Mar.)

community (**sangha**). The first festival falls on the full moon of the lunar month Magha (February–March) and is thus aptly named Magha Puja Day. An alternative appellation is Sangha Day in that it commemorates a large assembly of monks at Veruvana Monastery just prior to the Buddha's death. It is also called Fourfold Gathering Day, because it is said that four miracles were involved: the assembly was spontaneous; all of the monks were **arhats**; all of them had been ordained by Sakyamuni; and it was a full moon. On this occasion, the Buddha announced his pending death and delivered the Ovada-Patimokkha Gatha, a summary of the main points of his life's teachings.

The second festival occurs on the full moon of the month of Vaishakha (May–June) and thus is commonly known as **Vesak** or Buddha Day. Of all the Buddhist holy days, Vesak is the most important because it commemorates three critical events in the life of Sakyamuni: his birth, Enlightenment, and death – all of which were said to have occurred under a tree on the full moon of Vaishakha. Any one of these three would have given Vesak the same significance as Christmas or Easter in Christianity. In fact, these three events are often separated in Mahayana calendars such as in the Japanese Buddhist tradition.[13] In Theravada Buddhism, however, the threefold celebration on the one day concentrates an enormous amount of religious significance into Vesak. Practices vary according to local culture but often the laity flock to temples and monasteries to join the monks in honoring the Enlightened One by mantras, readings, sermons, meditation, and alms-giving. Customs include **circumambulation** of the temple or monastery three times to symbolize the Three Jewels; avoiding activities that may cause harm to small creatures; releasing caged birds as a sign of relinquishing anxiety; lighting lamps to signify the Buddha's illumination; and abstaining from meat for those who are not strictly vegetarian.

The third festival is celebrated two months later on the full moon of Asalha (July–August) and thus is called **Asalha Puja** Day. It marks the other crucial event in the life of Sakyamuni not included in Vesak – the Buddha's First Sermon to his five companions at **Sarnath**. Commonly described as the "turning of the wheel," it was this discourse that began the imparting of eternal truth once again. Asalha Puja Day (or Dharma Day, as it is also known) resembles Pentecost Sunday in Christianity, which celebrates the formation of the first believing community and the beginning of missionary outreach. Tibetan Buddhists mark Dharma Day (known in Tibet as Chokhor) by carrying scriptures on long rectangular wooden blocks in procession as a symbol of the spread of the Buddha's teachings.

As in Christianity, there are other festivals that mark various events taken from the Buddha's life on earth. One such commemoration is known as Ladhap in Tibet and Abhidhamma Day in the Theravada tradition. It recalls Sakyamuni's return to earth from one of the heavenly realms where he met his mother and preached the **Four Noble Truths** to her. Akin to Dharma Day, it is also a statement that the transmission of truth should have no bounds. In the **Pure Land** Mahayana tradition, where the stress on the celestial bodhisattva **Avalokiteshvara** (**Kwanyin** in China) is greater than on Sakyamuni, the key festivals commemorate her birth, enlightenment, and death.

Just as the main Buddhist feasts parallel those of Christianity by focusing on key events in the life of the founder, the Buddhist calendar also contains a Lent-like period during which believers should withdraw from everyday concerns and renew spiritual energy. Immediately after Asalha Puja Day, the **Vassa** period, or Rains Retreat, commences and, as the name suggests, lasts until the end of the wet season. Sakyamuni and the early generations of monks practiced itinerant preaching, but during the monsoon period travel was difficult as rivers swelled and roads became muddy. Moreover, their health could easily be undermined if they spent too much time outdoors in the rain. Thus the Buddha instructed monks to remain in one sheltered place for the duration of the season. A spiritual meaning subsequently arose from this practical necessity: it became a period of retreat spent in study and meditation. The rains also mean that fewer visitors come to the monasteries, enabling the monks to focus on such activities. Thus the **Vinaya Pitaka** stipulates that a monk may not spend a night away from his monastery during the Rains Retreat without the express permission of his superior. Special circumstances warranting such absence include illness in a family member or urgent work, but even then the monk has to return within seven days.[14]

The intensive spiritual activity of Vassa is not restricted to the monk or the nun. Lay persons often join a monastic community for part or all of the season and are sometimes appositely called "rain monks." In some Buddhist societies, such as Thailand and Burma, there is a strong expectation that a young man will become a temporary monk at some stage during his adolescence. For those who do not actually join a monastery, there are other ways of observing Vassa, such as adopting monastic vows privately, giving alms to the monks more frequently, abstaining from meat, alcohol, or tobacco, and practicing regular daily chants. In some cultures, families avoid planning weddings during this period. Many Buddhist communities hold special celebrations with meals to mark the end of the Vassa retreat on Pavarana Day. For many families it is also a time when their son returns home after his term in the monastery.

Within a month of the termination of the Vassa retreat, many communities hold a special ceremony during which the laity offer new robes to the monks. The **Kathina** ritual takes its name from the traditional wooden frame used for sewing clothes. The laity present the monastery with material that is used by several monks to cut and sew a set of robes. These are then presented by the lay community to a monk who has just completed the Vassa retreat and is nominated by the abbot. Kathina is highly symbolic because it captures in a simple gesture the fundamental relationship in Buddhism between the inner monastic community and the broader lay community. Just

Figure 10.2
Young Buddhists
often join a
monastery during
the wet season
(Vassa)

as the laity provide material support for the monks in the form of clothing and food, so the monks reciprocate by offering the good karma that they have accumulated by their more advanced spiritual way of life. Kathina ceremonies can attract large crowds and thus constitute an important opportunity for monasteries to raise funds as well.

Another major event on the Buddhist calendar, especially in the Mahayana tradition, is Ulambana, or the Festival of the **Hungry Ghosts**. One of the realms on the Buddhist wheel of life, into which the dead can be reincarnated, is that of the hungry ghosts. In that world, beings are doomed to incessant hunger as a result of their large stomachs and small mouths. The suffering will eventually purge away bad karma so that they can be reincarnated in a higher realm and eventually reach **nirvana**. According to popular Buddhist belief, the ghosts are released for 15 days at this time of year and allowed to wander the earth in search of food offerings. For many families, it is possible that some of their deceased relatives may be among the hungry ghosts and so it is imperative that action be taken to alleviate their suffering and help them along the road to liberation. A popular story told at this time concerns **Maudgalyana**, one of the earliest disciples of Sakyamuni and renowned for his miraculous powers. During meditation one day, Maudgalyana saw his deceased mother in a terrible state of suffering. Perturbed, he asked Sakyamuni for advice and was told to prepare food offerings for her and other deceased persons in the manner of the Hindu **shraddha** tradition. Thus Ulambana is a particularly appropriate time for Buddhists to pay their respects to the dead by visiting graves and making small offerings of food as Maudgalyana did. In Japan the festival is known as Obon and is characterized by paper lanterns displayed in front of homes and in cemeteries so that the wandering ghosts are able to find their resting place at the end of the period. Sometimes lanterns and candles are floated down rivers or out to sea to symbolize the return of the spirits to their proper abode. Obon dances held at night are a highlight of the festival, in memory of Maudgalyana's dance of joy upon freeing his mother. The festival of hungry ghosts reflects a fundamental belief in Buddhism that the actions of the living can in some way benefit the dead. It is a similar idea to that which underpins the Christian holy days dedicated to assisting the deceased such as All Souls' Day in the Catholic tradition and the eve of Pentecost in the Orthodox Church.

A myriad of other feast days populate Buddhist calendars, many of them culturally specific such as the Festival of the Tooth in Sri Lanka, the Elephant Festival in Thailand, and Guru Rimpoche's birthday in Tibet. However, Buddhist calendars in general are characterized by an emphasis on the key moments in the life of Sakyamuni in the Theravada tradition or of Kwanyin in the Mahayana tradition, as well as the insertion of a special season of spiritual renewal. In this respect, the Buddhist year resembles the Christian year which is heavily structured on the life of the founder and includes the Lenten season as a time of self-denial and replenishment. Even the numbering of the years is similar to the Christian system, although it is the death of Sakyamuni (traditionally understood to be 544 BCE), rather than his birth, that is considered Year One of the Buddhist Era.

However, the Buddhist concept of cosmic time is radically different from that of Christianity and the other **Semitic religions**. For Buddhists, the universe comes into being and dissolves again in an eternal series of cycles. Each cycle spans billions of years and is further subdivided into eons. The progression from one eon to the next is generally characterized by a gradual decline in wisdom and virtue. Sakyamuni himself predicted that, as the years went by, his teaching would eventually be forgotten and the next Buddha in the long series, **Maitreya**, would come to restore the lost truth.[15] Such a sweeping cyclic cosmology was inherited from its mother religion, Hinduism, which is the source of several notable features of the Buddhist calendar including festival dates determined by the lunar phases, the names of the months, and special religious significance attached to the wet season.

Day of Brahma

It is said that Hinduism has a longer list of festivals than any other religious tradition, with a celebration of some sort on almost every day of the year. Part of the reason for

Table 10.3　The southern Hindu calendar

Season	Month	Date	Time of month	Holy day
Spring	Chaitra	Mar.–Apr.	new moon	New Year
Summer	Vaishakha	Apr.–May		
	Jyaistha	May–June		
Rains	Ashadha	June–July	11th day of bright fortnight	Sleep of Vishnu commences
	Shravana	July–Aug.	full moon	Rakhi Bandan
Autumn	Badra	Aug.–Sept.	14 days of the dark fortnight	Ancestors' Fortnight
	Ashvina	Sept.–Oct.	10 days following the new moon	Navaratri–Dussehra
Winter	Kartika	Oct.–Nov.	new moon	Divali
	Agrahayana	Nov.–Dec.		
Cool	Pausha	Dec.–Jan.		
	Magha	Jan.–Feb.		
Spring	Phalguna	Feb.–Mar.	new moon	Holi
			full moon	Mahashivaratri

such a proliferation of feasts is the enormous regional and cultic diversity within Hinduism itself. For example, at the time of independence, the Indian government identified over 30 different religious calendars in operation. However, amid the bewildering variety there are some common traits, especially across the two calendars most widely used in India for religious purposes: the Vikram calendar in the north and the Shalivahana calendar in the south.

As with many religions, Hinduism defines its months by the phases of the moon. Thus, in the Shalivahana system, the month always begins with a new moon and is always divided into a bright half while the moon waxes (shukla paksha) and a dark half while the moon wanes (krishna paksha). Conversely, in the Vikram system the month commences with the full moon. In both systems, 12 lunar months equate to only 354 days and thus an adhik mas [extra month] is added every two or three years to maintain synchronicity with the the solar cycle.[16] The two calendars also differ in the way they reckon the beginning of the year. In the north, New Year is celebrated on the full moon of Kartika (October–November) while in the south it is the new moon of Chaitra (March–April). In both traditions, not only the New Year but the creation of the universe itself is commemorated since it is said to have occurred on this day. In many parts of India, houses are cleaned and decorated, greetings and sweets are exchanged, and people visit temples to hear a reading of the new almanac (pancanga), with its predictions for the coming year in terms of personal and public life.

The Hindu year is traditionally divided into six seasons: spring, summer, rains, autumn, winter, and cool season (see table 10.3). These are often arranged into pairs constituting a caturmasya – a period consisting of four months or one-third of the year. Each of these has its own particular tone, themes, and rituals, the most prominent of which is the caturmasya of the rains and autumn between July and October. While Buddhism sets aside the wet season as a time of retreat and spiritual renewal, the **Vaishnavite** tradition sees the period of monsoon rains as a dangerous and inauspicious time. On the eleventh day (ekadasi) of the bright fortnight of Ashadha, it is said that Vishnu retires below the ocean for four months of deep sleep. Caution and care are needed for the world is without its Lord and thus subject to malevolent forces. Hence, Hindus avoid weddings and abstain from a certain food each month, such as spinach, yogurt, milk, and lentils.

Despite the sense of dread, some of Hinduism's most important feast days are held during the Sleep of Vishnu, partly as a means of countering the spiritual danger. The first of these is **Rakhi Bandan** which occurs on the full moon of Shravana (August). The term literally means "a band of protection" which points to the central symbolic act. On this day each year, sisters, girlfriends, and wives tie a band or thread (rakhi) around the wrist of their brothers, boyfriends, and husbands as a sign of spiritual safeguard. The story behind the custom tells of how Indra's wife, Sachi, took a thread, prayed sacred mantras over it, and tied it to Indra's hand before a great battle. Hindus believe that the band will bring protection and security to the wearer. On occasions, women have tied rakhis to the wrists of unknown soldiers about to depart for war. Conversely, the tying of the band also signifies the duty incumbent on the brother, boyfriend, or husband to care for the woman he loves as a sibling or partner. Rakhi Bandan is thus a time to renew the mutual bonds of family love. Rakhis are often made of colored silk and are highly decorated. The rakhi is placed on a plate along with other objects such as a small lamp, some water, rice, sweets, and vermilion powder. As the rakhi is tied, the **tilak** is applied to the forehead and the sweets are eaten. In some places, Rakhi Bandan is also the occasion on which the **twice-born** males of the upper classes replace their sacred thread with a new one.

One month later, at the very heart of the dangerous period when Vishnu sleeps, Hindus dedicate the dark fortnight of the month of Bhadra to the dead. Prayers and offerings for deceased family members are a feature of every new moon (amavashya) throughout the year, but the Mahalaya Amavashya, or Ancestors' Fortnight, is a special time to assist those who have passed away on their journey to the higher worlds. Akin to the Buddhist Festival of the Hungry Ghosts, and the Christian All Souls' Day, Ancestors' Fortnight is characterized by shraddha food offerings for the

pretas as well as acts of charity for which good karma is generated and diverted for the benefit of the dead.

As the new moon of Ashvina brings the Ancestors' Fortnight to a close, it simultaneously ushers in the nine-day festival of **Navaratri** [Nine Nights] followed by a tenth day known as Dussehra. The main focus of Navaratri is the Mother Goddess – the manifestation of ultimate reality (**Brahman**) in feminine form. There are many ways in which Navaratri is commemorated, one of which is to dedicate three sets of three days to each of the main personifications of **Shakti** (the Mother Goddess): **Saraswati** (goddess of the arts and learning); **Lakshmi** (goddess of wealth and prosperity); and **Durga** (goddess of strength and fortitude). In other cases, believers place a different image of the goddess on a series of shelves known as a golu. Many visitors come to see a golu and it is a common custom to give them **prasad** and small gifts afterwards. In some parts of India, a statue of Durga is taken to the local riverbank or seashore and immersed in the water as a symbol of the purging away of accumulated unhappiness and bad karma.[17] Navaratri is an auspicious time to commence new projects and often people bring along items from their work such as tools or equipment to be blessed. On the tenth night, Dussehra, the main theme shifts from prayers for prosperity to the victory of **Rama** over the demon Ravanna as told in the Hindu epic the **Ramayana**. Huge paper and wooden effigies of Ravanna are constructed during the festival and burned on this night, symbolizing the destruction of evil.

The next new moon, at the start of the month of Kartika, is arguably the most popular and widely celebrated festival on the Hindu calendar – **Divali**. The name means "a row of lamps" and indeed light is the dominant symbol of the holy day which is linked to the New Year in the northern calendar. Under a dark moonless sky, the Indian landscape becomes ablaze with millions of lights emanating from sources that range from small oil lamps known as diyas to more sophisticated electric globes. Houses are cleaned and decorated with beautiful rangoli patterns on the floor; lamps are placed on window sills and porches; and brilliant fireworks are set off during the night. The theme of illumination is given various meanings, of which two are prominent. First, Divali commemorates the safe return to India of Rama and his rescued bride, Sita. According to the Ramayana, people lit the way home by placing lamps along the path in the darkness. Second, Divali is the time when Lakshmi, the goddess of prosperity, visits the earth bringing fortune and success to those she blesses. Thus the washing, decorating, and illuminating of homes are all intended to attract her attention and benevolence. Lakshmi's image is usually portrayed with coins falling from her hands, and many businesses prefer to commence their new financial year at this time. As with Christmas, Divali is not only an occasion for giving gifts and exchanging cards but also a powerful stimulus to the Indian economy.

The time following Divali is quieter, but two key festivals highlight the final month of the year according to the southern calendar system. The new moon at the

Figure 10.3
Hindu girls light lamps on the feast of Divali to welcome home Rama and Sita

commencement of Phalguna constitutes the important **Shaivite** holy day, **Maha-shivaratri** [Great Night of Shiva]. Unlike Divali and Navaratri, this is a time of self-discipline in the spirit of **Shiva** himself who is considered to be the supreme model of worldly renunciation. Followers observe strict fasting and abstinence. Often meat, curry, and cereals are avoided, and in some cases only water is taken. The mood is solemn rather than joyful. Believers visit temples and spend the entire night in vigil, chanting hymns, making food offerings, and bathing images of Shiva in foodstuffs such as milk, curds, ghee, sugar, and honey. The holy day has various meanings. One version claims that on this night Shiva performs the Tandava dance through which the universe was created and continues to be sustained. One of the most recognizable forms of Shiva in statues and paintings is **Nataraja**, the many-armed Lord of the Dance, surrounded by the fiery circle of the ever-changing physical world. A second theme associated with the Great Night is Shiva not as the detached ascetic but as the ideal husband who weds his consort **Parvati**. The night is considered especially auspicious for women. Young unmarried girls petition the god for a future groom, while wives pray for the well-being of their husbands.

In striking contrast to the ascetical mood of Mahashivaratri is the raucous, licen-tious festival **Holi** which falls on the full moon of the same month. Holi is an abbre-viation of Holika, sister of the demon king Hiranyakasyapu. According to the myth, Holika had the power to walk through fire unharmed. However, when she attempted to kill the child devotee Prahlad by taking him on her lap and sitting on a pyre of blazing wood it was Holika herself who was burned to death while Prahlad miraculously survived. The moral of the story is the triumph of good over evil. The myth is recalled every year via the burning of images representing Holika and Prahlad in huge bonfires at dusk. Usually the Holika figure is constructed of flammable materials while the Prahlad figure is non-combustible in order to achieve the appropriate effect. People participate by throwing branches and pieces of wood onto the fire. Coconuts and coins are tossed in and people circumambulate the flames a number of times for good karma. The following morning, believers gather the ashes which are considered to be holy and auspicious, smearing them on their bodies.

There is a second aspect to Holi for which it is more widely known. Alcohol and meat are more liberally consumed; verbal exchanges are less restrained and even ribald; wives may disagree with their husbands; lower castes may taunt upper castes; and general deportment becomes more riotous and merry. In a religion where caste and gender rules impinge heavily on social behavior, Holi, like the Christian Mardi Gras, is an occasion when these restrictions can be shifted if not altogether removed. The abiding image of Holi is of people indiscriminately throwing colored water or powder over each other in an atmosphere of gay abandonment. The result is that persons of all ages and classes and both sexes look the same color – usually a shade of pink or purple. For one day in the year, the color of one's class (**varna**) is irrelevant, suggesting a fundamental equality beneath the socio-religious superstructure. Thus, it is not surprising that Holi is one of the most loved festivals in India, especially among the lower classes. The most popular stories at Holi are those of the young **Krishna** who played mischievous pranks on the local cowgirls (gopis) and indulged in steamy affairs with them.

The Hindu calendar is also dotted with numerous birthdays of gods and heroes: Rama, **Hanuman**, Narasimha, Krishna, and Ganesha to name a few. While most key festivals are held on a new moon or a full moon, Hindus also celebrate the sankranti – the day on which the sun moves into a new zodiacal constellation. Two of these have particular significance. The Aries sankranti (Mesh Sankranti) represents the commencement of a new solar year when Hindus often begin wedding preparations for their sons and daughters. The Capricorn sankranti (Makar Sankranti) is associated with the winter solstice and, like Christmas, represents the return of the sun to the northern hemisphere and the gradual lengthening of the days.

Several systems provide the basis for a Hindu year number. The one endorsed by the official government calendar and prominent in southern India takes King Shalivahan's accession to the throne in 78 CE as the first year of the epoch. Thus on this reckoning the year 2000 was 1922. The Vikram calendar, prevalent in northern India, counts the years from King Vikramaditya's reign which commenced in 56 BCE. However, for religious purposes, the more significant and traditional system dates the

---

THE FOUR YUGAS (AGES) OF THE HINDU TIME SCALE   **BOX 10.2**

1   Satya Yuga: 1,728,000 years (age of perfect spiritual knowledge)
2   Treta Yuga: 1,296,000 years (age of advanced mental powers)
3   Dvapara Yuga: 864,000 years (age of rational thought)
4   Kali Yuga: 432,000 years (age of materialism)

---

current era from the death of Krishna. According to Hindu myth, this occurred in February 3012 BCE and ushered in the final phase of the fourfold cycle of Hindu cosmic time. Each phase or **yuga** in the cycle becomes progressively shorter and is characterized by a gradual decline in spiritual knowledge and morality. The current phase is the Kali yuga which will last for 432,000 years. The entire cycle consists of four such yugas and endures for over 4 million years (see box 10.2).

As in Buddhism, the vastness of Hindu time scales becomes even more apparent when it is realized that the lifespan of the current universe is said to be 1,000 of these cycles, or over 4 billion years. This is known as one Day of **Brahma** who wakes from a 4-billion-year-long night of sleep. After 100 such "days" and "nights," the present universe will descend into nothingness and the eternal cycle will begin again. For this reason, it is understandable why the moon is such a dominant factor in Hindu time and a key symbol in Hindu theology. Often seen in Shiva's hair, the ever-changing moon symbolizes not only the reincarnational nature of human existence but also the cyclic nature of cosmic existence on the largest scale imaginable.

The colossal scale and cyclic nature of Hindu–Buddhist time seems far removed from the more modest, linear view of history found in the Semitic religions. The eternal birth and death of the universe and the billions of years involved in just one Day of Brahma stand in strong contrast to the traditional biblical understanding of the world as a one-off project that is only about 6,000 years old. Yet, although the meanings differ, the Jewish year also has 12 lunar months, an occasional intercalary (extra) month, full moon feasts, a festival of light, a day of liberal alcoholic intake, a ceremony of casting evil into the waters, periods when weddings are avoided, and, most significantly, the absence of a series of biographical commemorations focused on a single founder (as in Christianity and Buddhism).

Harvests, History, and High Holy Days

For two days in September or early October each year, Jews gather in large numbers in **synagogue** for a long and solemn service. The usual colored cloths covering the

Ark and the Torah scrolls inside it are replaced by white, the color of purity. At various points during the prayers, the sound of a ram's horn (**shofar**) pierces the air announcing that the Books of Life and Death have been opened in heaven and a new religious year has begun. The festival is known by various names such as the Day of the Horn Blowing, the Day of Judgment, and the Day of Remembrance. However, its most popular title is **Rosh Hashanah** [Head of the Year]. Rosh Hashanah falls on the new moon that marks the first day of Tishri. This is the month in which it is traditionally believed God created the world in 3760 BCE, the basis for the calculation of the Jewish year number. Thus the year 2000 was 5760 on the Jewish calendar. Unlike the New Year tradition in many other cultures and religions, the Jewish year begins in an atmosphere of soul-searching and penitence rather than exuberant joy and revelry. Rosh Hashanah, the first of the **High Holy Days** of Judaism, ushers in a 10-day period known as the yamim noraim [days of awe].[18] During that brief time, each person strives to insure that their name is written in the Book of Life by honest self-examination and a sincere request for forgiveness from God and neighbor. Similar to the Hindu custom at Dussehra, **Ashkenazi** Jews perform tashlikh, in which they visit a riverbank or the seashore and throw away breadcrumbs from their pockets, symbolically casting off sins that have attached to their person during the previous year.[19] But Rosh Hashanah is not only about acknowledgment of guilt and purification: Jews also thank God for the sweet gift of another year, signified by dipping bread and apple in honey.

The ten days end with **Yom Kippur,** the second High Holy Day and arguably the most important day in the entire Jewish calendar. Sometimes described as the "sabbath of sabbaths," it is a time when almost all activity in Israel shuts down.[20] Like Christmas in Christianity, Yom Kippur is the one day of the year when non-practicing Jews are most likely to attend synagogue. In many ways it is as much about Jewish identity as about religious devotion. There are five synagogue services that run almost continuously from evening to evening and some devout Jews remain in the synagogue for almost the whole night and day.

The term *Yom Kippur* literally means Day of Atonement, and forgiveness of sin is the key theme. On the previous day, **Orthodox** Jews perform the kapparot ritual. Based on the biblical scapegoat ceremony, kapparot involves holding a rooster (for a man) or a hen (for a woman) over one's head and swinging it in a circle three times while reciting a prayer that transfers guilt onto the animal.[21] Alternatively, the animal is replaced by a small bag of coins. Some Jewish men also take a ritual bath (**mikveh**) in preparation. The evening service commences with the melodious chanting of the Kol Nidre, a traditional Aramaic prayer annulling unfulfilled vows to God. A litany of sins is then read out on behalf of believers who acknowledge their collective guilt and ask God for pardon. It is very rare that Jews kneel or prostrate for fear of idolatry but during the Yom Kippur service the cantor may prostrate himself as a gesture of sorrow and humility. As with Rosh Hashanah, white is used for synagogue adornments as a symbol of the purity that comes from divine forgiveness. Ashkenazi Jews may also wear the traditional white tunic or **kittel**.

Yom Kippur is perhaps best known for its strict 25-hour fast, which, it is said, brings one closer to the angels, who do not require food. The fast is also one of the five innuyim (forbidden activities) that represent the ascetical dimension of Yom Kippur. Apart from avoiding food and drink, Jews also abstain from anointing with oil, sexual intercourse, washing for pleasure, and wearing leather shoes. The final service is aptly named Ne'ilah, or the "closing of the gates." As the shofar sounds for the last time, the 10 days of awe come to an end, the heavenly books are closed, and the opportunity for formal reconciliation passes for another year.

There are several other fast days on the Jewish calendar, but only one that lasts the full 25 hours and involves the five innuyim as on Yom Kippur. **Tisha B'Av** [Av 9] commemorates the tragic destruction of the First and Second **Temples**, which are believed to have occurred on the same date. The colors of the synagogue are changed to dark blue, marking one of the saddest days on the calendar. Tisha B'Av is also one of the holy days on which one of the Five Scrolls (**Megillot**) is read (see box 10.3). In this case it is the book of Lamentations which narrates the devastation of Jerusalem under the Babylonian armies. Four other days impose a simple dawn-to-dusk fast:

*   Tishri 3 (the assassination of Gedaliah, governor of Israel, during the Babylonian invasion);
*   Tevet 10 (the beginning of the siege of Jerusalem by the Babylonians);
*   Adar 13 (the fast of Esther);
*   Tamuz 17 (the breaching of the city walls by the Romans).[22]

But the Jewish year is not restricted to days of fasting and penitence. There are also great feasts of cheerful celebration. While white in synagogues symbolizes an atmosphere of penitence and forgiveness, the synagogue is often adorned in green for three

---

THE FIVE SCROLLS AND THEIR CORRESPONDING HOLY DAYS

Box 10.3

Scroll	*Holy day*
Song of Songs	Passover
Ruth	Shavuot
Lamentations	Tisha B'Av
Qoheleth	Sukkoth
Esther	Purim

prominent annual religious festivals that acknowledge nature's bounty and God's gracious intervention in Israel's history. Together they are known as the pilgrim festivals because male believers in biblical times were required by law to make their way to Jerusalem as pilgrims and offer the first-fruits of the harvest to the Temple priests. The first is Pesah, or **Passover**. One of the best known of Jewish festivals, it commences on the full moon of the month of Nissan (March or April) and lasts for seven or eight days, depending on the branch of Judaism and whether or not one is in Israel. Nissan is actually the first month of the religious calendar whereas Tishri is the first month for matters of life and death. For this reason the extra thirteenth month, occasionally added to keep the calendar synchronized with the solar year, is inserted between Adar and Nissan and is aptly known as Second Adar. In terms of agricultural significance, Passover is associated with the spring barley harvest. But in terms of historical significance, it commemorates the most important event in Israel's past: the miraculous escape from Egypt.[23] The term *passover* actually refers to the moment when the angel of death passed over the homes of the Hebrew slaves during the final plague because they had marked their doorposts with the blood of a lamb.[24] Naturally, the key theme of the festival is liberation from all forms of slavery.

Table 10.4   The Jewish calendar

Hebrew month	Western months	Hebrew date	Holy day
Tishri	Sept.–Oct.	1	Rosh Hashanah
		10	Yom Kippur
		15	Sukkoth commences
		22	Simhat Torah
Heshvan	Oct.–Nov.		
Kislev	Nov.–Dec.	25	Hanukkah commences
Tevet	Dec.–Jan.		
Shevat	Jan.–Feb.		
Adar	Feb.–Mar.	14	Purim
second Adar (added in a leap year)			
Nisan	Mar.–Apr.	14–21	Passover commences
Iyar	Apr.–May		
Sivan	May–June	6	Shavuot
Tamuz	June–July		
Av	July–Aug.	9	Tisha B'Av
Elul	Aug.–Sept.		

As with many Jewish festivals, food is given a special religious meaning. One of the key symbols is the use of unleavened bread (**matzah***)* for the entire week. On the eve of the full moon, houses are emptied of all leaven (**hametz**) in a sort of spring-clean.[25] Special Passover crockery is brought out since it is possible that the set normally used may have absorbed some leaven. Matzah symbolizes the haste with which the Israelite slaves were forced to leave Egypt. Some also see in its flattened shape the rejection of "puffed up" vanity and pride. Unleavened bread is only one of the highly symbolic foodstuffs that are placed on the table during the **seder**, or evening Passover meal. Each food type represents an aspect of the **Exodus** experience: either the harshness of slavery or the sweetness of the escape (see chapter 7). As with most Jewish ceremonies, wine symbolizes the goodness of God, and four cups are drunk at Passover while a fifth is kept in case Elijah appears unexpectedly. Dress is usually formal and in Ashkenazi families, the head of the household often wears the kittel which also functions as a wedding gown, a burial shroud, and a garment for Yom Kippur. Passover is essentially a family affair, celebrated with happiness and gratitude around the domestic table, during which the youngest child asks four ritual questions designed to explain the meaning of the Exodus. The Megillah for Passover services is the joyous **Song of Songs**.

The second pilgrim festival comes seven weeks after Passover and thus is suitably named **Shavuot** [Weeks], or Pentecost (from the Greek for "fifty days"). A one- or two-day festival in May or June, Shavuot celebrates the summer wheat harvest but it also commemorates the revelation of the **Torah** to Moses on **Mount Sinai**. Hence the key theme is the gift of knowledge and learning. Shavuot was traditionally the time to commence one's religious education and to hold **confirmation** ceremonies in **Reform Judaism**. There are no specific rituals such as the Passover seder, but it is customary to decorate homes and synagogues with flowers and plants, symbolizing the height of the harvest season. Dairy products such as cheesecakes and blintzes (pancakes) are commonly served at Shavuot, based on the belief that the first Israelite community had no time to prepare a **kosher** meat dish on the day the Torah was revealed and thus ate dairy foods to avoid breaking the law. The special scroll for Shavuot is the book of Ruth, possibly because of its agricultural setting. The period between Pesah and Shavuot is known as the "Counting of the Omer [Sheaf]" and many families use a special omer board for this purpose, based on the biblical commandment to count the days between the two harvests.[26] Jews also see it as a reminder that the Exodus was not complete until the Torah was given. Freedom needs to be complemented with truth and purpose. According to the **Talmud** it is also a time of mourning for thousands of Rabbi Akiva's students who died in a plague.[27] Thus Jews refrain from weddings, parties, dances, and haircuts except on the thirty-third day when the plague is said to have lifted. A similar period of restriction is observed between the two fast days of Tamuz 17 and Ab 9, around July each year. The 50-day interval from Passover to Shavuot is mirrored in the 50 days from Easter Sunday to Pentecost Sunday on the Christian calendar.

The final pilgrim festival is **Sukkoth** which commences on the full moon of the first month Tishri, just five days after Yom Kippur. Like Passover, Sukkoth lasts for seven or eight days and coincides with the autumn fruit harvest. The term *sukkoth* means "booth" or "tent" and the festival commemorates the 40 years that the freed Hebrew slaves spent in the wilderness as tent-dwelling nomads prior to settling in the land of Israel.[28] Thus the key theme is divine protection. For the duration of the festival, Jews build a simple booth in their backyards with a partially open roof so that the stars can be seen at night.[29] In solidarity with the Israelites of old, believers take their meals inside the booth, and some even sleep in it. In the **Kabbalist** tradition, an invisible guest visits the booth on each evening: **Abraham**, **Isaac**, **Jacob**, Joseph, **Moses**, Aaron, and **David**. The other important symbolic action at Sukkoth is the four species. At morning synagogue services during the festival, Jews go in procession carrying a citron (lemon-like fruit) in the left hand and branches of palm, myrtle, and willow in the right. These items are waved in all directions, acknowledging the omnipresence of God and in fulfillment of the commandment to rejoice before the Lord.[30] The Megillah for Sukkoth is the book of Qoheleth. Its pessimistic tone is sometimes associated with the transition from summer to winter which is said to occur on Shemini Atzeret, the last day of the festival. The following day is known as **Simhat Torah**, on which the annual cycle of synagogue Torah readings ends and immediately recommences.

There are many other festivals scattered throughout the Jewish year, two of which deserve special mention. The feast of **Purim** occurs on the full moon of Adar in March. It is appropriate that the Megillah that is read is the book of Esther, for Purim commemorates the courage of the story's heroine who saves her people from destruction under the wicked king Haman. *Purim* literally means "lots" and refers to the casting of lots to determine the date for the planned massacre.[31] The Megillah is proclaimed publicly at evening and morning services, evoking noisy banging and shouting from the congregation as the enemy's name is read out. Although Judaism does not condone intoxication, the rabbinic tradition encourages the celebratory drinking of alcohol at Purim until one can no longer distinguish the phrases "Cursed be Haman" and "Blessed be Mordecai" (Esther's uncle).[32] Masks and costumes add to the carefree, carnival-like atmosphere of Purim which is reminiscent of Hindu Holi and Christian Mardi Gras.

While scholars have doubts as to the historicity of the Esther story, there is no uncertainty about the events behind the other prominent Jewish festival that celebrates victory over Israel's enemies. **Hanukkah** commences on the 25 Kislev and commemorates the recapturing of the Temple in 165 BCE from **Hellenistic** Syrian overlords by a small group of Jewish freedom fighters under Judas Maccabeus.[33] The term *Hanukkah* literally means "rededication" and refers to the fact that the Jews had to purify their holiest shrine after it had been desecrated by pagan practices and rituals. The festival lasts for eight days in memory of the miracle of the oil. According to the Talmud, the only uncontaminated oil found in the Temple was a small cruse that should have been exhausted after one day, but amazingly lasted eight days.[34] Thus foods cooked in oil such as potato pancakes, doughnuts, and fritters are popular at Hanukkah. Like the Hindu Divali, the predominant symbol is light. In place of the usual seven-branched **menorah** (candelabra), a special eight-branched version known as a hanukkiyah is used. Each evening after sunset, an extra candle is lit, building up to eight by the end of the feast. Of course, the candle is lit before sunset on the Friday to avoid contravening the sabbath law. The Talmud encourages Jews to place their candles in doorways and windows to proclaim God's miraculous intervention.[35]

Thus the Jewish calendar reflects the vicissitudes of Israel's experience in a fascinating blend of joy and sorrow, pleasure and austerity, feasting and fasting. At one level its key feasts express gratitude for the God of nature who insures the earth's fertility year after year via the harvests. At another level they also commemorate the saving intervention of the God of history at crucial moments in the past. As in Hinduism and Buddhism, the cycles of the moon and the seasons are used as a natural background against which to celebrate holy days of particular significance. This is possible because all three religions combine the lunar month with the solar year. Christianity, in contrast, adopted the Roman solar calendar in which the months have no connection to the moon. Conversely, the religion of the crescent moon and the star embraced a purely lunar year and thus disconnected its festivals from the natural cycle of the seasons. Moreover, Islam's calendar is not primarily constructed around the life of the founder as in the case of Christianity and Buddhism; its focal points are elsewhere.

Figure 10.4
Eight-branched menorah (with central lighting candle) used at Hanukkah

☪ Lunar Year

In September 622, the fledgling Muslim community emigrated from the town of Mecca to the town of Yathrib, some 250 miles to the north. After a decade of hostility and persecution, the epic relocation would bring security and consolidation. Yathrib was aptly renamed Al-Medina al-Nabi [The Town of the Prophet] which is usually shortened to Medina. From this new base, **Muhammad** would prove to be not only an authoritative spokesman for God but also a successful leader of men. Later, when the caliph **Umar** decided to number the years according to a new Islamic calendar, it was that journey, known as the **Hijra**, that was chosen as Year One.[36] Thus Islamic years are traditionally followed by "AH" (Anno Hegirae, or "in the year of the Hijra") in the same way as the Christian system used "AD" (Anno Domini, or "in the year of the Lord").

However, when one considers that 2000 CE was 1420 AH, it becomes apparent that the difference between the two systems is currently 580 years and not the expected 622. The reason is that the Islamic year is shorter than the Western year by 11 days and thus is slowly catching up. This is because the Muslim calendar uses a lunar year or 12 lunar months, each lasting only 29 or 30 days (see table 10.5). The **Qur'an** unambiguously states that the new religious community is to eschew the Arabian and Jewish practice of inserting an intercalary month:

> Surely the number of months with Allah is twelve months in Allah's ordinance since the day when He created the heavens and the earth, of these four being sacred; that is the right reckoning; therefore be not unjust to yourselves regarding them, and fight the polytheists all together as they fight you all together; and know that Allah is with those who guard (against evil).[37]

The consequence is that all annual Islamic festivals, which are set to lunar dates, drift through the seasons on a 33-year cycle.

Table 10.5   The Islamic calendar

Month	Date	Holy day
Muharram	1	New Year
	10	Ashura
Safar		
Rabi' al-awwal	12 or 17	Birthday of Muhammad (Mawlid an-Nabi)
Rabi' al-thani		
Jumada al-awwal		
Jumada al-thani		
Rajab		
Sha'aban	15	Birthday of the Mahdi, or Night of Forgiveness (Lailat al-Barah)
Ramadan (month of fasting)	23 or 27	Night of Power (Lailat al-Qadr)
Shawwal	1–3	Id al-Fitr
Dhu al-Qi'dah		
Dhu al-Hijjah	10	Id al-Adha

The Islamic year begins on the first day of the month of Muharram but there is only limited religious significance attached to the date. In some cultures cards are exchanged and the New Year is ushered in with thanksgiving and joy. However, for **Shi'ite** Muslims it is the beginning of 10 days of preparation for one of their most significant holy days. On the tenth day of Muharram, they commemorate the death of Muhammad's grandson, **Hussain**, at the Battle of **Karbala**[38] in 680. Popularly known as **Ashura** (tenth), it is a day of intense sorrow, akin to Tisha B'Av for Jews and Good Friday for Christians. Men gather in public for ceremonial chest-beating known as matham. Some even flagellate themselves using a zanjeer – a chain tipped with curved knives – although such extremism is officially discouraged. The climax of the event is a passion play re-enacting Hussain's death, much like the Christian Stations of the Cross. Emotions run high because Shi'ites consider Hussain to have been the rightful successor to the Prophet via his father, **Ali**. In contrast, **Sunnis** believe that **Abu Bakr** and his successors were chosen as the first caliphs according to God's will and thus do not ascribe the same significance to Ashura. Instead, Sunnis attribute to it a range of meanings including the day of creation, the day that Noah left the ark, the day Moses was saved from the Egyptians, the birth of Abraham, and the day on which the **Ka'bah** was built.

It is probable that a pre-Islamic fasting tradition on the tenth day of the first month existed, possibly influenced by the Yom Kippur fast of local Jews. However, as with the **qibla** and food laws, the Muslim faith developed its own fasting practices distinct

Figure 10.5
Shi'ite Muslims beating their chests during Ashura

from the Jewish tradition, the most important of which is **sawm**, the fourth pillar of Islam. Sawm refers to the annual fast during the ninth month of the year.[39] The choice of **Ramadan** was based on the fact that the first revelation of the Qur'an to the Prophet occurred in that month, although the precise date is unknown. Described by the Qur'an as **Lailat al-Qadr**, or **Night of Power**,[40] it falls by tradition on an odd-numbered date toward the end of Ramadan. Sunnis commemorate it on Ramadan 27 while Shi'ites prefer Ramadan 23. The anniversary of the victorious Battle of Badr (624) also occurs during the same month, adding to it another level of significance.

Among the five religions under consideration, there is no fasting regime incumbent upon ordinary adult believers as strict or as extensive as sawm. For the entire month, from sunrise to sunset, Muslims abstain from all food and drink including water. Sexual intercourse and smoking are also prohibited. The fact that Ramadan, like all events on the Islamic calendar, drifts through the seasons is often taken to be a sign of God's mercy since it will not always be in the long hot days of summer.[41] Those exempted from all, or part, of the demanding fast include children, the elderly, the sick, pregnant women, young mothers, menstruating women, soldiers in battle, and travelers. There is a general expectation that if the condition is temporary, then the number of days lost should be made up at a later date, prior to the next Ramadan. If the fast is broken intentionally then a penalty (kaffara) applies which involves compensatory fasting or feeding the needy for a specified number of meals.

Given the rigors of the daily fast, the evening meal (iftar) and the pre-dawn meal (suhoor) carry special significance during Ramadan, and many local communities run a type of soup kitchen. Of course, the physical act of fasting is accompanied by a range of spiritual activities that make Ramadan a particularly sacred time. Muslims not only give up eating and drinking during daylight hours, but they also endeavor to avoid other vices. The mastery of the stomach reflects a deeper mastery of the soul. Ramadan is also a time for extra prayer and reflection. Many Muslims attend tarawih at mosque each night during which one-thirtieth of the Qur'an is read so that the entire holy book is completed by the end of the month. Devout believers make a special retreat, known as i'tikaf, by spending the last 10 days of Ramadan inside a mosque in prayerful reflection and study. It is during this time that they "seek" the Night of Power. Ramadan ends with **Id al-Fitr** [Feast of the Fast-Breaking] which occurs on the first three days of the subsequent month, Shawwal. One of the two great festivals specified by Islamic law, Id al-Fitr not only celebrates another successful Ramadan fast but is also a time for reconciliation between families and friends. Fasting during Id al-Fitr is prohibited and faith communities often gather for a common celebratory meal, with gifts for children and accompanied with the greeting "Id mubarak" or "Happy Id."

The second Id occurs during the twelfth month of the year and is associated with the fifth pillar of Islam, the pilgrimage to Mecca (see chapter 12). **Id al-Adha**, or the Feast of the Sacrifice, is celebrated not only by those present in Mecca at the time but by all Muslims worldwide. While Ramadan is grounded in the revelation of the Qur'an, the pilgrimage focuses on events in the life of Abraham, the father of monotheism. The feast itself, which falls on the tenth day of Dhu al-Hijjah, recalls Abraham's willingness to sacrifice his son out of obedience to the one God.[42] In Jewish, Christian, and Islamic theological traditions, his decision is considered to be the outstanding paradigm of trusting faith. According to the story, God substituted a ram for the boy after the depth of Abraham's faith was proven. In commemoration, Muslims slaughter an animal for the main meal on the day of the feast. According to custom, one-third of the meat is for the family, one-third for neighbors, and one-third for the poor.

It is noteworthy that neither of the two great Islamic festivals directly concerns the life of the **Prophet** per se, in contrast to Buddhism and Christianity where the birth and death of the founders constitute major holy days. It is as if the Islamic calendar deliberately downplays the importance of Muhammad for fear of idolatrous deification – a position consistent with the decision to date the Islamic year from the Hijra. Muhammad's birthday (**Mawlid an-Nabi**) is celebrated in a modest manner by Sunnis on Rabi al-awwad 12 and by Shi'ites on the 17th of the same month. The **Wahhabi** school of Saudi Arabia rejects the day altogether as a later medieval innovation. Tradition holds that Muhammad died on the same date but his death does not carry anything like the theological weight of Good Friday, Vesak, or even Ashura. The priority given to Ramadan on the calendar suggests that it is not the life of the Prophet that is crucial but the revelation of the eternal truth of the Qur'an through him – more akin to the Buddhist Enlightenment of Sakyamuni, the Christian Epiphany, and the Jewish Shavuot.

One important birthday that is commemorated by Shi'ite Muslims on the fifteenth of Sha'aban is that of the twelfth imam, Muhammad al-Mahdi (born 868). In Islamic theology, the **Mahdi** is an **eschatological** figure who will appear at the end of time with the prophet Jesus and usher in a final age of justice and peace in which Islam will become the global religion. **Twelver Shi'ites** identify this future figure with the twelfth imam who is said to have disappeared at 5 years of age and is in "occultation" until the designated hour of his reappearance. Sunni Muslims accept the notion of a final Mahdi but do not identify him as the twelfth imam. Nevertheless, they celebrate mid-Sha'aban as Lailat al-Barah, or the Night of Forgiveness. It is believed that on this night God shakes the heavenly tree to determine who shall die in the coming year.[43] With one's immediate fate being determined on this night, believers seek divine forgiveness, in much the same way as Jews do during the Days of Awe while the heavenly books are temporarily open. The Night of Forgiveness is also a time when Muslims visit the graves of relatives and pray for the dead.

One outstanding event in Muhammad's life that is celebrated is his mystical **Night Journey** on the winged creature Buraq from Mecca to Jerusalem (**Isra**) and from there to heaven (**Mi'raj**). The term "Ascension of Muhammad" can be misleading because it may suggest a post-death ascent to the heavens similar to Jesus's ascension. The journey is said to have occurred in 621, just prior to the Hijra. The relevant verse in the Qur'an states: "Glory be to Him Who made His servant to go on a night from the Sacred Mosque to the remote mosque of which We have blessed the precincts, so that We may show to him some of Our signs."[44] During the night of Rajab 27, Muslims offer extra prayers in memory of the journey on which it is believed Muhammad received the command to pray the five daily prayers. Muslims mark the night with optional prayers and sometimes light up mosques and homes in celebration.

SUMMARY

Each major religion sanctifies the year in its own distinctive way with a unique mixture of feasts and fasts. No two religious calendars look the same and there is considerable variation within each tradition as well. However, there are also important connections and parallels worthy of note. In terms of basic structure, four of the five religions use the lunar month. The consequence is that many major religious festivals are held on a new moon or a full moon, with its consequent natural symbolism. Christianity is the exception with its purely solar year, but the dating of its great feast of Easter is still linked to the timing of the full moon of the Jewish Passover. Hinduism, Buddhism, and Judaism maintain a basic synchronicity with the sun by occasionally inserting an extra month, but Islam stands alone among the religions with its shorter lunar year and the result that its holy days drift through the seasons.

It is probably not surprising to find that the key to the Buddhist and Christian calendars is the founder. Significant events in the life of the Buddha and the Christ constitute the major festivals in both traditions, reflecting the elevated status that each founder holds in their respective faiths. The entire Christian calendar hinges on two focal points that celebrate the birth and the death and resurrection of Jesus, while the most important festivals in Buddhism celebrate the birth, Enlightenment, First Sermon, and death of Sakyamuni. Moreover, the year number in both systems is based on the founder's birth or death. One might expect a parallel pattern in Islam but there is a noticeable moderation in the way the Muslim calendar commemorates its founder, grounded in the conviction that Muhammad was the greatest of the prophets but not a divine incarnation. There has always been ambiguity as to the "founder" of Judaism and thus the focus of its calendar is the story of Israel itself as God's covenantal partner. Similarly, that Hinduism also has no single historical founder is reflected in its calendar which features the births and outstanding achievements of its pantheon of deities and their incarnations.

If the Islamic calendar avoids placing the Prophet in the spotlight, what it does focus on is the eternal truth of monotheism. Thus the main motif of the pilgrimage month and its climactic Feast of the Sacrifice is the faith of Abraham. Similarly, the month of Ramadan, with its mysterious Night of Power, commemorates the first revelation of the Qur'an to Muhammad. The celebration of transcendent truth made manifest in time is celebrated in other traditions such as the Christian Epiphany, the Jewish Shavuot, and the Buddhist Vesak and Asalha Puja. Of course there are many similar themes that can be traced across the five calendars. For example, the foundation of the believing community itself is a key theme in Jewish Passover, Christian Pentecost, Buddhist Asalha Puja, and the Islamic Hijra, which functions as the basis for the numbering of Islamic years. Another example is the theme of victory over evil that is a central aspect of Hindu Dussehra, Christian Easter, and the Jewish feasts of Passover, Hanukkah, and Purim. A third example is the special day or period set aside to pay respects to and to assist the dead such as the Hindu Ancestors' Fortnight, the Buddhist Festival of the Hungry Ghosts, Christian All Souls' Day and Pentecost Eve, and Islamic mid-Sha'aban. There are even moments during the year when the tradition appears to acknowledge the need for psychological release from the constraints of the faith and followers are allowed, or even encouraged, to indulge themselves such as on Hindu Holi, Jewish Purim, and Christian Mardi Gras.

The consecration of the year is not only about joyous celebration of divine truth, protection, and blessing. There are also times when the mood is more somber and austere, reflecting the need for self-denial, penitence, and spiritual replenishment. In their own individual ways, each of the five religions caters for this dimension of the religious experience. In Buddhism, the naturally restrictive impact of the wet season has given rise to the rains retreat when monks intensify their study and meditation, and the laity become monks albeit temporarily. The same connection with the annual monsoons is seen in the Hindu idea of Vishnu's Sleep during which more extensive fasting is undertaken and weddings are avoided. Similarly, Shaivite Hindus dedicate the Great Night of Shiva to rigorous fasting and prayer. Weddings, parties, and other social celebrations are taboo for Jews during the 50 days of the Counting of the Omer and the three weeks between the fast days of Tamuz and Av. However, the main Jewish period for penance and self-examination are the Ten Days of Awe at the very start of the Jewish year, culminating in Yom Kippur. Abstinence and penance are also the main features of Christian Lent which is based on Jesus's own 40-day fast in the wilderness and which is fundamentally a preparation for the Easter festival. Arguably the most demanding form of austerity and self-control for the ordinary believer is the Islamic month-long dawn-to-dusk fast of Ramadan.

The regular rhythm of the holy day and the annual cycle of the great feasts and fasts constitute a rich elaborate tapestry in which religious belief is symbolically and profoundly expressed. The ordinary units of day, week, month, season, and year are all taken up and transformed into a vast temporal framework in which faith is lived out. Time itself is consecrated and given transcendent meaning. However, human existence is not only temporal; it is also set within a three-dimensional world. Consequently, the sanctification of time is complemented by the sanctification of space. Religions not only have their sacred moments but also their sacred places.

DISCUSSION TOPICS

1   Compare the Hindu and biblical understandings of creation and time.
2   What are the main differences regarding the annual calendar and festivals between:
    (a)   Sunni and Shi'ite Muslims?
    (b)   Mahayana and Theravada Buddhists?
    (c)   Protestant, Orthodox, and Catholic Christians?
3   How do Buddhist, Christian, and Muslim calendars commemorate the life of their founders?
4   Identify common features between the sacred periods Ramadan, Lent, Vassa, and the Ten Days of Awe.
5   How do feasts like Holi, Mardi Gras, and Purim involve the relaxation of laws?
6   How is the theme of light used in festivals such as Divali, Hanukkah, and Easter (or Christmas)?
7   Which religious festivals celebrate fertility and new life?
8   Identify other themes that can be traced across the religious calendars?

FURTHER READING

Cohn-Sherbok, Dan (2003). *Judaism: History, Belief and Practice*. London: Routledge, pp. 474–82; 507–32.

De Lange, Nicholas (2000). *Introduction to Judaism*. Cambridge: Cambridge University Press, pp. 106–7; 141–6.

Goitein, S. D. (2006). "Ramadan, the Muslim Month of Fasting," in G. R. Hawting (ed.), *The Development of Islamic Ritual*. Aldershot: Ashgate, ch. 9.

Gordon, Matthew S. (2002). *Understanding Islam*. London: Duncan Baird, pp. 80–9.

Hertzberg, Arthur (ed.) (1998). *Judaism*. New York: Free Press, pp. 178–202.

Hickman, Hoyt, et al. (1992). *The New Handbook of the Christian Year*. Nashville, TN: Abingdon Press.

Knott, Kim (2000). *Hinduism: A Very Short Introduction*. Oxford and New York: Oxford University Press, pp. 56–63.

Lazarus-Yafeh, Hava (2006). "Muslim Festivals," in G. R. Hawting (ed.), *The Development of Islamic Ritual*. Aldershot: Ashgate, ch. 17.

Michaels, Axel (2003). *Hinduism: Past and Present*. Princeton, NJ: Princeton University Press, pp. 295–314.

Renard, John (1996). *Seven Doors to Islam: Spirituality and the Religious Life of Muslims*. Berkeley and Los Angeles: University of California Press, pp. 36–52.

Schauss, Hayyim (1996). *The Jewish Festivals: A Guide to their History and Observance*. New York: Schocken.

Segler, Franklin M., & Bradley, Randall (2006). *Christian Worship: Its Theology and Practice*. 3rd edn. Nashville: B & H Publishing Group, pp. 219–34.

Solomon, Norman (1996). *Judaism: A Very Short Introduction*. New York: Oxford University Press, ch. 4.

White, James F. (2001). *Introduction to Christian Worship*. 3rd edn. Nashville: Abingdon Press, ch. 2.

NOTES

1   Red is a popular color in the East during Winter Lent. In the West, the third Sunday of Advent is traditionally called Gaudete Sunday, when rose vestments may be worn, indicating a more joyous time.

2   Thus Christian churches that stress the imminent nature of Christ's second coming, and thus the end of the world, are often described as "Adventist" churches.

3   The Julian calendar was slightly too long, causing the equinox to slowly drift backwards. The solution was to remove three leap years every 400 years on the century year. Thus 1700, 1800, and 1900 were not leap years but 2000 was. Ten days were also removed from the calendar from October 4 to 15, 1582, although Britain and its colonies did not accept the revision until 1752. Today the difference between the Gregorian and Julian calendars is 13 days.

4   One of the earliest references to December 25 as Jesus's birthday is Sextus Julius Africanus in his *Chronographiai* (c.221 CE). The third-century Christian writer Origen condemned the idea of celebrating Christ's birthday on the basis that such a practice was only appropriate for human kings.

5   The link with the winter solstice is also evident in Germanic culture where Yuletide denotes the shortest day or the lowest point of the wheel (yule). Christmas symbols such as mistletoe, holly, and ivy originate here.

6   The Anglo-Saxon chronicler Bede used the Anno Domini system in his *Ecclesiastical History of the English People* (731) which was subsequently adopted by Alcuin during the ninth-century Carolingian renaissance under Charlemagne.

7   John 1:14.

8   See Matthew 2:1–12.

9   Leviticus 12:2–8. The feast is also called the Presentation of the Lord in the Temple (see Luke 2:22–39).

10   Mark 1:12–13; Matthew 4:1–11; Luke 4:1–13.

11   The Passover moon is the first full moon following the vernal equinox (taken as March 21). Thus Easter Sunday can fall anywhere between late March and late April.

12   John 1:3–5; Colossians 1:16.

13   In Japanese Buddhism, the Buddha's birth is celebrated on April 8, his Enlightenment on December 8, and his passing into nirvana on February 15.

14   Khandhaka, Mahavagga 3.5.4ff.

15   Samyutta Nikaya 16.13.

16   The month is added when two new moons occur while the sun is in same zodiacal constellation.

17   The same action is performed with images of **Ganesha** on his birthday – the fourth day of the bright fortnight of Bhadra.

18   Some Jews consider the days of awe to include the 30 days of the previous month, Elul. These 40 days correspond to the time Moses spent on Mount Sinai before descending with the **Decalogue** (see Exodus 34:27–8).

19   Micah 7:19.

20   Leviticus 23:32. See Talmud Yoma for laws pertaining to Yom Kippur.

21   Leviticus 16:5–22.

22   Except for Yom Kippur, all of these are either postponed or anticipated if they fall on a sabbath.

23   Exodus 14:10–31.

24   Exodus 12:21–7.

25   Exodus 12:15–20. This is also called the hametz hunt.

26   Leviticus 23:15–16.

27   Talmud Yebamot 62b.

28   Leviticus 23:42–3.

29   For details see Talmud Sukkah 1a.

30   Leviticus 23:40.

31   Esther 3:7.

32   Talmud Megillah 7b.

33   1 Maccabees 4:56.

34   Talmud Shabbat 21b. According to 2 Maccabees, the eight days of celebrations were based on the fact that Sukkoth lasts for eight days.

35   Talmud Shabbat 23b.

36   The Hijra is celebrated annually on 8 Rabi' al-awwal.

37   Qur'an 9:36–7.

38   Karbala is located about 60 miles southwest of Baghdad in present-day Iraq.

39   Qur'an 2:185.

40   Qur'an 97:1–5.

41   The word *Ramadan* is derived from the Arabic term for "scorching heat."

42   The Jewish and Christian traditions identify the boy as Isaac, Abraham's son by his wife, Sarah. However, Islamic tradition understands him to be **Ishmael**, Abraham's older son by his slave-girl (and wife) **Hagar**.

43   The tree mentioned in Qur'an 53:14 is considered to be the boundary of the seventh heaven, beyond which no creature can pass. The names of all living individuals are said to be written on its leaves.

44   Qur'an 17:1.

Chapter 11

BUILDING

CONTENTS

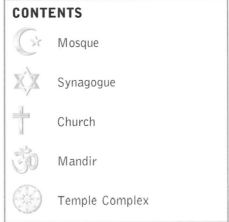

- Mosque
- Synagogue
- Church
- Mandir
- Temple Complex

Introduction

Religion not only casts a transcendent light on time but it also sanctifies the three-dimensional space that characterizes our world. Although most religions believe that the Absolute is ubiquitous, they also identify particular places where it can be more tangibly and powerfully experienced. In these final chapters we shall explore two ways in which ordinary space is given extraordinary, transcendent meaning: via religious buildings and sacred journeys. This chapter will focus on the physical edifices that serve as places of communal prayer and devotion. What is the religious building of each major faith? What primary and secondary functions does it serve? What are its salient architectural features? What religious beliefs are expressed by the details of its exterior and interior design?

☾ **Mosque**

Soon after **Muhammad** arrived in **Medina** in 622, the year of the **Hijra**, he built a residence for himself and his two wives Sawda and **Aisha**. According to one tradition, he chose the very place where his camel stopped after the long and perilous journey, purchasing the plot from two local orphans. It was a modest four-sided construction made of mud bricks, with his private chambers at the eastern end of a large court-yard.[1] For the next 10 years until his death in 632, the building functioned not only as his private domicile, but also as a place to settle disputes, receive official visitors, delegate administrative tasks, distribute aid, attend the sick and injured, plan military action, preach and lead community prayer. It was the political and religious center of the new faith that came to be known as the Masjid al-Nabawi – the Mosque of the Prophet.[2] Today, it is considered the second holiest place in Islam, containing the tombs of Muhammad and the first two **caliphs**, **Abu Bakr** and **Umar**.

Despite its early origins, the Masjid al-Nabawi is not considered to be the first Islamic **mosque**. That honor is usually bestowed upon the Quba mosque located just outside Medina. It is said that Muhammad laid its foundation stones as he approached the town during the last stage of the Hijra. Alternatively, some prefer to think of the **Ka'bah** in Mecca as the first mosque in the sense that Muhammad and his followers prayed there during the years prior to the Hijra.[3] The **Qur'an** records how local authorities prohibited the young community from the area around the Ka'bah, thus forcing them to recite their prayers in private homes or even in the streets of the town.[4] After Muhammad's triumphant return to Mecca in 630, the Ka'bah was converted into an Islamic symbol. Today it stands in the center of the magnificent Masjid al-Haram [Sacred Mosque] which is Islam's holiest site: the universal focus of daily prayer and the destination of the annual pilgrimage.[5]

But it was the Masjid al-Nabawi that became the model for all subsequent Islamic places of worship due to its key role in the early community during the crucial years of consolidation in Medina. As was the case with the prophet's mosque-residence, mosques today can still have a range of different purposes, both secular and sacred. A mosque and its surrounding complex can serve as a function hall, library, classroom, kitchen, infirmary, bazaar, and place of temporary lodging. But its primary purpose is reflected in the Arabic term from which the English word *mosque* is derived. A **masjid** literally means "a place of prostration."[6] In other words, a mosque is first and foremost a venue for communal prayer, a sacred space in which the religious community physically comes together in official worship. The Qur'an describes a mosque as a special "house" in which "Allah has permitted to be exalted and that His name may be remembered in them; there glorify Him therein in the mornings and the evenings."[7] Although the five daily prayers may be recited alone and in any place, men are obliged to pray in a mosque at Friday noon as a reminder of the public and collective aspect of religion. On this point, the **hadith** suggests that, although not mandatory, it is many times more meritorious to pray **salat** in the company of others than alone.[8]

From the beginning, the mosque has been a vital aspect of Islamic practice and a natural means of expressing religious belief in architectural form. As with many religions, the shape and design of Islam's holy building varies considerably depending on the period and the culture. Yet it is possible to identify the main features of a typical mosque and to explore what these tell us about the ways in which Islam sanctifies space.

The exterior of a mosque is characterized by a number of important features, in particular the dome, the **minaret**, and the place of **ablutions**. The earliest mosques, such as the Masjid al-Nabawi in Medina, were typically flat-roofed, rectangular buildings with a covered area for prayer and an enclosed courtyard. However, since the Ottoman era, mosques generally have had a domed roof above the main prayer hall that has subsequently become a trademark feature. It is probable that Islamic architects adopted the concept of the dome from existing Byzantine Christian churches, many of which were converted into mosques, for example the famous Hagia Sophia in Constantinople.[9] The usual shape of the dome is hemispherical although the **Mughals** of India preferred onion-shaped roofs. Whatever its precise form, the dome of a mosque represents the vault of the sky, reminding the worshiper of the splendor of the creator, who reigns over the heavens and the earth.

The second visible external feature of a mosque is the tall graceful tower known as a minaret. Appearing for the first time during the **Umayyad** period (seventh century) the minaret, like the dome, was probably an adaptation of the spire on Christian churches that had been converted into mosques. The term *minaret* literally means a lighthouse and it is possible that the earliest minarets functioned as a type of watchtower, illuminated by torches. However, the minaret quickly came to be used as the point from which the **muezzin** chants the call to prayer five times per day, in much the same way as the bell-tower of a Christian church traditionally summons the faithful to communal worship. Prior to the introduction of the minaret, the call to prayer was usually proclaimed from the roofs of nearby houses but the height of the minaret naturally facilitated the audibility of the summons. Today the call is often broadcast via loudspeakers and thus the minaret tends to play a decorative role or serves to indicate the sacred nature of the building over which it towers. Larger mosques often have up to four minarets, reflecting their importance and prestige.[10] Quite often a crescent moon and star adorn the very top of the dome or minaret. The image is recognized universally as a symbol of Islam and appears in many settings including the national flags of predominantly Muslim countries such as Turkey, Algeria, Azerbaijan, Malaysia, Pakistan, and Tunisia. In fact, the crescent and

Figure 11.1
A mosque with
two minarets in
Baku, Azerbaijan

star is only a relatively recent badge of Islamic identity. It was originally the symbol of Constantinople and was adopted throughout the **Ottoman Empire** after the Muslim conquest of that city in 1453.

The third important feature of mosque exteriors are the wells and fountains for the ablutions prescribed by Islamic law before commencing daily prayer. If the worshiper is in a minor state of impurity, they must perform the wudu, which comprises washing the face, arms, hands, and feet. Such a state is brought about by falling asleep, breaking wind, going to the toilet, or touching the skin of a person of the opposite gender who is of marriageable age. In the case of major impurity, which results from sexual intercourse or ejaculation, a full bath (ghusl) is required. Sometimes larger mosque complexes provide shower facilities for this purpose. Apart from the actual ablutions, the theme of cleanliness and purity applies in other ways to the mosque. For example, shoes should be removed before entering a mosque in the tradition of Exodus 3:5, where Moses takes off his sandals in the presence of God as symbolized by the burning bush. Analogously, the interior of a mosque is considered to be "holy ground." Islamic custom states that one should step through the doorway with the right foot first as an acknowledgment of the transition from profane to sacred space. Purity is also the reason for the argument that women should refrain from going to a mosque during their menstrual period, although the point is debated among jurists.[11]

The interior of a mosque is characterized by a striking lack of furniture. A mosque is essentially a prayer hall, and even the largest structures are devoid of any seating (unlike Jewish synagogues and Christian churches). Such uncluttered space facilitates the performance of Islamic prayer which involves a series of bodily movements including prostration – the etymological basis for the term *masjid*, as we saw earlier. Instead of benches and pews, the floor of the mosque is usually covered with carpets to insure that the ground on which the official prayers are uttered is clean. Many Muslims use their own private prayer mat when reciting salat outside of a mosque, as Muhammad himself did.[12] Another striking feature of mosques is the lack of statues, paintings, and icons of any sort. As was noted in chapter 1, Islam considers any attempt to depict Allah in a finite worldly manner as idolatry, the greatest of all sins. Thus it vigorously opposes sacred images. In the majority of Islamic schools, the ban extends to Muhammad and the major **prophets**, and even all human and animal figures, because it is considered to usurp the role of the creator.[13] Instead, the walls and ceilings of mosques are often adorned with more abstract designs such as geometric shapes or the images of plants. Calligraphy is also a popular means of decorating mosques, especially as the flowing Arabic script lends itself to decoration. Thus the names of Allah and Muhammad, as well as verses from the Qur'an, are used to enhance the aesthetic dimension of worship and to reinforce the religious nature of the space.

From the time of Muhammad, the believer has been obliged to face in a particular direction, known as the **qibla**, when reciting the five daily prayers. The original qibla was Jerusalem but soon after Muhammad arrived in Medina, it was changed to the Ka'bah. Muslims may recite their prayers anywhere (except for men at Friday noon) but they must insure that they are physically orientated toward the holiest point on earth in a global symbol of religious community. This fundamental aspect of official prayer is reflected in the most important internal feature of the mosque – the **mihrab**. The mihrab is a niche in the wall that faces Mecca (aptly known as the qibla wall). It is usually designed in the shape of an archway and is often highly decorated to emphasize its role as the focal point for prayer. Like the dome and the minaret, the mihrab may have evolved from the statue niches of Christian churches that were converted into mosques. Of course, there is no statue or image in the Islamic mihrab, which directs the worshiper's thoughts beyond the mosque wall to distant Mecca and ultimately to Allah in heaven.

The other important interior feature is the **minbar** – a term derived from the Arabic word for "high." The minbar is essentially the equivalent of a Christian pulpit from which a sermon is delivered to the congregation. Muhammad himself used to preach standing on a three-stepped platform at the end of the Masjid al-Nabawi so that he might be easily visible.[14] The minbar became a standard feature of all mosques and is usually located against the qibla wall near the mihrab. It is often richly adorned and shaped like a small tower with stairs, highlighting the importance of the spoken word in Islamic worship. The limitation of the visual image places greater weight on verbal expression: prayers recited from the mosque floor and faith preached from the elevated minbar.

Most mosques also have a separate space reserved for women. It may be defined by a partition or railing or even a separate room adjacent to the prayer hall. While women are not barred from attending mosque prayers,[15] they are not under the same obligation as men to attend at Friday noon. Thus men usually considerably outnumber women at communal prayers. Moreover, the law requires that women stand behind men during salat for modesty's sake because official prayer involves bowing and prostrating. With regard to access, the Qur'an implies that the mosque is not an appropriate place for "idolaters" but most Islamic law schools allow non-Muslims to enter mosques.[16]

From the humble house of the Prophet in Medina to the stupendous wonders of Islamic architecture, the "place of prostration" has been the sacred space within Islam where communal prayer is offered, wisdom imparted, and faith expressed by the design and contents of the building itself. The ban on idolatrous images, the emphasis on the word symbolized by the minbar, the segregation of the sexes, and the importance of the physical direction of prayer are all salient features of the Islamic mosque but they are also characteristic of sacred space within Judaism.

✡ Synagogue

In the year 586 BCE, the army of Nebuchadnezzar conquered the city of **Jerusalem**, destroyed the **Temple** and forced its king, its aristocracy, and a great number of other citizens into exile in **Babylon**.[17] The Temple had been constructed by King **Solomon** 400 years earlier and was the heart and soul of Israelite religious life. Faced with the prospect of existence without temple, priesthood, or sacrificial system, the exiled Jews began to create an alternative forum for worship in private homes where believers would come together to read the holy texts, listen to sermons, and pray as a community.[18] After the return to Israel in 537 BCE, and despite the rebuilding of the Temple in Jerusalem thereafter, the tradition developed into one of the most important of all Jewish institutions – the **synagogue**. For many, it was the more "portable" form of synagogue-based Judaism that enabled the faith to survive the destruction of the Second Temple by the Romans in 70 CE and the subsequent dispersal of the Jewish people throughout the empire and beyond. In time, the synagogue became the sacred space where communal, intellectual, and religious life was grounded. So central is the synagogue in the eyes of **Reform** Jews and some **Conservative** Jews that they prefer the designation "Temple."

The more common and less controversial term *synagogue* is derived from the Greek for "gathering" or "meeting." The Hebrew beit k'nesset, or house of assembly, conveys the same notion of a place where believers come together for a common purpose. As in Islam, a synagogue complex can be a venue for a range of cultural-religious events such as circumcisions, **bar mitzvahs**, weddings, as well as social welfare or organizational meetings. The Yiddish term *schul* (from the High German for school) and the alternative Hebrew term *beit ha-midrash* [house of study] both reflect the role of the synagogue in Jewish education. Often a synagogue will have a library and some classrooms where religious lessons for adults and children are conducted. However, the primary purpose of the synagogue, as with the mosque, is to provide a space for public communal prayer. For this reason a synagogue is sometimes called a beit tefillah, or place of worship.

Even more than Islam, Judaism is a congregational religion that expects its adherents to express their faith not only as individuals but also as members of a community. Certain prayers are ideally said at specified times in the company of fellow believers and the traditional quorum (**minyan**) required for certain official prayers is 10 adult men. Most synagogues hold prayer services on a regular thrice-daily basis: evening, morning, and afternoon. So what are the key physical features of a synagogue and how do they reflect elements of the Jewish faith?

The external appearance of synagogues varies considerably from culture to culture. In times past, Judaism's minority position in Christian or Islamic society was evident in that synagogues were often deliberately designed to be inconspicuous. Generally they were not allowed to be taller or more splendid in appearance than neighboring churches or mosques. After the Enlightenment, Western synagogues tended to become grander and more attractive as Jews emerged from the ghetto and found confidence to express their faith architecturally in the public sphere. Classical or even Christian styles were often chosen and adapted. However, unlike the mosque with its dome and minaret, synagogues are not possessed of specific universally distinctive external features. The unique identifying elements tend to be found inside the sacred space.

In contrast to mosques, synagogues tend to be fully furnished, with seating for the congregation whose bodily movements during services involve sitting, standing, and bowing but very rarely prostrating. In some synagogues, special boxes are located beneath seats where members may store their prayer shawls and books because Jewish law restricts what may be carried on a **sabbath**. Like mosques, the direction in which the congregation is orientated during communal prayer is highly pertinent. In the case of Judaism, the synagogue itself and the congregation gathered within it both face toward Jerusalem. When a synagogue is not able to be orientated in this direction for some reason, the congregation will turn toward Jerusalem at certain moments such as during the recitation of the **Amidah**.[19]

Similarly, just as the mihrab marks the qibla inside the mosque, the most important item in a Jewish synagogue is the **aron ha kodesh**, or Holy Ark, which is usually located on the wall pointing in the direction of the holy city.[20] As the name suggests, the aron ha kodesh is a sacred receptacle for the **Torah** scrolls just as the **Ark of the Covenant** (aron ha berith) housed the tablets of the Law in ancient Israel.[21] The aron ha kodesh is a cabinet either set into or mounted on the wall, and covered by a thick curtain known as the parokhet, reminiscent of the curtain in the Temple sanctuary that screened the **Holy of Holies**.[22] The congregation normally stands whenever the doors of the Ark are opened and a Torah scroll is brought out for the readings. It is considered an honor to be the one chosen to open or close the Ark doors and curtain. The Ark is usually the most lavishly adorned object in the synagogue, reflecting the precious nature of its contents. Sometimes it is embellished with an appropriate image such as the **Star of David** or an apt Hebrew phrase such as "Know before whom you stand." Nearby, the ner tamid [eternal flame] burns constantly, indicating the ongoing presence of God in this sacred space.[23] The ner tamid may be a specially designed electric light or a more traditional oil lamp, but it reminds Jews of the altar of incense that burned day and night in the Temple. As a source of light in a holy place, the ner tamid is often compared to the golden seven-branched candelabrum, or **menorah**, that stood in the sanctuary of the Temple. Tradition suggests that the shape of the menorah symbolizes the burning bush from which God first called Moses to his prophetic mission. The menorah has become one of the most widely recognized symbols of Judaism and features prominently in Jewish art and decoration. A

Figure 11.2
Torah scrolls
inside the holy
ark in a Jewish
synagogue

menorah is often found in synagogues and Jewish homes, although some Jews disapprove of an exact duplicate of the original version and thus avoid seven branches. An eight-branched version of the menorah is used during the eight-day festival of **Hanukkah**.

A central feature of a Jewish worship service is a series of readings from the holy texts through which it is believed God still addresses his people. On Monday and Thursday mornings and on Saturday mornings and afternoons, the Torah scrolls are removed from the Ark and respectfully carried in procession to a lectern on a raised platform known as the bimah.[24] The location and orientation of the bimah varies within Judaism. The traditional approach, still used by **Orthodox** Jews, is to place the bimah in the very center of the synagogue facing the Ark. Symbolically, this arrangement recaptures the moment when the people of Israel stood around Mount Sinai while the Torah was revealed to Moses. Practically, it enables everyone in the congregation to hear the sacred readings clearly. Orthodox synagogues also have a second lectern known as the amud at which the cantor (hazzan) stands and leads the singing. Traditionally the amud is located near the Ark so that the cantor might be inspired by the proximity of the sacred scrolls. In contrast, nineteenth-century Reform Judaism shifted the position of the bimah to the front of the synagogue, directly before the Ark and facing the congregation. The physical change resulted in a synagogue layout that resembled the plan of Christian churches and that reflected Reform Judaism's desire to assimilate itself into, rather than differentiate itself from, surrounding society. Similarly, Reform synagogues also introduced the use of organ music, choirs, and even vestments for prayer leaders.

The other important architectural innovation introduced by the Reform movement was the removal of the mehitza, the dividing barrier between the male and female seating areas. As in Islam, gender segregation during worship is still considered important in Orthodox Judaism in order to avoid distractions and focus the mind on spiritual matters. The mehitza may take the form of a curtain or a lattice. Alternatively, it can be a designated seating section at the side or back of the synagogue, or even an upstairs balcony. Despite these differences, Orthodox and Reform synagogues both share one characteristic that is also typical of mosques: the noticeable absence of any attempt to depict the deity in the form of a statue or icon. Three-dimensional sculptures of living creatures are also considered to constitute a form of idolatry and are thus banned. However, synagogues are not without aesthetic quality and many are beautifully decorated with symbolic imagery such as the Star of David, the menorah, the Tablets of the Law, and apposite quotes from the Hebrew scriptures.

The architectural changes brought about by Reform Judaism already hint at a certain basic similarity between the Jewish synagogue and the Christian church. In so far as both religions stress congregational worship, their respective places of gathering naturally play an important role in the practice of the faith. On the one hand, the centrality of an elevated place from which the holy text is read to the listening congregation and the avoidance of idolatrous images resonate strongly with Protestant Christian practice. On the other hand, the central focus on the receptacle of a sacred object and the use of a lamp to mark the divine presence have similarities with Catholic and Orthodox places of worship.

✝ Church

The contemporary English word *church* is a derivation from the Old English *cirice* which in turn was based on the Greek *kyriakon* [of the Lord]. It reflects the notion that the building in which believers gather to worship somehow belongs to the Lord in a special way. It is sacred Christian space. Of course, the first Christians were originally Jews and there are ample references in the **New Testament** to prayers that are held in both the Jerusalem Temple and synagogues throughout Israel and Asia Minor.[25] However, as Christianity gradually drew away from its mother religion, Christians began to worship in their own private dwellings.[26] By the second century, they were constructing their own edifices specifically designed for public congregational prayer. In Greek, such a building was called an ekklesia, which literally means "called out" or "called together." It is from this term that English words such as *ecclesial* and *ecclesiastical* are derived.

As with the Islamic mosque and the Jewish synagogue, the history of church architecture is long and varied. In Western Christianity, styles range from the early basilicas,[27] which were adaptations of Roman public buildings, through the classical forms of Romanesque, Gothic, and Baroque to more modern styles. Despite the enormous variety, it is possible to identify some of the enduring salient features of a church, which reflect key aspects of Christian belief and practice. One of the most common external features on a church, and which sets it apart as a religious building, is the steeple or spire. The steeple was originally adapted from military watch-towers and incorporated into church design as a bell-tower. As noted earlier, it was probably the historical inspiration for the Islamic minaret. Like its Islamic equivalent, the steeple traditionally served as the point from which the call to prayer was broadcast via the ringing of the church bells.

The spire is a conically pointed structure erected either as a continuation of the steeple or in its place. The term comes from the Anglo-Saxon for "spear," giving the impression of strength but also suggestive of prayer rising inexorably upwards. Like the crescent moon and star on mosques, a cross – the unambiguous badge of Christianity – is usually placed at the very highest point of the spire, as well as on many other parts of the building. Moreover, in many architectural styles, the building itself has a cruciform shape. In this scheme, the main axis consists of the nave and sanctuary while the shorter axis comprises the two transepts. Sometimes a dome was constructed directly over the intersection point, under which the main altar was located. As in Islam, the dome depicts the heavens over which the creator rules and under which believers worship. In classical Christian architecture, the entire structure ideally faced east toward the rising sun as a statement of faith in Jesus's resurrection, although in practice many churches are not orientated in any particular direction.

The interior of a church is designed fundamentally to provide space for the congregation at prayer. As in Jewish synagogues, Christian churches usually have seating that is orientated toward the focal point of the building. However, the physical focal point varies across denominations, reflecting a different **liturgical** emphasis. In traditions that stress the importance of the Eucharistic meal, like Orthodox, Catholic, and some Anglican churches, the architectural focus is on the altar (or table). The altar is often covered with a special cloth and adorned with candles and flowers to highlight its central role. The area around the altar/table is considered particularly holy and thus is known as the sanctuary or chancel. Usually access to the sanctuary during a service is restricted to the clergy and those with special roles. The sanctuary is often slightly elevated with steps and delineated by a low railing. In **Orthodox** churches, the boundary is marked by the iconostasis, a tall, highly decorated stand across the church on which icons of Christ and the saints are hung.[28] The remainder

Figure 11.3
Notre Dame
Cathedral, Paris

of the church is sometimes known as the nave, from the Latin *navis* [boat]. The term may have arisen from the fact that the vaulted roofs of medieval churches looked like the inside of a great ship. The nautical allusion is appropriate given that the **Catholic Church** has been nicknamed "Peter's bark," evoking the image of the church as a great boat similar to Noah's ark.[29]

Churches that prefer the term *altar* stress the idea that the communion ritual is essentially a memorial of Christ's sacrificial death which brings salvation to the world. The theme of sacrifice is also discernible in the Catholic practice of placing the relic of a saint in the altar-stone itself. Similarly in Orthodox churches, the bread and wine are placed on a small piece of cloth known as the antimension which is decorated with motifs of Christ's burial and in which a relic is sewn. In contrast, churches that prefer the term *table* place more emphasis on the **Eucharist** as a communion meal modeled on Jesus's **Last Supper**.

In most churches, the altar is separate from the wall so that the priest or minister stands behind it, facing the congregation. However, in pre-**Vatican II** Catholic churches, the altar was set against the back wall which meant that the priest faced the same way as the worshipers during the most sacred parts of the service. The decision by the Second Vatican Council in 1965 to move the altar away from the wall and reverse the direction of the priest's orientation was similar to the Reform Jewish initiative to move the bimah to the front of the synagogue so that it faced the people. In both cases, the change in physical configuration reflected a radical rethinking of the theology of worship and divine presence. In one system the leader and the congregation face outwards together, toward a transcendent deity beyond the group. In the other, the leader and congregation face each other, forming a closed circle in which an immanent deity resides.

The other distinctive architectural feature associated with the sanctuary is the receptacle for the sacred bread that is reserved for the sick. Its common designation **tabernacle** comes from the Latin word for "tent," which draws on the image of the Tent of Dwelling used by the Israelites to house the Ark of the Covenant during their wanderings in the Sinai wilderness. In Orthodox churches, the tabernacle is located on the altar, often in the shape of a miniature church building. In the Catholic Church, a tabernacle is usually a solid container made of stone, metal, or wood and covered with a colored cloth reflecting the liturgical season. In times past, the tabernacle was located in the center of the sanctuary directly behind the altar. However, current Catholic canon law recommends that it be placed at the side of the sanctuary or even in a separate chapel, because the Eucharistic actions at the altar should be the primary focus of attention during the service. In a similar manner to the Jewish ner tamid, a lamp burning near the tabernacle indicates that there is consecrated bread inside.[30]

Thus far the internal features described have been linked to the central act of blessing the bread and wine at the altar or communion table, and distributing them to the congregation for consumption. However, the first part of the Christian Eucharist involves a figurative feeding of the people via the word of God. In all Christian churches, scriptural readings and an accompanying sermon are considered essential nourishment for the spiritually hungry. Analogous to the Islamic minbar and the Jewish bimah, the Christian pulpit (from the Latin *pulpitum*, meaning elevated platform) is the point from which the spiritual leader proclaims the holy writings and their interpretation. In churches that emphasize the communion meal, such as Orthodox, Catholic, and Anglican denominations, the pulpit is usually located on the left side of the sanctuary as seen by the congregation. Traditionally it is from the pulpit that the gospel is read and the sermon is delivered. In some churches, a smaller lectern is placed opposite the pulpit on the right side of the sanctuary from which passages from the Old Testament and epistles from the New Testament are read. For this reason, the left side of a church was traditionally known as the "gospel side" and the right side as the "epistle side." In Protestant churches, which give priority to the proclaimed word over sacramental ritual, the pulpit is aptly located in a prominent central position with the communion table in front but less conspicuous.[31] Pulpits can vary from simple stands to highly ornate structures with staircase and canopy.

The contrast between altar-centered and pulpit-centered churches flows over into the question of images. In general, Orthodox and Catholic churches are characterized by a liberal use of statues, paintings, and icons which can be found on any part of the building including ceilings, walls, doors, and windows. One example in Catholic churches is the 14 "stations of the cross" which commemorate **Jesus**'s final journey from his trial to his burial (see box 10.1) The various episodes are artistically depicted along the walls and are used to mark pauses ("stations") during meditative processions around the church, especially in the season of Lent. In contrast, Protestant churches prefer to minimize the use of such imagery for fear of idolatry and superstition, in much the same manner as Jews and Muslims. Even crucifixes (crosses which include the corpus of Christ) are avoided and the empty cross is preferred – a practice based on fulfill-ment of the second commandment but also intended to stress Jesus's resurrection.

Churches also contain secondary features which pertain to rituals other than the celebration of the communion meal or the Service of the Word. For example, a baptismal pool is often located behind the central pulpit in a **Baptist** church, while a baptismal font might be situated in the sanctuary or near the main doorway of an Orthodox, Catholic, or **Anglican** church. Catholic churches also have small fonts at all entrances so that the faithful may "bless" themselves as they enter by dipping their hand into the holy water and making a sign of the cross. The gesture not only calls to mind the waters of baptism but also suggests the need for purification as one enters holy space, not unlike the Islamic wudu. Catholic and some Anglican churches also contain a space for the sacrament of reconciliation in which the believer confesses their sins to a priest and receives absolution. Traditionally this occurred in special booths inside the church although today the booth is often replaced by a small interview room.

While Christian churches have several features in common with the mosques and synagogues of the other **Semitic religions**, there are also interesting parallels with the sacred buildings of the sanatana dharma. The tower that reaches to the skies, the inner sanctuary at the heart of the edifice, statues and images that evoke a sense of the divine presence, the use of candlelight, flowers, and incense, the purifying water fonts at entrances, and the offering of blessed food are aspects of not only the altar-centered Christian church but also the Hindu temple.

Mandir

There is a Hindu legend that tells the story of a primeval struggle between the god **Shiva** and the demon Adhisaka during which a drop of sweat fell to the ground from Shiva's forehead. A thunderous clap was heard and the drop was transformed into a dangerous monster that threatened to devour the world. The gods rushed down and pinned him to the ground in order to restrain him. The monster was subdued and subsequently became the patron deity of land plots and buildings. He was aptly named Vastu Purusha [Lodging of the Gods].[32] The legend gave rise to a sacred diagram (**mandala**) in which Vastu Purusha is pictured lying on the ground in the shape of a great square with his head in the northeast corner, his feet in the southwest corner, and his elbows and knees in the opposite corners (see figure 11.4). The very center of the square lies precisely over the figure's navel, symbolizing fertility. The mandala is usually divided into 64 or 81 squares so that each part of the anatomy corresponds to a particular section of the square. Not only is the Vastu Purusha mandala a fascinating offshoot of ancient Hindu lore, but it also constitutes one of the fundamental templates for important building projects, especially sacred buildings. Perhaps in no other major religion is the pattern of a sacred building specified in such precise detail and with such extensive imagery as in the case of the Hindu temple.

Figure 11.4
Vastu Purusha Mandala

The common term for a Hindu temple is mandir which literally means a "house of god."[33] As the term implies, a mandir is a place where the deity "resides" in the sense that the worshiper is able to experience the divine presence in a more powerful and tangible manner. As was noted in chapter 1, such an encounter often takes the form of a "seeing" (**darshana**) of the deity represented in physical form by the sacred image (**murti**). Wherever there is a murti, this profound and personal spiritual encounter with transcendent reality is facilitated. The most common place for darshana is the home where a special room or space is dedicated to the images. Unlike the Semitic religions, Hinduism is not primarily a congregational faith that expects attendance at a communal service on a regular basis. Devotional worship is first and foremost a domestic affair. However, Hindu practice is not without its communitarian dimension, and groups of believers often gather in the mandir for darshana.

Mandirs are found in all parts of India and wherever Hindu communities exist around the world. The larger ones may be associated with a pilgrimage destination or a center of spirituality (ashram) and are often served by a resident priest or a community of priests. Mandirs may be located in the heart of a city, on a river bank, on a mountain slope, or deep in a forest. Whatever the setting, the actual site is chosen with great care and an eye for a range of factors including the soil color which can determine the **caste**. The process commences with the ankura–arpana ritual, in which a seed is planted to symbolize the impregnation of mother earth and to test the level of fertility. If the plant germinates satisfactorily then the site is accepted. The ground is leveled and the Vastu Purusha mandala is applied as the basic floor plan.[34] As with the cruciform Christian church, the shape of the temple as seen from above reveals a holy pattern: the compacted body of the god of buildings. Hindu mandalas combine basic geometric shapes, especially the square which represents the four-cornered terrestrial world, and the circle which represents the perfection of the celestial realms. The implication is that the mandir, built on the mandala, is a meeting place of earth and heaven.

While the image of the body defines the basic floor plan of the mandir, two other natural images are the key to the structure of the building as seen at ground level. The first such image is the cave. As dark, quiet places removed from the dazzle and noise of society, caves have been used as places of spiritual retreat in many religious traditions.[35] Hinduism is no exception and the cave is associated with the radical self-renunciation of those who have reached the final life stage of the **sannyasin**.[36] The deep, dark recesses of the cave are also linked symbolically to the womb from which human life springs. Thus it is not surprising that the Hindu mandir is designed to represent a journey into the depths of a sacred womb-cave, an inward spiraling pathway toward immanent holiness.[37] At the same time it is also a reflection of the individual's journey through various states of meditation toward ultimate awareness and liberation.

As the believer approaches the exterior of the mandir, they are greeted by hordes of sculpted figures covering almost every surface of the structure representing the infinity of being. Many of the scenes are explicitly erotic and sensual, typical of the lowest level of spiritual life engrossed in the transient features of the physical world. Inside the temple, classical scenes from Hindu mythology begin to elevate the worshipers' minds to a plane beyond mundane reality. As the devotees move inward toward the center of the structure, decorations become less and less elaborate until finally they reach the inner sanctum directly above the center of the sacred mandala and the navel of Vastu Purusha. This sacred space is known as the **garbhagrha** (womb-house) because it contains the most important object in the entire temple: the murti of the main deity. There are no windows or lavish sculptures in the garbhagrha; only the stark simplicity and darkness of the cave which directs the observer toward the primary focus of their devotion. Sometimes entry to the garbhagrha is restricted to the temple priests alone, in which case the worshipers sit in an anteroom. The main murti is usually fixed, but there are portable temple murtis that are brought out of the sanctum to be displayed or carried in procession on festivals. In Hinduism, encircling a sacred object is a common means of expressing devotion and turning one's mind to the divine. Thus, the passageway that leads to the garbhagrha often traces a spiral route inwards, creating the effect of circumambulating the sacred image. The direction is always clockwise so that the impure left side of the body is facing away from the symbol of the divine.[38]

The second natural image used in temple design is the mountain. As with caves, many religions regard mountain peaks as places where the sacred is more readily experienced. In the Hindu tradition, the mythical **Mount Meru** is the abode of the gods and the vertical axis that joins heaven to earth. Thus it makes sense that the distinctive external shape of a Hindu temple is that of a holy mountain rising upwards toward the sky. If the womb-cave represents the journey inward toward immanent divinity at the heart of being, the mountain evokes the idea of reaching upwards toward transcendent reality which presides over the cosmos.

Commentators speak of two major styles of temple architecture, based on the shape and position of the tower-mountain. The Dravidian style, typical of southern India, is characterized by the gopura or gateway tower. Gopuras typically have a stepped pyramidal shape with gradually receding levels divided by horizontal bands. Like most things Hindu, they are elaborately decorated with carvings, sculptures, and paintings featuring themes from Hindu literature. Although not necessarily part of the temple itself, the gopura is usually the highest structure in the complex. The northern or Nagara style of temple design is typified by its tower which is known as a shikara, meaning "summit" or "peak." In contrast to the Dravidian model, the shikara usually has a more semi-conical shape with curved edges and bulging sides, perhaps more suggestive of a mountain (see figure 11.5). Like the gopura in the south, the shikara is the highest

Figure 11.5
Hindu mandir (temple) at Khajuraho, India

part of the structure. Unlike the gopura, it is located directly above the garbhagrha, joining mountain and cave: the convergence of the immanent and the transcendent. Horizontally approaching the murti within the womb-house puts one directly on the vertical axis that joins heaven and earth.[39]

Because the mandir is considered a sacred place, purity and propriety are import-ant issues for devotees and visitors. Shoes and sandals are not permitted and the soles of the feet must always point away from the sacred image. Modest clothing should be worn and many cover their heads out of respect, especially women. Meat, alcohol, and tobacco are avoided and, as in Islam, tradition requires that women not enter the mandir during menstruation. Near the altar there is often a bowl of water (charanamrita) that is used to bathe the feet of the deity. In a manner reminiscent of Catholic Christians, devotees sip or sprinkle this holy water on their heads for blessing and purification.

The basic threefold imagery of body, cave, and mountain provides the key to understanding the architectural patterns and the theological significance of the Hindu mandir. Worshipers stand on a holy mandala fashioned in the shape of a divine body. They spiral inwards toward a visual encounter with the deity symbolized by the murti located in the depths of the womb-cave. They gaze upwards toward the holy moun-tain in the hope of ultimate transcendence and liberation. Although Hinduism is not primarily a congregational faith, its places of communal gathering and worship are rich in spiritual symbolism and artistic beauty. The same is true of its daughter religion which also stresses the importance of the visual image, the offering of food and incense, and the cosmic symbolism of the tower.

Temple Complex

One of the most popular and widely used mantras in Buddhism is known as the **Three Jewels**: "I go for refuge to the Buddha; I go for refuge to the Dharma; I go for refuge to the Sangha." The believer seeks haven in the teacher (Buddha), in the truth that he imparted (**dharma**), and in the community which he founded (**sangha**). As the metaphor suggests, these three dimensions of Buddhist life are considered priceless possessions for they provide safe passage to final liberation.

The third jewel suggests that there is more to Buddhism than simply individual accept-ance of the wisdom of Siddhartha Gautama. Although the way of the **Buddha** is essen-tially about one's own personal search for enlightenment which cannot be delegated to another, the reference to the sangha suggests that there is also a communal dimen-sion to the religion. Buddhism may not be a congregational faith to the same degree as the Semitic religions but the individual Buddhist is not alone. One can and should turn to the sangha for support. Thus, although a great deal of devotional worship is carried out before Buddha images in the privacy of an individual's own home, there are also special places that Buddhists may visit from time to time to worship along-side others, to gain counsel from the wise, to honor the memory of the dead, or to be inspired by the example of past saints. Such a place is the Buddhist temple complex with its cluster of buildings, three of which are the most significant.

The first important building in a temple complex is hinted at by the word *sangha*. In the broad sense, sangha means the larger community of the Buddhist faithful not only in one's own nation or culture but across the globe. In the narrow sense, it refers to the local community of Buddhist monks or nuns who live out the dharma in a radically dedicated manner. The third jewel not only means taking consolation in that one is a member of a worldwide family of fellow believers. It can also have the very practical meaning of visiting a nearby monastery. It is noteworthy that the Sri Lankan term *vihara* and the southeast Asian term *wat* are both commonly translated as "temple" but their primary meaning is a monastic residence or school. In cultures like Thailand, Cambodia, and Laos, many temples are attached to monasteries and thus the two terms are virtually synonymous.

The earliest Buddhist monks were itinerant and often found hospitality in the homes of the laity. During the wet season they would stay in simple huts or natural abodes such as caves. As Buddhism expanded, permanent residences began to be erected under the sponsorship of wealthy patrons. Ideally the monastery was located near enough to a town so that the daily alms round was possible, but secluded enough to provide a peaceful ambience for meditation and study. The architectural style of monasteries varies from culture to culture, and may be inspired by the design of an imperial palace, a military fortress, or a rustic farmhouse. Monasteries are essentially residential and thus consist of individual cells with spartan conditions. A typical monastery also has a study hall, a library, and a guest area where laity are able to attend talks, sermons, and other forms of spiritual education. One of the holiest rooms, especially in Thai monasteries, is the bot, or ordination hall. Here monks convene on a regular basis for the recitation of the rule and on special occasions for the ordination of new monks. The bot is built on consecrated ground and is surrounded by eight stones (stima) which provide spiritual protection.

The second type of building that constitutes a vital part of any Buddhist temple complex is the main shrine hall. Usually the most central and publicly accessible section, the shrine hall contains the main Buddha images that are popular aids to meditation and devotion by resident monks and lay visitors.[40] The space is usually highly ornate with a selection of prominent figures organized in particular patterns. In the **Theravada** tradition, the historical Buddha **Sakyamuni** may be depicted alone or flanked by his closest companions. In the **Mahayana** tradition, Sakyamuni is often accompanied or even replaced by a variety of celestial Buddhas and **bodhisattvas** such as **Amitabha, Avalokiteshvara, Maitreya, Manjusri,** and others. The different position of the hands (**mudra**) on a Buddha statue indicates different themes such as meditation (hands in the lap), instruction (hands in front of the chest), resistance to temptation (hand touching the ground), or humble begging (hands holding a bowl). A Buddha image in the reclining position indicates the death of the Buddha and his passing from this world into **nirvana**. As in certain Hindu and Christian traditions, sumptuous offerings of flowers, candles, incense sticks, and food are placed before the images by devotees seeking assistance from above. Placing gold leaf on a Buddha statue is also a common gesture intended to gain good **karma**. Near the entrance of the shrine hall there is usually an instrument such as a drum or a bell for announcing scheduled times for meditation and devotion. As in other religious cultures, such as Islam and Hinduism, visitors to Buddhist temples are asked to remove their footwear at the door and insure that the soles of their feet never point to a Buddha image or a monk.

In Tibetan Buddhism, the walls of the shrine hall and other parts of the monastery are often adorned with special cloth paintings known as thangkas. These images depict episodes from the life of Sakyamuni, scenes from the **Jataka Tales**, or icons of celestial Buddhas and bodhisattvas. The observer will also notice rows of prayer wheels of varying size around the complex. Small texts containing holy **mantras** are attached to the wheel which is spun by the believer, symbolizing the multiple recitation of the mantra. A similar principle underlies the practice of Tibetan prayer flags which are common features in monastic complexes, private homes, and across the countryside. It is Buddhist belief that, as the wind blows through the colorful flags, the mantras written on them are carried upwards to the celestial Buddhas and bodhisattvas. In contrast, Japanese **Zen** Buddhist complexes are distinguished by the lack of such visual aids and the emphasis on inner reflection. Hence exquisitely manicured gardens of rocks, sand, and trees are the main external aid to peaceful meditation.

The third important building type in the Buddhist temple complex is usually the most conspicuous structure due to its height. The feature is known by various names in different cultures: stupa in south Asia; dagoba in Sri Lanka; chedi in Thailand; chörten in Tibet and Bhutan; pagoda in China and Vietnam. Outsiders frequently mistake its prominent size and shape to mean that it is the place where Buddhist devotional worship occurs. In fact, the stupa or pagoda is the part of the complex in which sacred relics and the ashes of the deceased are stored.

After the death of Siddhartha Gautama, his ashes were distributed among eight kingdoms and placed in simple structures known as **stupas**. The bell-like shape of the stupa is based on Indian burial mounds and cairns that were used to cover the remains of cremated nobility. Relics and memorabilia of Sakyamuni were later distributed to other sites and housed in stupas, as were the remains of other holy persons.[41] Consequently, the stupa emerged as the first type of Buddhist religious monument. Pilgrims came to pay their respects and meditate near the sacred relics, while monks

Figure 11.6
Kuthodaw Buddhist Temple in Mandalay, Burma

and nuns established residences nearby to care for the site. Thus the stupa developed into the stupa-shrine and eventually into the stupa-shrine-monastery complex that is often described as a temple today.

Over time the design of the stupa became more complex and took on new religious meanings. Eventually the typical stupa, especially in south Asia and Tibet, came to consist of five main layers, each of which stood for one of the five fundamental elements of the universe. The entire structure rests on a square base with four sides facing the cardinal points, symbolizing earth. Above this is the original hemispherical or bell-shaped dome that, in this new cosmic imagery, stands for water. It is here that relics and the ashes of the dead are usually housed. A stepped spire sits above the dome, representing the element of fire. The number of steps in the spire often carries a symbolic meaning such as the stages of enlightenment. Above this lies a crescent moon or parasol which stands for the element of air or wind. At the very apex of the stupa, a jewel or pointed finial signifies the final element, ether (see figure 11.7). Alternatively, stupas can be designed to symbolize the **Four Noble Truths** and the Noble Eightfold Path, with nirvana as the crowning tip.

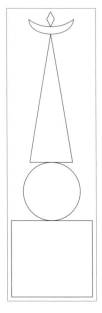

Figure 11.7
Basic geometric patterns of a stupa design

As Buddhism expanded into eastern Asia, the stupa evolved into a more pyramidal design known as the **pagoda**. The term *pagoda* is probably a derivation of the Sanskrit *dhatu garba*, meaning a womb that contains something precious. The Singhalese term *dagoba* is also etymologically related. Another possibility is that the term goes back to a Chinese word for an eight-sided tower. Pagodas often have either 4, 8, or 12 sides but the octagonal design is considered particularly auspicious in Chinese culture. Eight is also a highly significant number in Buddhism itself, based on the Buddha's noble Eightfold Path to Enlightenment.

In ways similar to the Hindu mandir, Buddhist temple complexes are often designed to reflect the body of the meditating Buddha. Moreover, moving through the complex is sometimes interpreted as a symbolic journey from ignorance to enlightenment. Perhaps the best-known example of such symbolism is the great Buddhist temple at Borobudur in central Java. On the lowest levels the sculptured reliefs feature events in the life of the historical Buddha and the Jataka Tales. As visitors move upwards, they pass images relating to more advanced Buddhist thinking such as the vocation of the bodhisattvas. Finally, at the summit, three concentric terraces house 72 stupas, symbolizing the attainment of nirvana. There are other buildings in the typical Buddhist temple complex but the mix of monastic residence, devotional shrine hall and reliquary tower constitutes the kernel of Buddhist sacred space and a practical expression of the third jewel's promise that the sangha will provide safe haven for the spiritual traveler.

SUMMARY

As a fundamental aspect of human society, buildings are used for a vast array of activities including religious worship and devotion. Although religions teach that transcendent reality is literally everywhere, practice indicates that it is encountered in a special way within the sacred building where space itself is sanctified and earth meets heaven. All five major religions have such places where communities gather for congregational worship or individuals come for private devotion and inspired meditation. As with all buildings, the shape and design of the structure itself reflects not only the devotional practices that are carried out within them but also the religious beliefs that lie behind the practices. Although the designs, practices, and beliefs are unique to each religion, it is also possible to identify some interesting points of similarity between the traditions.

In some cases the entire edifice itself is a statement of faith. Hindu and Buddhist temples are both fashioned on the shape of the human body albeit in different ways. The Hindu mandir is traditionally erected on consecrated land according to the pattern of a mandala or sacred diagram. The classical mandala used as the floor plan for Hindu temples is the body of Vastu Purusha, the god of buildings and land. Similarly

Buddhist temples are often designed to imitate the shape of the meditating Buddha seated in the lotus position as seen from a lateral perspective. Traditional Christian churches often had a cruciform pattern so that, from above, the building itself formed the unmistakable symbol of the cross. Although Islamic places of worship do not necessarily have any such overall pattern, an external feature on almost all mosques (as well as many Christian churches) is the domed roof symbolizing the heavens in which God dwells and under which the worshiping community gathers. Historically, the capacity to express Jewish faith through the external appearance of the synagogue was limited as a result of restrictions imposed by the Muslim or Christian social major-ity. When greater freedom was granted in nineteenth-century Europe the tendency was to borrow from classical and even Christian building styles, with the result that the truly distinctive nature of a synagogue is more apparent internally than externally.

The other external feature that is common to many sacred buildings is the tower that reaches upwards toward the sky. In Christianity, it takes the form of a steeple or spire. The steeple usually functioned as a bell-tower from which the call to prayer was tolled in traditional times. With or without a spire, the steeple also symbolizes prayers and human hope rising up to God. A cross is often placed at the very apex of the structure, thus stamping the building as a Christian place of worship. In an Islamic mosque, the tower feature takes the form of the minaret which may originally have been an adaptation of the Christian steeple. In one sense the minaret serves the same purpose as the steeple since it is the elevated place from which the voice of the muezzin calls believers to prayer five times per day.

The tower feature of the Hindu mandir is a symbol of the holy mountain Meru where the gods abide, which makes it a counterpart to the basic floor plan of the mandi the dome of the mosque and the church. However, as the tallest feature of the mandir, it also represents the vertical axis connecting heaven and earth. In northern India, the tower is known as a shikara which is located directly over the central part of the mandir, while in the south it is the gopura which forms part of the gateway to the temple. In the Buddhist temple, the tower feature is known by a variety of names including stupa or pagoda. Although often mistaken for the main part of the complex, it is actually the place for housing relics and the cremated ashes of the deceased. The original bell shape of the stupa was based on the traditional Indian funeral mound. Over time it evolved into a multilayered symbol of the cosmos with each level representing one of the fundamental elements: a square base as earth; a bell-shaped dome as water; a tapered spire as fire; a parasol as air; and a finial or some other symbol at the very apex as the ether. In eastern Asia, the stupa evolved into the slender pyramidal shape of the pagoda. Just as the dome sits above mosque and church representing divinity's dominion over the cosmos, the stupa-pagoda rises above the temple complex symbolizing the cosmos itself in all of its levels through which the individual must journey toward ultimate liberation.

The interior of the sacred building is also replete with religious symbolism and meaning. The main issue is the focus of attention. The interior of a mosque is strikingly empty of seating, creating an open atmosphere but also reflecting the need for space given that much of Muslim prayer involves bodily prostration, as the etymology of the term mosque suggests. The key feature is the arch-shaped wall niche (mihrab) indicating the direction of Mecca (qibla) toward which every official prayer must be directed. Thus every mosque physically orientates the believing community toward the symbol of Islamic unity. The original qibla was Jerusalem until it was later changed. As in Islam, the direction of Jewish prayer is also an important consideration. Like mosques, synagogues indicate the direction of the holy city via the positioning of their most important interior feature, the aron ha-kodesh (holy ark).

Apart from being a direction indicator, the holy ark is essentially a receptacle for the Torah scrolls which are read during synagogue services on an annual cycle. A lamp burns alongside the ark, indicating the presence of the scrolls inside. That the holy writings occupy pride of place inside the sacred building attests to the unrivaled importance accorded to the inspired word in the Jewish tradition. In a similar manner, Protestant churches often give prominence to an enthroned Bible over the communion table. It is no coincidence that Judaism, Islam, and Protestant Christianity all share a pronounced emphasis on the word rather than the image as the principal way to approach divinity. Thus, synagogues, mosques, and Protestant churches are also notable for their lack of icons, statues, and any other image that might be considered idolatrous. Moreover, a key feature in each of them is the platform from which the holy texts are recited and interpreted: the bimah, the minbar, and the pulpit.

In contrast, the sacred image is an essential part of worship and devotion in other mainstream Christian churches, as well as in Hindu mandirs and Buddhist temples. Although Catholic, Orthodox, and Anglican churches have scriptural readings during their services, the pulpit is usually not in the center of the sanctuary but to one side. Central position is given to the altar or communion table on which the Eucharistic bread and wine are consecrated. Like the Jewish ark, these churches also have a holy receptacle, known as the tabernacle, with a lamp burning beside it. However, unlike the Jewish ark, the Christian tabernacle contains sacred bread rather than sacred texts. Moreover, these churches warmly endorse the use of icons, statues, and other images in the sacred building. Often the faithful will pray before the image and light candles as a gesture of devotion. Similarly, the main focus within the Buddhist temple complex is the shrine hall which houses images representing the historical Buddha or a selection of celestial Buddhas and bodhisattvas. Here the faithful meditate or make offerings of incense, flowers, lighted candles, and food.

In the same tradition, Hindu worship involves offerings of the same sorts of substances before the sacred image (murti) through which the devotee gains a vision (darshana) of the deity. As with Buddhism, much Hindu devotion occurs in the privacy of the domestic shrine, but the Hindu mandir is typically replete with images and sculptures of Brahman's many manifestations. The central space inside a Hindu mandir is the inner sanctum in which the image of the main god is kept. As a small, cave-like space set deep within the structure, it is appropriately described as the garbhagrha (womb-house). The very act of entering a Hindu mandir – passing from the highly ornate and brightly lit exterior, circumambulating the inner sanctum via the ever-narrowing passageway, and finally encountering the garbhagrha – is a powerful metaphor for the spiritual journey. In northern Indian mandirs, the garbhagrha lies directly beneath the shikara tower and directly above the navel of the Vastu Purusha, thus representing the convergence of transcendence, immanence, and origin at this crucial point in space.

The sacred building has been a source of inspirational architectural design through the centuries and across the religions. At a practical level it functions as the forum for public worship. At a theological level, it stands as a statement of faith in stone, metal, wood, and glass. In many ways mosques, synagogues, churches, mandirs, and temple complexes have their own unique characteristics that reinforce the distinctiveness of each religion. Yet beneath the visible differences there also lies a basement of commonality. Whether the emphasis is on congregational or individual devotion, the priority of the verbal or the visual, the heights of transcendence or the depths of immanence, in all cases the sacred building is the place where the sacred meets the profane, where heaven touches earth, and where ordinary space is given extraordinary meaning.

DISCUSSION TOPICS

1 How do religious buildings use height and depth symbolically?
2 What does a sacred building tell us about that religion's concept of transcendent reality?
3 Explore how water, light, and other symbolic substances are used in sacred buildings.
4 How is purity an issue in sacred buildings?
5 Is the Hindu home more important than the temple for worship?
6 How do Catholic, Orthodox, and Protestant churches differ in their fundamental design features?
7 How do Muslims and Jews adorn their sacred buildings without falling into idolatry?
8 Examine the historical development of the Buddhist stupa or pagoda.
9 What are some recent trends in religious architectural design?

FURTHER READING

Bhaskarananda, Swami (2002). *The Essentials of Hinduism*. 2nd edn. Seattle: Viveka, pp. 151–5.

Cohn-Sherbok, Dan (2003). *Judaism: History, Belief and Practice*. London: Routledge, pp. 483–7.

Davies, J. G. (1984). *Temples, Churches and Mosques*. Oxford: Blackwell.

De Lange, Nicholas (2000). *Introduction to Judaism*. Cambridge: Cambridge University Press, pp. 125–40.

Fisher, Robert E. (1993). *Buddhist Art and Architecture*. London: Thames & Hudson.

Frishman, Martin, & Khan, Hasan-Uddin (2002). *The Mosque: History, Architectural Development and Regional Diversity*. London: Thames & Hudson.

Gordon, Matthew S. (2002). *Understanding Islam*. London: Duncan Baird, pp. 72–9.

Holm, Jean, & Bowker, John (eds.) (2000). *Sacred Place*. London: Continuum.

Meek, Harold (1995). *The Synagogue*. London: Phaidon.

Michell, George (1988). *The Hindu Temple: An Introduction to its Meaning and Forms*. Chicago: University of Chicago Press.

Reynolds, Frank E., & Carbine, Jason A. (eds.) (2000). *The Life of Buddhism*. Berkeley and Los Angeles: University of California Press, ch. 1.

Segler, Franklin M., & Bradley, Randall (2006). *Christian Worship: Its Theology and Practice*. 3rd edn. Nashville: B & H Publishing Group, pp. 205–18.

White, James F. (2001). *Introduction to Christian Worship*. 3rd edn. Nashville: Abingdon Press, ch. 3.

Wilkinson, John (2002). *From Synagogue to Church: The Traditional Design*. London: RoutledgeCurzon.

NOTES

1　See Qur'an 49.4: "Those who call out to you from behind private chambers." Surah 49 is aptly named "The Chambers."

2　See Sahih Muslim 4.1068–70.

3　Some see an oblique reference to the Quba mosque in Qur'an 9:108 which speaks of a mosque built on piety "from the first day."

4　Qur'an 2:217; 5:2; 8:34; 22:25.

5　The Masjid al-Haram's present structure was completed by Sultan Selim II in the late sixteenth century.

6　The Arabic term *masjid* is rendered as *masqid* in Egyptian and *mezquita* in Spanish. The Qur'an also uses *masjid* to refer to places of worship in general, including the pre-Islamic Ka'bah.

7　Qur'an 24:36. Because of its aptness, this verse is a popular calligraphic theme in mosques.

8　Sahih Bukhari 1.8.466.

9　Another example of the adaptation of pre-existing styles is the typical Iranian mosque, which is often a converted **Zoroastrian** fire temple, characterized by a domed roof and an open courtyard.

10 The Masjid al-Haram in Mecca is distinguished by its seven minarets while the Blue Mosque in Istanbul has six minarets. The builder of the Blue Mosque, Sultan Ahmed I, was criticized for having the same number of minarets as the Masjid al-Haram at the time (c.1616). Consequently, he sponsored the seventh minaret for the Meccan mosque.

11 Sunan Abu Dawud 1.232.

12 Sahih Bukhari 1.8.376.

13 Other Islamic schools, especially the Shi'ite tradition, are less concerned about the artistic depiction of Muhammad and the prophets. Moreover there are many historical examples of Islamic artwork in which the Prophet is depicted either in full or with his face veiled.

14 Sahih Bukhari 1.8.374, 411, 466.

15 Sahih Muslim 4.884–96; Sahih Bukhari 2.13.23: these hadith indicate that women should not be prevented from attending mosque but they should not wear perfume.

16 Qur'an 9:17–18.

17 2 Kings 24:1–15; 25:9–12.

18 See Ezekiel 8:1; 14:1. Ezekiel 11:16 speaks of God becoming a "sanctuary" for the exiles which is often interpreted as the nascent synagogue.

19 Traditionally all seats face the **Ark** in **Ashkenazi** synagogues while the seating in **Sephardic** synagogues tended to follow the perimeter of the sanctuary although worshipers faced the Ark when they stood up to pray.

20 The term *aron ha kodesh* is used among Ashkenazi Jews. The Sephardic tradition prefers the term *heikhal*.

21 Exodus 25.10–23; 37.1–9. There is no strict etymological link with the word for Noah's ark (teyvat), although it too was a vessel that contained something precious.

22 Exodus 26:31–7; 36:35–8.

23 See Exodus 27:20.

24 *Bimah* is the Ashkenazi term while the Sephardim prefer *tebah* or *taivah*.

25 Mark 1:21; 3:1; etc.; Acts 13:5; 14:1; 17:10, etc.

26 Acts 2:46; 12:12; 20:7.

27 Originally a basilica was a Roman public building usually in the forum of a town but eventually the word came to mean a large Christian church modeled on a similar design.

28 The iconostasis usually has three doors that are open or closed depending on the festival or ceremony.

29 See Genesis 6:14–19.

30 Catholic Code of Canon Law, canons 938–40. Some Anglican parishes also use tabernacles that are located behind, above, or on the altar with a presence lamp nearby.

31 A single pulpit from which all scriptural readings are read and the sermon is preached is technically called an *ambo* from the Greek word meaning 'both.'

32 The story is told in the Matsya Purana. See also Brihat Samhita 53.1–3.

33 *Devalaya* and *devagrha* are also common terms for a Hindu temple and carry the same meaning, namely "dwelling of a god."

34 During construction, a gold or silver casket filled with auspicious items such as jewels, plants, and soil is buried near the temple door.

35   For example, the cave features in the spiritual experiences of Elijah, Saint Benedict, and Muhammad in the Jewish, Christian, and Islamic traditions respectively.

36   Svetashvatara Upanishad 2.10.

37   Some Hindu temples are constructed inside caves, for instance the classical fifth-century examples at Ellora in Maharashtra, India.

38   Similarly in Hindu puja, the worshiper moves a flaming lamp of camphor around in a clockwise manner emulating the act of **circumambulation**.

39   The equivalent of the shikara in southern temples is the vimanam, but it is not the most prominent part of the structure.

40   The shrine hall is called a kondo in Japan and vihara in Thailand.

41   Thai Buddhism distinguishes between various types of stupa, or chedi: those that contain relics of the historical Buddha or his companions (prathart chedi); those that contain personal belongings of the Buddha and his companions (boriphoke chedi); and those that contain written records of his teachings (dhamma chedi).

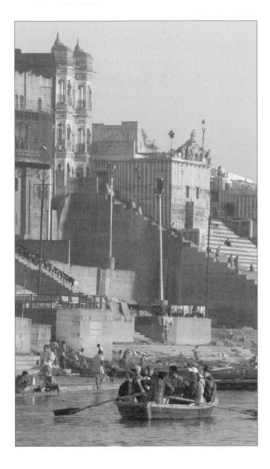

Chapter 12

JOURNEY

CONTENTS

 The Sacred Ford

 Traces of Tathagata

 The Quest of the Magi

 Aliyah

 Hajj

Introduction

Transcendent reality can be experienced in the special space within the house of worship, but it is also sought after in more distant places of exceptional significance. Such locations beckon the believer to visit them and to draw on their unique ethos, even if only once in a lifetime. Ordinary space is rendered extraordinary not only by the sacred building but also by the sacred journey. In this chapter we explore the sanctification of space via the experience of the pilgrim. What are the main pilgrimage destinations in each of the five religions? Why are these particular places so significant? What physical features mark the sacred location and what specific actions and rituals are performed there? What are the main motives for such journeys and what aspects of belief are highlighted and expressed?

The Sacred Ford

In the Forest Chapter (Aranyaka Parvan) of the great Hindu epic, the **Mahabharata**, the sage Pulastya describes a grand circuit encompassing all of India and taking in hundreds of interesting sites. The litany of mountains, rivers, and cities is not only a revealing insight into ancient Indian geography but also one of the more explicit references in Hindu scripture to the concept of the religious journey. Although naturally disinclined to leave Mother India and travel across the contaminating "black waters" (kala pani) of her seas, Hindus have always felt a powerful urge to travel within her borders to places of outstanding religious significance. From ancient times to the modern day, pilgrimage has occupied an important place in Hindu belief and practice.

The traditional Hindu term for pilgrimage is tirthayatra, which literally means "a journey to the ford." It is an apt metaphor for the special threshold where the spiritual traveler is able to cross over a figurative river from the profane to the sacred. As with all pilgrim destinations, the tirtha [ford] is a liminal point – a place at the edge of the mundane where the transcendent is more powerfully experienced. In the Hindu imagination the sky is a river that separates earth and heaven, but that is traversed by the gods who descend into our world. In pilgrimage, the movement is in the opposite direction as the human subject crosses over to the other side and ascends to a higher level of existence, even if for only a brief moment. So important is pilgrimage that it is often included as one of the five basic duties of all Hindus alongside daily worship, festivals, rites of passage, and a virtuous lifestyle.[1] The development of modern forms of transport has served only to further stimulate the practice in contemporary India. Millions take advantage of train, bus, and plane to visit sacred sites which are scattered like jewels across the subcontinent.

The specific reasons why Hindus embark on pilgrimages are many and varied. Often the pilgrimage is a form of petitionary prayer in the sense that the effort invested may persuade the gods to answer a request such as conceiving a child, finding romance, or succeeding in business. Conversely some people undertake the journey as an expression of gratitude for a blessing already granted, or to fulfill a vow made in perilous circumstances. Many believe that holy sites possess a special ethos and that devotions and sacrifices are naturally more efficacious offered there than elsewhere. For example, many Hindus journey to places where funeral offerings (**shraddha**) are thought to have a greater effect. Elderly pilgrims travel to hallowed places in the hope that dying there will guarantee them liberation from the wheel of **reincarnation**. For others pilgrimage is primarily about purification from bad **karma**, usually symbolized by bathing. The site may also be associated with incarnations of particular deities, for example their birthplace, childhood home, royal palace, or last dwelling place on earth. Visiting such auspicious places brings the pilgrim into more tangible, intimate contact with the deity. Ultimately, the pilgrim has come to "see" the divine and be transformed in the process. They come to cross the ford.

The journey itself may be long and arduous, especially when a pilgrimage site is located in a remote place such as high in the mountains or deep within a forest. The time and energy invested in traveling to a sacred site are an essential part of the overall experience and generate good karma along the way. Upon arrival, the Hindu pilgrim engages in a series of activities that express inner faith and symbolize the purpose of the journey. One of the first actions usually performed is bathing in the purifying waters of the river, lake, or ocean. Thus, many popular pilgrimage sites are located on or near the banks of rivers, seven of which are considered to be particularly holy in the Hindu tradition: the Ganges, the Yamuna, and the (underground) Sarasvati in northern India; the Narmada in central India; the Godavari and the Kaveri in the south; and the Indus in present-day Pakistan. In particular, the Ganges is considered to be the most sacred of all rivers. In Hindu mythology it flows from its celestial source (the Milky Way) down through the hair of **Shiva** and on to the earth where it brings life, fertility, and purification. Many of India's great pilgrimage cities are located on its banks and are often literal as well as figurative fords.

Most sacred sites have a temple or series of temples in which pilgrims are able to experience a "seeing" (**darshana**) of the deity. They may circumambulate the temple or the image within the temple in the usual clockwise direction, keeping their unclean left side away from the object of veneration. Offerings are made to the god whose powerful presence is mediated via the image. Quite often the pilgrim will also make an offering to the temple priests, providing much appreciated practical support for those who maintain the site as well as generating good karma for the donor. Pilgrims will often listen to discourses or receive spiritual counsel from the local priests or gurus.

Traditionally, a tirthayatra involves a high degree of self-denial. In this way, the pilgrim, at least temporarily, emulates the radical detachment of the Hindu **sannyasin** who is described as a wanderer on the earth. Going on pilgrimage often means fasting, abstaining from foods such as meat, fish, and alcohol, shaving the hair, and avoiding sexual activity. The journey to the ford is a time of austerity and discipline, during which the bodily passions are subdued and spiritual matters given priority. The metaphor of the ford is appropriate since, during this special journey, ordinary persons are invited to cross over to the other side and adopt the lifestyle of those who have attained the final stage of the **ashramas**.

There is also another sense in which tirthayatra involves crossing over: namely, the dilution of **caste** and gender boundaries. Commentators have noted how Hindu pilgrimage tends to highlight equality rather than hierarchy in that everyone and anyone is able to make the sacred journey. People who may be ordinarily separated by geographical, social, and religious barriers converge on sacred sites and discover

Figure 12.1

Major pilgrimage sites in Hinduism

themselves to be fellow companions. Thus, pilgrimages are especially popular among women, lower-caste Hindus, and all who are excluded from the traditional brahmanical rites. As the Mahabharata text above suggests, there are thousands of such places scattered across the landscape of India, making a detailed consideration impossible in the space available here. However, it is worthwhile taking a closer look at three prominent examples of tirtha in the Hindu world: the char dham, the Kumbha Mela, and the holy city of Varanasi.

According to Indian tradition, the eminent eighth-century CE sage **Shankara** once made an epic journey around India, establishing shrines at the four cardinal points. The all-embracing route came to be known as **char dham** [the four abodes] and is still looked upon as the archetypal Hindu pilgrimage. Few have had the time, the resources, or the energy to emulate Shankara's extraordinary feat in a single journey, although many Hindus aspire to visit each of the four dhams at least once during their lifetime. Traditionally the pilgrimage begins at the eastern dham situated in the coastal city of Puri, in the province of Orissa. The main temple houses three enormous statues of Jagganath (**Krishna**), his brother Balarama, and his sister Subhadra. Each year, during the month of Ashadha (June–July), hundreds of thousands of pilgrims flock to the city to witness the grand procession through the town to the nearby Gundicha Temple. The statues are placed on huge chariots known as rathas, which are dragged through the streets by dozens of the faithful pulling on enormous hemp ropes. Sometimes ardent devotees attach the ropes to their backs with hooks to demonstrate their radical devotion. Fanatical followers have even prostrated themselves under the huge wheels of the chariots and have allowed themselves to be run over by Jagganath. The practice is the origin of the English term *juggernaut* which signifies a massive unstoppable vessel.

The char dham follows a clockwise direction, imitating the normal **circumambulation** of a sacred image. From Puri, the sacred route takes the pilgrim to the southern shrine at Rameshvaram, in Tamil Nadu. As the name implies, Rameshvaram is considered to be the site where **Rama** worshiped Shiva prior to his battle with the demon Ravanna in Sri Lanka. It is considered to be the same site where Rama built a shrine in thanksgiving after his victorious return. The extensive temple is located on a small island off the coast, and is reputed to have over 1,000 stone pillars and more than a mile of corridors. Inside the complex are 22 special pools, each of which cleanses the pilgrim who bathes in them from a particular type of impurity. The temple is also believed to be one of the 12 locations scattered around India where Shiva manifested himself as a gigantic column of light (jyotirlinga). Two sacred **linga** stones are housed in the temple, their phallic shape symbolizing the life-giving power of the deity.

The third dham is the city of Dwarka on the western coast of Gujarat, facing the Arabian Sea. According to Hindu legend, Krishna founded the city and reigned there as king until the end of his earthly life. Dwarka is also listed among the sapta pura, or seven holy cities of India that bring liberation from the wheel of reincarnation for those who die within their borders.[2] A beautiful temple located between the town and the sea marks the actual pilgrimage site. The fourth and northern dham is Badrinath, nestled over 10,000 feet above sea level in the snowy peaks of the Himalayan mountains. For many, Badrinath is the final and most important of the traditional dhams. So extreme is its altitude that the temple can be opened to visitors only during the summer months. The track to Badrinath is an arduous one, promising an abundance of good karma for those who make the effort to reach their destination. The name of the town is derived from a legend that narrates how the goddess **Lakshmi** turned herself into a badri tree to protect Vishnu, her partner.

In place of the four classical dhams, a more local Himalayan version has evolved known as the chota [little] char dham which attracts thousands of pilgrims each year. The spiritual journey begins in Yamunotri, source of the Yamuna river, and progresses to Gangotri at the headwaters of the Ganges. From here the pilgrim walks for two days to remote Kedarnath, another of the 12 Shaivite jyotirlinga sites. The circuit terminates in Badrinath, as it does in the case of the traditional char dham. It is interesting to note that both forms of the char dham include shrines dedicated to Vishnu and Shiva, revealing an ecumenical spirit and appealing to followers of both major Hindu sects. The **Advaita** school of Hinduism also regards the four classical dhams as among the holiest of places, for the shrines were originally established by its founder, Shankara. In other words, tirthayatra not only cuts across caste and gender boundaries but also unites believers from different spiritual traditions within Hinduism itself.[3]

The second example of Hindu pilgrimage constitutes one of the largest gatherings of human beings on the planet – the **Kumbha Mela.** The term literally means a jar of nectar and refers to an episode in Hindu mythology in which the demons stole the pitcher of immortality from the gods. After a struggle, the gods retrieved the container but, as it was being transported back to the heavens, four drops of the precious nectar fell to earth. Four cities now stand where the drops landed: Prayag (Allahabad),

Hardwar, Ujjain, and Nashik. Every three years, a colossal religious festival is celebrated in each of the cities in turn, thus creating a 12-year cycle. The actual dates of the Kumbha Mela are determined astrologically by the position of the sun, moon, and the planet Jupiter which has a 12-year synodic period.[4] Although Hardwar and Ujjain are counted among the seven sacred Hindu cities, the largest gatherings in the cycle occur at Prayag where crowd estimates in 2001 ranged from 10 to 20 million. Activities include worshiping in temples, listening to the teachings of distinguished gurus, feeding the poor, and especially ritual bathing. Thousands of sadhus and sannyasins emerge from their reclusive lifestyles to attend the festival. Traditionally they are given the honor of bathing before all others.

The third example is arguably the best-known pilgrimage site in all of India, a place whose image is virtually synonymous with being Hindu. Situated on a ford of the Ganges river in Uttar Pradesh, **Varanasi** derives its name from two nearby tributaries: the Varuna and the Assi. Its alternative name, **Benares**, was popular during the British regime but in ancient times it was known as Kasi. It is said that Shiva lived as an ascetic in Varanasi which is also one of the 12 jyotirlinga sites of Shaivism. The city is the premium destination for pilgrims from all Hindu sects and more than a million come each year to bathe at the famous **ghats** [steps] along its riverbanks.[5] There are over 1,000 temples in Varanasi where pilgrims offer **puja** to their personal deity. In traditional Hindu

Figure 12.2
The holy city
of Varanasi
(Benares) on
the Ganges

fashion, many visitors circumambulate the entire city by walking the Panchkosi Road and stopping at the many shrines along the way. The circuit is nearly 35 miles long and can take up to five days to complete on foot.

For most Hindus, the greatest motive for making the tirthayatra to Varanasi is to die there and have one's ashes scattered on the waters of the Ganges. Death in Varanasi, as in all seven holy Hindu cities, circumvents the cycle of **samsara** and offers the deceased instant access to ultimate liberation. Thus many elderly Hindus migrate to Varanasi to live out their final days while those who pass away elsewhere have their corpses transported hundreds of miles to the sacred city for cremation. At places along the river, such as the Manikarnika Ghat, funeral pyres fueled by sandalwood burn day and night, releasing deceased spirits from their mortal bodies for the most important of all journeys. As the holiest Hindu city on the banks of Mother Ganges, where death brings final release from the wheel of rebirth, Varanasi is the epitome of tirthayatra in the world of Hinduism. But Varanasi is a significant pilgrimage destination in another major religious tradition, for a key event occurred many centuries ago in a deer park on its outskirts.

Traces of Tathagata

According to Buddhist scripture, as **Sakyamuni** approached the end of his life, his cousin and close companion **Ananda** asked how his followers would be able to pay their respects to the master after his death. In response the Buddha spoke of four places where the believer could go to experience his abiding presence.

> Bhikkhus, after my passing away, all sons and daughters who are of good family and are faithful should, as long as they live, go to the four holy places and remember: Here at Lumbini, the enlightened one was born; here at Bodhgaya he attained enlightenment; here at Sarnath he turned the wheel of Dharma; and there at Kusinegara he entered Parinirvana.[6]

The **Tipitaka** text goes on to describe how the Buddha predicted that believers would make their way to these sites and perform acts of devotion such as circumambulation and offerings. The visitors would be reminded of the Buddha truth and achieve advanced states of mental awareness via meditation. In effect, Sakyamuni was predicting the future emergence of a Buddhist pilgrimage tradition. Like Hinduism, Buddhism acknowledges the intrinsic value of the sacred journey and shares with its mother religion many related beliefs and practices. Pilgrimage is an act of faith requiring discipline but promising good karma in return. Pilgrimage involves the adoption of a simple lifestyle and many pilgrims donate gifts of food and clothing to the resident

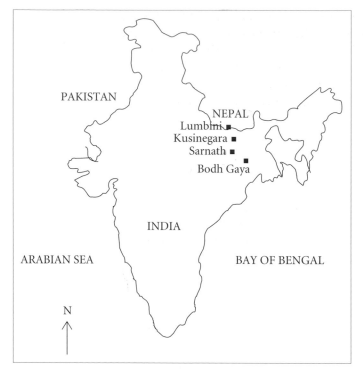

PAKISTAN

NEPAL

Lumbini ■
Kusinegara ■
Sarnath ■
■
Bodh Gaya

INDIA

ARABIAN SEA

BAY OF BENGAL

N
↑

Figure 12.3

Major pilgrimage
sites in Buddhism

monks who maintain the sacred sites. Pilgrimage holds out the promise of rebirth in a higher realm of heavenly happiness for those who die on the way. As in Hinduism, the motivations behind Buddhist pilgrimage include the expression of devotional faith, the earning of karma by self-denial, and the reaping of benefits prior and subsequent to death.

There are many holy places in the Buddhist world but the above text identifies the four principal sites and highlights the key that links them: the historical founder. Unlike Hinduism which has no such figure and whose sacred places are primarily associated with mythological events or natural symbolism, the main destinations for the Buddhist pilgrim are locations where the devotee can draw closer to the Enlightened One. Sakyamuni is often described as **Tathagata**, the one who has thus come and gone: he is both absent and present. In the physical sense he is no longer here since his body was cremated long ago. Yet Buddhist faith holds that he left "traces" in this world that provide powerful and tangible links with his person. One obvious form of such traces is the relics and personal possessions of the Buddha that are stored in temples and shrines across Asia. According to tradition, the Buddha's ashes were housed in eight **stupas** until the Emperor **Ashoka** redistributed them to tens of thousands of shrines. But another type of trace is a place where a significant event in his life occurred, and there are no more significant events than the four enunciated above: his birth, Enlightenment, First Sermon, and death.

The historical origins of Buddhist pilgrimage are obscure but it appears that believers began to make their way to places that figured in the life of Sakyamuni at a relatively early stage. The most important impetus given to the practice of pilgrimage came from the Emperor Ashoka, a convert to Buddhism and one of its greatest political sponsors. In obedience to the sutta text, Ashoka set out on a dhammayatra [journey of truth] in 249 BCE, visiting the four sites as well as others where the Buddha was reputed to have worked various miracles.[7] He erected a monument in each place, and despite the vicissitudes of history, the four main locations are once again on the itinerary of Buddhist pilgrimages and religious tours today.

Lumbini, the site of Sakyamuni's birth, is located in the Rupandehi district of Nepal near the Indian border. Tradition has it that the Buddha's pregnant mother, Maha Devi, was on her way to her parents' home when she went into labor. She disembarked from the royal carriage and gave birth to her son while leaning against a tree in the grove. As with many other Buddhist holy places, Lumbini fell into neglect and ruin for centuries until it was rediscovered and restored by archaeologists in the late nineteenth century. It was declared a World Heritage Site by UNESCO in 1997. The visitor to Lumbini is first greeted by the remains of Ashoka's great stone pillar with the following inscription:

> Twenty years after his coronation, King Ashoka ("Beloved of the Gods") visited this spot in person and worshiped at this place because here Buddha Sakyamuni was born. He caused to make a stone (capital) representing a horse and he caused this stone pillar to be erected. Because the Buddha was born here, he made the village of Lumbini free from taxes and subject to pay only one-eighth of the produce as land revenue instead of the usual rate.

The horse capital was destroyed long ago but a nearby tree with a vermilion-colored base represents the original tree that supported Maha Devi during childbirth and miraculously bent over in reverence when the baby was born. Its branches are usually adorned with colored prayer flags and offerings. Near the tree are the ruins of the original Ashokan shrine where a womb-shaped commemorative stone sits on a platform of bricks. According to tradition, this is the precise spot where the young Prince Siddhartha first saw the light of day. The new shrine contains a bas-relief depicting the birth scene and a pond (pushkarini) where the Buddha's mother is said to have bathed after the nativity.

Although Lumbini marks the beginning of the last reincarnation of the Buddha, greater prestige is bestowed upon the place where the prince became the Buddha. **Bodhgaya** lies approximately 120 miles east of the holy city of Varanasi. Like many Buddhist shrines, it was devastated by the Muslim invaders of the twelfth century and became a Hindu place of worship for many centuries. The renowned British archaeologist, Sir Alexander Cunningham, excavated the site in the 1880s and it was eventually returned to the Buddhist community in the twentieth century. Consequently, the pilgrimage tradition has been revived and Buddhist faithful from all over the globe visit the complex every year. The earliest buildings date from the time of Ashoka but the present Mahabodhi Temple was erected in the second century CE. It is thought that the relics stored in the stupa are those of Siddhartha Gautama himself. The interior is dominated by a giant golden statue depicting the Buddha sitting in a serene earth-touching posture, just as Sakyamuni would have sat under the bodhi tree on that fateful night. The gesture of reaching down to the earth

Figure 12.4
Buddhists
meditating at
the bodhi tree,
Bodhgaya

symbolizes how the Buddha resisted the temptations of Mara during the process of **Enlightenment**. Pilgrims circumambulate this most holy place by following a marble walkway around the temple. In 2002, five years after Lumbini, the Mahabodhi Temple was also declared a World Heritage Site.

The two most venerated objects in all of Buddhism are located behind the temple: the bodhi tree and the diamond throne. The tree under which Sakyamuni became the Buddha is a peepal tree (*Ficus religiosa*). Sadly it has been destroyed, intentionally and unintentionally, on a number of occasions but each time it has either been revived or replaced with cuttings from saplings taken from the original tree.[8] It is said that each Buddha attains enlightenment under a tree of their choice which becomes the bodhi tree for that epoch. According to tradition, the tree in Bodhgaya was chosen by Siddhartha because no other place on earth could support the weight of the **dharma**. In front of the tree are the remains of Ashoka's shrine known as the Vajrasana, or Diamond Throne, which is thought to be the very place where Sakyamuni sat in meditation. The precise spot is now marked by a red sandstone slab and considered by Buddhists to be the holiest place on earth. There are also markers indicating where the Buddha spent the next seven weeks after his Enlightenment absorbed in the bliss of nirvana on earth.[9]

After the seven weeks passed, Sakyamuni left Bodhgaya in search of his five former companions whom he found in a deer park at **Sarnath**, just outside Varanasi.[10] It was there that he conveyed to them the **Four Noble Truths** in his First Sermon, known as the Dhammacakkappavattana Sutta [The Turning of the Wheel Sutta]. Thus Sarnath which, like other sites, has experienced moments of destruction and protracted periods of neglect, became the third major destination for pilgrimage.[11] Once again, it was nineteenth-century archaeological excavations that reclaimed the site for posterity. The park itself still exists and the ancient Dhamek Stupa indicates the traditional place where the First Sermon was delivered. A short distance away, the pilgrim can visit the Dharmarajika Stupa which once held bodily relics of Sakyamuni before they were inadvertently consigned to the Ganges by well-meaning Hindus in the late eighteenth century. The main ruins are thought to be the house where Sakyamuni spent his first rains retreat. According to legend, a rich man donated the place to the Buddha and his community and immediately a mansion appeared for him in the celestial realms as a reward for his generosity. An Ashokan pillar indicates the place where the Buddha sent out 60 monks to go forth and spread the teaching in all directions. The famous lion image that once stood atop the pillar is now housed in the local museum.

The fourth sacred site is **Kusinegara** in Uttar Pradesh, about 60 miles south of Lumbini. It was here that the Buddha lay down in a grove of trees and passed into **nirvana**. The immediate cause of his death was tainted food that had been offered to him by a blacksmith in Pava.[12] His body was cremated and the ashes distributed between eight local kingdoms. Pilgrims made their way to the site of his passing for centuries until it was left deserted after the twelfth-century Islamic conquests. Kusinegara was identified and restored as part of Cunningham's archaeological projects during the late nineteenth century. Today pilgrims visit the Mahaparinibbana Temple with its 20-foot-long statue of a recumbent Buddha in the process of passing into nirvana. The figure of the dying Buddha bears the 32 marks of the Enlightened One and is surrounded by statues of three disciples: Ananda, Dabba Malla, and Subhadda. Within the same complex, the Makutabandhana Stupa is erected on the traditional place where Sakyamuni's remains were cremated. Residential monasteries from Chinese, Japanese, Sri Lankan, Burmese, and Tibetan communities testify to the international character of a religion whose founder passed from the world on this site 2,500 years ago.

There are many other shrines, temples, monasteries, and holy sites throughout the Buddhist world that attract pilgrims and religious visitors. Part of the attraction in many cases is that they contain relics of the founder and other saintly figures from the past. While Hinduism has an extensively developed pilgrimage tradition, the lack of a historical founder means that its holy sites tend to be associated more with natural spiritual beauty or significant events from its vast mythology. In contrast, Buddhism's most important pilgrimage destinations, like its religious festivals, are linked to the life of Sakyamuni. The pilgrim who visits the place of the Buddha's birth, Enlightenment, First Sermon, or death is ultimately seeking the Buddha himself. The traces he left on earth in the form of relics and holy sites are a powerful, tangible point of spiritual contact for the believer. This quest for the founder via the actual locations in which he lived and died is a feature not only of Buddhism. Sacred sites such as Lumbini, Bodhgaya, Sarnath, and Kusinegara have their Christian equivalents in places such as Bethlehem, Nazareth, and Jerusalem.

 ## The Quest of the Magi

In the second chapter of Matthew's gospel, the evangelist describes how "wise men" (**magi**) from the East saw a new star in the heavens and recognized it as a portent of some imminent and momentous event. Following the celestial sign, they eventually came to a stable in the village of **Bethlehem** where they discovered a newborn infant lying in a manger. In recognition of the holiness and royalty of the child, they offered gifts of gold, frankincense, and myrrh, and then returned home without betraying the location to the jealous King Herod.[13] The story of the wise men, which has become a popular aspect of the celebration of **Christmas**, carries many layers of profound theological meaning for the Christian. One of them concerns the journey from a distant country to the scene of Christ's birth and back home again. For many Christians, the visit of the magi is the archetype of all sacred journeys made by the believer in search of the divine. In one sense, it is the scriptural basis and model for all Christian pilgrimages.

Like Hinduism and Buddhism, Christianity is also characterized by a long, esteemed history of pilgrimage. The idea of a journey undertaken in faith to a place of great religious significance has, if anything, become even more widely practiced in recent times with advances in the means of transport. Throughout history, Christians have traveled to an impressive range of holy sites. One of the earliest forms of pilgrimage was to visit living saints who dwelt at the edge of civilization in the deserts of Egypt, Syria, and the eastern Mediterranean. Even today, **Orthodox** Christians often travel to remote monasteries, such as **Mount Athos** in northern Greece, to seek spiritual counsel from the startsy, or holy men, who reside there.

In time, a more common form of pilgrimage emerged that involved visiting not the home of a living saint but the grave of a deceased one. The tombs of the saints, especially martyrs, were considered to be exceptionally sacred places where faith could be reinvigorated, sins forgiven, and blessings bestowed. Probably the best-known European example is the ancient imperial capital itself where Christian tradition holds that **Saints Peter** and **Paul** were executed and buried, although historical divisions within Christianity have meant that Rome is now associated primarily with **Catholic** pilgrimage. Since the fourteenth century, popes have declared special "Jubilee Years" during which Christians are encouraged to make their way to the Eternal City and pray in the two basilicas which are said to have been constructed on the gravesites of the two apostles. The other prominent example of an apostolic tomb that has attracted great numbers of Christian pilgrims, since medieval times at least, is Santiago de Compostela in northwest Spain. According to legend, the remains of the apostle James (Spanish *Iago*) are housed in the crypt of the cathedral.[14] Pilgrims would travel to Compostela by various routes that were described collectively as the Way of Saint James. Other later examples of popular saints include the tombs of Saint Thomas Becket at Canterbury (England), Saint Francis in Assisi (Italy), and Saint Theresa in Avila (Spain).

A third type of Christian pilgrimage has come to prominence in the Catholic tradition in recent centuries. Every year, crowds of the faithful flock to places such as Guadalupe (Mexico), Fatima (Portugal), Lourdes (France), and Medjugorje (Bosnia-Hercegovina) where it is claimed that miraculous apparitions of Mary, the mother of **Jesus**, have been seen. But as in the case of Buddhism, the most important Christian pilgrimage destination throughout history and across denominations is the place where the founder himself lived and died. Although Christianity eventually spread across the Roman Empire and beyond, it never lost sight of its geographical origins. Mary and the saints are important figures in many churches, but there is no one more central to Christian belief than the incarnate Son of God who once walked the earth in the land of Palestine.

Historical records indicate that small numbers of Christians were visiting the Holy Land as early as the second century CE. However, as in Buddhism, the most important impetus came from an imperial source.

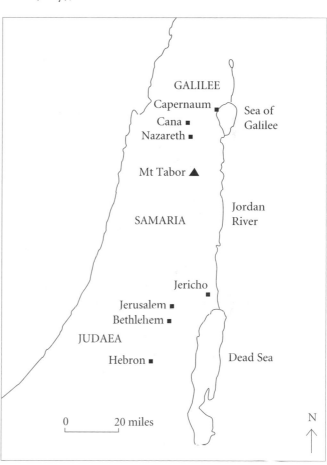

Figure 12.5

Major Christian pilgrimage sites in Israel

Just as Ashoka's tour of holy sites was responsible for the consolidation of Buddhist pilgrimage practice in northern India, it was Saint Helen, mother of the Roman Emperor **Constantine**, who turned Christian eyes and hearts irreversibly toward Palestine. She visited Jerusalem in 326 when she was in her eighties, soon after the **Council of Nicea**, and erected shrines at principal places associated with the life of Jesus. Tradition also has it that she discovered the cross on which Jesus was crucified, buried beneath a pagan temple that had been erected on what is considered to be **Calvary**. Thus began a stream of visitors to the holy sites where churches, monasteries, and various forms of lodgings were established as part of a supportive infrastructure for pilgrims.[15] The tradition continued even when the land fell under Muslim control, although one of the ostensible motives for the Crusades was to recapture the Holy Land from the "infidel" and secure a safe route for pilgrims. Military religious orders such as the Knights Templar were specifically founded to provide escorts for travelers. In the nineteenth and twentieth centuries, biblical scholars and archaeologists contributed to a more accurate historical appreciation of the Holy Land. Today, the tradition of returning to the place where it all began is as strong as ever.

Most Christian pilgrimages to the Holy Land take in the main places mentioned in the **gospels**, as well as other significant **Old Testament** sites. In Galilee, a typical pilgrim group would visit the Church of the Annunciation in **Nazareth** where it is believed the angel Gabriel "announced" to Mary that she would become pregnant with the holy child. At nearby Cana, Christians recall Jesus's first miracle of turning water into wine at a wedding feast and many couples take the opportunity to renew their wedding vows. Similarly Christian pilgrims either renew their baptismal vows or are actually baptized in the waters of the river **Jordan**. Other popular sites include Capernaum on the shores of the Sea of Galilee, where the synagogue ruins date to Jesus's time, and Mount Tabor which is considered to be where Jesus was gloriously transfigured for a few brief moments in the presence of his closest disciples.

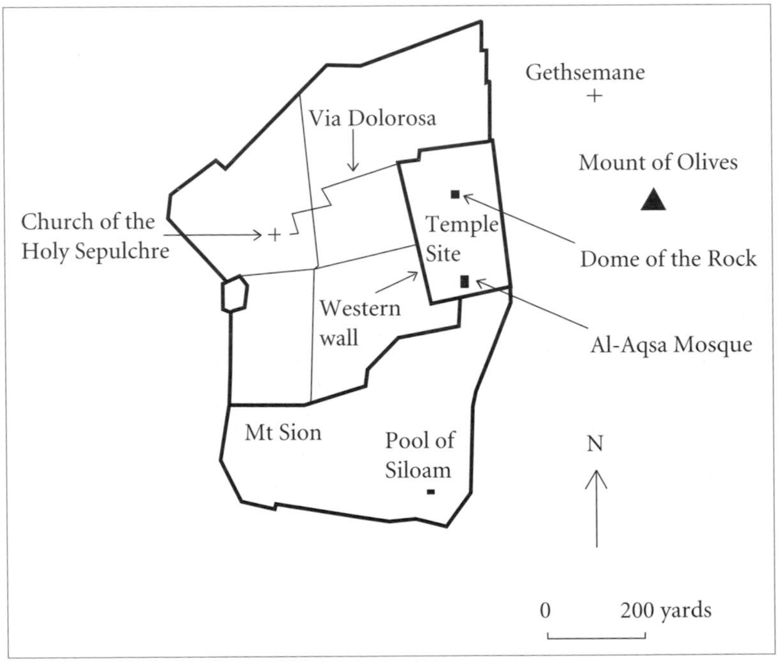

However, the climax of the pilgrimage is **Jerusalem** itself where the most sacred sites in Christianity are located. The Church of the Nativity in Bethlehem, about six miles south of the city, com-

Figure 12.6 The old city of Jerusalem

memorates the birth of Jesus and the image of the magi's star set in the floor before the main altar marks the traditional spot. Just west of Jerusalem pilgrims visit the Mount of Olives from where, it is believed, Jesus ascended to heaven. Nearby, the garden of

Gethsemane still contains a grove of olive trees where Jesus experienced his "agony in the garden" on the night before his death. In the same district, the medieval "Cenacle" church (from the Latin for "evening meal") contains an upper room that commemorates the **Last Supper**. Arguably the most striking expression of Christian pilgrimage in Jerusalem is to walk the Via Dolorosa [Way of Suffering], re-enacting the final journey of Jesus who was forced to carry his own cross to his death. The Via stretches from the Antonia Palace, where Jesus was probably tried by Pontius Pilate, through the ancient city streets to the most important shrine of all, the Holy Sepulchre Church just outside the old city walls. Here the pilgrimage reaches its apex. This edifice stands on what is believed to be **Golgotha** (Calvary), where Jesus was crucified and died. Today, all one can see of the original hill is the gray stone visible beneath the altar. Inside the same edifice is a small chapel surrounding an ancient rock tomb from which the church takes its name. Of all the sites visited by the pilgrim, this is without rival. In this holiest of places, Christians believe that the most important event in human history took place: the Son of God died, was buried, and rose again for the salvation of the world.

What actually happens during a Christian pilgrimage? Typically there are readings from the relevant scriptures at each site. It is thought that the Christian calendar of feasts was influenced by the pattern of pilgrims visiting places in the Holy Land and selecting appropriate gospel passages to mark each spot. These biblical readings are

Figure 12.7
Church of the Holy Sepulchre in Jerusalem

often accompanied by spiritual talks, prayer sessions, and communion services. The Holy Land is littered with churches, chapels, shrines, hostels, and other facilities to cater for such purposes.

As with Hinduism and Buddhism, the motives for embarking on Christian pilgrimage are multiple. Often the pilgrim hopes to obtain some spiritual or material blessing such as forgiveness of sin or physical healing. In this respect Christian leaders have often pointed out the inherent dangers of superstition and a misplaced emphasis on shrines and relics. **Protestant Christianity** has been most vocal in expressing such concerns. For example the Augsburg Confession described pilgrimage as foolish and idolatrous.[16] Instead Protestantism has traditionally stressed not so much pilgrimage to a particular shrine as the pilgrimage of the soul itself from birth to its final destination in heaven. The individual's exile in this world and its epic return to its true home with God is an element in **New Testament** theology but its classical expression is John Bunyan's *Pilgrim's Progress* (1642).[17] In one sense, every Christian pilgrimage is a mirror of life itself. Even the common term *parish*, which denotes the basic organizational unit in many Christian denominations, is derived from the Greek word *paroikia*, which means "to live in exile." The Catholic Church took up the theme of the pilgrim church at the Second **Vatican** Council, stressing that not only individuals but the entire Christian community throughout the ages is on an epic journey toward God under the guidance of the Holy Spirit.[18]

In the main, Catholic and Orthodox churches admit the veracity of Protestant concerns and endeavor to guard against abuse and excess. Ideally, the journey to a tomb or shrine should not fuel superstition but enable the believer to be inspired by the legacy and charism of the saint. The principle applies above all in the case of the founder himself. Just as visits to Lumbini, Bodhgaya, Sarnath, or Kusinegara are ultimately about discovering traces of Sakyamuni, so too a Christian pilgrimage to the Holy Land must ultimately be about drawing closer to the person of Jesus of Nazareth. Although pilgrimage is not an obligation for the Christian, experiencing at first hand the places where the founder lived and died has the potential to deepen personal faith in him. Like the magi of old, the Christian pilgrim comes to the land of the gospels to gain a glimpse of the Savior.

If Christian pilgrimage resembles Buddhist pilgrimage in that both involve traveling to places that were significant in the life of the founder and other holy figures from the past, it also shares a fundamental geographical intersection with its mother faith. **Luke** portrays Jesus's entire ministry as a fateful yet necessary journey from Galilee to Jerusalem where the great events of salvation would be accomplished. As a Jew, Jesus himself would have visited Jerusalem three times each year, as **John**'s gospel notes during his public life.[19] All the canonical gospels agree that it was during one of these visits, in the proximity of the Temple, that Jesus was arrested and executed. Eventually Christians would describe Christ as the new Temple – a living holy of holies where divinity and humanity meet. But long before the advent of Christianity, the ancient Temple was the focus of national religious attention and the regular destination of Jewish citizens who were obliged by divine law to "go up" to the holy city as pilgrims.

Aliyah

Among the 150 sacred hymns that comprise the **Book of Psalms** in the Hebrew Bible, there are 15 that are prefaced with the phrase "Song of Ascent." Psalms 120 through to 134 are short joyful expressions of faith that dwell on a number of themes, including that of journeying to Jerusalem. As the preface to each psalm suggests, these were canticles sung by groups of religious travelers on their way to the holy city:

> I was glad when they said to me, "Let us go to the house of the Lord!"
> Our feet are standing within your gates, O Jerusalem.
> Jerusalem – built as a city that is bound firmly together.
> To it the tribes go up, the tribes of the Lord.[20]

In fact, Jerusalem is situated in the hill country of Judea and a journey to the gates of the ancient capital would have meant a real physical ascent – one which appropriately symbolized the ascent of the mind and heart toward God. The Songs of Ascent reflect the most prominent example of pilgrimage in ancient Judaism – **aliyah** le regel [going up for the festivals]. According to the Torah, every Jewish adult male was obliged to make their way to Jerusalem three times each year:

> Three times a year all your males shall appear before the Lord your God at the place that he will choose: at the festival of unleavened bread, at the festival of weeks, and at the festival of booths. They shall not appear before the Lord empty-handed; all shall give as they are able, according to the blessing of the Lord your God that he has given you.[21]

The Deuteronomy text specifies the three occasions as the feasts of Passover, Shavuot, and Sukkoth. These feasts still constitute three of the most important religious holidays on the Jewish calendar, commemorating key events in Israel's past: the escape from Egypt; the giving of the Torah on Sinai; and the wanderings in the desert before the settlement of the promised land. But the three feasts also marked key harvest times in the agricultural cycle. The feast of **Passover** is also known as the festival of spring. It is a week-long celebration commencing on the full moon of the Hebrew month of Nissan (March–April) and coincides with the barley harvest in the land of Israel. The feast of **Shavuot**, often called the feast of gathering, comes seven weeks after Passover and corresponds with the wheat harvest, the last grain harvest for the year.

The third festival, **Sukkoth**, commences on the full moon of the month of Tishri (September–October). As an early autumn feast, Sukkoth celebrates the fruit harvest but is also a general thanksgiving for the entire harvest season. The four species of plants that are carried in procession and waved about during the Sukkoth ceremony (willow, palm, myrtle, and citron) symbolize the richness of the harvest and the fertility of the land.

According to the Torah, these three feasts had to be celebrated in the city of Jerusalem. Consequently Passover, Shavuot, and Sukkoth are collectively known as shalosh regalim [the foot festivals]. In addition, the believer was obliged not only to go up to Jerusalem for the feasts but also to insure that they did not arrive empty-handed. In other words, the pilgrim was required to make an offering of the first-fruits (bikkurim) to the Temple priests who would grant a special blessing in return. Importantly, the daily and seasonal offerings sustained the priests, who owned no land and were reliant on the community for their sustenance. Traditionally the offerings were carried in colorful baskets to the sound of singing and dancing in the streets of the holy city. The offering of the first-fruits is essentially an act of thanksgiving to the creator whose beneficence makes the harvest possible in the first place.[22] Furthermore, the most appropriate place to celebrate God's mighty actions in the past and to offer the fruits of the harvest as a gesture of gratitude was the Temple.

Although the Jewish scriptures mention earlier shrines such as Gilgal, Shechem, and Shiloh, the city of Jerusalem came to prominence as the religious center of the nation when King **David** captured it from the Jebusites and established it as his new capital. His son, **Solomon**, subsequently constructed the First **Temple** on a hill within the city known as **Mount Zion**. It is believed that this is the same place where **Abraham** was prepared to sacrifice his son, **Isaac**, to God in obedience.[23] The Temple was not only the primary place of worship but it also housed the **Ark of the Covenant** within its inner sanctum. Sadly the Temple has had a turbulent history. It was first destroyed by the Babylonians in 586 BCE but was rebuilt after the return of the exiles 50 years later. It was desecrated by **Hellenistic** overlords in the middle of the second century BCE, an act that sparked the **Maccabean** revolt and the events commemorated at **Hanukkah**. The temple was expanded by Herod the Great at the turn of the epoch only to be destroyed a second time by Roman armies in 70 CE.

After the destruction of the Second Temple and the ban on Jews entering the holy city, the aliyah le regel lapsed. The three pilgrim festivals remained a very important part of the religious calendar, but the aliyah [going up] eventually took on a new form and meaning: the return of the Jewish exiles to their homeland. With the loss of the Temple and its priesthood under the Romans, Jewish prayers began to include the hope that one day the Temple would be rebuilt and the nation gather again in Eretz Yisrael, the land of Israel. At daily **synagogue** service Jews would face toward the land of Israel and pray for a return. At the Passover meal and at the end of the **Yom Kippur** fast, Jewish prayers speak of gathering "next year in Jerusalem." At Jewish weddings, a glass is broken in commemoration of the destruction of the Temple, and the seven blessings speak of the hope that one day the streets of Zion will be filled with her own children.

As the centuries went by, Jews gradually began to make their way back to the land of their fathers. Religious persecution in Europe and the expulsion of Jews from places such as England (1290), France (1391), Austria (1421), and Spain (1492) were interpreted by many as a sign of the end days, prompting large numbers to migrate to Israel. However it was the **Zionist** movement in the late nineteenth century that led to the establishment of the modern Israeli state in 1948 and the mass return of Jewish exiles that followed. Today the term *aliyah* still primarily means immigrating to Israel as an individual or as a group. Its converse, emigration from Israel, is considered to be "going down" (yeridah). The exiled Jews go up to their true home just as their forefathers also "went up" to Israel from Egyptian slavery and Babylonian captivity.[24] For many Jews, aliyah is considered to be a religious duty and those who do so are known as olim. The Law of Return guarantees assistance for any Jew who wishes to immigrate and automatic citizenship upon arrival. Thus today, the journey up to Jerusalem, which was once to celebrate the three festivals after which the pilgrims returned home, is now for many a one-way journey to a religious homeland given to Abraham by God long ago.

Of course not all Jews make the modern aliyah and migrate permanently to Israel. The majority still live in other parts of the world and no longer consider themselves literally "in exile." However, many often visit Israel for religious reasons, especially to see for themselves places associated with prominent figures from the past such as **patriarchs**, kings, and holy persons. Examples of modern-day Jewish pilgrimage sites include the tombs of Abraham, Isaac, and **Jacob** in Hebron; the tomb of King David in Jerusalem; and the graves of Rabbi Simeon Bar Yohai in Meron and Rabbi Meir Ba'al Na Nes in Tiberias. But the holiest space in the Jewish world and the main focus of all journeys to the land of Israel is the last visible remnant of the primary symbol of a nation's faith and the destination of its ancient pilgrimages: the HaKotel HaMa'aravi, or **Western Wall**.

When the Roman army destroyed the Second Temple in 70 CE, it left part of Herod's outer retaining walls still standing. Some say that it was deliberately spared by Titus as a constant reminder of Roman power. For Jews, however, it was seen as a divine sign providing a tangible link with the great building in which a nation once worshiped. For many Jews, the divine presence that occupied the **Holy of Holies** moved into the Western Wall, transforming it into a sacred place. For 2,000 years, Jews who made their way to Jerusalem would visit the Temple Mount and pray before the Wall. The sorrow they expressed at the destruction of Israel's most sacred building led

Figure 12.8
The Western
Wall, Jerusalem

non-Jewish observers to call it the "Wailing Wall," but the preferred term within the Jewish community is Western Wall.

The growth of the Jewish population in Israel from the nineteenth century saw an increase in the religious and political significance of the Western Wall. Jews were prevented from visiting the Wall when it came under Jordanian control in 1948. In June 1967, Israeli forces captured the city and the Moghrabi residential quarter adjacent to it was demolished. On the first day of Shavuot that year, a quarter of a million Jews converged at the Wall to celebrate the ancient pilgrim festival. Today a wide paved plaza has been created in front of it for easier access. One of the most widely recognized images of Judaism is that of Jews praying before the Wall and placing petitionary prayers written on a small piece of paper (tzetel) into its crevices.

The Western Wall has also become a popular place for the **bar mitzvah** ceremony in which a young Jewish male is considered to enter spiritual adulthood. In one sense it is an appropriate location since at bar mitzvah the young man has the privilege of reading the Torah at synagogue for the first time. The term for approaching the bimah in order to read the sacred text is *aliyah la-Torah*: hence the physical movement of "going up" to the elevated platform that holds the word of God here takes on the special resonance of the ancient practice of "going up" to the Temple to celebrate the great pilgrim festivals. The movement may involve a few yards or thousands of miles, but in both cases it is an aliyah, a sacred journey upwards from the mundane into the presence of the divine.[25]

As we have seen, the old city of Jerusalem, in particular the Temple Mount, is a holy place of pilgrimage for both Christians and Jews. For Christians these are the streets where **Jesus** spent his last days on earth prior to his saving death and glorious resurrection. For Jews, it is David's city in which believers would gather three times each year to celebrate God's past intervention in their history and his ongoing blessing of their fields. But today, when visitors cast their eyes toward the site of the ancient Temple, what they see above the Western Wall is not a Jewish or Christian shrine but two mosques.

Hajj

Soon after he captured the city of Jerusalem in 637 CE, the **caliph Umar** erected a mosque next to the place where, according to Islamic belief, **Muhammad** had paused on his mystical **Night Journey** from **Mecca** to heaven. The building was named after the Qur'anic reference to "the furthest mosque," Al-Masjid al-Aqsa.[26] Several decades later, the caliph Abd al-Malik erected a shrine over the actual rock where Muhammad is said to have set foot, just to the north of Umar's mosque. It was aptly named the **Dome of the Rock**. These two buildings, which dominate the Temple Mount today, constitute what Muslims call the "Holy Sanctuary." The nearby Western Wall is described as the al-Buraq Wall, after the creature that is said to have transported Muhammad on his nocturnal flight.

Thus Jerusalem is not only a sacred city of pilgrimage for Jews and Christians. It also figured prominently in Muhammad's religious vision from the earliest times. The original **qibla**, or direction of prayer, was toward Jerusalem, which is still considered to be the third holiest city in Islam and one of the few places Muslims are encouraged to visit as pilgrims. However, soon after the **Hijra**, the qibla was moved to Mecca, the birthplace of the Prophet and the principal focus of Islamic pilgrimage.

Of the five major religions under consideration, the obligation to go on pilgrimage is strongest in Islam where it constitutes the last of the five pillars of faith for **Sunnis** and one of the ten "branches" of religion for **Shi'ites**.[27] The **Qur'an** declares that "pilgrimage to the House is incumbent upon men for the sake of Allah, (upon) every one who is able to undertake the journey to it."[28] The "House" referred to is understood to be the **Ka'bah** in Mecca, which was already a center of Arabic pilgrimage before Muhammad. When the Prophet captured the town in 630, he removed the Ka'bah's idols, converting it into a central symbol of Islamic unity and the destination for all Islamic pilgrimages. Although Muhammad continued to reside in Medina and was eventually buried there, he made several pilgrimages to Mecca in the last years of his life, thus consolidating the practice as an essential aspect of the new religion. The fifth pillar was named **hajj**, an Arabic term that means "to set out on a journey." The Muslim who completes a hajj is given the honorific title *haji*, which carries a degree of social status and has sometimes been handed down as a family name.

The fifth pillar requires that all adults who are physically and financially capable make the pilgrimage to Mecca at least once in their lifetime. However, Islamic tradition acknowledges that this is not possible for everyone. In fact, only a small proportion of the world's Muslims are able to afford to make the journey, especially those who live at a considerable distance from Saudi Arabia. A Muslim should not go into debt to pay for the hajj, nor should he jeopardize the welfare of his family who are his primary responsibility. Moreover, money used for the hajj should be purified beforehand by the Islamic religious tax known as **zakat**.

Pilgrims traditionally travel with family or friends from the local mosque. In past times, many joined the main caravans from places such as Egypt, Syria, and Iraq to insure safety on what could be an arduous and perilous journey. Today, millions of pilgrims converge on the holy city by modern means of transport. The hajj proper commences when the pilgrim arrives at a miqat, a marker that indicates the boundary of the sacred territory around Mecca. Traditionally there are six miqats to serve pilgrims arriving from different directions.[29] Since Muhammad's final visit in 632, only Muslims have been allowed to pass the miqats and enter Mecca. The holy city is a place of religious pilgrimage, not secular tourism, although there have been occasions when non-Muslims have entered clandestinely.[30]

At the miqat, the pilgrim is required to bathe and don a special garment known as an **ihram,** symbolizing entry into the sacred state. Men wear a white, seamless, two-piece garment. Their heads must be bare and sandals are normally worn on the feet. There is no particular dress for women although many often wear a white gown with head-covering. The color white suggests purity while the uniform look indicates the fundamental equality of all pilgrims before God in a manner reminiscent of grave clothes. As with other religious traditions, pilgrimage involves purity and self-denial. Shaving, clipping hair and nails, wearing jewelry and perfume, eating meat, using profane language, or engaging in sexual activity are all prohibited.[31] The pilgrim acknowledges that they have entered sacred time and space by reciting the talbiyeh prayer:

> Here I am at Your service, O God, here I am. Here I am at Your service. You have no partners. Yours alone is all praise and all bounty. Yours alone is the sovereignty. You have no partners.

There are actually two types of pilgrimage in Islam. The "lesser hajj," or umra, may be performed at any time of the year and consists of two basic activities. The first is the tawaf, or sevenfold circumambulation of the Ka'bah. Unlike Hindu circumambulation, which is clockwise so that the unclean left side of the body is facing away from the holy object, the tawaf is performed in an anti-clockwise direction so that the heart is closer to the Ka'bah. Pilgrims walk at a fast pace for the first four circuits and then at a more leisurely pace for the final three, reciting verses from the Qur'an and other spiritual texts as they go.

The Ka'bah is a cube-shaped building approximately 40 feet high and constructed from the gray stone of the surrounding Meccan hills. According to Islamic belief, it was originally built by Adam but, somewhat like the tree in Bodhgaya, it has been destroyed and reconstructed many times in its history. On one occasion it was Abraham and his son **Ishmael** who rebuilt the edifice. The Ka'bah is said to be located directly under the heavenly mosque used by the angels and is thus the spiritual axis of the world. As noted above, it originally housed the idols of the pre-Islamic Arabic religion before they were destroyed by Muhammad. Today it is an empty shrine with a simple unfurnished interior and lamps hanging from the ceiling. It is covered by a black cloth known as the kiswa, on which Qur'anic verses are embroidered in gold. The pilgrims are not required to enter the building but as they circumambulate they reach out their arms toward the Black Stone which is inserted in the eastern external corner. The Black Stone itself is not an object of worship and probably become part of hajj practice because Muhammad used to reverence it on his visits to Mecca. Providentially, geologists have declared that it is probably a meteorite – literally a stone from heaven.

The second component of the umra is the sa'y circuit. Pilgrims walk seven times back and forth between two small hills (Safa and Marwah) that are now housed at either end of a long corridor extending from the main courtyard of the Ka'bah. The walk is a re-enactment of the desperate search for water in the desert by Abraham's wife **Hagar** in order to save their son Ishmael from dying of thirst.[32] According to the biblical story, God provided her with a spring of water that saved their lives. Islamic tradition claims that the Well of Zamzam, located near the Sa'y walk, is the same spring. Like Catholics at Lourdes, Muslims drink from the well and take containers home as gifts for relatives and friends because it is believed that the water has miraculous healing power. At this point the pilgrim is allowed to shave or cut some hair to indicate the end of the sacred state and the completion of the umra.

In contrast to the umra, the "greater hajj" always occurs on three specific days during the twelfth month of the Islamic calendar which is known as Dhu al-Hijjah [Month of the Hajj]. It is during these days that millions of pilgrims descend on Mecca every year to fulfill the obligations of the fifth pillar. On the eighth day of Dhu al-Hijjah, the pilgrims put on the ihram again and travel to the village of Mina which is located about five miles east of Mecca. There they spend the remainder of the day, reciting **salat**. On the morning of the ninth, they continue for another 10 miles to the Plain of Arafat. Here, from noon until sunset, millions of pilgrims engage in the wuquf

Figure 12.9
Muslim pilgrims
at the Ka'bah
in Mecca

[standing] ceremony. As the name implies, the great sea of believers stands in silent meditation, reflecting on themes such as the day of judgment and Abraham's willingness to sacrifice his son Ishmael out of obedience to God, which is believed to have occurred nearby. According to Islamic tradition, the Prophet asked God to forgive the sins of those who stand at Arafat. Thus pilgrims believe that wuquf wipes away sin and enables them to make a fresh start in life.[33]

At the center of the plain is a small hill known as the Jabal ar-Rahmah, or Mountain of Mercy. It is said that **Adam and Eve** were separated for some time after their descent from Paradise and found each other again here. It is also the location of Muhammad's "Farewell" Sermon in 632 to over 100,000 followers who had gathered for the hajj. Today, a sermon is still preached during hajj from the same place by the chief qadi (Islamic judge) of Mecca. On the evening of that same day, pilgrims set out for Muzdalifa where they collect some small pebbles. On the tenth, the pilgrims return to Mina where they throw seven pebbles at a jamrah (originally a pillar but recently converted into a wall for safety reasons). The gesture recalls how Abraham resisted the temptation of **Satan** to disobey God and not proceed with the sacrifice of Ishmael. The tenth day of Dhu al-Hijjah is also known as **Id al-Adha**, or the Feast of the Sacrifice. The pilgrims in Mecca, and all Muslims around the world, sacrifice a sheep or goat in memory of the animal that God provided in place of Ishmael. Traditionally the meat of the animal is shared out: one-third for the family, one-third for neighbors, and one-third for the poor. With this, the greater hajj comes to an end. Pilgrims make a final tawaf at Mecca, have a haircut, and remove their ihram. Many relax at Mina for a few days during which more pebbles may be thrown at the jamrahs. Some visit Medina to see the graves of Muhammad, **Abu Bakr**, and Umar but this is never done wearing the ihram because it is not part of the official hajj. Muslim authorities have always been concerned about possible deification of the Prophet at his final resting place. To this end, visitors are advised not to prostrate themselves or kiss or touch the grave as they do at the Ka'bah.

The annual hajj is one of the largest gatherings of human beings on earth, rivaling events such as the Hindu Kumbha Mela and Catholic Jubilee Year pilgrimages to Rome.

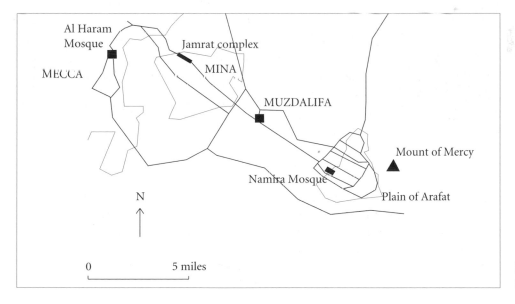

Figure 12.10

Sites of the Hajj

Like pilgrimages in other religions, the hajj is also a powerful symbol of a worldwide faith community, a gathering of believers from different cultures and nationalities, dressed in simple, uniform garments, in the city toward which all Muslims face during their daily prayers. Somewhat surprisingly, the hajj does not emphasize links with the founder as Buddhist and Christian pilgrimages do. As noted, the tomb of Muhammad is not an official part of the hajj and there are deep concerns about any idolatry associated with it. Although Mecca is the birthplace of the Prophet and the place where his religious mission began, the symbolic acts of the hajj are more about Abraham than Muhammad. The Ka'bah is a symbol of the Abrahamic covenant; the sa'y circuit recalls the miraculous survival of Abraham's wife Hagar and his first son Ishmael; the wuquf ceremony at Arafat focuses on Abraham's obedience; the stoning of the jamrah commemorates Abraham's resistance of temptation; and the feasting on Id al-Adha recalls God's intervention in Abraham's sacrifice. It is as if Islam's great pilgrimage deliberately deflects attention away from the final Prophet and toward the first believer in the one God. In that sense it is a sacred journey back to the very origins of monotheism.

SUMMARY

All five religions agree that ultimate reality is truly omnipresent and can be accessed in any place within the physical world. Yet each religion also acknowledges that there are special loci in which the transcendent is more readily experienced within time and space. These are the holy sites that attract religious visitors in large numbers from all parts of the global faith community. While the tradition of pilgrimage is quite ancient in each case, the popularity of pilgrimage today has been greatly facilitated by the advances in transport.

In some religions, the act of pilgrimage is an obligation. This is particularly so in Islam where the hajj constitutes the fifth pillar within the Sunni tradition and one of the ten branches of religion in Shi'ite Islam. The expectation, based on explicit Qur'anic verses, is that all adult Muslims visit Mecca at least once in their lifetime, with exemption for those who are not financially or physically capable. Thus one should not go into debt nor jeopardize the welfare of one's family in order to make the hajj. Pilgrimage was also a religious duty in the ancient Jewish tradition when adult males were obliged to "go up" to Jerusalem three times each year on the "foot festivals" of Passover, Shavuot, and Sukkoth. These three pilgrimage festivals celebrated the saving intervention of God in Israel's history as well as the ongoing fertility of the land. With the destruction of the Temple, the obligation has lapsed, but the duty of "going up" to Jerusalem has taken a new form in some branches of Judaism as the migration of Jewish exiles to the land of Israel.

In other religions the act of pilgrimage may not be compulsory but it is keenly felt by believers as a worthy act of devotion. The reasons why individuals make a pilgrimage are multiple and varied. Many seek a material good such as healing from illness or success in a venture. For example, Muslims believe that the water from the well of Zamzam in Mecca has healing properties, just as Catholic Christians take home water from the shrine at Lourdes. Jewish pilgrims place tzetels into the cracks of the Western Wall, while Hindus who die on the banks of a holy river hope for immediate liberation from the wheel of reincarnation. But many also seek more spiritual benefits such as good karma, a deeper faith, the forgiveness of sins, or some blessing or grace. Ultimately, a pilgrimage is both an external expression of inner faith and a means to strengthen that same faith. Belief and commitment are deepened by the anticipation generated on the journey and the inspiration generated upon arrival in a place of enormous significance.

The source of the destination's significance varies somewhat across the religions. In Buddhism and Christianity, the holiest pilgrimage sites are associated with the life of the founder. According to Buddhist tradition, the four most important places to visit correspond to the most crucial events in Sakyamuni's career: his birth, Enlightenment, First Sermon, and passing to nirvana. Similarly, the main Christian shrines in the Holy Land are found at the location of Jesus's birth, miracles, sermons, last meal, arrest, death, burial, resurrection, and ascension. In both traditions, the pilgrim seeks to draw closer to the historical person who is considered to be the definitive source of truth and liberation.

One might expect a similar pattern in the third religion with an identifiable founder, yet the main focus of the hajj is not Muhammad. The place of pilgrimage, Mecca, is where the Prophet was born and the Qur'an was first revealed, yet the hajj is not explicitly concerned with either event. Its main theological focus is Abraham: the Ka'bah that he rebuilt; the sa'y circuit of Hagar and Ishmael; the stoning of the jamrahs; the meditation themes at Arafat; and the sacrifice of the sheep on Id al-Adha. Although the Islamic hajj was established by Muhammad during his lifetime, the center of attention is the person considered by Jews, Christians, and Muslims to be the first believer in the one God.

An even greater overlap between the three **Abrahamic religions** is evident in the importance that each places on Jerusalem. Christian pilgrimages come to their climax in the city where Jesus spent his last days, with visits to the Cenacle, Gethsemane, the Via Dolorosa, and the Church of the Holy Sepulchre. Muslims consider Jerusalem to be the third holiest city on earth. It was the original qibla and Muhammad is said to have paused on the hill of Zion during his mystical journey to heaven. Today, the Dome of the Rock and the al-Aqsa mosque testify to its significance in Islamic eyes. The overlap is also a source of considerable tension, for this is also the site of the ancient Jewish Temple. Although Jewish pilgrims visit the tombs of patriarchs, kings, and abbis, there is no single founder-figure as in Christianity, Islam, or Buddhism. Instead, the heart of religious life and the focus of pilgrimage in ancient Israel was the Temple. Today, the remains of that Temple have become the most sacred place in Judaism and the destination of Jewish pilgrims from other parts of Israel and the entire Jewish world. As Jews stand before the Western Wall in prayer, they express their sorrow at the tragic loss of their holiest shrine, but draw strength from its enduring stones that God has not abandoned his people.

While Hinduism has a highly developed pilgrimage tradition, unlike the other four religions its sacred journeys do not focus on a historical founder or a single unifying temple-shrine. In contrast, it has thousands of holy places dotted around the subcontinent like jewels in a tiara – locations linked to deities from Hindu mythology rather than historical memory. Its natural features are considered to be places where **Brahman** can be encountered in unusually powerful ways: mountains, forests, and especially sacred rivers. The holiest cities lie on the banks of rivers where pilgrims bathe to rid themselves of bad karma, and hope to die in order to obtain immediate **moksa**. In one sense, India itself is a holy shrine to be circumambulated via the Four Dhams. The abiding Hindu paradigm of pilgrimage as a tirtha (ford) applies to the other religions as well. The image of crossing a river to the other side powerfully captures the ideal of all pilgrims whether they stand in the streets of Varanasi, Bodhgaya, Mecca, or Jerusalem. Pilgrimage is not merely a physical journey to a distant destination involving time, effort, and risk. Pilgrimage is also a spiritual journey of the mind and heart seeking out the bedrock of religious belief. Pilgrimage is a mirror of the journey of human life from birth to death and beyond those shores to the other side. In the end, pilgrimage, like so many other aspects of religious practice, is crossing over from the ordinary to the extraordinary.

DISCUSSION TOPICS

1   How does a religious pilgrimage reflect the "journey of life"?
2   What are the main motives for embarking on a religious pilgrimage?
3   Why is Jerusalem so important to Jews, Christians, and Muslims? What problems have arisen as a result?
4   What are the main events in the history of the Jewish Temple? Do all Jews believe that the Temple should be rebuilt?
5   What was the significance of the Ka'bah before Islam? Why is it so important to Muslims?
6   Why is the Ganges so significant in Hinduism? Are other rivers also considered holy?
7   What are the main Marian pilgrimage sites in Catholicism and why are they so popular?

8   What are some important Buddhist pilgrimage sites outside of India?
9   Compare pilgrimages associated with the tomb of a holy person in different religions.

FURTHER READING

Ali Shari Ati (2005). *Hajj: Reflection on its Rituals*. Houston: Free Islamic Literatures.

Bhardwaj, Surinder M., & Lochtefeld, James G. (2004). "Tirtha," in Sushil Mittal (ed.), *The Hindu World*. Abingdon: Routledge, ch. 21.

Coleman, Simon, & Elsner, John (1997). *Pilgrimage: Past and Present in the World Religions*. Cambridge, MA: Harvard University Press.

Feldhaus, Anne (2003). *Connected Places: Region, Pilgrimage and Geographical Imagination in India*. Basingstoke: Palgrave Macmillan.

Forbes, Duncan (1999). *Buddhist Pilgrimage*. New Delhi: Motilal Banarsidass.

Fuller, C. (1992). *The Camphor Flame*. Princeton, NJ: Princeton University Press, ch. 9.

Granoff, Phyllis, & Shinohara, Koichi (eds.) (2003). *Pilgrims, Patrons, and Place: Localizing Sanctity in Asian Religions*. Vancouver: University of British Columbia Press.

Harpur, James (2002). *Sacred Tracks: Two Thousand Years of Christian Pilgrimage*. Berkeley and Los Angeles: University of California Press.

Hertzberg, Arthur (ed.) (1998). *Judaism*. New York: Free Press, ch. 5.

Holm, Jean, & Bowker, John (eds.) (2000). *Sacred Place*. London: Continuum.

Hurgronje, C. Snouck (2006) "The Meccan Feast," in G. R. Hawting (ed.) (2006), *The Development of Islamic Ritual*. Aldershot: Ashgate, ch. 14.

Levine, Lee I. (1999). *Jerusalem: Its Sanctity and Centrality to Judaism, Christianity, and Islam*. London: Continuum.

Peters, F. E. (1996). *The Hajj*. Princeton, NJ: Princeton University Press.

Scott, Jamie, & Simpson-Housley, Paul (eds.) (1991). *Sacred Places and Profane Spaces*. London: Greenwood.

Stoddard, Robert H., & Morinis, E. Alan (eds.) (1997). *Sacred Places, Sacred Spaces: The Geography of Pilgrimages*. Baton Rouge, LA: Geoscience Publications, Louisiana State University.

Storper Perez, Danielle, & Goldberg, Harvey E. (2001). "Meanings of the Western Wall," in Harvey E. Goldberg (ed.), *The Life of Judaism*. Berkeley and Los Angeles: University of California Press, ch. 12.

Subhadra Sen Gupta (2003). *Chaar Dhaam: A Guide to the Hindu Pilgrimages*. New Delhi: Rupa.

NOTES

1   The five fundamental duties are referred to as the panca kriya: upasana (worship); utsava (holy days); dharma (virtuous living); tirthayatra (pilgrimage); and samskara (rites of passage).

2   The seven holy cities are Ayodhya, Mathura, Hardwar, Varanasi, Kanci, Ujjain, and Dwarka.

3   The char dham is an important practice in the Advaita school of Hinduism. The Shakta school, which focuses on the Mother Goddess, has its own special pilgrimage sites, such as Kanyakumari, Madurai, Vaishno Devi, and the Temple of Kali in Calcutta.

4   The festival is held at Prayag when Jupiter is in Taurus; at Ujjain when Jupiter is in Leo; at Nashik when Jupiter is in Scorpio; and at Hardwar when Jupiter is in Aquarius.

5   A popular custom involves bathing at the five main ghats: Asi, Dashashwamedha, Adi Keshava, Panchganga, and Manikarnika.

6   Maha Parinibbana Sutta 5.16–22.

7   Apart from the four main sites, Ashoka also visited Savatthi, Sankasia, Rajagaha, and Vesali where the Buddha worked various miracles.

8   The present tree is over 100 years old and was taken from the former tree which collapsed during a storm in 1876.

9   According to tradition, the Buddha spent a week in each of seven places near the original tree, meditating on the dharma.

10   The five companions became the first Buddhist monks: Kondanna, Vappa, Bhaddiya, Mahanama, and Assaji.

11   It suffered under the sixth-century Hun invasion and again under the Islamic invasions in the late twelfth century.

12   The contents of the Buddha's last meal are described as sukara-maddava which can be translated as either "pork" or "food consumed by pigs" (e.g. truffles). See Maha-Parinibbana Sutta 4.17.

13   Matthew 2:1–12.

14   Unlike the more reliable tradition that Peter and Paul are buried in Rome, the popular claim that James traveled to Compostela and died there is difficult to reconcile with Acts 12:1–2 which states that he was executed in Jerusalem. The 1884 Bull of Pope Leo XIII accepted the authenticity of the relics but Catholic scholarship remains ambivalent.

15   The *Pilgrimage of Etheria* (c.400 CE), which records the journey of a Spanish nun to the Holy Land, speaks of a well-organized system of guides and lodgings for pilgrims.

16   Augsburg Confession 12.14; 21.16.

17   See Hebrews 11:13–16; 13:14; 1 Peter 1:17; 2:11.

18   See Second Vatican Council's Constitution on the Church (*Lumen Gentium*), ch. VII, "The Pilgrim Church."

19   See John 2:13; 7:10; 11:55.

20   Psalm 122:1–4.

21   Deuteronomy 16:16–17. See also Exodus 23:17; 34:23.

22   See Talmud Moed, Treatise 12 (Hagigah) which deals with the pilgrimage festival offerings.

23   See Genesis 22:1–3.

24   See Genesis 13:1; 46:4; 50:14; Numbers 32:11; Ezra 1:3; 2:1.

25   The term *aliyah* also refers to the miraculous ascension to heaven of holy persons such as Enoch and **Elijah**. See Genesis 5:23–4; 2 Kings 2:11.

26   Qur'an 17:1:"Glory be to Him Who made His servant to go on a night from the Sacred Mosque to the remote mosque of which We have blessed the precincts."

27 Shi'ite Islam speaks of the five "roots" of religion (monotheism, justice, prophethood, leadership, and the day of judgment) and the ten "branches" of religion (daily prayer, fasting, alms, tax, pilgrimage, struggle, goodness, avoidance of evil, loving the community, and hating the enemies of the community).

28 Qur'an 3:97.

29 The six traditional miqats are: Zu'l-Hulafa, near Medina, and Al-Johfa, near Jeddah, for those arriving from Egypt and Syria; Zat-i-'Irq, northeast of Mecca, for those coming from Iraq; Qarnu l-Manazil, east of Mecca; Yalamlam, south of Mecca, for those arriving from Yemen; and Taneem, situated in Mecca, for its citizens. Pilgrims arriving by the airport in Jedda are required to put on their ihram about one hour before landing.

30 See Sir Richard Francis Burton, *Pilgrimage to Al Madina and Mecca* (1885).

31 Qur'an 2:197–8.

32 Qur'an 2:158.

33 Qur'an 2:198–9.

CONCLUSION

At the end of our comparative tour of practice in five major religions, it is time to gather together and identify the salient features that have emerged. How similar or different are these five great traditions? What points of intersection can be seen from our juxtaposition of thematic cross-sections? The first general observation to be noted is that each religion is different from all of the others and thus is genuinely unique. The ever-present danger of the comparative approach is to force similarity at the expense of authentic difference. An overemphasis on the areas of common ground can easily neglect the fact that each religion has its own distinctive qualities that differentiate it from others and provide it with its identity. This is true in the broadest sense. Hinduism is really different from Buddhism; Judaism is not the same as Islam or Christianity. It is also true in terms of particular practices. For example, although they can all be described as festivals of light, Hanukkah, Divali, and Easter are very different in their meanings and their specific combination of symbols, words, and actions. Similarly, although they are all holy texts, the Qur'an, Tanach, and the Tipitaka are very different in content and context. Again, although they are all sacred buildings where believers occasionally gather, a synagogue is not a mosque, and a mandir is not a church.

The need to recall the differences between the religions is reinforced by the fact that each religious tradition is not monochrome but consists of a multicolored spectrum of subdivisions. There are not only real differences between the religions but also within each of them. Not only is Divali different from Hanukkah and Easter, but not all Hindus celebrate Divali and those who do approach it according to their particular Hindu sect. Theravada and Mahayana Buddhists interpret and use the Tipitaka in quite different ways. A church is very different from a synagogue but the shape, furnishings, and use of a church can vary considerably for Orthodox, Catholic, and Protestant Christians.

Yet it would be inaccurate to simply stop there and be satisfied with the statement that all religions are fundamentally unique. While it is important to acknowledge the variations within each religion as well as the real differences between them, it is also important to recognize that there is also a considerable degree of similarity. The glass is both half empty and half full. But in what sense are they similar? At the most basic level, the five are similar because they are all members of the category of "religion," even though for many people Buddhism sits uneasily there. The fact that, in most cases, the 12 practical themes chosen for this book found resonance in each religious tradition confirms this fundamental level of commonality. All five religions profess that the ultimate meaning of human existence is found in reference to a transcendent reality that can be fully encountered only beyond physical death. All five religions believe that truths pertaining to this transcendent reality and its relevance for human existence have been mediated to us via a corpus of writings. These texts are consequently revered as holy and are thus determinative of belief and practice. All five religions are committed to the idea that part of the journey toward our ultimate destiny is the duty to live a moral life according to a shared core of fundamental norms. Each religion celebrates the key moments of that journey – such as birth, marriage, and death – in ways that highlight their transcendent nature. Each religion takes up common aspects of human existence – such as food and clothing – and imparts to these a transcendent significance that gives expression to religious faith. Finally, all five religions consecrate the very fabric of our spatio-temporal world. Time itself is given transcendent meaning via the cycles of holy days, weeks, months, seasons, and years while space is sanctified via the architecture of the sacred building and the common tradition of pilgrimage to holy places. In other words, although the five religions are unique, they are also fundamentally very similar, at least in the sense of possessing these practical features of a religion. There are real resemblances as well as differences.

However, simply pointing out that the five religions share these 12 aspects of practice is still very general. It has also been possible to identify more nuanced patterns of similarity and difference between them. These specific points of intersection are reflected in the order in which each religion is treated in each chapter. When the religions are set out beside each other on the table, where do the natural bridges appear? The most obvious pattern that emerges is not surprising because it reflects the historical mother–daughter connection between two pairs of religions: Hinduism–Buddhism and Judaism–Christianity. In both cases, the latter has sprung from the former and, although it eventually evolves into a distinctive religion in its own right, the daughter also naturally inherits and retains many of the elements of its mother.

Thus, Hinduism and Buddhism both share a quasi-cyclic reincarnational understanding of human existence as an extended series of birth, death, and rebirth leading eventually to final liberation. The relative unimportance of the physical body is reflected in the common (but not universal) funeral practice of cremation which facilitates advancement toward final emancipation. Progress toward liberation is also gained by the fulfillment of ethical-religious duties summed up in both traditions by the term *dharma*, understood as an intrinsic cosmic order or truth rather than a code of law given by an external creator God. In both Hinduism and Buddhism, the more advanced stages of the samsaric path are characterized by renunciation of worldly pleasures and the adoption of the celibate lifestyle as in the ideal of the Buddhist monk and the Hindu sannyasin. Both traditions also profess that spiritual advancement involves a commitment to non-violence toward living creatures that is reflected in the practice of vegetarianism in higher-caste Hinduism and Buddhist monastic life. The cyclic Hindu–Buddhist world view is also symbolized in the religious calendar via an emphasis on the lunar cycle, especially in the calculation of regular holy days such as ekadasi and uposatha. Both traditions also give religious meaning to the annual monsoon season as a special time of spiritual retreat or caution while the gods sleep. Finally, Hindu and Buddhist sacred buildings commonly contain a special room housing sacred images that assist the believer in their encounter with transcendent being either in the form of the many Hindu deities, the glorious body of Sakyamuni, or the celestial Buddhas and bodhisattvas of the Mahayana tradition.

Similarly, Judaism and Christianity share an extensive area of overlap based on their historical connection. Both are commonly referred to as monotheistic faiths given their explicit belief in a single personal God. Judaism's emphasis on the transcendent, invisible nature of God and the concomitant danger of idolatry is evident in the traditional lack of visual images in synagogues. This is most clearly reflected in Protestant Christianity's version of the Ten Commandments and its churches which are usually devoid of statues or icons. One very important point of intersection is the corpus of sacred writing known as Tanach for Jews and the Old Testament for Christians. Although interpreted in very different ways by each tradition, this common set of holy texts is read in both synagogue and church over annual cycles and constitutes a vital part of official worship, private devotion, and theological study. Synagogues and churches are both places where the divine word is reverently stored, liturgically proclaimed, and theologically interpreted for the gathered faithful. Embedded in that sacred corpus is the Decalogue which lists the principal religious and moral precepts for what is often referred to as the "Judeo-Christian tradition." In contrast to the Hindu–Buddhist reincarnational world view, Judaism and Christianity generally adhere to a linear understanding of human existence in which an individual is born, lives, and dies just once. One's unique physical body carries much greater significance and is considered to be an essential part of one's being both now and beyond death. Thus both religions traditionally profess a belief in the resurrection of the body and both have historically preferred burial over cremation. Jews and Christians understand marriage as part of the divine dispensation and see the love of husband and wife as an earthly symbol of the vertical relationship between the divine and the human. Christianity has also inherited and transformed other Jewish practices including the ritual use of bread and wine, the weekly day of rest and prayer, the punctuation of the day with official prayer times, the 50-day season from Passover to Shavuot (Easter to Pentecost), and the recognition of the land of Israel, and in particular the city of Jerusalem, as a place of unparalleled religious importance.

Because Muhammad and the first Muslims were not Jews, Islam is not a daughter religion of the Jewish tradition in the same sense as Christianity. Nevertheless, it is properly included with its two monotheistic cousins under the label of the Abrahamic religions. In fact, a comparison of practices reveals an extensive range of similarities between the religions of the Qur'an and the Torah. Unlike Christianity, which is more nuanced on both issues, Islam shares with Judaism an uncompromising stress on the oneness of God and an absolute ban on divine images. Thus the interior of a mosque and a synagogue both display the same absence of icons and the same preference for adornment via abstract symbol or scriptural text. For both Jew and Muslim, the verbal has priority over the visual. Space also has its relevance for both traditions in that synagogues and mosques are physically orientated toward a particular location on earth: Jerusalem and Mecca respectively, although the original qibla was also Jerusalem. Islam consecrates five parts of each day to prayer in much the same way as the threefold practice of the Jewish tradition, and it is likely that the insistence on congregational worship at Friday noon in Islam was historically linked to sabbath preparations. Muslims hold to a linear view of existence and thus agree with Jews and Christians on the eternal relevance of the physical body. Islamic belief in the resurrection of the dead is thus accompanied by a strict prohibition on cremation. Along with Jews and Christians, Muslims also pray for the dead in the hope that divine judgment will be clement and merciful, although Islam agrees with Christianity, in contrast to Judaism, on the possibility of eternal damnation for the most wicked. Muslim and Jewish birth rituals both include circumcision, a ransom ceremony, and the custom of weighing for alms-giving. Both traditions also see marriage and procreation as fundamental religious duties and thus share a distrust of religious celibacy. Finally halal and kosher food laws are strikingly similar although the Islamic version is somewhat more lenient.

At points where Islam and Judaism converge, the third Semitic faith appears to shift toward the Hindu–Buddhist end of the spectrum. Whereas synagogues and mosques (and Protestant churches) are devoid of divine images, Catholic and Orthodox Christian churches are full of icons and statues, making them more similar to the Hindu mandir. The difference, of course, is that Christianity claims a single historical incarnation that underscores a fundamental likeness between the divine and the human and justifies the use of the sacred image. While this is anathema to Judaism and Islam which stress God's transcendence and otherness, it is very close to the Hindu concept of the avatar and the prolific use of the murti as a bridge between heaven and earth. Similarly the Christian understanding of God as Trinity is a more explicit acknowledgment of plurality within the one God which echoes the Hindu notion of one Brahman manifest in a host of forms or deities. Moreover, the traditions of Christian Eucharist and Hindu prasad both utilize the symbol of a sacred meal to express tangible connection with transcendent yet immanent divinity. Finally, Christianity and Hinduism, in their own distinctive ways, accept the legitimate place of both marriage and celibacy, in contrast to the Islamic and Jewish caution with regard to the celibate life.

Similarly, there are times when Christian practice also shares significant similarities with Buddhism, even though the latter is at best ambiguous about the existence of both an external God and an inner soul, or atman. The crucial link is the role and impact of the founder in both cases, a feature reflected in that the names of both religions are based on their theological titles: the Buddha and the Christ. Similarly, the heart of the scriptural canon of both Buddhism and Christianity is grounded in the teachings and authority of the founder who is understood as the personification of eternal truth. The main festivals in the annual religious calendars are key moments in their respective lives including their birth and death, and the main places of pilgrimage are venues of those key moments. Finally, traditional priority is given to the monastic way of life which is reinforced by both founders' option for celibacy.

This is not to say that there are no specific points of connection between Judaism and Islam on one side and Hinduism and Buddhism on the other. For example. Jewish tradition acknowledges a form of reincarnation and there are many elements of the richly symbolic Jewish wedding ceremony that resonate with the Hindu equivalent, including the use of the canopy and the number seven. Similarly, certain aspects of Muslim birth rituals resemble Hindu practices and Muslims share with Buddhists the same explicit concern for the compromising effects of alcohol and drugs. The Islamic calendar also marks the birthday and death of the Prophet as in Buddhism (and Christianity), but Islam downplays the importance of its founder in terms not only of its calendar but also of its pilgrimage tradition for fear of deifying God's greatest human messenger and descending into idolatry.

Such are the general patterns that emerge from a comparative look at the practical dimensions of the five major religions. As noted in the Introduction, Ninian Smart posited other dimensions – doctrine, narrative, spirituality, ethics, and institution – and a similar comparison of these may turn up a very different set of patterns. Hopefully this exploration, with its practical-ritual focus, has contributed to a deeper appreciation of not only the undeniable uniqueness of each of the five major religions, but also their rich interrelationship. Hopefully it has highlighted not only the points where each religion appears singular and distinctive, but also where it shares common ground with others. The poet John Donne's classical statement of the fundamental connectivity between human beings can perhaps be paraphrased and aptly applied here: "No religion is an island."

GLOSSARY

ablutions: ritual cleansing to remove spiritual impurity.

Abraham (c.1800 BCE): patriarch of the Israelite people and recognized by Jews, Christians, and Muslims as the first believer in the one God.

Abrahamic religions: Judaism, Christianity, and Islam.

Abu Bakr (c.573–634): one of the first converts to Islam, a close companion of Muhammad, and the first caliph.

Acts of the Apostles: New Testament book composed by Saint Luke which recounts the story of the early Church.

Adam and Eve: according to the book of Genesis, the names of the first human beings.

adhan: Islamic call to daily prayer chanted by the muezzin.

Advaita Vedanta: one of the major theological schools of Hinduism which stresses that all beings are essentially part of Brahman and that individuality is an illusion.

Advent: first season of the Christian calendar.

Agni: Hindu god of fire.

ahimsa: principle of non-violence.

Aisha (c.614–678): daughter of Abu Bakr and third wife of Muhammad.

Al-Fatiha [The Opening]: first chapter of the Qur'an.

Ali (c.599–661): cousin and son-in-law of Muhammad and husband of Fatima; regarded by Sunni Muslims as the fourth caliph but by Shi'ite Muslims as the true successor to Muhammad.

aliyah [going up]: (1) return of Jewish emigrants to Israel; (2) going up to read from the Torah scrolls at synagogue; (3) making a pilgrimage to Jerusalem in ancient times.

Allah: Arabic term for (the one) God.

alms round: daily reception of food and other material items from the laity by Buddhist monks.

Amidah [Standing]: Jewish prayer consisting of 18 benedictions that constitutes a vital element in the three daily synagogue services.

Amitabha (or **Amida**): Buddha of the Western Pure Land.

Ananda: cousin of Sakyamuni and one of his earliest disciples.

Anglican Church: originally the Church of England, which separated from Rome in 1534 under Henry VIII; today it consists of an international communion of autonomous churches, known under various names such as the Episcopal Church in the USA.

aniconism: the belief that divinity cannot be depicted in human or worldly form.

apocrypha: books excluded from a sacred canon, especially in Judaism and Christianity.

aqiqah: series of Islamic birth rituals.

Aramaic: Semitic language written in Hebrew script and widely spoken in the period of the Second Temple.

arhat: in Buddhism, someone so advanced in the spiritual life that they are assured of nirvana after physical death.

Arjuna: one of the heroes of the Hindu epic the Mahabharata.

Ark of the Covenant (aron ha berith): container that held the stone tablets on which the Ten Commandments were written.

aron ha kodesh [holy ark]: an adorned cabinet or receptacle in a synagogue where sacred scrolls are stored.

Arya Samaj: Hindu reform movement founded in the late nineteenth century that rejected ritualism and caste discrimination.

Asalha Puja: festival that commemorates the Buddha's First Sermon.

Ashkenazi: form of Jewish culture associated with central and eastern European communities (see also **Sephardic**).

Ashoka (third century BCE): Mauryan ruler who converted to Buddhism and extensively promoted the religion throughout his empire.

ashrama: the four traditional Hindu life stages according to the Laws of Manu: student (brahmacarin), householder (grihasthin), forest-dweller (vanaprasthin), and ascetic (sannyasin).

Ashura: Shi'ite holy day that commemorates the death of Hussain.

atman: in Hinduism, the inner spiritual essence or true self that lies beneath the temporary features of each reincarnation.

aum (or **om**): in Hinduism, the fundamental sound of the universe and the source of all mantras.

Avalokiteshvara: important bodhisattva in Mahayana Buddhism who personifies compassion; also known as Kwanyin in China and Kwannon in Japan.

avatar: an incarnation of a Hindu god (especially Vishnu) in human or animal form.

Babylonian Exile (586–537 BCE): period during which many Israelites were taken in captivity to Babylon after the fall of Jerusalem.

baptism: Christian initiation rite.

Baptist Christianity: branch of Christianity that rejects infant baptism and teaches that baptism requires the personal faith of the recipient.

bar mitzvah [son of the commandment]: Jewish ceremony that initiates a 13-year-old boy into religious adulthood.

Benares: see **Varanasi**.

Bethlehem: town five miles south of Jerusalem and considered to be the place where Jesus was born.

Bhagavad Gita [Song of the Lord]: one of the most important texts in Hinduism; it is found in the sixth book of the Mahabharata and consists of a dialogue between Arjuna and Krishna.

bhakti: in Hinduism, the path to liberation based on loving devotion.

bhikkhu/bhikkhuni: a Buddhist monk/nun.

Bodhgaya: traditional site of the Buddha's Enlightenment.

bodhisattva [being of enlightenment]: in Mahayana Buddhism, a being who out of compassion delays nirvana to assist others.

Brahma: one of the three main gods who form the Hindu trinity or Trimurti (with Vishnu and Shiva).

brahmacarin [student]: the first life stage (ashrama) of Vedic Hinduism.

Brahman: Hindu term for ultimate reality or the impersonal absolute beyond all attributes.

brahmin (or **brahman**): the priestly class – the highest of the four traditional classes in Hindu society (see **varna**).

b'rit milah: Jewish rite of circumcision.

Buddha [Enlightened One]: (1) title given to the historical founder of Buddhism, Siddhartha Gautama; (2) any enlightened being, especially in Mahayana Buddhism.

Byzantine: generally pertaining to Eastern Orthodox Christianity.

cakras: in Hinduism, points on the human body where spiritual energies converge.

caliph: a successor to Muhammad.

Calvary (also **Golgotha**): site of Jesus's crucifixion.

Calvinism: branch of Christianity that follows the teaching of Protestant reformer John Calvin (1509–64) and is characterized by a strong emphasis on the sovereignty of God.

canon: set of authoritative religious texts, often considered to have been divinely inspired.

caste: see **jati**.

Catholic Church: (1) the "universal" Church; (2) the Roman Catholic Church whose organization and governance is centered on the bishop of Rome (the Pope).

char dham: traditional Hindu pilgrimage consisting of four sites located near the eastern, southern, western, and northern extremes of India.

Christ [Anointed One]: title given to Jesus by Christians, who recognize him as the true Messiah.

Christmas: Christian festival held on December 25 celebrating the birth of Jesus.

circumambulation: movement around a sacred object as an expression of devotion.

cohen (or **kohen**): member of the priestly line in Judaism.

commandments: see **mitzvot**.

Communion, Holy: see **Eucharist**.

confirmation: Jewish or Christian adulthood initiation ceremony.

Conservative Judaism: a branch of Judaism between Orthodox and Reform Judaism.

Constantine (c.280–337): the first Roman emperor to legalize Christianity.

Council of Nicea (325): early Christian council that defined Jesus as the incarnation of the divine Son of God.

Dalai Lama: title given to the spiritual and political leader of Tibetan Buddhism.

darshana: in Hinduism, viewing or "seeing" a deity especially via a sacred image.

David (c.1000 BCE): one of the earliest kings of Israel.

Dayananda Saraswati (1824–83): founder of the Hindu reform movement Arya Samaj.

Dead Sea Scrolls: writings of the Jewish Essene community which was based at Qumran, near the Dead Sea.

Decalogue [Ten Words]: see **Ten Commandments**.

Deuteronomy [Second Law]: the fifth book of the Jewish Torah.

Dhammapada [Verses on the Truth]: popular collection of over 400 sayings attributed to the Buddha.

dharma: (1) in Hinduism, the fundamental order of the universe which holds all things in being and which is manifest in natural, ethical, and socio-religious laws; (2) in Buddhism, the Buddha's teaching.

dharmashastras: ancient Hindu writings on morality and law.

Divali: prominent Hindu festival celebrated in October–November which focuses on Lakshmi, the goddess of prosperity and wealth.

Dome of the Rock: the main mosque situated on the Temple Mount in Jerusalem.

Durga: warrior-like Hindu goddess of strength and fortitude, and consort of Shiva.

Easter: Christian festival held in March–April celebrating Jesus's resurrection from the dead.

Eastern Christianity: general term for the family of Orthodox churches in communion with the Patriarch of Constantinople.

ecumenical council: an official gathering of bishops and leaders representing the entire Church. All Christians recognize 7 such councils between 325 and 787, but Catholics recognize another 14, the last of which was Vatican II.

Eighteen Benedictions: see **Amidah**.

Elijah: Israelite prophet from ninth century BCE; in Judaism, Elijah will return to herald the coming of the Messiah.

Enlightenment, the: night on which Siddhartha Gautama gained supreme insight and became the Buddha for our epoch.

eschatology: branch of theology that deals with death, the afterlife, and the end of the world.

Eucharist [thanksgiving]: the central Christian ritual modeled on Jesus's Last Supper.

Exodus: (1) the second book of the Torah; (2) the miraculous escape of the Israelites from Egypt under the leadership of Moses.

Fatima: daughter of Muhammad and wife of Ali.

Four Noble Truths: the four key principles of the historical Buddha's teachings.

Gandhi, Mohandas (**Mahatma**) (1869–1948): Hindu spiritual and political leader who contributed profoundly to India gaining independence from British rule.

Ganesha: elephant-headed Hindu god of good fortune and blessing.

garbhagrha [womb house]: the inner chamber of a Hindu temple that contains the main image.

Gayatri Mantra: important Hindu mantra recited on a daily basis and conferred during the sacred-thread ceremony.

Genesis: the first book of the Jewish Torah.

gentiles: traditional term for non-Jewish peoples.

ghats: steps on a river bank often used for ritual washing and cremations.

Golgotha: see **Calvary**.

Good Friday: Christian holy day commemorating the death of Jesus.

gospel [good news]: a faith-inspired biography of Jesus.

grihasthin [householder]: the second life stage (ashrama) of traditional Hinduism during which it is obligatory to marry and have children, especially sons.

gunas: the three fundamental components of all things according to the Hindu Samkhya school: sattva (lightness), rajas (movement), and tamas (dullness).

hadith: the authorized accounts of Muhammad's words and deeds that constitute an important complement to the Qur'an; the two most reliable collections are those of Al-Bukhari (810–70) and Muslim bin Al-Hajjaj (821–75).

Hagar: mother of Ishmael; in Judaism, the slave-girl of Abraham's wife, Sarah; in Islam, one of Abraham's wives.

hajj: the fifth pillar of Islam: annual pilgrimage to Mecca.

halal: Islamic term indicating that a certain act is permissible (see also **haram**).

hametz: Hebrew term for leaven, which is forbidden during Passover.

Hanafi: one of the four main Sunni law schools, Turkey, Syria, Egypt, Iraq, and central and south Asia.

Hanbali: one of the four main Sunni law schools, prevalent in the Arabian peninsula.

Hanukkah: eight-day Jewish festival in November–December commemorating the re-dedication of the Temple in 165 BCE.

Hanuman: monkey-god who assists Rama in the rescue of his wife, Sita, as told in the Hindu epic the Ramayana.

haram: Islamic term indicating that a certain act is forbidden (see also **halal**).

Hasan (624–69): first son of Ali and Fatima and considered to be the second caliph by Shi'ite Muslims.

Hasidism: form of Judaism that originated in eighteenth-century Europe and that stresses spiritual joy and constant communion with God; Hasidic Jews are often recognizable by their distinctive dress.

Hebrew: (1) a member of the people who escaped from Egypt under Moses and eventually settled in the land of Israel; (2) the traditional language of the Jewish religion.

Hellenism: Greek thinking and culture disseminated by the conquests of Alexander the Great that profoundly influenced much of the ancient world.

henotheism: worship of one God while acknowledging the existence of other gods.

High Holy Days: the two main Jewish festivals of New Year and the Day of Atonement.

hijab: veil worn by Islamic women.

Hijra: emigration of Muhammad and the first Muslims from Mecca to Medina in 622.

Holi: Hindu festival in February–March characterized by a general relaxation of rules and the throwing of colored water or powder.

Holy of Holies: Central sanctuary of the ancient Jewish Temple that housed the Ark of the Covenant.

hungry ghost: see **preta**.

huppah: the Jewish wedding canopy.

Hussain (626–80): second son of Ali and Fatima who was killed at Karbala by Umayyad forces and is thus honored as the greatest of martyrs by Shi'ite Islam.

iconoclasm: the rejection of the use of icons and images for worship, especially in Christianity.

Id al-Adha: Islamic Feast of the Sacrifice which marks the end of the annual pilgrimage in Mecca.

Id al-Fitr: Islamic Feast of the Fast-Breaking which marks the end of Ramadan.

ihram: Islamic pilgrimage garment.

imam: (1) a leader of Islamic congregational prayer; (2) according to Shi'ite Islam, one in the line of authentic successors to Muhammad.

incarnation: (1) a divine being in human form; (2) in Christianity, the belief that the eternal Son of God took human form in Jesus of Nazareth.

Isaac: son of Abraham and Sarah, and father of Jacob; in Judaism, Abraham is asked to sacrifice Isaac as a test of his faith.

Isaiah: Israelite prophet from the eighth century BCE after whom a book of the Hebrew Scriptures is named.

Ishmael: son of Abraham and Hagar; in Islam, it is Ishmael whom Abraham is asked to sacrifice.

Isra and Mi'raj: mystical journey of Muhammad from Mecca to Jerusalem and then to heaven.

Jacob: son of Isaac and Rebecca, and grandson of Abraham; his 12 sons are the forefathers of the 12 tribes of Israel.

Jainism: ancient Indian religious movement that teaches a radical form of asceticism and non-violence.

Jataka Tales: stories of previous incarnations of the Buddha.

jati [caste]: caste is determined by birth and profoundly affects marriage, meals, and general social mixing.

Jerusalem: city in Judea originally conquered by David and established as the capital of Israel; it contains sites of outstanding religious importance to Jews, Christians, and Muslims.

Jesus of Nazareth (c.6 BCE–30 CE): founder of Christianity; in Christian theology, Jesus is the long-awaited Messiah of Israel and the unique incarnation of the Son of God; in Islam, Jesus is one of the prophets in the line from Adam to Muhammad.

jihad [struggle]: primary meaning is the moral struggle against evil but also refers to armed defense of the faith.

Jodo-Shinsu: Japanese Pure Land Buddhist school founded by Shinran (1173–1262), which emphasizes devotion to Amitabha and disavows celibate monasticism.

John the Baptist: Jewish prophetic figure considered by Christians to be the precursor to the Messiah.

John, Saint: traditionally identified as the author of the fourth canonical gospel and referred to as the "beloved disciple."

Jordan: river in Israel that runs southward from the Sea of Galilee to the Dead Sea.

Josephus: prominent first-century Jewish historian.

Ka'bah: cube-shaped building in the center of the Great Mosque of Mecca toward which all Muslims are required to face during the five daily prayers; it is also an important part of Islamic pilgrimage customs.

Kabbalah: Jewish mystical tradition that stresses intimate knowledge of God via contemplation and illumination.

Kaddish: an important prayer recited during Jewish services including funerals.

Karbala: city in Iraq that contains the tomb of Muhammad's grandson Hussain.

karma: the concept that good and bad actions carry corresponding consequences not only in this life but also in terms of the next reincarnation.

Kathina: Buddhist ceremony during which laity present monks with cloths for their robes.

Khadijah (c.555–619): the first wife of Muhammad.

kippah: Jewish skullcap.

kittel: white garment worn by Ashkenazi Jews on certain religious occasions including Passover and weddings; it also functions as burial clothing.

kosher: in Judaism, something that is permissible, especially in relation to food laws.

Krishna: eighth avatar of Vishnu.

kshatria: the warrior class – the second of the four traditional classes in Vedic Hindu society (see **varna**).

Kumbha Mela: Hindu pilgrimage held every three years over a 12-year period at Prayag (Allahabad), Ujjain, Nashik, and Hardwar.

Kusinegara: site of the Buddha's death.

Kwannon: Japanese name for Avalokiteshvara.

Kwanyin: Chinese name for Avalokiteshvara.

Lailat al-Qadr: see **Night of Power**.

Lakshmi: consort of Vishnu and Hindu goddess of wealth and prosperity.

Last Supper: Jesus's final meal with his disciples at which it is believed he established the rite of the Eucharist.

Laws of Manu: the most influential of the ancient Hindu law codes known as dharmashastras and thought to date from about 200 BCE to 200 CE.

Lent: Christian liturgical season prior to Easter and characterized by fasting, abstinence, and charitable works.

levite: in Judaism, a descendant of the priestly tribe of Levi.

Leviticus: the third book of the Jewish Torah.

linga: phallic symbol common in Shiva worship.

liturgy: official worship, especially in Christianity.

Luke, Saint: traditionally identified as the author of the third canonical gospel and the Acts of the Apostles.

Lumbini: site of the Buddha's birth.

Lutheran: Christian churches whose theology and practice are inspired by the teachings of the key Protestant reformer Martin Luther (1483–1546).

Maccabean wars: military campaign fought by Judas Maccabeus and his followers against Hellenistic Syrian overlords (168–165 BCE).

magi: according to the gospel of Matthew, wise men from the East who visited the child Jesus in Bethlehem.

Mahabharata: Hindu epic that narrates the battle between the five Pandava brothers and their evil cousins, the Kauravas; it contains the Bhagavad Gita.

Mahashivaratri [Great Night of Shiva]: Hindu festival in February–March characterized by fasting and abstinence.

Mahayana Buddhism [Greater Vehicle]: major subdivision of Buddhism predominant in China, Vietnam, Japan, Korea, Mongolia, and Tibet; it stresses the importance of compassion for other beings, typified in the concept of the bodhisattva (see also **Theravada Buddhism**).

Mahdi: in Islam, a future figure who will appear at the end of the world; Twelver Shi'ites identify him as the twelfth imam who entered into "occultation" in 874.

Maimonides (1135–1204): distinguished Jewish philosopher and author, also known as Moses ben Maimon or Rambam.

Maitreya: the future Buddha who is expected to come at the end of this age.

Maliki: one of the four main Sunni law schools, prevalent in north and west Africa.

mandala: in Buddhism and Hinduism, a sacred diagram usually of concentric design used during meditation and ritual.

Manjusri: important bodhisattva in Mahayana Buddhism, usually linked to wisdom and learning.

mantra: a sacred verse repeatedly chanted as part of worship or meditation.

Mark, Saint: traditionally identified as the author of the second (and earliest) canonical gospel.

Mary: the mother of Jesus.

masjid: see **mosque.**

Mass: see **Eucharist.**

Matthew, Saint: traditionally identified as the author of the first canonical gospel.

matzah: Hebrew term for unleavened bread.

Maudgalyana: early companion of the Buddha who was renowned for working miracles.

Mawlid an-Nabi: Islamic holy day celebrating the birthday of the prophet Muhammad.

Mecca: place of Muhammad's birth and the center of the Islamic pilgrimage tradition.

Medina: the town to which Muhammad and the first Muslims emigrated in 622 (see **Hijra**); it is also the location of Muhammad's tomb.

Megillot, Five [Five Scrolls] (*sing.* **Megillah**): five biblical scrolls read at certain festivals during the Jewish year: Esther, Lamentations, Qoheleth, Ruth, and Song of Songs.

mehendi: elaborate designs made with henna on the hands, feet, and body of a Hindu bride.

menorah: Jewish seven-branched candlestick.

Mesopotamia [Between the Rivers]: region between the Tigris and Euphrates rivers (now Iraq), where the earliest civilization emerged.

Messiah [Anointed One]: (1) in Judaism, a future descendant of King David who will usher in an era of justice and peace; (2) in Christianity and Islam, the title given to Jesus and rendered as "Christos" in Greek.

mihrab: a niche-shaped feature inside a mosque indicating the direction of Mecca.

mikveh: Jewish ritual bath.

minaret: a tower attached to a mosque, from which the call to prayer is traditionally chanted or broadcast.

minbar: a pulpit in a mosque.

minyan: official quorum of 10 adult men for certain Jewish prayers and ceremonies.

mitzvot [commandments]: religious duties incumbent upon Jews once they reach adulthood; the rabbinic tradition identified 613 commandments in the Torah.

mohel: a ritual circumciser in Judaism.

moksa: Hindu concept of final liberation from the cycle of reincarnation (see **nirvana**).

monism: the philosophical belief that there is ultimately only one reality and that all forms of plurality or individuality are illusory.

monotheism: belief in one God.

Mormonism: religious movement founded by Joseph Smith in the USA in the early nineteenth century which claims that Jesus appeared in North America after his resurrection.

Moses (c.1250 BCE): leader of the Hebrews during the escape from Egypt and the period of wandering in the desert; Moses received the Law from God on Mount Sinai and is considered the greatest prophet in Judaism.

mosque (**masjid**): Muslim place of worship.

Mother Goddess: see **Shakti**.

Mount Athos: famous center of Orthodox Christian monasteries in northeast Greece.

Mount Meru: in Hinduism and Buddhism, the mythical mountain that forms the axis of the world and is the abode of the gods.

Mount Sinai: mountain on which Moses received the Ten Commandments.

Mount Zion (or **Sion**): traditional name for the hill on which the Jewish Temple was built.

mudra: the position of the hands on a Buddha statue.

muezzin: the one who calls the faithful to daily prayer in Islam.

Mughals: Islamic rulers of northern India from 1526 to 1857.

Muhammad (c.570–632): founder of Islam and considered by Muslims to be the last and greatest of the prophets.

murti: Hindu sacred image.

Nataraja [Lord of the Dance]: Shiva depicted performing the dance that sustains the cosmos.

Navaratri [Nine Nights]: Hindu festival in September–October which focuses on the Mother Goddess (see **Shakti**).

Nazareth: town in Galilee and the home of Jesus.

New Testament: the 27 Christian writings that constitute the second part of the Christian Bible.

Nicene Creed: major Christian statement of faith issued at the Council of Nicea (325) and expanded at the Council of Constantinople (381).

Night Journey: see **Isra and Mi'raj**.

Night of Power (**Lailat al-Qadr**): a night toward the end of Ramadan that commemorates the descent of the Qur'an from heaven.

nirvana: Buddhist term for final liberation from the cycle of reincarnation (see **moksa**).

Noah: Biblical figure commanded by God to save his family and a pair of every animal species from the waters of the Great Flood by building an ark.

Numbers: the fourth book of the Jewish Torah.

Old Testament: Christian term for the Hebrew Scriptures that are included in the Christian Bible; Catholic and Orthodox Christians also include other Jewish writings known variously as apocryphal or deutero-canonical books.

om: see **aum**.

Orthodox churches: family of autonomous (Eastern) Christian churches that recognize the Patriarch of Constantinople as a symbolic figurehead; they officially separated from Rome (see **Western Christianity**) in 1054.

Orthodox Judaism: traditional forms of Judaism that stress fidelity to the oral and written law as handed down (see also **Reform Judaism**).

Ottoman Empire: extensive Islamic empire that lasted from the thirteenth century to World War I.

pagoda: a common form of the Buddhist stupa in east and southeast Asia.

Pali: Indo-Aryan language in which the Buddhist Tipitaka [Three Baskets] is written.

Pancasila [Five Virtues] (or **Five Precepts**): five fundamental ethical principles of Buddhism.

Panchen Lama: Tibetan spiritual leader traditionally based in Tasilhunpo; the current Dalai Lama identified Gedhun Choekyi Nyima as the eighth Panchen Lama in 1995 but the Chinese government has produced its own candidate, Gyaltsen Norbu.

Parvati: Hindu goddess and consort of Shiva.

Passion, the: Christian term for the sufferings and death of Jesus.

Passover (Pesah): major Jewish festival commemorating the escape from Egypt as recounted in the book of Exodus.

Patriarchs, the: Abraham, Isaac, and Jacob.

Paul, Saint: convert from Judaism who championed the spread of Christianity in the first decades after the death of Jesus.

Pentateuch: see **Torah**.

Pentecost [Fiftieth Day]: (1) in Judaism, the Feast of Weeks (or Shavuot) which falls 50 days after Passover; (2) in Christianity, the seventh Sunday after Easter, which commemorates the descent of the Holy Spirit on the first Christians.

People of the Book: Islamic term for Jews and Christians that acknowledges their common monotheistic faith.

Pesah: see **Passover**.

Peter, Saint: one of Jesus's closest companions and the first leader of the Christian community, especially in Catholic Christianity where the Pope is regarded as his successor.

polygyny: marriage of a man to more than one wife.

polytheism: belief in the existence of many gods.

prasad: food offered to a Hindu deity that is subsequently distributed to believers for consumption.

preta: (1) in Hinduism, the intermediate state of a deceased person between death and the land of the ancestors; (2) in Buddhism, an inhabitant of one of the six realms into which one can be reincarnated.

prophet: in the Abrahamic religions, a person who speaks on behalf of God.

Protestant Christianity: broad subdivision of Christianity comprising churches and communities that arose as a result of the sixteenth-century Reformation, including the Lutheran, Anglican, Calvinist, and Baptist traditions.

Psalms, Book of: collection of 150 sacred songs in the Hebrew Bible.

puja: Hindu devotional worship often involving the use of a murti (image).

Puranas: ancient Hindu poems considered part of the smriti literature.

Pure Land Buddhism: a form of Mahayana Buddhism that emphasizes devotion to a Buddha who dwells in a spiritual "pure land"; the aim of the devotee is to be reincarnated into the pure land from which attainment of nirvana is guaranteed.

Purim: annual Jewish festival celebrating the biblical story of Esther who prevented a massacre of the Jewish people by her courage and intelligence.

qibla: the direction of the Ka'bah, toward which all Muslims must face during official daily prayer.

Qur'an: Islam's holiest book which consists of a collection of the divine revelations experienced by Muhammad during his lifetime.

rabbi: leader of a Jewish community.

Rabbi Akiva (or Akiba) (c.50–135): Jewish scholar and martyr under the Romans.

rabbinic Judaism: main form of Judaism that arose as a result of the destruction of the Temple in 70 CE and the subsequent loss of the priesthood and sacrificial system.

raka: certain words and bodily movements that constitute a basic (repeated) unit of Islamic daily prayer.

Rakhi Bandan: annual Hindu festival during which women place bands on the wrists of male members of the family.

Rama: hero of the Ramayana and the seventh avatar of Vishnu.

Ramadan: ninth month of the Islamic year during which Muslims fast from sunrise to sunset.

Ramayana: Hindu epic that narrates the story of Rama and the rescue of his kidnapped wife with the help of an army of monkeys.

Ram Mohan Roy (1772–1833): Indian scholar and reformer who professed a monotheistic form of Hinduism and opposed traditional practices such as widow-burning, child marriage, and caste laws.

Reform Judaism: a liberal form of Judaism that is more open to the adoption of contemporary ideas such as the use of vernacular language in worship and the rabbinic ordination of women.

reincarnation: see **samsara**.

resurrection of the body: in religions such as Zoroastrianism, Judaism, Christianity, and Islam, the idea that the body will be raised up and transformed into a new, glorious state beyond death, usually at the end of the world.

resurrection of Jesus: the Christian belief that Jesus was raised bodily from the dead soon after his crucifixion.

Rg Veda: oldest and most sacred of the four Vedas.

rishis: authors of the Vedas.

Rosh Hashanah: Jewish New Year festival.

sabbath: seventh day of the Jewish week on which no work is to be performed.

sacraments: official Christian rituals that use visible objects and actions to symbolize invisible spiritual benefits; in the Catholic, Orthodox, and Anglican traditions there are seven sacraments (see box 4.2); in most Protestant churches only two are acknowledged as having scriptural basis (baptism and the Eucharist).

sacred thread: see **Upanayana**.

Sakyamuni [Sage of the Sakya People]: common title for Siddhartha Gautama, the historical Buddha.

salat: the second pillar of Islam: the five official daily prayers.

samadhi: advanced state of mental awareness as a result of intense meditation.

samsara: the belief that a deceased person is reborn into the world in a new bodily form (reincarnation) that is determined by the amount of good or bad karma generated during their life; the cyclic process of birth, death, and rebirth continues until one achieves final liberation.

samskara: traditional Hindu life-cycle ritual.

sangha: Buddhist monastic community.

sannyasin [ascetic]: the fourth and final life stage (ashrama), according to classical Hinduism, during which all ties with family and society are severed.

Sanskrit: classical language of Hindu, Buddhist, and other south Asian religious traditions.

Saraswati: Hindu goddess of the arts and learning, and consort of Brahma.

Sarnath: site near Varanasi where the Buddha delivered his First Sermon.

Satan: the main enemy of God in Judaism, Christianity, and Islam.

sati (or suttee): in Hinduism, self-immolation of a widow at her husband's cremation.

sawm: the fourth pillar of Islam: the annual fast during the month of Ramadan.

seder: the Jewish Passover meal.

Semitic religions: see **Abrahamic religions**.

Sephardic: form of Jewish culture associated with communities from Spain, Portugal, and northern Africa (see also **Ashkenazi**).

Sermon on the Mount: an episode in the gospel of Matthew in which Jesus delivers a collection of his sayings to a crowd.

seudat mitzvah: Jewish festive meal celebrating a religious ritual or event.

Shafi'i: one of the four main Sunni law schools, prevalent in east Africa and south-east Asia.

shahadah: the first pillar of Islam: a concise declaration of faith in the one God and his prophet, Muhammad.

Shaivite: major Hindu tradition in which Shiva is the main object of worship.

Shakti: Mother Goddess, often manifest as a consort of Shiva; sects devoted to the worship of Shakti constitute one of the main subdivisions of Hinduism.

Shankara (c.788–820): prominent Hindu thinker and proponent of the Advaita Vedanta school.

shari'a [path]: Islamic law.

Shavuot (or **Pentecost**): Jewish festival commemorating the giving of the Law on Mount Sinai.

Shema: key Jewish prayer derived from several Torah passages and recited at evening and morning synagogue services.

Shemoneh Esrei: see **Amidah**.

Shi'ite Islam: minority subdivision of Islam which claims that the true successors to Muhammad were Ali and his descendants.

Shinto: the indigenous religion of Japan.

shirk: Islamic term for idolatry.

Shiva: one of the three main gods of Hinduism along with Vishnu and Brahma; he is often depicted in art as Nataraja, Lord of the Dance.

shofar: ram's horn sounded during Jewish New Year and Yom Kippur.

shraddha: in Hinduism, food offerings for the deceased.

shruti: category of Hindu sacred writings considered to have been directly revealed by the gods, in particular the Vedas and the Upanishads (see also **smriti**).

shudra: the servant class – the fourth and lowest of the traditional classes in Vedic Hindu society (see **varna**).

Shulhan Aruch: code of Jewish law compiled by Joseph Caro (1488–1575) and widely used among Ashkenazi Jews.

Siddhartha Gautama (c.560–c.480 BCE): personal name of the historical Buddha.

Simhat Torah [Rejoicing with the Law]: the final day of the Jewish feast of Sukkoth and the day on which the annual cycle of Torah readings recommences.

Sita: wife of Rama.

smriti: category of Hindu sacred writings that are authoritative but secondary to shruti literature.

Solomon (c.950 BCE): king of Israel who succeeded his father, David, and builder of the First Temple in Jerusalem.

Song of Songs: a book in the Jewish Bible in the form of love songs that are interpreted as an allegory of God's love for Israel.

Star of David: six-pointed star often used as a symbol for Judaism.

Stations of the Cross: in Christianity, a series of meditations and prayers that follow the journey of Jesus from his condemnation to his burial.

stupa: bell-shaped construction widely used in Buddhism for storing relics and the ashes of the dead.

Sufi: Islamic mystic.

Sukkoth: major Jewish feast also known as the Feast of Tabernacles (or Booths) which commemorates the wanderings of Israel in the desert.

Sunni Islam: majority subdivision of Islam that accepts the legitimacy of the first four caliphs and their successors.

surah: a chapter of the Qur'an.

sutra (or **sutta**) [thread]: (1) in Hinduism, ancient manuals for various purposes; (2) in Buddhism, collections of the Buddha's teachings.

sutta: see **sutra**.

synagogue: place for Jewish congregational worship and other communal activities.

synoptic gospels: the gospels of Matthew, Mark, and Luke which (unlike the gospel of John) are similar in structure and content and thus considered to be historically interrelated.

tabernacle [tent]: in Christianity, an adorned receptacle in Catholic churches in which consecrated bread is stored.

tallit: Jewish prayer shawl.

Talmud: extensive body of written commentary on the Jewish scriptures composed by rabbinic experts during the centuries after the destruction of the Second Temple.

Tanach: acronym for the Jewish Scriptures, derived from the three main subdivisions: Torah (Law), Neviyim (Prophets), and Ketuvim (Writings).

tantrism: alternative stream within Hinduism and Buddhism that emphasizes the bipolar (masculine/feminine) nature of reality and the need to unite the two by a range of practices, some of which are considered unorthodox by the mainstream.

Tathagata [Thus Gone]: the Buddha's preferred self-designation.

Temple, Jerusalem: main focus of worship in biblical times, initially constructed by Solomon; it was destroyed by the Babylonians in 586 BCE, rebuilt under Ezra after the return from Exile, and destroyed a second time by the Romans in 70 CE.

Ten Commandments: the fundamental moral-religious principles given by God to Moses on Mount Sinai in the form of two stone tablets.

Theravada Buddhism: main form of Buddhism in south and southeast Asia which emphasizes the authority of the Pali Canon (see also **Mahayana Buddhism**).

Three Baskets: see **Tipitaka**.

Three Jewels: the three most precious items in Buddhism: the Buddha, the dharma (his teaching), and the sangha (the monastic community).

tilak: in Hinduism, a painted mark on the forehead or other parts of the body that can signify various things such as sect membership, marriage, or the third eye.

Tipitaka (or **Tripitaka**) [Three Baskets]: threefold collection of Buddhist canonical writings: the Vinaya Pitaka (monastic code), the Sutta Pitaka (the Buddha's teachings), and the Abhidhamma Pitaka (higher learning).

Tisha B'Av [Ninth of Av]: Jewish holy day commemorating the destruction of the First and Second Temples.

tithi: in Hinduism, a lunar day.

Torah: first five books of the Jewish Bible, also known as the Law or the Pentateuch.

Trimurti: the three main gods of Hinduism: Vishnu, Shiva, and Brahma.

Trinity: in Christianity, the concept that there is a threefold plurality (Father, Son, and Holy Spirit) within the one God.

Twelver Shi'ites: major Shi'ite school that recognizes 12 imams in contrast to the Seveners.

twice-born: adult males of the upper three classes of Hindu society who receive the sacred thread and are thus given access to the Vedas.

Umar (or **Omar**; c.584–644): second caliph and key architect of the Islamic expansion following the death of Muhammad.

Umayyads (661–750): first hereditary dynasty of caliphs in Islam that began when Mu'awiyya prevailed over Ali during a period of civil war.

Upanayana: the sacred-thread ceremony in Hinduism during which a young male of the upper three classes is initiated into spiritual adulthood (see also **twice-born**).

Upanishads: collections of Hindu philosophical writings that are attached to the Vedas but move beyond their emphasis on ritual by seeking the meaning of human existence.

uposatha: in Buddhism, a regular day of intensive spiritual observance in monasteries, usually marked by the phases of the moon.

Uthman (c.580–656): the third caliph.

Vaishnavite: major Hindu tradition in which Vishnu is the main object of worship.

vaishya: the merchant class – the third of the four traditional classes in Hindu society (see **varna**).

vanaprasthin [forest-dweller]: according to classical Hinduism, the third life stage (ashrama), during which one severs ties with family and society and lives as a celibate.

Varanasi (also **Benares** or **Kasi**): one of the holiest cities in Hinduism located on the Ganges.

varna [color]: the four classes of traditional Vedic Hindu society.

Vassa (or **Rains Retreat**): period of retreat and spiritual renewal for Buddhist monks that corresponds to the wet season.

Vatican II (1962–5): the most recent ecumenical council of the Catholic Church during which many significant reforms in theology and practice were implemented.

Vedanta [End of the Vedas]: major Hindu philosophical tradition based on the Upanishads and similar literature.

Vedas: the four ancient texts that constitute the oldest and most sacred stratum of Hindu sacred writings: the Rg Veda, the Yajur Veda, the Sama Veda, and the Atharva Veda.

Vesak: annual feast commemorating the birth, Enlightenment, and death of the Buddha.

Vinaya Pitaka [Basket of Discipline]: the part of the Tipitaka that contains the rules for Buddhist monastic life.

Vishnu: one of the three main gods of Hinduism along with Shiva and Brahma; often described as the preserver of the cosmos, Vishnu becomes incarnate during times of crisis (see **avatar**).

Wahhabi Islam: conservative Islamic movement that is predominant in Saudi Arabia and follows the Hanbali school of law.

Western Christianity: general term for churches in the Latin tradition, especially after the Great Schism of 1054; as a result of the sixteenth-century Reformation, Western Christianity was further divided into the Catholic and Protestant Churches.

Western Wall: part of the remains of the Second Temple in Jerusalem, which was destroyed by the Romans in 70 CE.

Yiddish: a mixture of German, Hebrew, and other languages used by Ashkenazi Jews.

Yom Kippur: Jewish Day of Atonement.

yugas: the four main stages or eras in the Hindu cyclic concept of time.

zakat: the third pillar of Islam: a religious tax for the benefit of the poor and needy.

Zen: form of Buddhism that derived from the Chinese "Chan" school and became widespread in Japan and Korea; it stresses inner meditation and the gaining of insight outside the scriptures.

Zionism: Nineteenth-century political-religious movement aimed at establishing a homeland for the Jews.

Zoroastrianism: religion founded by the prophet Zoroaster (or Zarathustra) in the tenth century BCE; professing one good God (Ahura Mazda) and an opposing evil force (Angra Mainyu), it became the state religion of the Persian Empire during the sixth century BCE.

SELECT BIBLIOGRAPHY

Ali Shari Ati (2005). *Hajj: Reflection on its Rituals*. Houston: Free Islamic Literatures.

Bahadur, Om Lata (2000). *The Book of Hindu Festivals and Ceremonies*. 2nd edn. Delhi: UBS.

Bechert, Heinz, & Gombrich, Richard (eds.) (1984). *The World of Buddhism: Monks and Nuns in Society and Culture*. London: Thames & Hudson.

Berkwitz, Stephen, & Korom, Frank (eds.) (2006). *Buddhism in World Cultures: Comparative Perspectives*. Santa Barbara, CA: ABC-CLIO.

Bhaskarananda, Swami (2002). *The Essentials of Hinduism*. 2nd edn. Seattle: Viveka.

Binns, John (2002). *An Introduction to the Christian Orthodox Churches*. Cambridge: Cambridge University Press.

Black, Naomi (ed.) (1989). *Celebration: The Book of Jewish Festivals*. London: Jonathan David.

Bowden, John (ed.) (2006). *Christianity: The Complete Guide*. London: Continuum.

Bowen, John (2004). *Religions in Practice: An Approach to the Anthropology of Religion*. 3rd edn. Boston: Allyn & Bacon.

Bowker, John (2006). *World Religions: The Great Faiths Explored and Explained*. Harlow: Dorling Kindersley.

Brown, Daniel James (2003). *A New Introduction to Islam*. Oxford: Blackwell.

Brown, Raymond (1997). *An Introduction to the New Testament*. New York: Doubleday.

Browning, Don S., Green, M. Christian, & Witte, John Jr. (eds.) (2006). *Sex, Marriage and Family in World Religions*. New York: Columbia University Press.

Burke, T. Patrick (2004). *The Major Religions: An Introduction with Texts*. 2nd edn. Oxford: Blackwell.

Buswell, Robert E. Jr. (1992). *The Zen Monastic Experience*. Princeton, NJ: Princeton University Press.

Cabezon, Jose Ignacio (ed.) (1992). *Buddhism, Sexuality and Gender*. Albany, NY: SUNY Press.

Carmody, Denise Lardner, & Carmody, John Tully (1990). *Roman Catholicism: An Introduction*. Upper Saddle River, NJ: Prentice Hall.

Charing, Douglas, & Cole, W. Owen (eds.) (2004). *Six World Faiths*. London: Continuum.

Chaudhuri, Nirad (1979). *Hinduism: A Religion to Live By*. New York: Oxford University Press.

Chilton, Bruce (2002). *Redeeming Time: The Wisdom of Ancient Jewish and Christian Festal Calendars.* Peabody, MA: Hendrickson.

Cohn-Sherbok, Dan (2003). *Judaism: History, Belief and Practice.* London: Routledge.

Coleman, Simon, & Elsner, John (1997). *Pilgrimage: Past and Present in the World Religions.* Cambridge, MA: Harvard University Press.

Conze, Edward, et al. (eds.) (2006). *Buddhist Texts through the Ages.* Whitefish, MT: Kessinger.

Cook, Michael (2000). *The Koran: A Very Short Introduction.* Oxford: Oxford University Press.

Cooper, John (1994). *Eat and Be Satisfied: A Social History of Jewish Food.* Lanham, MD: Jason Aronson.

Corrigan, John, et al. (1997). *Jews, Christians, Muslims: A Comparative Introduction to Monotheistic Religions.* Upper Saddle River, NJ: Prentice Hall.

Coward, Harold (ed.) (1997). *Life after Death in World Religions.* Maryknoll, NY: Orbis.

Cragg, Kenneth, & Speight, R. Marston (2002). *The House of Islam.* 3rd edn. Belmont, CA: Wadsworth.

Creel, Austin B. (1977). *Dharma in Hindu Ethics.* Calcutta: Firma KLM.

Crook, Roger (2006). *Introduction to Christian Ethics.* 5th edn. Upper Saddle River, NJ: Prentice Hall.

Davies, Douglas James (2002). *Death, Ritual and Belief: The Rhetoric of Funeral Rites.* London: Continuum.

Davies, J. G. (1984). *Temples, Churches and Mosques.* Oxford: Blackwell.

De Lange, Nicholas (2000). *Introduction to Judaism.* Cambridge: Cambridge University Press.

Denny, Frederick Mathewson (2005). *An Introduction to Islam.* 3rd edn. Upper Saddle River, NJ: Prentice Hall.

Dessing, Nathal M. (2001). *Rituals of Birth, Circumcision, Marriage and Death among Muslims in the Netherlands.* Leuven: Peeters.

Domnitch, Larry (2000). *The Jewish Holidays: A Journey through History.* Lanham, MD: Jason Aronson.

Eastman, Roger (ed.) (1999). *The Ways of Religion: An Introduction to the Major Traditions.* 3rd edn. New York: Oxford University Press.

Eck, Diana (1998). *Darsan: Seeing the Image in India.* 3rd edn. New York: Columbia University Press.

Edwards, D. L. (1997). *Christianity: The First Two Thousand Years.* London: Cassell.

Eisen, Arnold M. (1999). *Rethinking Modern Judaism: Ritual, Commandment, Community.* Chicago: University of Chicago Press.

Elbogen, Ismar, & Scheindlin, Raymond (1993). *Jewish Liturgy: A Comprehensive History.* Philadelphia: Jewish Publication Society of America.

Ellwood, Robert S., & McGraw, Barbara A. (2004). *Many Peoples, Many Faiths: Women and Men in the World Religions.* 8th edn. Upper Saddle River, NJ: Prentice Hall.

Eskenazi, Tamara, et al. (eds.) (1991). *The Sabbath in Jewish and Christian Traditions.* New York: Crossroad.

Esposito, John (2002). *What Everyone Needs to Know about Islam.* Oxford and New York: Oxford University Press.

Esposito, John (2004). *Islam: The Straight Path.* 3rd edn. New York: Oxford University Press.

Esposito, John, et al. (eds.) (2005). *World Religions Today*. 2nd edn. New York: Oxford University Press.

Etzioni, Amitai, & Bloom, Jared (eds.) (2004). *We are What We Celebrate: Understanding Holidays and Rituals*. New York: New York University Press.

Fadwa El Guindi (2003). *Veil: Modesty, Privacy and Resistance*. Oxford: Berg.

Falk, Nancy (2005). *Living Hinduisms: An Explorer's Guide*. Belmont, CA: Wadsworth.

Faure, Bernard (1998). *The Red Thread: Buddhist Approaches to Sexuality*. Princeton, NJ: Princeton University Press.

Feldhaus, Anne (2003). *Connected Places: Region, Pilgrimage and Geographical Imagination in India*. Basingstoke: Palgrave Macmillan.

Fellows, Ward J. (1998). *Religions East and West*. 2nd edn. Belmont, CA: Wadsworth.

Fine, Lawrence (ed.) (2001). *Judaism in Practice: From the Middle Ages through the Early Modern Period*. Princeton, NJ: Princeton University Press.

Fisher, Mary Pat (2005). *Living Religions*. 6th edn. Upper Saddle River, NJ: Prentice Hall.

Fisher, Robert E. (1993). *Buddhist Art and Architecture*. London: Thames & Hudson.

Flood, Gavin (1996). *An Introduction to Hinduism*. Cambridge: Cambridge University Press.

Flood, Gavin (ed.) (2003). *The Blackwell Companion to Hinduism*. Oxford: Blackwell.

Forbes, Duncan (1999). *Buddhist Pilgrimage*. New Delhi: Motilal Banarsidass.

Fowler, Jeaneane (1997). *Hinduism: Beliefs and Practices*. Brighton: Sussex Academic Press.

Frishman, Martin, & Khan, Hasan-Uddin (2002). *The Mosque: History, Architectural Development and Regional Diversity*. London: Thames & Hudson.

Fuller, C. (1992). *The Camphor Flame*. Princeton, NJ: Princeton University Press.

Gatje, H. (1996). *The Qur'an and its Exegesis*. 2nd edn. Oxford: Oneworld.

Geffen, Rela M. (ed.) (1993). *Celebration and Renewal: Rites of Passage in Judaism*. Philadelphia: Jewish Publication Society of America.

Goldberg, David F., & Rayner, John D. (1989). *The Jewish People: Their History and their Religion*. London: Penguin.

Goldberg, Harvey E. (ed.) (2001). *The Life of Judaism*. Berkeley and Los Angeles: University of California Press.

Goldman, Ari L. (2000). *Being Jewish: The Spiritual and Cultural Practice of Judaism Today*. New York: Simon & Schuster.

Göle, Nilüfa (1997). *The Forbidden Modern: Civilization and Veiling*. Ann Arbor, MI: University of Michigan Press.

Goodman, Hananya (ed.) (1994). *Between Jerusalem and Benares: Comparative Studies in Judaism and Hinduism*. Albany, NY: SUNY Press.

Gordon, Matthew S. (2002). *Understanding Islam*. London: Duncan Baird.

Granoff, Phyllis, & Shinohara, Koichi (eds.) (2003). *Pilgrims, Patrons, and Place: Localizing Sanctity in Asian Religions*. Vancouver: University of British Columbia Press.

Greenberg, Irving (1988). *The Jewish Way: Living the Holidays*. New York: Touchstone.

Harpur, James (2002). *Sacred Tracks: Two Thousand Years of Christian Pilgrimage*. Berkeley and Los Angeles: University of California Press.

Harris, Elizabeth (1999). *What Buddhists Believe*. Oxford: Oneworld.

Harvey, Peter (1990). *An Introduction to Buddhism: Teaching, History and Practices*. Cambridge: Cambridge University Press.

Hauer, Christian E., & Young, William A. (2000). *An Introduction to the Bible: A Journey into Three Worlds*. 5th edn. Upper Saddle River, NJ: Prentice Hall.

Hawley, John Stratton, & Narayanan, Vasudha (eds.) (2006). *The Life of Hinduism*. Berkeley and Los Angeles: University of California Press.

Hawting, G. R. (2002). *The Idea of Idolatry and the Emergence of Islam: From Polemic to History*. Cambridge: Cambridge University Press.

Hawting, G. R. (ed.) (2006). *The Development of Islamic Ritual*. Aldershot: Ashgate.

Hedayetullah, Muhammad (2002). *Dynamics of Islam: An Exposition*. Victoria, BC: Trafford.

Heehs, Peter (ed.) (2002). *Indian Religions: A Historical Reader of Spiritual Expression and Experience*. London: Hurst.

Heilman, S. C. (1999). *Synagogue Life: Study in Symbolic Interaction*. Somerset, NJ: Transaction.

Hertzberg, Arthur (ed.) (1998). *Judaism*. New York: Free Press.

Hick, John, & Hebblethwaite, Brian (eds.) (2001). *Christianity and Other Religions*. 2nd edn. Oxford: Oneworld.

Hickman, Hoyt, et al. (1992). *The New Handbook of the Christian Year*. Nashville, TN: Abingdon Press.

Hinnells, John R. (ed.) (1991). *A Handbook of Living Religions*. Ringwood, Vic.: Penguin.

Hoffman, Lawrence A. (1996). *Covenant of Blood: Circumcision and Gender in Rabbinic Judaism*. Chicago: University of Chicago Press.

Holm, Jean, & Bowker, John (eds.) (2000). *Sacred Place*. London: Continuum.

Hopfe, Lewis M., & Woodward, Mark R. (2006). *Religions of the World*. 10th edn. Upper Saddle River, NJ: Prentice Hall.

Isaacs, Ronald H. (1998). *Every Person's Guide to the High Holy Days*. Lanham, MD: Jason Aronson.

Johnson, Maxwell E. (1999). *The Rites of Christian Initiation: Their Evolution and Interpretation*. Collegeville, MN: Liturgical Press.

Juergensmeyer, Mark (ed.) (2003). *Global Religions: An Introduction*. Oxford and New York: Oxford University Press.

Kaufman, Michael (1992). *Love, Marriage, and Family in Jewish Law and Tradition*. Lanham, MD: Jason Aronson.

Keene, Michael (2006). *World Religions*. Louisville, KY: Westminster John Knox Press.

Keown, Damien (2000). *Buddhism: A Very Short Introduction*. Oxford and New York: Oxford University Press.

Keown, Damien (2001). *The Nature of Buddhist Ethics*. Basingstoke: Palgrave Macmillan.

Klein, Isaac (1979). *A Guide to Jewish Religious Practice*. New York: Ktav.

Klostermaier, Klaus (1994). *A Survey of Hinduism*. 2nd edn. Albany, NY: SUNY Press.

Knott, Kim (2000). *Hinduism: A Very Short Introduction*. Oxford and New York: Oxford University Press.

Kraemer, David (1999). *The Meanings of Death in Rabbinic Judaism*. New York: Routledge.

Kramer, Kenneth (1986). *World Scriptures: An Introduction to Comparative Religions*. Mahwah, NJ: Paulist Press.

Kuban, Dogan (1997). *Muslim Religious Architecture: Development of Religious Architecture in Later Periods*. Boston: Brill.

Kuhns, Elizabeth (2003). *The Habit: A History of the Clothing of Catholic Nuns*. New York: Doubleday.

Lamm, Maurice (2000). *The Jewish Ways of Death and Mourning*. Middle Village, NY: Jonathan David.

Levine, Lee I. (1999). *Jerusalem: Its Sanctity and Centrality to Judaism, Christianity, and Islam*. London: Continuum.

Lipner, Julius (1998). *Hindus*. London: Routledge.

Lippman, Thomas (1995). *Understanding Islam: An Introduction to the Muslim World*. 2nd edn. New York: Penguin.

Lopez, Donald S. Jr. (ed.) (1995). *Buddhism in Practice*. Princeton, NJ: Princeton University Press.

Lopez, Donald S. Jr. (ed.) (1995). *Religions of India in Practice*. Princeton, NJ: Princeton University Press.

Lopez, Donald S. Jr. (ed.) (1996). *Religions of China in Practice*. Princeton, NJ: Princeton University Press.

Lopez, Donald S. Jr. (ed.) (1997). *Religions of Tibet in Practice*. Princeton, NJ: Princeton University Press.

Lopez, Donald S. Jr. (ed.) (2002). *Religions of Asia in Practice: An Anthology*. Princeton, NJ: Princeton University Press.

Madan, T. N. (ed.) (1997). *Religion in India*. 4th edn. New York: Oxford University Press.

Madan, T. N. (ed.) (2004). *India's Religions: Perspectives from Sociology and History*. New Delhi and Oxford: Oxford University Press.

Marcus, Ivan G. (2004). *The Jewish Life Cycle: Rites of Passage from Biblical to Modern Times*. Seattle: University of Washington Press.

Martimort, A., et al. (eds.) (1992). *The Church at Prayer: An Introduction to the Liturgy*. Collegeville, MN: Liturgical Press.

Masuzawa, Tomoko (2005). *The Invention of World Religions: Or, How European Universalism was Preserved in the Language of Pluralism*. Chicago: University of Chicago Press.

Matthews, Warren (2006). *World Religions*. 5th edn. Belmont, CA: Wadsworth.

McArthur, Meher (2002). *Reading Buddhist Art*. London: Thames & Hudson.

McGrath, Alister E. (1997). *An Introduction to Christianity*. Oxford: Blackwell.

Meek, Harold (1995). *The Synagogue*. London: Phaidon.

Michaels, Axel (2003). *Hinduism: Past and Present*. Princeton, NJ: Princeton University Press.

Michell, George (1988). *The Hindu Temple: An Introduction to its Meaning and Forms*. Chicago: University of Chicago Press.

Millgram, Abraham (1971). *Jewish Worship*. Philadelphia: Jewish Publication Society of America.

Mittal, Sushil (ed.) (2004). *The Hindu World*. Abingdon: Routledge.

Mittal, Sushil, & Thursby, Gene (eds.) (2006). *Religions of South Asia: An Introduction*. Abingdon: Routledge.

Molloy, Michael (2006). *Experiencing the World's Religions: Tradition, Challenge and Change*. 4th edn. New York: McGraw-Hill.

Morgan, David (2005). *The Sacred Gaze: Religious Visual Culture in Theory and Practice*. Berkeley and Los Angeles: University of California Press.

Narayanan, Vasudha (2004). *Hinduism*. New York: Oxford University Press.

Nasr, Seyyed Hossein (2003). *Islam: Religion, History and Civilization*. San Francisco: HarperSanFrancisco.

Neusner, Jacob (ed.) (2003). *World Religions in America: An Introduction*. 3rd edn. Louisville, KY: Westminster John Knox Press.

Neusner, Jacob, et al. (eds.) (2000). *Judaism and Islam in Practice*. London: Routledge.

Newman, Louis E. (2004). *An Introduction to Jewish Ethics*. Upper Saddle River, NJ: Prentice Hall.

Noss, David S. (2002). *A History of the World's Religions*. 11th edn. Upper Saddle River, NJ: Prentice Hall.

Novak, Philip (1994). *The World's Wisdom: Sacred Texts of the World's Religions*. San Francisco: HarperSanFrancisco.

Obayashi, Hiroshi (1991). *Death and Afterlife: Perspectives of World Religions*. New York: Praeger.

Oxtoby, Willard G. (ed.) (2001). *World Religions: Eastern Traditions*. 2nd edn. Don Mills, Ont.: Oxford University Press.

Oxtoby, Willard G. (ed.) (2001). *World Religions: Western Traditions*. 2nd edn. Don Mills, Ont.: Oxford University Press.

Panati, Charles (1996). *Sacred Origins of Profound Things: The Stories behind the Rites and Rituals of the World's Religions*. New York: Penguin.

Parry, Jonathan P. (1994). *Death in Banaras*. Cambridge: Cambridge University Press.

Partridge, Christopher H. (ed.) (2005). *Introduction to World Religions*. Minneapolis: Augsburg Fortress.

Pauling, Chris (2004). *Introducing Buddhism*. 3rd edn. Birmingham: Windhorse.

Peters, F. E. (1996). *The Hajj*. Princeton, NJ: Princeton University Press.

Powell, Barbara (1996). *Windows into the Infinite: A Guide to the Hindu Scriptures*. Fremont, CA: Asian Humanities Press.

Powers, John (1995). *Introduction to Tibetan Buddhism*. Ithaca, NY: Snow Lion.

Prasad, R. C. (1997). *The Upanayana: The Hindu Ceremonies of the Sacred Thread*. New Delhi: Motilal Banarsidass.

Pratt, Douglas (2005). *The Challenge of Islam: Encounters in Interfaith Dialogue*. Aldershot: Ashgate.

Renard, John (1996). *Seven Doors to Islam: Spirituality and the Religious Life of Muslims*. Berkeley and Los Angeles: University of California Press.

Reynolds, Frank E., & Carbine, Jason A. (eds.) (2000). *The Life of Buddhism*. Berkeley and Los Angeles: University of California Press.

Ridgeon, Lloyd (2003). *Major World Religions*. London: RoutledgeCurzon.

Riemer, Jack (ed.) (2002). *Jewish Insights on Death and Mourning*. Syracuse, NY: Syracuse University Press.

Rinehard, Robin (ed.) (2004). *Contemporary Hinduism: Ritual, Culture, and Practice*. Santa Barbara, CA: ABC-CLIO.

Rippin, Andrew (2000). *Muslims: Their Religious Beliefs and Practices*. 2nd edn. London: Routledge.

Robinson, N. (2004). *Discovering the Qur'an: A Contemporary Approach to a Veiled Text*. 2nd edn. London: SCM.

Robinson, Thomas A., & Rodrigues, Hillary (eds.) (2006). *World Religions: A Guide to the Essentials*. Peabody, MA: Hendrickson.

Rosen, Lawrence (2004). *The Culture of Islam: Changing Aspects of Contemporary Muslim Life*. Chicago: University of Chicago Press.

Rutherford, Richard (1990). *Death of a Christian: The Order of Christian Funerals*. Collegeville, MN: Liturgical Press.

Ruthven, Malise (1997). *Islam: A Very Short Introduction*. New York: Oxford University Press.

Saeed, Abdullah (2003). *Islam in Australia*. St Leonards, NSW: Allen & Unwin.

Sandmel, Samuel (1978). *The Hebrew Scriptures: An Introduction to their Literature and Religious Ideas*. New York: Oxford University Press.

Sangharakshita (1985). *The Eternal Legacy: An Introduction to the Canonical Literature of Buddhism*. Birmingham: Windhorse.

Schauss, Hayyim (1996). *The Jewish Festivals: A Guide to their History and Observance*. New York: Schocken.

Scott, Jamie, & Simpson-Housley, Paul (eds.) (1991). *Sacred Places and Profane Spaces*. London: Greenwood.

Segler, Franklin M., & Bradley, Randall (2006). *Christian Worship: Its Theology and Practice*. 3rd edn. Nashville: B & H Publishing Group.

Sharma, Arvind (ed.) (1994). *Our Religions: The Seven World Religions introduced by Preeminent Scholars from Each Tradition*. San Francisco: HarperSanFrancisco.

Sharma, Arvind (1997). *Hinduism for our Times*. New Delhi: Oxford University Press.

Sharma, Arvind (ed.) (2003). *The Study of Hinduism*. Columbia, SC: University of South Carolina Press.

Shearer, Alistair (1993). *The Hindu Vision: Forms of the Formless*. London: Thames & Hudson.

Sherwin, Byron L. (2000). *Jewish Ethics for the Twenty-First Century: Living in the Image of God*. Syracuse, NY: Syracuse University Press.

Shirazi, Faegheh (2003). *The Veil Unveiled: The Hijab in Modern Culture*. Gainesville, FL: University Press of Florida.

Singer, Peter (ed.) (1993). *A Companion to Ethics*. Oxford: Blackwell, chs. 4–9.

Smart, Ninian (1989). *The World's Religions: Old Traditions and Modern Transformations*. Cambridge: Cambridge University Press.

Smart, Ninian (1998). *The World's Religions*. 2nd edn. Cambridge: Cambridge University Press.

Smith, Brian K. (1998). *Reflections on Resemblance, Ritual and Religion*. New Delhi: Motilal Banarsidass.

Smith, Huston, & Novak, Philip (2004). *Buddhism: A Concise Introduction*. San Francisco: HarperSanFrancisco.

Smith, Jane I., & Haddad, Yvonne Y. (2002). *The Islamic Understanding of Death and Resurrection*. Oxford: Oxford University Press.

Solomon, Norman (1996). *Judaism: A Very Short Introduction*. New York: Oxford University Press.

Stietencron, Heinrich von (2005). *Hindu Myth, Hindu History: Religion, Art and Politics*. New Delhi: Permanent Black Press.

Stoddard, Robert H., & Morinis, E. Alan (eds.) (1997). *Sacred Places, Sacred Spaces: The Geography of Pilgrimages*. Baton Rouge, LA: Geoscience Publications, Louisiana State University.

Strassfeld, Michael (1993). *The Jewish Holidays: A Guide and Commentary*. New York: Harper.

Subhadra Sen Gupta (2003). *Chaar Dhaam: A Guide to the Hindu Pilgrimages*. New Delhi: Rupa.

Swearer, Donald K. (2004). *Becoming the Buddha: The Ritual of Image Consecration in Thailand*. Princeton, NJ: Princeton University Press.

Tanabe, George J. Jr (ed.) (1999). *Religions of Japan in Practice*. Princeton, NJ: Princeton University Press.

Tarlo, Emma (1996). *Clothing Matters: Dress and Identity in India*. Chicago: University of Chicago Press.

Teshima, Jacob (1995). *Zen Buddhism and Hasidism*. Lanham, MD: University Press of America.

Turner, Victor Witter, & Turner, Edith L. B. (1995). *Image and Pilgrimage in Christian Culture*. New York: Columbia University Press.

Waines, David (1995). *An Introduction to Islam*. Cambridge: Cambridge University Press.

Ward, Keith (2000). *Christianity: A Short Introduction*. Oxford: Oneworld.

Ware, Timothy (1993). *The Orthodox Church*. New York: Penguin.

Weaver, Mary Jo, et al. (1997). *Introduction to Christianity*. Belmont, CA: Wadsworth.

Welbon, Guy R. (ed.) (1982). *Religious Festivals in South India and Sri Lanka*. New Delhi: Manohar.

White, James F. (2001). *Introduction to Christian Worship*. 3rd edn. Nashville: Abingdon Press.

Wijayaratna, Mohan (1990). *Buddhist Monastic Life: According to the Texts of the Theravada Tradition*. Cambridge: Cambridge University Press.

Wilkinson, John (2002). *From Synagogue to Church: The Traditional Design*. London: RoutledgeCurzon.

Witty, Abraham, & Witty, Rachelle (2001). *Exploring Jewish Tradition: A Transliterated Guide to Everyday Practice and Observance*. New York: Doubleday.

Woodhead, Linda (2004). *Introduction to Christianity*. Cambridge: Cambridge University Press.

Woodhead, Linda, et al. (eds.) (2001). *Religions in the Modern World: Traditions and Transformations*. London: Routledge.

Young, William A. (2004). *The World's Religions: Worldviews and Contemporary Issues*. 2nd edn. Upper Saddle River, NJ: Prentice Hall.

Zerubavel, Eviatar (1989). *The Seven Day Circle: The History and Meaning of the Week*. Chicago: University of Chicago Press.

Zibawi, Mahmoud (1993). *The Icon: Its Meaning and History*. Collegeville, MN: Liturgical Press.

INDEX